CAMBRIDGE SOUTH ASIAN STUDIES

THE RISE OF
BUSINESS CORPORATIONS
IN INDIA

1851–1900

CAMBRIDGE SOUTH ASIAN STUDIES

These monographs are published by the Syndics of Cambridge University Press in association with the Cambridge University Centre for South Asian Studies. The following books have been published in this series:

1 S. GOPAL: *British Policy in India, 1858–1905*
2 J. A. B. PALMER: *The Mutiny Outbreak at Meerut in 1857*
3 A. DAS GUPTA: *Malabar in Asian Trade, 1740–1800*
4 G. OBEYESEKERE: *Land Tenure in a Village in Ceylon*
5 H. L. ERDMAN: *The Swatantra Party and Indian Conservatism*
6 S. N. MUKHERJEE: *Sir William Jones: A Study in Eighteenth-Century British Attitudes to India*
7 ABDUL MAJED KHAN: *The Transition in Bengal, 1756–1775: A Study of Saiyid Muhammad Reza Khan*

THE RISE OF
BUSINESS CORPORATIONS
IN INDIA

1851-1900

BY

RADHE SHYAM RUNGTA

*Senior Lecturer in Business Administration,
University of Khartoum*

CAMBRIDGE
AT THE UNIVERSITY PRESS
1970

PUBLISHED BY
THE SYNDICS OF THE CAMBRIDGE UNIVERSITY PRESS
Bentley House, 200 Euston Road, London, N.W.1
American Branch: 32 East 57th Street, New York, N.Y. 10022

Library of Congress Catalogue Card Number: 69–10573
Standard Book Number: 521 07354 5

Printed in Great Britain by
Unwin Brothers Limited
The Gresham Press
Old Woking, Surrey
England

Produced by Letterpress

TO MY MEMORIES OF L.S.E.

CONTENTS

Preface   *page* ix
Acknowledgements   xiii
A Note on Statistics   xv
Abbreviations   xvii
Glossary   xviii

Chapter

1 The Rise of Business Corporations in India   1
2 The Promotion and Finance of Companies to 1850   18
3 Problems of Company Law up to 1850   36
4 Growth of the Corporate Sector, 1851–1860   46
5 The American Civil War and the Banking Inflation in
   Bombay, 1861–1865   72
6 The Boom in the Tea Industry   94
7 Growth of the Corporate Sector, 1866–1882   109
8 The Gold Rush in Southern India   136
9 Growth of the Corporate Sector, 1882–1900   149
10 Savings, Insurance and the Gold Mining Companies   187
11 Trends in Corporate Financing and Legal Develop-
   ments   203
12 Corporate Management: The Managing Agency System   219
13 Concluding Observations   256

Appendices

1 Early European Chartered Companies in India   270
2 Institution of Guilds in Ancient India   272
3 List of Indian and Foreign Banks to 1850   273
4 List of Industrial Companies in India, 1817–50   274
5 Brief History of the Iron and Steel Industry in India   276
6 Tea Companies of Northern India Incorporated in U.K.   279
7 Table showing the Number and Paid-up Capital of
   Companies registered in India from January 1866 to
   March 1882   283
8 Table showing, by Industries, the Number of Com-
   panies registered, wound-up, and working in India
   between 1851 and 1865, 1866 and 1882, and 1851 and
   1882   284

Contents

9 A Double Frequency Table showing, by Size of Capital and Age, the Number of Companies formed during 1863–5 and wound-up by 31 March 1882   286

10 A Double Frequency Table showing, by Capital and Age, the Number of Companies formed in India between 1851 and 1882   287

11 A Double Frequency Table showing, by Capital Groups, the Life Span of Companies between 1851 and 1882   288

12 Table showing, by Industries, the Paid-up Capital of Companies registered in India between 1851 and 1882   289

13 Graphs showing, in Select Industries, the Number of Companies registered each year in India from 1851 to 31 March 1901   290

14 Table showing Sources and Uses of Funds in the Cotton Mills of Bombay, 1893–4   291

15 History of the Shipping Industry in India   292

16 Table of Dividends paid by Gold Mining Companies in Mysore from 1886–1900   295

17 Table showing the Number and Paid-up Capital (in rupees) of each Class of Company in existence at the end of each year since 1881–2   296

18 Table showing the Number of Companies at Work in India, and their Nominal and Paid-up Capital (in rupees) at the end of each year since 1884–5   300

19 Table showing the Number of Companies and their Paid-up Capital in each Province at the end of each year since 1891–2   301

20 Table showing the Number of Companies registered, ceased, and working, with capital, at the end of March from 1882–3 to 1900–1   302

21 Graph showing the Number of Companies registered and dissolved each year from 1851 to 1900–1 in India   303

22 Graph showing the Paid-up Capital of Tea, Jute, Cotton and All Companies working at the end of the calendar year from 1866 to 1881   304

23 Graph showing the Paid-up Capital of Companies registered and dissolved annually from January 1851 to March 1882   305

Select Bibliography   306

Index   321

PREFACE

The late Sir Winston Churchill once said: 'If we say the past is past, then we surrender the future.' The importance of the study of history is implicit in these words but very often this has meant simply the study of political history, for as late as 1927, Professor L. H. Jenks was able to write:

The change of organisation in man's financial behaviour seems often to be strangely missing from the chronicles of the historian. The very omnipresence of the corporate form of business dulls the curiosity as to its antecedents, and perplexes effort to distinguish its characteristics. Yet it can not be doubted that the Corporation, the 'Joint stock company', the '*Société Anonyme*', the '*Aktien-Gesellschaft*', is at least one of the most important institutions in the great society which in the past fifty years the world has been becoming.

(The Migration of British Capital to 1875, 1927, p. 233)

How true this statement is, in relation to India today, can be seen from the following excerpt from the *Progress of Joint Stock Companies in India*, issued in 1955 by the Research and Statistics Division, Department of Company Law Administration, Ministry of Finance, New Delhi:

While it is proposed to review the growth and the role of Joint Stock Companies in the economic development of this country ever since their birth in 1850, the dearth of adequate data renders this task a great deal difficult. The statistical evidence for the first three decades since 1850 is completely lacking, and some fragmentary information is available for the next two decades in a solitary source named *Statement Exhibiting the Moral and Material Progress of India* (p. 11).

Available information on the progress of joint stock companies in India in the period subsequent to 1850, related mainly to the number of companies and their paid-up capital under six broad groups like banking and loan, mills and presses, etc., in three specific years: 1882, 1892, and 1900. These data raised more questions than they answered. Why, for instance, was the first Companies Act passed in 1850? Was there a demand for such a measure at that particular time? If so, what had led to such a demand? Why, again, was this Act modelled after the British

Act of 1844? Was there no Indian experience to be used? Were there no companies in India before 1850? Did the law prohibit their formation? How was large business organised in India before the Act? Did the ancient Hindus have any notion of corporate organisation? If so, what were the peculiar features of these bodies? Why did modern companies in India not grow out of older Indian institutions? What happened to these earlier corporate bodies?

Knowledge about the number, capital, industrial and regional classification of companies was completely lacking before 1882. Moreover, it was not known who promoted such companies as might have existed then nor how they were financed.

Actually, the figures in the *Progress of Joint Stock Companies in India* proved to be more disturbing than illuminating. For instance, of the 407 banking and loan companies in India at the end of 1900, only about a dozen could possibly be classified as banks, and the figures for insurance companies were likewise misleading. Moreover, certain developments such as the intense gold mining speculation of 1890 in Calcutta remained completely unreported. How and when the managing agency system had started in India was unknown. In particular, the process and extent of growth in the corporate sector had been left unexplained. At the end of March 1900, 1,340 companies operated in India. Their paid-up capital amounted to Rs.354 million (not Rs.347 million as the report states). Most importantly, why was growth not bigger?

The growth of joint stock companies may be studied from various angles, such as the growth of corporate management or corporate finance or corporate law. To have confined my study only to one or other of these facets would have simplified the task considerably, but much valuable material bearing on related aspects discovered during the research would have had to be rejected. Nor would detailed treatment of one selected aspect provide the overall view of joint stock company growth in India which seemed so desirable. Incidentally, selecting the overall approach may well stimulate further research in greater depth on specific issues.

Paucity of authoritative texts necessitated systematic search for what might be available in the libraries of the London School of Economics, India House, the British Museum, and the India

Office. Very little of importance relating to the growth of joint stock companies in India could be found, apart from a few company histories, Cooke's *Banking* (1863), and Wacha's *A Financial Chapter in the History of Bombay*.

Turning to potentially useful primary sources, I went through the *Legislative Proceedings of India*, where papers connected with the Companies Act of 1850 proved to be directly relevant. No idea about the characteristics, process or extent of growth of companies could be formed from these papers, although some light was shed on the state of commercial banking and the views held by government officials and businessmen on the subject of incorporating banks and extending limited liability to them.

The discovery of the *Statistical Tables for British India*, a very important source rarely used hitherto, filled much of the gap, as they give the number of companies formed in India since 1850, the objects for which they were formed, their paid-up capital and their place of business. Even so, the problems associated with company promotion and development, and the ways in which they were resolved continued to elude me. Why were particular enterprises promoted rather than others? What were the reasons for their success or the failure of others? How were they financed and managed? How did government policy or the social and religious attitudes of the people influence the growth of these enterprises? What was the impact of agriculture and transport on the corporate sector?

Trying to find answers to satisfy some of these questions, I searched the files of the *Times of India* (Bombay) and the *Friend of India* (Calcutta) over a period of sixty years. The files of the *Madras Mail*, which I only sampled, produced very little of interest, probably because the number of companies in South India was comparatively small. Regional studies were necessary; lacking adequate means of communications, publications then carried little inter-regional news. The task proved very time-consuming; nineteenth century newspapers carried few headlines, nor were they indexed, so that literally every paragraph had to be scanned.

I found Trade Directories valuable, particularly in providing information on companies prior to 1850 and about the origin of the managing agency system. Secondary sources were used in particular for the study of the general economic, political and social conditions of India. One potential source which I was unable to investigate—the files of individual companies likely to exist in the offices of the Registrar of Companies or the High Courts could conceivably have thrown more light on the composition of shareholding, the size and asset structure, besides other possible data.

Work on this study began in January 1959, at the London School of Economics. During 1959–60 lack of finance forced me to seek a paid post, when only a small part of my time could be spared for research, but by June 1962 the draft had been completed. Having meanwhile been appointed Lecturer in Finance at the University of Nigeria, I could not present my research as a Ph.D. thesis to the University of London until 1965.

Indian economic history has received increasing attention from scholars in India, Britain and America during the last five years. The limited library facilities available to me during that period prevented me from keeping myself as up to date as I would have liked, and I am indebted to the publishers' referee for drawing my attention to points which called for reconsideration.

ACKNOWLEDGMENTS

I am indebted to Professor F. W. Paish and Dr Vera Anstey, who supervised this work in its Ph.D. stage. I have greatly benefited from the critical comments of my colleagues Professors F. de P. Hanika and Syed Ahmed in revising the work for publication. They are, however, in no way responsible for any views expressed here. I owe, too, a debt of gratitude to Mrs C. G. Minty for pointing out blemishes in my English and typing drafts of much of the original thesis and to Mrs Alison Hanika who very kindly typed the whole of the revised version.

Thanks are also due to the librarians and staff of the libraries of the London School of Economics, the India Office, India House, the British Museum and the Delhi School of Economics.

I am deeply grateful for financial help to the following persons and institutions: Messrs B. L. Jalan, N. L. Jalan, the All-India Marwari Sammelan Educational Trust, the Jayashree Charity Trust, the Swadeshi Cotton Mill Company Ltd., the London School of Economics for the Leverhulme Research Studentship for Oversea Students, the University of London for grants from the Central Research Fund and the Convocation Trust Fund, the Lady Edwina Mountbatten Grants for Commonwealth students, the Sir Richard Stapley Education Trust, and the Henry Foyle Education Trust.

I am also grateful to the editors for allowing me to adapt and reprint my articles published in the following journals: the *American Journal of Legal History*, the *Indian Journal of Economics*, and the *Indian Economic and Social History Review*.

University of Khartoum   R. S. RUNGTA
Sudan
January 1968

A NOTE ON STATISTICS

All statistics relating to joint stock companies unless otherwise stated, are derived from the *Statistical Tables for British India*, first published in 1877 and changed to the *Financial and Commercial Statistics for British India* in 1894.[1] It was an annual publication of the Government of India, published from Calcutta.

Company registration in India began in 1851 and the information on companies was reported in a fragmentary way for the first time in 1877 in that publication. *The Statistical Tables*, 1882, contained a list of 1,149 companies registered from 1851 to the end of March 1882, under the following heads: serial number, name of company, date of registration, nominal capital, paid-up capital, objects, and whether still working.

Information about the registration of companies outside Bengal was published only from 1859. The coverage was extended to other areas in the next two years. Whether this means that no company had been registered outside Bengal until 1859 cannot be said.

The last column 'whether still working' contained such words as 'defunct', 'no papers received', etc., and it was not always possible, therefore, to say exactly when a company was wound-up or struck off. Thirty-seven such companies had, of necessity, to be grouped separately, and the annual statistics for companies wound up to 31 March 1882, are therefore understated to that extent. Statistics given in the chapters dealing with the period 1851–82 are based on an analysis of the information contained in the 1882 publication. They are classified according to calendar years up to the end of 1881. The figures for 1882 are only for the first three months of that year.

From April 1882 to 31 March 1896, the publication contained only a list of such companies as were working at the end of each Financial Year, 1 April to 31 March, under similar headings, except that the last column disappeared. It was not possible, therefore, to find out from it the number of annual registrations and liquidations. An attempt to ascertain these figures indirectly had to be abandoned because of the frequent changes in its

[1] Their British Museum Catalogue numbers are I.S. 190 and I.S. 190/2.

A Note on Statistics

industrial classification of companies. Because of the difference in classification, the data for 1881–2 in Appendices 8 and 12 are not strictly comparable with the data in Appendix 17.

For the next two years, 1896–7 to 1897–8, the publication contained only details of companies registered and wound-up in these years, and in the two closing years of the century, a mere summary of new registration and liquidation. The statistics as found in the official publications from 1883, although containing some errors of calculation and rather unhappy classification of companies as regards industries, have been retained undisturbed, since these short-comings are insignificant. The various divisions of the period under study and the style of exposition have been influenced by the nature of the statistics available.

ABBREVIATIONS

C.P.	Central Provinces
EHR	*Economic History Review*
EJ	*Economic Journal*
EW	*Economic Weekly*
F.O.I.	*Friend of India*
IEJ	*Indian Economic Journal*
IER	*Indian Economic Review*
IESHR	*Indian Economic and Social History Review*
IJE	*Indian Journal of Economics*
JAS	*Journal of Asian Studies*
JCII	*Journal of the Chartered Insurance Institute*
JEH	*Journal of Economic History*
J.P.	*Judicial and Public Department Register*
L.P.	*Legislative Proceedings of India*
P.P.	*British Parliamentary Papers*
Rs.	*Rupees*
S.T.B.I.	*Statistical Tables for British India,* first published in 1877 and changed to *Financial and Commercial Statistics for British India* in 1894
T.O.I.	*Times of India*

GLOSSARY

Rupee	Indian currency equal to about 2s. up to 1872, and 16d. in 1900; now 13·3d. approximately
Anna	1/16th of a rupee
Pie	1/12th of an anna, e.g. Rs. 11–10–6 is 11 rupees, 10 annas and 6 pies
Lakh	Rs.100,000 (Indian notation Rs.1,00,000)
Crore	Rs.10,000,000 (normal Indian notation Rs.1,00,00,000)
Bania	Trader (a caste)
Mofussil	Provinces, interior
North-West Provinces (N.W.P.)	Now the Uttar Pradesh
Ryot	Subject, peasant
Zamindar	Landlord
Zilla	District
Shroff	Money lender and gold- and silver-trader
Sicca	Rupees issued during the rule of the East India Company

CHAPTER I

THE RISE OF BUSINESS CORPORATIONS IN INDIA

Modern business corporations in India owe their existence to foreign influences and traditions. It was mainly from the operations of the European chartered companies that the Indian merchants learnt about this form of business organisation.[1] The ancient indigenous institutions of the guild type and the territorial groups of businessmen and artisans, plausibly regarded as akin to modern companies, had almost withered away by the end of the fifteenth century in the wake of political disturbances preceding and following the advent of European merchants on Indian waters.[2]

SOUTH INDIAN JOINT STOCK COMPANIES

A form of joint stock company had come into existence about the middle of the seventeenth century in South India; understandably, as it was here that Indians first came into contact with European merchants.[3] During the seventeenth century there was a considerable expansion of trade between India and Europe, and European companies were competing in South India to buy Indian merchandise of which cotton textiles constituted a very important part.[4] So far the European companies had followed the

---

[1] See Appendix 1 for a short account of chartered companies.

[2] See Appendix 2 for a short account of the institution of guilds in ancient India.

[3] The earliest instance of such a company is found in the 1660's when Laurens Pit was Dutch Governor of Coromandel. *Memoir of Governor Laurens Pit to his successor Cornelis Speelman*, Koloniaal Archief, Overgekomen Brieven 1664, inv. nr. 1132 fo. 791–811, 25 June 1663, The Hague. See S. Arasaratnam, 'Indian Merchants and their Trading Methods (*circa* 1700)', a paper presented to the International Conference of Economic History, Munich, August 1965, and published in the IESHR, Vol. III, No. 1, March 1966, pp. 85–95. For two specific examples see my Ph.D. thesis, London, 1965, pp. 22–5.

[4] Arasaratnam, IESHR p. 85. See also a paper by Tapan Raychaudhuri, 'European Commercial Activity and the Organisation of India's Commerce and Industrial Production, 1500–1750' in B. N. Ganguli (Ed.) *Readings in Indian Economic History*, 1964, pp. 69–71.

practice of procuring supplies through individual Indian merchants who were paid advances. The Indian merchants in their turn advanced money to weavers to secure the output. In a period of expanding trade it was natural that the European companies had to deal more and more with a greater number of smaller merchants to procure supplies. This necessarily increased the cost of supplies as well as created uncertainty with regard to the quality and quantity of goods supplied. Recovery of debts became a great problem. It was primarily to overcome these difficulties that the European companies seem to have fostered among the Indian merchants the idea of organising on the basis of a joint stock company. The small merchants of Coromandel who were often badly hit by the result of their own competition eagerly accepted the idea, but the wealthy Surat merchants did not really favour it and secretly competed with their own joint stock companies in buying goods from the market.[1]

Generally a joint stock company consisted of between five and ten merchants who together subscribed an amount varying from 10,000 to 150,000 pagodas.[2] From the 1660's many such companies are mentioned in the records of the English and the Dutch East India companies. Their number begins to decline after about 1720 until they disappeared almost completely by the end of the eighteenth century.[3] The limited purpose for and the manner in which they were formed sealed the fate of these companies from the start. The document by which they were constituted was primarily a contract for the supply of goods by certain merchants to a European company. For the most part this document contained details of the goods to be supplied, period of delivery, prices, terms of payment, privileges conferred on the merchants by the European company within the jurisdiction of its fortified settlement (as for example, exemption from tolls in certain cases), and the nature of protection afforded to merchants in the case of political troubles.

Mixed together in this contract were four or five clauses which could easily find a place in a memorandum or an article of association or for that matter in a partnership agreement. These clauses

---

[1] See my thesis, pp. 24–5. Also Raychaudhuri, pp. 74–5.

[2] Gold coins current in South India. One pagoda was equal to approximately 12 shillings.

[3] Arasaratnam, IESHR, pp. 85–6.

were mainly that merchants together should trade with the European company concerned, remaining one with another, in an association; that they should together subscribe a stated capital according to the number of shares allocated to each; that the junior among them should in turn willingly go to the weaving centres to collect goods and further that they should defer to the judgement of senior merchants, the elected 'heads', in the management of the affairs of their company, and (in most cases) that the accounts should be settled annually. Among other important features of this document were the provisions whereby the European company forbade the use of the funds of these associations for any purpose except its own trade, any violation being punishable at its discretion. The European companies could, in their own interest, add a new merchant to these associations at any time, and, finally, the terms of this document could not be varied without their consent.[1]

The way these companies were constituted therefore left no scope for their future growth. It was as if a few merchants had got together to tender for the supply of goods required by a European company and, having won the contract, could not take on new business from other sources. In such a situation these companies had no incentive either to create permanent capital and increase it or to establish an independent executive. The absence of the latter often created a conflict of interest between the merchants as a joint body and as individuals, particularly when the supply and demand conditions in the market changed. When, therefore, the impetus provided by the European companies was removed the reason for the existence of these companies disappeared. It never seems to have occurred to the Indian merchants to make their joint stock organisationally independent of the European companies. Neither did they think of establishing joint stock companies for carrying on other types of businesses. According to S. Arasaratnam one reason why the partnership idea failed to be popular among Indian merchants was that the commercial castes in South India were evenly divided between two factions which frequently quarrelled.[2] He does not, however, advance any reason why the idea could not be taken up within

---

[1] For a copy of such a contract translated into English see Arasaratnam, IESHR, pp. 91–5.

[2] *Ibid.*, pp. 90–1.

each caste group or how it was that for nearly one century joint stock companies kept on being formed in South India. In the Indian context one must remember that partnership does not generally mean partnership between two or more individuals but between two or more joint family businesses, a relationship more difficult to achieve and sustain. Sociological explanations must therefore take into account the limitations of the Hindu joint family institution.[1] On the other hand, sufficient economic incentives may well have been lacking.[2]

ORGANISATION OF TRADE AND INDUSTRY—SOME TRENDS
AND FEATURES

The emergence of the English East India Company, in the second half of the eighteenth century, as the sole arbiter of India's destiny had many repercussions.[3] Not only did it end the influences of the other chartered companies but the monopoly instinct of the Company dictated the closing of all avenues, British or Indian, which were incompatible with its own trading interests. For example, up to 1834,[4] the Company pursued a policy of keeping other Europeans away from Indian shores, thus depriving India of much valuable enterprise, skill and capital. This was not all. It is said 'even merchants from upper parts of Hindostan were expelled and those concerned with export by sea discouraged'.[5]

[1] See pp. 163–7. For a provocative view of the Hindu joint-family living, see Nirad C. Chaudhuri, *The Continent of Circe*, 1965, pp. 230–1.

[2] See p. 9.

[3] The English East India Company started dominating the scene from about the beginning of the eighteenth century. Its position was further reinforced in 1717 by the grant of exclusive privileges by the Moghul emperor. Raychaudhuri, pp. 75–6.

[4] Some of the monopoly privileges of the East India Company had, however, been abolished at the time of its charter revision in 1813 and India had been partially opened to the free private enterprise of British traders in 1815. Helen B. Lamb, 'The "State" and Economic Development in India' in Simon Kuznets, Wilbert E. Moore and Joseph J. Spengler (Eds.), *Economic Growth: Brazil, India, Japan*, 1955, p. 467.

[5] Lord Cornwallis, quoted by R. K. Mukerjee in N. C. Sinha, *Studies in Indo-British Economy*, 1946, p. 4. In fact more than one hundred years before the battle of Plassey, the system of 'passport' introduced by the Dutch East India Company and the English East India Company was, in the following years, already having the effect of introducing far-reaching changes in the structure and volume of coastal as well as the South-east Asian and Middle-eastern trade of the Bengal merchants; and although the Bengal merchants benefited in some ways, on the whole their trade diminished very significantly

As a result of this policy, much of the free private trade passed into the hands of European servants of the Company and some 'free merchants'. A 'free merchant' was a merchant permitted by the Honourable East India Company to enter a Presidency in India and trade there under licence. 'The Company did not like them' but 'they were tolerated . . . because they were necessary; while the civil and military gentlemen were making their fortunes, they required some dependable person—British for choice—with whom to bank their takings'.[1] The secret of a free merchant's success lay in 'his personal tact, his scruples—or lack of them— and in his skill in spotting a stayer in the rapidly changing field of those whose interest was worth cultivating. Between sudden death, sudden disgrace and sudden caprice, it was difficult to depend on anyone.'[2] In 1710, there were only twenty-nine free merchants in Madras, then the seat of the East India Company, and 'at the most, they would have trebled or quadrupled by the end of the eighteenth century'.[3]

At a later stage, when Company servants were prevented from taking part in private trade they, 'finding their habits better adapted for commercial pursuits, obtained permission to resign their situations and engaged in agency and commercial business'.[4] Thus a substantial portion of private trade came to be concentrated in the hands of a few agency houses, which were partnership concerns, and which became the characteristic units of private British trade. The agency house was not simply a merchant firm, dealing in indigo or the coastal trade, but combined all sorts of diversified operations, such as ship-owning, house-owning, farming, manufacturing, banking, bill-broking, insurance etc. These houses were the bankers of the non-trading European community in India and their capital resources ran into millions of pounds

---

from the activities of these Companies. The secret of the powers of these Companies lay in their naval strength which enabled them to dictate the terms of trade. Om Prakash, 'The European Trading Companies and the Merchants of Bengal, 1650–1725' in IESHR, Vol. 1, No. 3, Cf. Raychaudhuri, pp. 73–6.

[1] Hilton Brown, *Parry's of Madras*, 1954, pp. 4–5. On 'fortunes' made by the Company servants see p. 6, note 2 and also essays on Lord Clive and Hastings in *The Works of Lord Macaulay*, Vol. 2, n.d. N. K. Sinha, *Economic History of Bengal*, Vol. 1, 1956, *passim*. D. H. Buchanan, *The Development of Capitalist Enterprise in India*, 1934, pp. 32–5. W. W. Hunter, *The Annals of Rural Bengal*, 1897, pp. 352–4. P.P. 1831–32, X, Part 1, p. 102.

[2] Brown, pp. 4–5.

[3] *Ibid.*   [4] P.P., 1831–2, X, Pt. II, App. 3, p. 496.

sterling.[1] By the close of the eighteenth century they had attained such an ascendency as to form, in effect, an oligopoly, controlling a large portion of the internal and coastal trade of the country.[2] Their dominance was due, among other things, to their capital resources and superior skill in organisation.

It should also be remembered that until the British established the 'rule of law' after the Sepoy Rebellion (1857) the country had been almost continuously engaged in internecine wars, both during the reign of the Moghuls and after Plassey.[3] The essential concomitants of economic growth, such as peace and security, and the creation of 'social overheads' by the State, were largely absent. Before the damage done by an invading army could be repaired, and conditions could return to normal, they would once again be upset by political events. The people of India were relatively poor, and the yield from agriculture was low.[4] It has

[1] Some idea of their resources can be gathered from 'the losses sustained by the East India community, in consequence of the failure of the conjoint private bankers and merchants in India . . .' (C. N. Cooke, *The Rise, Progress and Present Conditions of Banking in India*, 1863, p. 348.) on account of the commercial crisis of the mid-1840s. The deficiencies on six houses alone in Calcutta were as follows:

Palmer & Co.	£2,600,000
Alexander & Co.	3,440,000
Mackintosh & Co.	2,470,000
Ferguson & Co.	3,260,000
Colvin & Co.	1,210,000
Cruttenden & Co.	1,350,000
	£14,330,000

[2] '. . . the coasting trade in India, and between the islands, as well as the internal trade of India, were the monopoly of the higher employees of the Company'. Karl Marx in *Das Kapital*, Vol. 1, quoted in J. Beauchamp, *British Imperialism in India*, 1934, p. 19. 'The servants of the Company obtained—not for their employees but for themselves—a monopoly of almost the whole internal trade.' *The Works of Lord Macaulay*, 'Essay on Lord Clive', Vol. 2, p. 402.

[3] After 1858 there were two Indias: British India and the India of the princely states. The latter India contained some six hundred states with one fourth of the population and two-fifths of the area of the Indian subcontinent.

[4] According to Morris 'traditional Indian society was supported at a lower level of real income per capita than was the case in early modern Europe or even Tokugawa, Japan'. To support his view he quotes Thomas Kerridge, who wrote in 1669, 'though this countrie be esteemed rich, we find the common inhabitants to be verie needie . . .', cited in W. Foster, *The English Factories in India, 1618–1621*, 1906, p. 138. See Morris D. Morris, 'Towards a Reinterpretation of Nineteenth Century Indian Economic History', JEH, Vol. XXIII, December 1963, No. 4, fn. 16.

The implication is not that the Indian agricultural techniques were under-

long been asserted that until about the end of the eighteenth century India was by no means backward in world trade and was a great manufacturing nation. But no-one has as yet assessed the importance of India's trade and industry in relation to the size of her population and the proportion of people involved. The general impression is that much of India consisted of thousands of self-sufficient villages with the bulk of her trade, commerce and industry centred around the ports, religious places, and in the capital cities of rajahs and nawabs.[1] But the likelihood of specialisation in the production of textiles, brass and copper wares and animals above the village level makes self-sufficiency a doubtful proposition.

The proportion of Indian population living in large cities would seem to have been higher than many countries in Europe and America until about the middle of the nineteenth century. In the subsequent period the rate of change towards urbanisation became slower in India.[2] No definitive statement can be made about the comparative levels of technology although it has been claimed

---

developed or that the agricultural sector was insensitive to innovation, but extremes of temperature, very short growing seasons, and the restricted supply of soil moisture made it impossible to achieve high yields. Rotation, fallowing, green manuring, and double cropping were known in India. Similarly, tobacco, potato, ground nuts, and plantation crops such as tea, coffee and rubber were quickly introduced and some rapidly spread. *Ibid.* See also Louise E. Howard, *Sir Albert Howard in India*, 1953, and Sir Albert Howard and J. A. Voeleker, *Report on the Improvement of Indian Agriculture*, 1893.

After the book had gone to the Press the IESHR published in its March 1968 issue a debate on Morris' paper. No alteration anywhere in this book has, therefore, been made on this account.

[1] For political and economic conditions in India in the late eighteenth and early nineteenth centuries, see W. H. Moreland and A. C. Chatterjee, *A Short History of India*, 1957. A Tripathi, *Trade and Finance in Bengal Presidency, 1793–1833*, 1956. R. D. Choksey, *Economic Life in the Bombay Deccan, 1818–1839*, 1955, also *Economic Life in the Bombay Konkan, 1818–1839*, 1960. A. Sarda Raju, *Economic Conditions in the Madras Presidency, 1800–1850*, 1941. D. R. Gadgil, *Origin of the Indian Business Class*, mimeographed, n.d., India Office Library.

On village self-sufficiency and later changes in the economic life of a village, see Daniel Thorner, 'Emergence of an Indian Economy, 1760–1960', *The Encyclopedia Americana*, Vol. 15, pp. 12–19 (1960 Edn.), reprinted in Daniel and Alice Thorner, *Land and Labour in India*, 1962, pp. 51–69. Also M. N. Srinivas (Ed.), *India's Villages*, 2nd Edn. 1960, and M. N. Srinivas and A. M. Shah, 'The Myth of Self-Sufficiency in the Indian Village', EW, 10 September 1960.

[2] For some comparative figures see Kingsley Davis, 'Social and Demographic Aspects of Economic Development in India' in Kuznets *et al.* (Eds.), pp. 269–77.

contrary to popular belief, that India was significantly behind Europe in this respect.[1] This may well be true but with our present knowledge of the facts, the question cannot be settled. There is no doubt, however, that the rate of progress in science and technology had been meagre. For this the explanation may lie in the fact that the size of the trading community was limited by caste; occupations such as metal ware, which form the basis of an industrial community, were restricted to inferior castes.

---

[1] According to Morris, a comparison with the European technical development between 1400 and 1700 would show that the Indian technology was at about the productive levels of late medieval Europe. He argues, 'while India produced fine textiles and a few examples of remarkable craftsmanship, we must not mistake manual dexterity for productivity nor assume that dexterity implied the presence of sophisticated tools and manufacturing techniques. In fact, the reverse is true'. He is right when he says that we cannot assume the presence of sophisticated tools but by the same token we cannot assume the contrary. He is wrong when he says, 'we must not mistake manual dexterity for productivity'. Why not? Logically, manual dexterity or skill in manipulation can certainly lead to greater productivity like any other skill. The fact that India exported large quantities of cotton textiles to Europe almost to the end of the eighteenth century would justify the assumption that India had substantial comparative-cost advantage in this field. Either Europe did not have the skill to produce such fine textiles or the cost of producing them must have been higher. A substantial part of the total cost must be represented by the cost of labour. The wage rates may have been cheaper in India and the raw materials may have been locally grown, but could the two of these alone account for the vast difference in prices between India and Europe? To my mind, no. It is more likely that the productivity was higher in India. The change of direction of trade in the subsequent period is a pointer in this regard. As further evidence to support his argument, Morris says that 'early European travellers often noted the primitive character of Indian technology when compared with their own' and that the 'English factory records of the seventeenth century constantly stress the inelasticity of textile supplies and low productivity'. I am not an expert on the literature of this period but the evidence shows that much greater quantities of textiles were exported from India during the seventeenth century as compared to earlier periods. The supply, therefore, must have increased. T. Raychaudhuri explains this on the assumption that existing idle capacity was brought in use to match demand. The views of Morris and Raychaudhuri can be reconciled if we assume that increasingly less efficient workers were employed. Morris also believes that India '*used*' very little metal'. To support this he adduces the evidence that an examination of Indian imports from 1500 to 1800 shows that imports included a substantial proportion of metals in various stages of fabrication. To my mind, his evidence proves the contrary. My knowledge does not warrant me to make any definitive statement, but it would seem that even the Indian metallurgy was not behind Europe before the Industrial Revolution if the gold and silver ornaments, the brassware, copperware and iron and steel products made in India are any evidence.

See Morris, JEH, section III and Raychaudhuri, p. 72.

Capital was thus divorced from technology, which must adversely affect technical progress. Though this division was due to the caste system, it could have been overcome by applying the concepts of the joint stock company and the factory system of production. Combined, these two institutions held far reaching possibilities and both of them were known to Indians from the latter half of the seventeenth century. Such a situation would suggest that the Indians lacked initiative but it is difficult to be sure. Even in England it was only by the end of the seventeenth century that 'some idea had been gleaned of one of the primary functions of the company concept—the possibility of enabling the capitalist to combine with the entrepreneur'.[1] Moreover, it seems reasonable to assume that when goods were produced or manufactured by a craftsman at his home, cost items such as wages, rent, lighting, depreciation, etc. were likely to be understated in computing the total unit cost of a product and this may have influenced prices to be on the low side. The cost of production in a factory could therefore be easily higher. Tapan Raychaudhuri's suggestion that the incentive for introducing a factory system was lacking because demand for textiles was easily met, could not be regarded as sufficient explanation, since if a businessman could see possibilities for economies of scale one would expect him to change over to the factory system of production.[2] Further research must be done before one can be sure.

Stages of Company Growth before 1850

The growth of companies in India was not continuous and during certain periods no progress was made at all. During the hundred years up to 1850 their development can be conveniently divided into four stages: the first period is marked by the foundation of banks and insurance companies, and the second by the stimulus given to the development of banking companies by the break-up of the great Calcutta agency houses in 1829; the invention of the

---

[1] L. C. B. Gower, *Modern Company Law*, 1957, p. 26.

[2] Raychaudhuri, p. 72. The European companies introduced the factory system of production on a limited scale in India; the following reasons may explain their action. Rent was not a true cost inside a fortified settlement. Workers were more willing to shift there for reasons of security. Middlemen profits and bad debts were saved. Such a system allowed greater control over supply in quantity and quality (including styles).

steamship and expansion of trade and commerce opened the third phase, and the last and most revolutionary stage owes its character to the coming of the railways to India and the development in England of economic conditions and a climate of opinion favourable to the growth of Indian industry.

The first period, that of the founding of banks and insurance companies, dates from the 1780's. The capital market was suffering from an acute scarcity of money and credit, which was damaging the whole trade and commerce of the country. The establishment of a banking company was considered necessary to improve the situation, and the plan of the 'General Bank' was adopted, though not without opposition, in a public meeting held in Calcutta on 17 March 1786.[1] The Articles of Association of the Bank contained remarkably modern features and it is interesting to note here that they purported to limit the liability of the shareholders to the face value of their holdings.[2] After rendering gallant service, this bank went into voluntary liquidation under the

---

[1] In the preceding two decades, the following two companies are also known to have existed, but their details are lacking. The first, the 'Exclusive Society of Trade', established by Lord Clive and his Select Committee in August 1765, after the privilege of private trade had been withdrawn from the servants of the Company, must be regarded as extraordinary both as to its constituents and objects. It had the 'monopoly of the trade in salt, betel nut and tobacco, to be carried on exclusively for the benefit of the superior servants of the Company'. 'There were three classes of proprietors and the capital stock was divided into 56 one-third shares, the Governor having 5 shares, the Second-in-Council 3, the General 3, two colonels each 2 shares. The second class was to consist of 18 persons. They were to have in all 12 shares. The third class consisted of 28 persons. They were to have altogether 9⅓ shares.' 'In the second year, the capital stock was divided into 60 shares.' But the Court of Directors of the Company ordered the abolition of this Society and it ceased to exist on and from 1 September 1767. N. K. Sinha, pp. 72, 73, 96. The second company, an earlier General Bank, was formed by Warren Hastings in an effort to mitigate the stringency of the money market. The Bank had two chief offices, one at Calcutta, and another at Murshidabad, with 14 branches. 'The statement of accounts ... showed considerable profits between June 1773 and June 1775, of which the Government took half share. The directors, however, failed to grasp the full utility of the scheme and it was dissolved.' (*Ibid.*, p. 144), see also H. Sinha, *Eearly European Banking in India*, 1927, pp. 9–11 and 98.

[2] Unless there was a formal contract between the parties, statements alleging limited liability in deeds of settlement and prospectuses were eventually held to be ineffective in England in Re *Sea, Fire & Insurance Co.* (1854), 3 De G.M. & G. 459.

See Gower, p. 35, fn. 65 and 66. Also B. C. Hunt, *The Development of the Business Corporation in England, 1800–1867*, 1936, pp. 33–4, 72 and 99–101.

impact of the monetary crisis caused by the Mysore war and was finally dissolved on 31 March 1791.

The experience of the General Bank, however, had already shown its usefulness in mitigating the monetary stringency in the capital market and in 1806 another bank—the Bank of Calcutta— was formed as an instrument of government policy. In 1809, this bank received the first known charter granted to an Indian company and on that date it also changed its name to the Bank of Bengal.[1] For the next twenty-three years it remained the only banking company in the country and continued to exist until its identity was merged in that of the Imperial Bank of India on 27 January 1921.

Insurance on modern lines began in India during the eighteenth century in course of her trade with the western countries. Marine insurance was the first to start. There was a considerable volume of shipping to and from ports in India, and between India and other eastern ports, for which cover was required. During the last quarter of the eighteenth century Indian international trade was mainly in the hands of European agency houses. Originally all marine insurances were placed in London but very often underwriters there had only an imperfect knowledge of the risks undertaken by them because communications were difficult. Insurances had to be written before the name of the ship could be known. This required great caution on the part of the underwriters since they could not tell what their overall liability might be on any one ship.[2] In fact, as Smallwood writes, 'it was probably not uncommon for an insurance to have terminated before the extent of the underwriters' liability was known'.[3] The result was that the premiums were quite high; considerably higher on the goods on the unnamed ship than on the named. Indeed it was difficult at times to get the required cover from reputable firms.[4] These factors ultimately led the British merchants in India to establish local marine insurance companies during the last decade of the eighteenth century. One of the earliest to be mentioned was the Calcutta Insurance Company, which was established in 1798.[5] One can also read the names of thirteen other insurance com-

---

[1] H. Sinha, pp. 5–6.

[2] R. P. F. Smallwood, 'The Nature and Structure of Insurance Markets in the Far East', JCII, Vol. 59, p. 79.

[3] *Ibid.*   [4] *Ibid.*

[5] Harold E. Raynes, *A History of British Insurance*, 1948, p. 184.

panies together with their 'Committee of Directors' and 'Agents'[1] in *The Bengal Almanac and Directory for 1815*.[2] Their main business would seem to have been marine insurance and some of them probably originated in the last decade of the eighteenth century. The exact nature of their organisation and operations must, however, remain obscure until further research proves successful.

Having gone into the field of insurance, the agency houses took the next step almost immediately and started life insurance companies. The earliest, the Calcutta Laudable Society, started, it seems, in 1797. This is based on the assumption that the Third Calcutta Laudable Society, a life insurance company founded in 1809 for a term of six years, had already enjoyed two similar leases of life. In reality, the Calcutta Laudable and another company, the Union Society of Calcutta, founded on 23 April 1814 were of the nature of a mutual contribution society, a more complex form of friendly society. In these societies the policy holders were also the proprietors but, since policies were assignable, provided the approval of the directors was obtained, something in the nature of a stock of freely transferable shares was achieved.[3] The idea of insurance, begun at Calcutta, had spread to other major Indian cities during this period.[4] Life insurance companies were no longer temporary laudable societies but were started on a commercial basis with corporate form though without its legal privileges. The first of these was the Oriental Life Insurance Company founded in 1822 in Calcutta.[5] It was started mainly by

---

[1] Agents here mean managing agents and not commission agents or brokers.

[2]
1. Amicable Insurance Office	2. Aramean Insurance Company
3. Asiatic Insurance Company	4. Bengal Insurance Society
5. Calcutta Insurance Company	6. Canton Insurance Company
7. Canton Insurance Company	8. Ganges Insurance Company
9. Globe Insurance Company	10. Hindostan Insurance Company
11. Hope Insurance Company	12. India Insurance Company
13. Phoenix Insurance Company	14. Star Insurance Company

There were two companies both named Canton Insurance Company, both founded in Canton with agencies in Calcutta. They amalgamated on 1 January 1815.

[3] *Ibid.*

[4] Morris mentioned that by 1851 there were twenty-five insurance companies carrying on business in Bombay, but does not give any details. See M. D. Morris, *The Emergence of an Industrial Labour Force in India: A Study of the Bombay Cotton Mills, 1854–1947*, 1965, p. 15.

[5] The date of establishment of this company can be worked out from a memorandum submitted by the New Oriental to the Government of India

Europeans to insure European lives. The Company was reconstructed in 1834 under the name of New Oriental Insurance
Company and through the influence of Motilal Seal accepted to
underwrite Indian lives as well. In promoting the business of
insurance in Bengal, the names of Dwarka Nath Tagore, Ramtanu
Lahiri and Rustomji Cowasji must also be mentioned. By 1850 at
least eleven other companies were working in India, but only six
of them originated there.[1]

The second stage in company development is marked by the
break-up of the Calcutta agency houses in 1829, following the
commercial crisis in England. The European community had
always deposited their savings with these agency houses. After
the failure of these houses the Europeans naturally wished to
promote banking companies so that banking and trading activities
could be separated. From this year onwards, the banking companies in India registered a continuous progress which, though
not spectacular, was not insignificant. Thus between 1829 and
1850, fourteen new banking companies were formed; the Union
Bank of Calcutta and the Benares Bank, however, failed in 1848.
A few others were also incorporated outside India, mainly with a
view to operating in the Indian market.[2]

With the development of steamships in the 1820's and the
possibilities now opened for greatly increased traffic in passengers,
cargo and mails, the third phase of growth began. A number of
shipping, dock, tug-boat and warehouse companies were set up
during the thirties.[3] As a result of the sudden rise in the demand

which was dated 30 January 1850, and in which it stated 'During the 28 years
which have elapsed since the New Oriental Life Insurance Company was
established . . .', *Legislative Proceedings of India*, 27 December 1850. But
according to N. R. Sircar, the Oriental was started in 1818 and reorganised
as New Oriental in 1834. Quoted in R. M. Ray, *Life Insurance in India*, 1941.

[1] *Companies established in India*	Date	Place
Bombay Life Insurance Co.	1823	Bombay
Madras Equitable	1829	Madras
Madras Widows	1834	Madras
Christian Mutual	1847	Punjab
Tinnevalley Diocesan Council Widows' Fund	1849	Madras

Companies established in Britain
Albert Life Assurance Co.   European Life Assurance Co.
Universal Life Assurance Co.   Colonial Life Assurance Co.
Royal Insurance Co.
(R. M. Ray, *passim*.)
[2] See Appendix 3 for a list of Indian and foreign banks established between
1829 and 1850.   [3] See Appendix 4 for a list of companies to 1850.

for coal for ships some coal mining companies were launched in the Ranigunj, Mirzapore and Sylhet areas.[1]

Elimination of political instability from large parts of India and the construction and repair of roads directly led to the expansion of trade.[2] The abolition of the East India Company's trade monopoly in 1833 provided another stimulus to economic activity, particularly to tea plantations, and many companies were formed in this period with a view to establishing indigo factories, cotton-textile mills, iron and steel works, and coffee and tea plantations.[3] But these pioneering efforts were mostly shortlived. As yet, conditions were not favourable for the sucessful launching of industrial enterprises.

So far as cotton was concerned, the traditional view was that the prohibitory and sumptuary laws against the use of Indian calicos in England,[4] the dumping of cheap goods by Lancashire and 'a murderous system of anti-Indian tariffs and duties'[5] killed an industry which was capable of threatening the very existence of its rival. No doubt these measures did a great deal of harm to the export side of the Indian textile industry, but the difficulties of transport and communications of those days among other things must have greatly limited the impact of Lancashire on the interior parts of the country.[6] The distress of the Indian hand-loom industry probably became really serious as the result of the

[1] See appendix 4 for a list of Companies to 1850.

[2] After the defeat of the Maratha empire in 1818 British hegemony had been established over almost the whole of Western India, leading directly to the expansion of commerce. See Kenneth Ballhatchet, *Social Policy and Social Change in Western India, 1817–1830*, 1957. The opening of the Bhore Ghat in 1830, the first major roadway through the Western Ghats, further stimulated trade. See Morris, *Emergence of a Labour Force*, p. 14.

[3] See Appendix 4.   [4] Mukerjee, in N. C. Sinha, pp. 5–6.

[5] Brown, p. 5.

[6] The cotton textile industry would seem to have suffered most during the period 1813–33 and the resulting distress in terms of unemployment was probably most severe in the 1820's and 30's. See H. R. Ghosal. 'Changes in the Organisation of Industrial Production in the Bengal Presidency in the Early Nineteenth Century', in Ganguli (Ed.), pp. 124–33. See also 'Report on the discussion', *ibid.*, p. 152–3. It is conceivable that the East India Company could have debarred British manufactures from entering India though nobody can seriously suggest that it was practicable politics. Britain could certainly not be expected to have continued to import from India. The handloom industry had to suffer if not at British hands, certainly from Bombay mills. The structural changes had to occur although the period of adjustment could have been artificially extended. After the initial Lancashire impact, the hand-loom industry had to live continuously under the threat of competition from the

rise of the cotton mills in Bombay and the spread of communications.

Sugar was in rather a different position. European agency houses had taken an interest in its plantation and manufacture since the 1820's, but 'West Indian interests with, it was said, as many as ninety M.P.'s in their pocket, were able to debar the East Indian produce from the English market by prohibitive tariffs'.[1]

In addition, the occasional apprehensions of the East India Company that 'the destruction of the Indian manufactures would ultimately lead to the diminution of remittances to England . . . and loss of revenue'[2] stood in the way of immediate replacement of antiquated types of enterprise and thus had the effect of causing a 'definite hiatus between the decay of the indigenous industries and the rise of factories and large-scale concerns. . . .'[3]

Moreover, 'the British Government sought to maintain a relative superiority in skill, knowledge and enterprise by prohibiting the emigration of artisans and the export of [important] machinery' from England.[4] The proximity of the European countries to England frustrated the attainment of this object in Europe.[5] Whether or not these provisions applied to India,[6] the distance that separated her from the seat of this new industrial

---

Indian mills, which must have grown increasingly severe with the increase in the capacity and rise in productivity of mills and the spread of communications. Yet the handloom industry managed to survive on a large scale. In explaining this, account must be taken of the fall in the cost through using mill-produced yarn, and the Indian taste, e.g., for handloom sarees, towels, and certain types of silk. The growth in population, plus the above mentioned factors, other things being equal, would cause a shift of the demand curve to the right as well as a downward movement along the demand curve. The greatest danger to the handloom industry would probably come from nylon and such fabrics, as the income rises, but this is beyond the point. See also Morris, JEH.

[1] Brown, p. 5. Despite this by 1846 the export of sugar to England averaged 60,000 tons per year. But the subsequent policy of *laissez-faire* hit the sugar industry and the country became an importer of sugar which came mostly from Java and Mauritius. Sunit Kumar Sen, *Studies in Economic Policy and Development of India, 1848-1926*, 1966, pp. 71-2. See also Ganguli (Ed.), pp. 152-3.

[2] Mukerjee in N. C. Sinha, p. v (Introduction).

[3] G. E. Hubbard, *Eastern Industrialisation and its Effects on the West*, 1938, p. 251.

[4] C. K. Hobson, *The Export of Capital*, 1914, p. 107. The first Act was passed in 1774, but the export of machinery was freed partially in 1825 and completely in 1843. L. C. A. Knowles, *Industrial and Commercial Revolutions in Great Britain during the Nineteenth Century*, 1937, p. 129.

[5] *Ibid.*, p. 107.   [6] A reading of the 1774 Act shows that they did.

knowledge, coupled with the religious superstitions and other social prejudices of her own people, effectively hindered the acquisition of new industrial techniques. At the same time the Government of India did not, like that of Japan, follow a policy of sending students abroad for technical education.[1] As regards difficulties of inland transport, even where they did not act as a deterrent, procuring raw materials, fuel, machinery and its components proved always to be very costly and time-consuming.[2] Moreover, the significance of the company concept was not seen in its true perspective right up to the 1830's. It was regarded, even among the educated, to be a necessary evil for raising large sums of capital.[3]

Halfway through the nineteenth century came, however, the last phase, ushering the country into an unprecedented era of company development. By this time, the economic climate of England had so changed as to be highly conducive to the accumulation of capital;[4] this, plus rising wages,[5] and the precarious position of cotton supply from America[6] turned the attention of

[1] Hubbard, p. 250.

[2] 'Even before the railway era, attempts had been made to establish modern industries [such as cotton mills and iron works] in India, but these had failed, owing to the absence of transport facilities . . .', Hubbard, p. 250. See also V. Anstey, *The Economic Development of India*, 1929, pp. 128–9, and D. H. Buchanan, pp. 128–9. Lack of efficient means of transport was certainly a great obstacle but not the main reason for the failure of industrial enterprises in the 1820–50 period. Several other reasons, among them poor organisation, bad management, and poor location were also important.

[3] The following comment on the subject of steam communication with England is illuminating in this regard. 'A steam company, with joint stock capital contributed with the express object of getting an adequate dividend, and with reasonable directors and servants would make a very different turnout. And if any mercantile firm had capital enough at their disposal to undertake the whole themselves, perhaps they would manage the business better still.' (Leading article, F.O.I., 21 May 1833.)

[4] 'Capital was accumulating at a rapid pace and joint stock enterprises were looking beyond Europe. So in the third quarter of the century capital began to flow in bulk towards the East and ultimately ushered in the era of modern industry in India.' N. C. Sinha, p. 10.

[5] '. . . trade union organisation and the growing solidarity of the British workers in the nineteenth century were forcing the jute manufacturers to yield to the demand for better wages and more humane conditions; they [British manufacturers] found that by transferring their capital to India and building jute mills there, they could increase the rate of exploitation by getting destitute Indian ex-peasants to work for them for almost nothing . . .' Beauchamp, p. 44.

[6] 'The mania of 1845 produced nearly a dozen companies in London which proposed to build railways in India.' But 'only two of them survived the panic'.

Rise of Business Corporations

British investors towards India, and in the later 1840's, a number of railway companies were floated to connect the coal districts of Burdwan and the cotton belt near Nagpur to the ports of Calcutta and Bombay respectively. The laying of railway tracks in India started a whole chain of foreseen and unforeseen results.[1] In particular it provided the foundation of capitalist enterprise.

But the growth of companies in the second half of the nineteenth century owes much to the contribution made earlier by the pioneers—the civil and military servants of the East India Company, the European agency houses, and the Indian mercantile community. In particular the passing of the first Companies Act of 1850 removed the greatest obstacle to the growth of companies by according them the privilege to sue and be sued. The part played by the servants of the East India Company, the agency houses and the Indian communities in promoting and financing companies and the legal problems faced by companies in the era up to 1850 are discussed in the following two chapters.

'There was the East India Railway Co., promoted by Macdonald Stephenson who seems to have been the earliest person to plan railways for India. Stephenson was backed by Cockrill and Co., Fletcher, Alexander and Co., Crawford, Colvin and Co., Palmer, Mackillop and Dent, and several others of the great East India Houses, and by the shipping interests, the new P. & O., desirous not only to expand the volume of Indian trade, but also to procure access to the Burdwan coal mines. Another railway company, the Great Indian Peninsular, contemplated a line from Bombay to tap the great cotton producing districts of Nagpoor. Its support came from Bombay and Liverpool, and the Lancashire mill owners made its cause their own through lobbyists at London. The cotton famine of 1846 reminded Lancashire of its dependence on the United States and during the session of 1847-8 a Parliamentary committee headed by John Bright investigated the growth of cotton in India and agreed that deficient transportation was the main difficulty.' L. H. Jenks, *The Migration of British Capital to 1875*, 1927, pp. 210–11.

[1] D. H. Buchanan, p. 181. It has been argued that the British failed to anticipate the political consequences of railway development in India. See Beauchamp, p. 42.

CHAPTER 2

THE PROMOTION AND FINANCE OF COMPANIES TO 1850[1]

Up to the middle of the eighteenth century Indian merchants invested their capital mainly in the large inland trade of the country.[2] They were generally prosperous and important as middlemen for purchasing goods for the European companies, particularly for the 'investments' of the English East India Company and the private trade of its servants. But the change in the Company's 'investment' policy, as well as its *de facto* assumption of political power in the country in the 1750's, revolutionised the structure of internal trade.[3] After 1757 the role played by the Indian middlemen gradually diminished in importance and they were largely superseded by the servants of the Company in making its purchases.[4] The servants were also allowed to trade on their own account but this privilege, having been greatly abused, was subsequently withdrawn by the Company.[5] The persons who most benefited from these changes were the 'free merchants' who soon afterwards established the well-known agency houses. The agrarian situation was also unstable during this period, rendering human and capital resources somewhat idle. Beginning in the 1890's, for half a century afterwards the British introduced far-reaching changes in the landholding, land revenue, education and legal systems of the country, which made investment in land and a job in the civil service attractive. The resultant flow of

[1] Pp. 18-35 are adapted, by permission, from my article in the *Indian Journal of Economics*, Vol. XLVI, No. 183, April 1966, pp. 477-86.
[2] Mukerjee in N. C. Sinha, p. vi says that the merchants also invested in the handicraft industry, by which I think he means the money paid by the merchants to the artisans as an advance for the supply of goods. Such a treatment of advance payment is, to my mind, wrong since the merchants had no stake in the profit or loss of these handicraft establishments.
[3] N. K. Sinha, pp. 21, 23-4.
[4] *Ibid.*
[5] *Ibid.*, p. 90. The privileged private inland trade of the servants lasted in its varied enormity from 1757 to 1767 and lingered on till 1771.

capital into land property is said to have adversely affected the development of modern enterprises.[1]

It is generally believed that Indian participation in the growth of modern enterprises was very disappointing. Judged by absolute standards this may be true, but this failure is understandable in view of what has been said above. If, however, their contribution is judged in relation to what was achieved in the corporate field during this period, it was in no way small, except, perhaps, in the limited area of insurance, which was then concentrated in European hands. The major Indian contribution came in the field of promoting banking companies. There was not a single banking company of any importance which did not owe its existence partly to the enterprise and capital of Indians.[2] The Bengal Tea

[1] Mukerjee in N. C. Sinha, p. vii; N. C. Sinha, pp. 30–1, 36–7; Tripathi, p. 223, and S. K. Sen, *Economic Policy*, pp. 58–9. Opinion is divided on whether Cornwallis consciously meant to discourage industrial development or simply expected agriculture to benefit from a fresh inflow of capital when he said, 'there is every ground to expect that large capitals possessed by many Natives ... will be applied to the purchase of landed property as soon as the tenure is declared to be secure'. (Quoted in Tripathi, p. 18.) At any rate the process of change was much slower than what is popularly believed. The Permanent Settlement took at least half a century to be completed and temporary settlements continued in what is now Bihar as late as 1860. See 'Report on Discussion' by Raychaudhuri in Ganguli (Ed.), pp. 151–3. Large parts of India were never affected by the changes introduced by the British in the land revenue system.

[2] *Banks* — *Promoters and/or Directors*
   1. Bank of Bengal — Maharaja Sookmoy — p. 96*
   2. Oriental Bank — Dadabhoy Rustomjee† / Jugonnath Sunkersett
   3. Union Bank — D. Tagore / Prosunnocomar Tagore (p. 187) / Promothonath Day
   4. The Delhi Bank Corporation — Lalla Choonni Mull, Trustee — p. 234
   5. Dacca Bank — Kajeh-alleemoollah (p. 234) / Babu Nandlal Dutt / Kajee Abdul Gunni
   6. Benares Bank — Babu Huri Chund (p. 237) / Lala Sambhunath

In an important meeting of the shareholders of this Bank, 15 out of 23 shareholders were Indian.
   7. Agra Savings Fund — Peetambur Dutt — p. 324
   8. Commercial Bank of India — Byramjee Jejeebhoy / Sorabjee Jejeebhoy / Limjee Monockjee / Mangaldas Nathoobhoy

* The page references are to Cooke.
† Refers to L.P., 27 December 1850.

Association is an outstanding example of their enterprise. The Assam Company, formed in 1839, in London, was not the first in the field of tea cultivation in India. It is worth mentioning here that the proposal to form the Bengal Tea Association originated from the office of Carr, Tagore and Company, Calcutta, who were Secretaries of the Calcutta Steam Tug Association and were also connected with the formation of the India General Steam Navigation Company.[1] The extent of Indian participation, however, was by no means uniform throughout the country, but varied quite considerably in different parts.[2]

The vast majority of Europeans then in India were the servants of the East India Company, since, according to statistics, for every free merchant who sailed to India there were 11 writers, 87 cadets, 11 surgeons and 110 'mariners'.[3] It would be difficult to find a parallel in economic history anywhere for such direct participation by the military and civil servants of a government in trade generally and in the growth of joint stock enterprises in particular. The key to this peculiarity lies in the privileged private trade permitted to the Company's servants which enabled them to amass fabulous wealth. As their gains could not always easily be sent to England, they sought safe and profitable investments in India.[4] After this privilege had been withdrawn and they could

---

Among its promoters were four other Parsee names. Its auditors were also Parsees—Sorabjee Pestonjee Framjee, pp. 330, 335.

9. Chartered Mercantile Bank of India, London, and China, projected by, among others:
Jugonnath Sunkersett
Cowasjee Jehanghier Heerjee
Mangaldas Nathoobhoy
Cowasjie Nanabhoy   p. 357

[1] Among the promoters of the Bengal Tea Association were the following Indians:
Dwarkanath Tagore
Prossonocomar Tagore
Rustomjee Cowasjee
Motee Lall Seil
Hadjee Ispahanie

Motee Lall Seil also became one of the first directors and Prossonocomar Tagore, subsequently, of the Amalgamated Assam Company. H. A. Antrobus, *A History of the Assam Co., 1839–1953*, 1957, pp. 39, 401, 404.

[2] (See pp. 22–6).

[3] Brown, p. 4.

[4] 'This ill-gotten wealth had to be remitted home. But the E.I. Co., would not let them remit their fortunes through their channels. Nor would their servants think it prudent to do so. . . .' N. K. Sinha, pp. 10–11.

no longer trade on their own account, it would seem that they found in the company concept a way of circumventing the orders of their employer. The General Bank, the first unincorporated company formed in 1786 was the result of their enterprise.[1] Not only did they have plenty of capital, but many of them had technical knowledge in various fields. In the course of their duties they were posted to various parts of India which enabled them to discover the mineral wealth of the country and they were quick to realise its commercial potential. Thus, the first iron works, the Porto Novo Steel and Iron Company, was set up by one Heath, an engineer in the employ of the Company.[2] Similarly, the first person to undertake coal mining appears to have been a British magistrate of Chhotanagpur, serving the Company.[3] The servants of the Company also possessed the administrative experience necessary to run a company, with the added asset of a host of friends in the Government. They were, therefore, well qualified to promote, finance, and direct companies, and were particularly prominent in the field of banking. In other branches, they were not so successful, perhaps because they tended to lack true business acumen or perhaps because India was not yet ripe for ventures such as they attempted.

The rise of the agency houses coincided with the abolition of the privileged inland trade, when the scramble for wealth gave way to regulated commercial ventures. The 'free merchants' organised themselves in large partnerships later called the 'Agency Houses'.[4] These had become firmly established towards the end of the eighteenth century and in the following years the glory of their wealth was such that they became known as the 'Merchant Princes of India'.[5] Between 1790 and 1830 these houses were the centres of large capital resources, enterprise, and administrative and organisational skill, and wielded great economic and political powers.[6] Unlike the Indian firms or the Company servants, they

---

[1] See H. Sinha, *op. cit.*   [2] Brown, pp. 64–5.
[3] Viz., S. G. Heatly, D. H. Buchanan, p. 255.
[4] 'The East India agency houses numbered 29 in 1803', N. K. Sinha, p. 90. *The Bengal and Agra Directory and Annual Register for 1850* contained the names of 99 merchants and agency houses, out of which 29 agency houses were members of the Bengal Chamber of Commerce.
[5] Cooke, p. 18.
[6] 'There were, by 1830, 7 principal and 3 secondary houses of agency and 20 smaller mercantile houses at Calcutta. . . . The Government at Calcutta supported their efforts and on various occasions between 1812 and 1828 loaned

were interested in all branches of trade and industry and were largely responsible for the spread of the company concept in the fields of shipping, sugar, coal, and insurance. The managing agency system is one of their unique contributions.[1]

If, however, one takes into account the capital resources, the commercial ability, and the remarkable knowledge of the country which members of these agency houses possessed, the extent of their achievement seems comparatively small. This may have several explanations. Firstly, their capital resources, though large, were fully employed in their traditional businesses of indigo, cotton, cotton piece goods, and opium; as is evidenced by the fact that speculations in these commodities were chiefly responsible for the ruin of many of these houses during the two commercial crises of 1825 and 1845.[2] Secondly, the very brisk business in these trades made the agency houses less inclined to venture into new fields and developed in them a rather over-cautious attitude towards industrial enterprises, which by all accounts were extremely risky and difficult to launch.[3] Lastly, they had vested interests in certain fields, particularly banking, and they did not like the idea of sharing their profits with others, as their attempts to obstruct the formation of the General Bank and the Bank of Bombay illustrate.[4]

It is possible to make some assessment of the relative importance of the three classes, the Indians, the Company servants, and

in all 88 lakhs (8,800,000) of rupees to the Houses . . .', C. H. Phillips, *The East India Co., 1784–1834*, 1940, p. 277.

[1] See pp. 219–55.

[2] Phillips, p. 277. *The Bengal and Agra Directory*, etc., *op. cit.*, contained a list of 42 agency houses which were insolvent and in liquidation in 1849–50.

[3] Commenting on the cotton twist mills established in India, Thomas Bracken, partner of Alexander & Co., said, 'I have great doubts whether they will be able to compete with the cotton mills in England. The reason being that there is great difficulty at Calcutta at present in repairing the machinery employed, and any accident happening to it is likely to stop the whole. Cotton twist already made there is not liked by natives as much as the English. It may be a matter of fancy, but there is a prejudice in favour of that which comes from England.'

Again, commenting on the possibility of a large scale machine-making establishment in Calcutta he observed, '. . . that will depend in great measure upon the success of the Glouster Mills. Parties at present are scarcely likely to venture on such establishments till they see whether the making of cotton twist or piece goods in India becomes a profitable speculation or not.'

P.P. *Minutes of Evidence before the Select Committee on the Affairs of the East India Co.*, Pt. II, Finance, 24 March 1832, p. 154.

[4] H. Sinha, p. 71. Cooke, pp. 162–3.

the agency houses, from an analysis of the shareholders of three incorporated companies—the Bank of Bombay, the Bank of Madras, and the Bengal Bonded Warehouse Association, situated in Bombay, Madras, and Calcutta respectively. These companies were established about 1840 and as far as Bombay and Madras were concerned, the banks named above were the only incorporated companies.

The Bank of Bombay was established by an Act of the Legislative Council of India in 1840, with a share capital divided into 5,225 shares of Rs.1,000 each. In the first instance 5,090 shares were taken up by 387 persons. Of these 146 or 38% were Indians, subscribing to 1,553 shares or 30·5% of the total.[1] Cooke gives the following classification of its shareholders at a later date (not mentioned) in 1840:[2]

Community	Shareholders				Shares Held	
		No.	%		No.	%
Europeans:						
Resident in India		173	52		3,261	66·2
Indians:						
Native Christians	12			49		
Mohammedans	3			55		
Parsees	109			1,233		
Hindus	35			327		
	—	159	48	—	1,664	33·8
		332	100		4,925	100

The Bombay Government also held 300 shares.

It will be observed by comparing the shareholding pattern in the above two cases that the Indian proportion of the total had increased by 10%, but the increase in their holdings was only 3·3%. In other words, they represented a little less than half the numerical strength of the shareholders and held a little more than a third of the total shares. Thus, the part played by Indian shareholders in Bombay cannot be regarded as small. It is also clear from Cooke's table that, among the Indian shareholders, Parsees were the most important group, both in the number and size of their holdings. The European shareholders were mainly officers in the military and civil services of the Company.[3]

In 1848 the pattern of shareholding in this Bank was as follows:

[1] G. W. Theobald, *Legislative Acts of the Governor General of India-in-Council, 1834–71.* [2] Cooke, p. 165. [3] *Ibid.*

Business Corporations in India, 1851–1900

Community	Shareholders No.	%	Shares Held No.	%
Europeans:				
Resident in India	91		1,473	
Non-resident	95		2,365	
	— 186	59·4	— 3,838	78
Indians:				
Native Christians	13		62	
Mohammedans	1		18	
Parsees	88		877	
Hindus	25		130	
	— 127	40·6	— 1,087	22
	313	100	4,925	100

Besides 300 shares continued to be held by the Bombay Government.

It is interesting to compare the preceding two tables. Between the years 1840–48 the percentage of Indian shareholders in the total decreased from 48 to 40·6. The fall in their holdings was still sharper, from 33·8% to 22%. There are two possible reasons for this. Firstly, the 1840 table is bound to contain a certain element of speculative buying,[1] and secondly, the commercial crisis in 1845–6 had rendered the bank shares relatively less attractive than other investments.[2]

Another interesting point to notice is the change in the nature of the European shareholders. During the intervening eight years more than half of the Europeans, in the usual changes to which Indian society was then subject, had retired and settled in England. In terms of shareholding, the percentage of Europeans who had retired comes to about 61·6. This led Cooke to fear that 'in the course of a few years the largest proportion of the capital will be held by parties resident in England'.[3]

The Indian share in Madras was very meagre indeed. The first shareholders' list of the Bank of Madras, incorporated in 1843, contained the names of 237 persons who subscribed for 2,700 shares of Rs.1,000 each. Only eighteen of these were Indians.[4] A breakdown of the Indian names shows nine of them to be North-Indian, the rest belonging to the wealthy South-Indian community of Chettis.

[1] '. . . the natives . . . are not to be found . . . such extensive investors in the Government stocks as our own countrymen, except for speculative or temporary purposes'. *Ibid.*, p. 74.
[2] *Ibid.*, p. 332.   [3] *Ibid.*   [4] Theobald, Act IX of 1843.

Among the European shareholders as many as sixty-one were military officers, varying from the rank of Captain to a Major-General, and of the remainder, thirteen were qualified surgeons and physicians. It would seem, therefore, that without the support of the servants of the Company, it would have been extremely difficult, if not impossible, to promote even such an important institution as the Bank of Madras.

At this time Calcutta had three statutory companies: the Assam Company, the Bank of Bengal, and the Bengal Bonded Warehouse Association, compared to one each at Bombay and Madras. The Assam Company was formed in England in 1839 with the object of carrying on the cultivation of tea in India. The capital stock of the Company was divided into 10,000 shares of £50 each. There was already in existence in India another company, the Bengal Tea Association, and an amalgamation was brought about, one of the conditions being that 2,000 shares should be issued for subscription in India, out of which 1,400 should be reserved for the promoters of the Bengal Tea Association. The 2,000 shares were taken up with avidity; in the first list of shareholders of the Assam Company there were only nine Indians, possessing a total of 275 shares or 14% of the total shares allocated to India,[1] but this may not represent the true picture in so far as the potential Indian participation was concerned, for 1,400 of the 2,000 shares were already reserved for a certain group who were largely Europeans and the rest also may not have gone beyond that group.

The first subscription list of the Bengal Bonded Warehouse Association provides a much better index of the extent of Indian participation in Bengal. This body, incorporated in 1838, had a subscribed capital of Rs.1,000,000 divided into 2,000 shares of Rs.500 each. It is important to note here that the subscription of its share capital was restricted by statute to the residents of Bengal Presidency. Of the first 171 shareholders forty-five were Indians, of whom all, with one possible exception, were Bengalis.[2] Indians, therefore, represented 26·3% of the shareholders, but this does not mean that they held a proportionate interest in the shareholding. Unfortunately, the details of shareholdings are not available.

[1] Antrobus, *Assam Company*, p. 40.
[2] Namely, Brijbullub Dass and Gokul Dass (jointly held). These names are common throughout India. Theobald, Act V of 1838.

An analysis of the European shareholders shows a great concentration of shares in the hands of European agency houses and their partners; there were only nine military officers, a very small number compared with Madras. This can be explained by the fact that commercially this undertaking occupied a rather important place in the coastal and foreign trade of the country, so that naturally the agency houses were very intimately concerned and in order to protect their interests, took as many shares as they could get. Conversely, it must have been very difficult for others to obtain these shares.

To sum up, each of the three classes played an important part in developing joint stock enterprises. The combined European element—the servants of the Company and the agency houses—made the major contribution, of course, but the Indian share was by no means small or insignificant, although, as has been said, it was not equally important in all parts of the country. In Bombay, the Parsees, a small community with a sustained zeal for trade and industry, took a very keen interest in promoting and supporting joint stock enterprises. In Calcutta, Bengalis represented a little more than one-fourth of the total shareholders of the Bengal Bonded Warehouse Association, a significant fact considering that Bengalis were traditionally held to be more interested in the liberal arts than in matters of trade.[1] The Indian contribution in Madras was clearly poor but, at the same time it must be admitted that commercially, Madras was relatively less important as compared with Bengal and Bombay, as can be seen from the following comparison of annual figures of notes in circulation issued by the three Presidency banks.[2]

Bank of Bengal   Rs.11,600,000 (in 1835)
Bank of Bombay   Rs.12,812,000 (highest total before 1862)
Bank of Madras   Rs. 3,000,000 (highest total before 1862;
                                    generally under Rs.2,000,000).

SOME FEATURES OF CAPITAL MARKET AND COMPANY FINANCE

It must first be stressed that at this time there was no organised capital or stock market in India; indigenous bankers and the

---

[1] On Bengali enterprise, see pp. 58–9; also S. K. Sen, *Economic Policy*, pp. 57–73.   [2] Cooke, pp. 105, 152, 168.

Promotion and Finance to 1850

European agency houses were then responsible for channelling savings into productive fields. Until the year 1829, as we know, there was only one bank in India on the modern European lines, the Bank of Bengal. But this was primarily a government bank and laboured under various disabilities under its charter. Thus, when, in 1829, the Union Bank of Calcutta was formed, one of its main objects was to 'fill up the space in the money market occasioned by the restrictions imposed on the Bank of Bengal by its charter'.[1] The next two decades saw an unprecedented growth of banking companies all over the country but this development had its foundations in the ashes of the agency houses, and its immediate effect, therefore, was to fill the gap in the money market left by their decline. But the growth of the companies is significant as the first sign-post towards the creation of an organised capital market.

The use of multifarious metallic currencies and the lack of safe and fast means of remittance made the cost of placing funds in different parts of the country very high.[2] This may have also adversely affected the growth of *mofussil* banks. Absence of banking facilities encouraged people to hoard their savings in the form of gold and silver ornaments and may have been a significant factor in diverting funds in landed property.[3] These reasons operated to restrict the flow of funds from the *mofussil*. Yet, capital scarcity does not seem to have been a major factor impeding industrial growth in this era.[4] No doubt the promoters of some manufacturing enterprises did not find it easy to raise the necessary capital; yet it would be hard to find any instance where a scheme had to be shelved or an enterprise discontinued for want of capital alone.[5] There is also no evidence to suggest that the Company

[1] Cooke, p. 177, footnote.

[2] There were 80 different kinds of coins in India; and until 1836 even the British Government in India issued as many as five different kinds of rupees. N. C. Sinha, pp. 20–1.

[3] On hoarding and investment in landed property see also pp. 54–6.

[4] It is interesting to note that N. C. Sinha quotes a contemporary writer as saying, 'India's capital resources were enough, only they were lying scattered', p. 22.

[5] In this connection, see R. H. Mahon, *Report upon the Manufacture of Iron and Steel in India*, 1899. It gives an account of the Porto Novo Iron Works started by Heath. For the Bowreah Cotton Mill complex started in 1818, see P.P. 1831–32, X, Paper 735–II, evidence of T. Bracken, pp. 154–55; P.P., 1840, H.C. VIII. Paper 527 evidence of H. Gouger, pp. 116–19. For other case histories of this period see Antrobus, *Assam Company, op cit.; Andrew Yule & Company*, 1863–1963 (Managing Agents of the Bengal Coal Company),

servants, the free merchants or the agency houses had to import any capital from abroad[1] although in one or two cases it was thought better to raise funds in London.[2] At least in Bombay and Calcutta the more orthodox form of investment did not suffer from want of capital. People readily subscribed to bank shares and government loans.[3] The fact was, if anything, that there was not much demand for industrial capital;[4] the number of industrial ventures known to have been conceived and/or started, was very small.

Companies altogether were very few. The market for shares was therefore 'aristocratic' in nature, its scope being limited to the relatively small number of Europeans in the country and, among Indians, to a handful of wealthy Chettis in Madras, a small community of Parsees in Bombay and the Bengali elite of Calcutta, for the man-in-the-street had neither the means nor the knowledge to take part in this intricate institution.[5] Even the *Zilla* bankers who were the depositories of the landed aristocracy preferred the

---

Calcutta, 1963; Alfred Brame, *The India General Steam Navigation Company*, 1900; and Blair B. Kling, 'The Origin of the Managing Agency in India', JAS, Vol. XXVI, No. 66, pp. 37–47. Kling's article gives an account of the companies with which the firm of Carr, Tagore and Company was concerned such as the Calcutta Steam Tug Association, the India General, the Bengal Coal companies.

[1] N. C. Sinha quotes Sleeman as saying that the agency houses did not import 'a particle of capital from home', p. 23.

[2] See Antrobus, *Assam Company*, p. 40.

[3] See p. 29. In the case of the Bank of Asia, projected in London, the number of shares subscribed in India was 5,283 against only 1,392 in Britain, and the demand was so great in India that the shares commanded a premium of 12% on the issue price. Cooke, p. 342.

[4] At one place Cooke says, 'No country, whatever be its form of government—whatever be the industry and skill of its people, or the vegetable and mineral riches of its soil, can thrive while the interest on money is at 20, 30, 40 and 50% per annum' (p. 349). At another place he says capital scarcity was felt because 'Surpluses [were] being either taken from the country or locked up in the different loans opened by the government' (p. 74). If interest rates were generally so high nobody would be normally willing to buy government securities for a return of 5% or so. High interest rates were generally charged by the village moneylender. Interest on business loans was never anywhere so high. The fact that people were willing to invest in government loans at 4 or 5% and clamoured to buy bank shares, while banks reduced their paid-up capital sometimes because funds could not be invested, goes to show that there was probably not much demand from the private sector.

[5] What could be a better index of the poverty of the people than the fact that 'the smallest change is represented by shells, called cowries, of which eighty go to the smallest copper coin, and consequently, no less than 5,120 to the rupee', Cooke, p. 20.

devil they knew to the devil they did not know and continued in their age-old trades.[1]

In the absence of an organised market for the securities of new enterprises, various interesting methods were used to sell them. No distinct group of individuals devoted themselves primarily to this phase of promotion. During the 1840's there were only six stockbrokers in Bombay, and although the number in Calcutta is not known, it could not have been much higher,[2] but as there were so few companies in existence even those few must have depended for their income largely on dealing in government securities.[3]

Contact with the prospective shareholders was primarily established through the medium of public meeting[4] and advertisements in newspapers.[5] Where banking companies were concerned, the subscription list was easily filled, particularly in the cities, because the military and civil servants of the East India Company were so enthusiastic that mere knowledge of a scheme would make them vie with one another and with the mercantile community in supporting it.[6] As a result, such companies found it absurdly easy to raise capital, and their offices were flooded with applications for shares far in excess of the issued capital. Additional capital was generally issued to meet this demand.[7] Banking shares commanded almost an immediate premium of 60 to 70%.[8] It was because of this persistent demand that almost every such company in the country was able to increase its capital with comparative ease by issuing fresh shares every year and even every half-year.[9]

---

[1] Cooke, pp. 13–14.

[2] *Bombay Stock Exchange Enquiry Committee Report*, 1924, p. 3.

[3] *Calcutta Stock Exchange Official Year Book*, 1940, p. 34. See also V. R. Cirvante, *The Indian Capital Market*, 1956, p. 34.

[4] H. Sinha,, p. 10; Cooke, p. 163.

[5] See for instance the prospectus of the New Bank, F.O.I., 1838, p. 149.

[6] Cooke, p. 163.

[7] 'The Bank of Bombay was obliged to increase its share capital from Rs.3,000,000 to Rs.5,225,000 to meet the wishes of its numerous applicants.' *Ibid.*, p. 164.

[8] *Ibid.*, p. 164.

[9] For example: the Union Bank of Calcutta increased its capital on the following dates: January, May 1836; April 1837; January, May 1838; June 1839. During these years the capital was increased from the original figure of Rs.1,500,000 to Rs.10,000,000. *Ibid.*, pp. 178–9. Similarly, the Agra and

The situation was, however, very different if a company had mismanaged its affairs or its prospects seemed otherwise dubious. Appeals for capital under these circumstances often took the form of an approach to a selected group, generally of wealthy Indians, as happened in the case of the Assam Company. The first 2,000 shares allotted to India having been taken up immediately, the Calcutta Board, at its own request, was allotted 223 more shares by the main Board in London; but interest had flagged by the time they were received in Calcutta. The Minutes of the Calcutta Board's proceedings of 6 March 1841, records the following:[1]

The Secretary having found no demand for the shares in the market at present, it was resolved that the individual members of the Committee, do use their efforts for the disposal of the unappropriated shares, and that the aim of the Company's objects be brought to the notice of the most influential natives.

The following letter, and other extracts from letters written to a shareholder by a director of the Benares Bank, provides an illuminating example of high pressure salesmanship and the unhealthy financial practices in this era:[2]

My dear Graham,
In reply to yours of the 17th ultimo, I say, yes; I advise you to buy as many more shares as you possibly can, for this will be a glorious Bank—and no mistake, and I think I can promise you old shares carrying new as on 31st January last on the same terms on which you got your last (i.e. 50% premium); but you must be quick in writing me your wishes, that I may instruct the Secretary, who will lend you any sum you may need to pay for them, and you can repay him by instalments, big or small, as may suit your convenience.
In haste, Sincerely yours, P. L. Pew

United Services Bank and the North Western Bank of India increased their capital as follows:

| | Agra and United | North Western | | |
Date	shares Issued	Date	No. of Shares	Amount Rs.(000's)
1841	1,000	July 1844	1,000	500
1842	3,000	Jan. 1845	2,000	1,000
1844	1,000	Jan. 1846	2,000	1,000
1845	2,000	May 1847	1,000	500
1846	1,000	Sept. 1847	1,000	500
1847	1,555			

Ibid., pp. 209, 224–5.

[1] Antrobus, *Assam Company*, p. 413.   [2] Cooke, pp. 267–9.

'... you should strain every nerve to come into this Bank largely, now, before a number of shares be created; you would not only be getting thumping dividends, but new stock, at par, every half-year. Bring in all your rich friends—for 'twill be the best of Banks, with a glorious business ...'

'... Don't at all inconvenience yourself about payments. ... Debnam will lend you funds, as long as you require them ...'

No wonder the Bank went bankrupt.

Sometimes stockbrokers were appointed to help with the original issue.[1] This method was very effective, and almost imperative for those companies, Indian or foreign, which offered shares beyond their own immediate locality. For, in those days of extremely difficult and hazardous communications, the use of the post for individual applications, letters of allotment, remittances, and issues of scrip would have been fatal.

Once a company had disposed of its original issue, the problem of handling subsequent issues was not so great. They were always offered to the existing shareholders and in nine cases out of ten were taken up by them.[2]

Once an investor had acquired shares, he could either advertise in local newspapers or employ a local stockbroker if he wished to sell them subsequently. A search through the newspapers of the period suggests that the latter method was the more common.

In spite of the many difficulties, banking issues were almost always over-subscribed since there was no real strain on capital resources as there were only a few companies. The very high face value of shares suggests that issues were intended only for wealthy people. The number of Indians who could buy shares of the face value of Rs.1,000 must have been small indeed. Yet, this may have been a blessing in disguise, for the issue of shares of low denomination has often led to unscrupulous practices.[3]

---

[1] For example, the Bank of Asia, projected in London, appointed the following as stockbrokers in India:

     Grey and Russel—Bombay
     Cauter and Company—Calcutta
     Line and Company—Madras.

Cooke, pp. 343–4.

[2] *Ibid.*, pp. 267–9.

[3] Speaking about France under the Second Empire, A. B. Levy writes: 'The most unscrupulous promotions were based on the issue of shares of very small amount; bogus companies frequently had their capital divided into one franc shares, by which the poorer and more gullible members of the public were

A ruling of the Government of India in the 1840's had a slightly adverse effect on the capital market. Government employees had to furnish security in certain connections and the practice, hitherto, had been to deposit shares in private companies. This was now forbidden as the growing use of such shares naturally caused anxiety in Government circles, but the little dis-investment that this may have caused would have been more than compensated by the growing tendency of insurance companies and banks to invest in shares.[1]

The sentiments of the shareholders played a great part in determining the price of shares which was not always finely adjusted to the calculated yield and to pressure on the money market. For example, an agreement between the Government and the Bank of Madras regarding the limit of the Bank's note circulation pushed its shares from a premium of 14% to 100%,[2] although the limit fixed was, in fact, a little lower than its average note circulation in past years, and the dividends, if anything, actually decreased.[3] Similarly, the Bank of Bengal, as a result of certain forgeries in 1834, for the first time in its existence did not declare any dividend, the whole of the profits of the previous half-year having unwisely been written off the profit and loss account. This created such 'great consternation' in the market that the Bank shares fell from a premium of Rs.6,000 on the nominal value of Rs.10,000 to par.[4]

A contrasting feature of the share market was the stabilising influence of the servants of the East India Company. They protected shares against falls in price due to occasional pressure in the money market, since they looked for safe and long-term investments rather than quick profits.[5] This, however, made the shares of private companies particularly sensitive to the issue of Government loans. Thus, in 1843–4, after the 5% loan of 1841–2 had closed, and 4% paper was at par, the Bank of Bombay's shares were at a premium of 52% and in 1846–7 when the 5% loan was reopened, the shares fell to 36% premium, although during the

---

attracted and deprived of their savings.' *Private Corporations and Their Control*, Vol. I, 1950, p. 90.

[1] 'The Company may purchase and sell bullion and Government Bills . . . and shares in the chartered banks of India, as the Directors shall think fit', Deed of Settlement of the Commercial Bank of India. Cooke, p. 331. Article XXIV of the Fourth Calcutta Laudable Society also empowered the Directors to invest in bank shares. *The Bengal Almanac, op. cit.*

[2] Cooke, p. 152.   [3] *Ibid.*, p. 154.
[4] *Ibid.*, p. 104.   [5] *Ibid.*, p. 176.

latter years the dividend was increased from 7% to 8%.[1] The adjustment in price may not seem unreasonable, but at that time the fall was considered to be great.

The capital structure of companies was very simple, as the entire capital was invariably raised in ordinary shares. They showed a short-sighted approach towards the raising of their initial capital, which was generally very small, and it was partly for this reason that it had to be increased almost annually or even bi-annually, the capital being raised by further calls on what were apparently fully paid shares.[2]

The absence of limited liability meant that the failure of a company could cause a scare in the whole share market, as the history of the Union Bank of Calcutta shows.[3] The use of preference shares was incompatible with unlimited liability. Preference shares and debentures had been developed in England by chartered companies with limited liability as a result of the special problems encountered in financing the construction of canals and railways, but in India at that time there were no comparable enterprises.[4] There was almost a complete absence of public utilities and the construction of railways started only in the early fifties.

Some industrial companies did, from time to time, feel the need for emergency finance, but such funds generally were borrowed from banks on the security of company properties.[5] In special circumstances the Government also granted loans and, as in the case of Porto Novo Steel and Iron Works, such a loan was guaranteed by individual shareholders.[6]

---

[1] Cooke, p. 176.

[2] 'the stock was doubled by call for an additional payment of 250 per share, the shares being raised to Rs.500 each, thus making the capital . . ." *Ibid.*, p. 209.

[3] *Ibid.*, p. 293.

[4] 'Preference shares grew out of the financial embarrassments of the early transportation companies. Such projects were almost invariably started without an adequate understanding of the engineering difficulties to be overcome, and in consequence the construction costs exceeded expectations. . . .'
'Mortgages, annuities, promissory notes and other debt instruments were not always in high favour. . . .'
'. . . it was not until about 1800, during the period of extensive canal building, that new types of shares gained a firm footing . . .' '. . . the railways gave rise to further need for this method of financing, with the result that by 1850 more than 100 railway preference shares had been marketed . . .'. G. H. Evans, *British Corporation Finance, 1775–1850*, 1936, pp. 149–50.

[5] Cooke, pp. 188–91.

[6] Brown, p. 65.

33

In terms of pure economic theory some modern economists would find the dividend policy of companies in this era highly satisfactory[1] but whether it was applied consciously is a different matter. Companies, as a rule, appropriated the entire profits for dividends, generally ascertained every half-year. No thought was given to stabilising the dividends and consequently they varied enormously from year to year.[2] Mining and other companies of this nature follow this practice everywhere even now. Although the idea of creating reserves as a buffer goes back to the time of the General Bank of India,[3] the practice did not become common until late in the period, when commercial crises or unexpected losses, whether trading or otherwise, had finally brought home to them its utility. Where a reserve was created, it was done by setting aside a certain percentage of profits every half-year until it stood at a certain percentage of paid-up capital. In one instance, a minimum dividend of 6% on the capital had to be paid before anything could be appropriated for reserves.[4] But reserves were always used to meet contingencies and never to equalise dividends. Sometimes a cash bonus of one pound per share would be paid out of these reserves. The idea of ploughing back profits is of later development.

The implications of paying dividends out of capital were well understood and in many cases the articles or the statute incorporating a company would prohibit such a payment.[5] But instances are not wanting when dividends were paid out of capital,[6] and in the case of the Union Bank they were paid even out of deposits received from the public.[7]

---

[1] 'If we assume that directors are endeavouring to maximise the net returns to the shareholders, then clearly no portion of the earnings ought to be reinvested unless the return upon the increment of capital employed promises to be at least as large as could be earned upon the same capital employed elsewhere, i.e. outside the enterprise.' See the marginal principle in dividend distribution in N. S. Buchanan, *The Economics of Corporate Enterprise,* 1940, p. 234.

[2] Cooke, pp. 188–91.

[3] Article XI of the General Bank recited, '. . . no dividends to be made of a larger amount than two-thirds of the net profits . . .'. But it was deleted in a general meeting held on 1 December 1787. H. Sinha, p. 17.

[4] Cooke, pp. 142–3.

[5] Article 2 of the Royal Charter of the Oriental Bank Corporation read, '. . . no dividend may be paid out of capital . . .'. *Ibid.,* p. 146.

[6] See the Union Bank of Calcutta and Benares Bank in Cooke, *op. cit.,* and the Assam Company in Antrobus, *Assam Company,* all of whom paid dividends out of capital.

[7] '. . . that the dividends it [Union Bank] declared, and of which it made so

The history of banking presents probably no greater instance of mismanagement than that which has brought this establishment with a paid-up capital of one million sterling to ruin. The proprietors have lost the whole of their capital by the acts of their own directors . . . are further liable to the public to the extent of the whole of their private property for the outstanding engagement of the concern.[1]

This extract from a minute signed by, among others, Lord Dalhousie, gives an example of the type of mismanagement which ultimately led the Government to pass the first Companies Act in India. The legal problems faced by companies in this era will be discussed in the following chapter.

---

great a parade, were taken, not from the capital, for that had gone long before, but from the deposits that people were still confiding . . .'. Cooke, p. 186.

[1] *Proceedings of the Governor General in Council in the Financial Department*, 27 May 1848 (No. 29 of 1848).

CHAPTER 3

PROBLEMS OF COMPANY LAW
UP TO
1850 [1]

Unlike today, when corporate status is a necessary and automatic accessory to the creation of companies, it could be obtained at the beginning of the last century only through a Royal Charter, Letters Patent, an Act of the British Parliament, or, later, an Act of the Indian Legislature. It was a privilege rarely granted. The difficulties were even greater in the case of British companies which sought to operate in India on account of the intervention of the East India Company, which was consulted on all such matters. [2] The East India Company offered relentless opposition to any grant of charters for India, especially as regards banking companies. It claimed that, under an Act of Parliament, [3] the power to charter banks in India had been delegated to the local government of India and, therefore, unless a bank first obtained the approval of the Company, the establishment of such an institution in India would be invalid.

The Company had laid down two rules for considering applications for grant of banking charters: (a) that additional banking facilities were required in India; and (b) that, if so, the proposed bank was likely to provide such facilities with benefit and security to the public interest. Even if, contrary to the emerging spirit of *laisser-faire*, there was nothing *prima facie* objectionable in these rules, but as it turned out they served only as pretence to turn down requests for charters, as is sufficiently illustrated by the attempts of the Bank of India, Australia and China, and the Bank of Asia.

[1] This chapter is adapted, by permission, from my article in the *American Journal of Legal History*, Vol. 6, No. 3, July 1962, pp. 298–308.

[2] 'The Board of Trade was responsible for advising the Privy Council on Royal Charters in general but those relating to the colonies were always referred to the Treasury which as a matter of course in turn consulted the Board of Control for India about Indian matters so that the views of the East India Company might be ascertained.' C. Mackenzie, *Realms of Silver, 100 Years of Banking in the East*, 1954, p. 16.

[3] 47 George III, C. 68, S. 8.

No charters were granted to any bank for India before 1850. In October 1851, the Company, which was still powerful, inadvertently consented to the grant of a charter to the Oriental Bank Corporation. This error was to result in opening the doors of India to other banks. Indignation among manufacturing interests in Britain had been growing as a result of the manipulation, by the East India Company, of the English rate of exchange with India. The mounting protests put the Treasury in a quandary and the East India Company reluctantly gave way, allowing charters to be granted to other banking companies, 'in as much as it was not possible to dispute the validity of the Oriental Bank's charter and it would have been against the public interest to grant that corporation a monopoly of the exchange business'.[1] The grant of a charter was still an advantage at this time, since it carried prestige value and generally permitted shareholders to limit their liability whereas, although an Act of general incorporation had been passed in 1850, limited liability under it was not permitted until 1860.

In India only five Acts of incorporation proper were passed up to the end of 1850, including those enacted in connection with the three Presidency banks of Calcutta, Bombay and Madras,[2] which were instruments of government policy. The Union Bank of Calcutta, formed in 1829, could not acquire even the partial privilege of sueing and being sued through its officer until 1845. An alternative method of acquiring the advantages of incorporation was to procure an obsolete charter or amalgamate with a chartered body, but this means was used still more rarely and there is only one known instance of it in India.[3]

For the rest, lawyers in India fell back, like their counterparts in England, whom they largely emulated, on the existing resources of the law. To some extent, the partnership form of organisation could be adapted to the needs of the joint stock company. The

[1] Mackenzie, p. 16. For a list of applications for charters and their results, see P.P. 1854 (299) LXV. 611. For an account of the various contemporary banks see Cooke, *op. cit.*

[2] The other two incorporated companies were the Bengal Bonded Warehouse Association and the Assam Company, incorporated by Act V of 1838 and Act XIX of 1845 respectively. The three principal cities of India—Calcutta, Bombay and Madras—were called the Presidency towns and the Bank of Bengal, the Bank of Bombay and the Bank of Madras, in which the government held one-third of the total shares, were called the Presidency banks.

[3] The Oriental Banking Corporation acquired the charter of the Bank of Ceylon. Cooke, pp. 144–5.

joint property of a company could with some ease and effectiveness be held through the medium of a trust and the management of directors.[1] The resulting hybrid organisation differed very little in structure from a chartered company, but in law it was regarded rather as a large partnership, for the legal distinction, so clear today between a partnership and a joint stock company, was not established then. Down almost to the end of the first quarter of the last century, under the Bubble Act,[2] the establishment of these corporate bodies was illegal in England. Fortunately, in India there was no such law.

The device of a trust was a partial answer to companies' difficulties in bringing and defending suits in law,[3] but the failure to distinguish them from partnerships made joint stock companies subject to the legal provisions concerning partnerships, and was the cause of some of their greatest difficulties. These arose from applying certain rules of English common law and equity.

The rules of common law were, first, that no action could be sustained between partners where any matter of account was involved, or where the damages sought would, when recovered, belong to the firm; second, that in an action against a debtor to the

[1] S. D. Murray, Manager of the Commercial Bank of India which was established on 1 October 1845, in Bombay, with an authorised capital of Rs.1,000,000 and had 348 shareholders, stated that the Bank 'suffers great inconvenience from the application of the law of partnership to their association by which they are compelled to place their property in great jeopardy by the frequent use of the names of trustees and intervention of third parties'. L.P., 27 December 1850.

[2] The Bubble Act (6 Geo. I, c. 18) was passed in England with a view to prevent the formation of joint stock companies without the specific grant of a charter or a like instrument. It remained on the statute books for almost a century, but failed to achieve its purpose on account of the various ingenious legal devices resorted to by businessmen and industrialists. See B. C. Hunt, *The Development of the Business Corporation in England, 1800–1867*, 1936, especially Chapters 1 and 2.

[3] '... the difficulties, the Bank experiences in recovering its debts at law, are altogether insurmountable and if generally known might prove most injurious to the interest of the shareholders'. Memorandum by W. W. Cargill, Managing Director, Oriental Bank, Bombay. L.P., 27 December 1850. The memorandum also included a letter from the Bank's solicitor who stated that 'in the action by the Trustees of the Bank against . . . the judge . . . after commenting on the great inconvenience to which the public and the Bank are exposed from want of an express act of legislature authorising the Bank to sue and to be sued by one of its officers intimated that his present opinion was that the Bank could not sue without joining all the shareholders as plaintiffs'. In England these difficulties were met by making extensive use of arbitration. See A. B. DuBois, *The English Business Company after the Bubble Act, 1720–1800*, 1938, p. 221.

partnership all the partners should be joined as plaintiffs (as the firm itself was not recognised as a legal entity); and, third, that any partner might bind his co-partners by contracts made within the scope of the partnership business.

The consequence of applying the first of these rules to companies was that no call could be enforced against a shareholder by directors, for the directors were considered partners of the shareholders. The numerous shareholders made it a practical impossibility to bring a legal action under the second rule. As to the third, the scope it offered for confusion or mischief was considerable.

The relevant rules in equity laid down, first, that a general account had to be taken before a partner could be compelled to pay money at the suit of another partner; second, that a partner seeking an account or any other interference in partnership matters had to pray dissolution; and third, that the court would not interfere unless all the partners were before it.

Another rule, that the partnership could be dissolved at will by any partner, if no term was fixed, would have led to strange results if it had been applied in the case of companies.[1]

Lastly, the liability of the shareholders of an unincorporated company was always unlimited.

These rules caused special hardship to banking companies whose whole business consisted of borrowing and lending money.

Companies were not alone in this difficult situation. Creditors were in much the same boat. The paid-up capital of a company was no security for their money for it could be reduced to nothing at the will of the management, there being no law to prohibit a reduction of capital at this time. Even when it was not so reduced it was difficult to say whether it had not in fact been lost in the absence of full and fair accounts. The impossibility of discovering and assembling all the shareholders made it fruitless to bring an action against the company, and creditors had, therefore, to single out and sue shareholders individually to recover their debts. Since companies were not subject to any winding-up or insolvency law a vigilant creditor could outsmart his fellows by being the first to attack the properties of wealthy shareholders.

Lastly, the plight of the shareholder was worst of all. He was liable to be singled out for the debts of the company and he had no means of reimbursing himself.

[1] Whitley Stokes, *Indian Companies Act, 1866*, 1866, Preface.

Strangely enough, there was prior to 1847 hardly any move to get an alteration of the law—only in two cases was an effort made to obtain the right to sue and be sued through officers.[1] The absence of any representation from the three Presidency Chambers of Commerce is most striking.[2]

The government, on the other hand, in response to a request from the East India Company, had conducted an inquiry in 1846 among the three Governors of the North-West Provinces, Bombay and Madras into the condition of private banking in India and the desirability of legislative interference in the matter. Opinion was divided, but the President-in-Council of the Indian Legislature concluded that banking in India was neither 'so advanced' nor 'in so unsound a state' as to call for any legislative interference beyond allowing the several establishments to sue and be sued in the name of their officer and for the protection of the public bringing the proprietors and their several and joint responsibilities more readily within the reach of the law.[3]

Shortly afterwards came the failure of the Union Bank of Calcutta and the Benares Bank and the revelation, in both cases, of the directors' misdeeds and fabrication of the accounts. These events impressed the government beyond all doubt of the advantages that accrued to the public from allowing them to sue without the need of joining all the shareholders, but even they did not make them see the need for further reform and it is clear from the statements of the time that the government was looking at the problem from two points of view only; that of the creditors and that of the management. The interests of the shareholders were ignored.[4]

The companies themselves had still not come forward with petitions or proposals for relief; the one request for a general measure came from a few merchants of Agra. It happened, however, that the Law Member of the Supreme Council of India,

[1] See memos. by the Commercial Bank, Bombay and the Oriental Bank, Bombay. L.P., 27 December 1850.

[2] The precursor of the Bengal Chamber of Commerce, the Calcutta Chamber of Commerce, was founded in 1834. The Madras and the Bombay Chambers of Commerce were founded in 1836. Their members were chiefly the European agency houses in the Presidency towns and so they were representative of educated commercial opinion of the time.

[3] *The Proceedings of the Governor-General-in-Council in the Financial Department*, 27 May 1848 (No. 29 of 1848).

[4] *Ibid.* Stokes,

Bethune,[1] disliked the practice of framing individual Acts where the object, if desirable, could be attained by general legislation. His first draft outlined a very simple measure, restricted to conferring on partnerships of over six people the right to sue and be sued through their officers. But this was not what the shareholders wanted; they sought a measure which would stop them being primarily exposed to the suits of creditors. Legal opinion was uniformly favourable to them in this and in the opinion of one judge: 'there were reasonable grounds for requiring a resort to company's funds in the first instance'.[2]

At the time of its second reading the Bill was completely recast and, despite abortive constitutional objections,[3] the Companies Act was passed on 27 December 1850.

Every unincorporated company of seven or more persons whose shares were transferable without the consent of all the shareholders was entitled to be registered under the Act. Registration was, however, not compulsory. The Act dealt only with the registered companies. It conferred certain privileges on them and in return put some restrictions on the freedom of management which the latter thought, particularly in Bombay, far outweighed the advantages.[4] The result was that for a number of years to come, apart from a few companies in Calcutta, companies all over India refrained from registering.[5]

---

[1] J. E. D. Bethune (1801–51) was appointed fourth ordinary or legislative member of the Governor-General-in-Council (Supreme Council of India) in 1848. He soon achieved fame as an eminent Indian legislator and educationist. *Dictionary of National Biography, IV*, London, 1885, pp. 434–5. On the administrative developments concerning India and the structure of the Indian legislature during 1818–58, see the *Cambridge History of India*, Vol. VI, London, 1932, pp. 1–8. [2] L.P., 27 December 1850.

[3] The judges of the Supreme Court of Madras argued that the Companies Act that the Legislative Council of India intended to pass was *ultra vires* the powers of the Governor-General-in-Council-of-India on the ground that it trenched upon one of the Prerogatives of the Crown by creating institutions which had the quality of a corporation. Under statute *3 and 4 Wm. IV, c. 85, S. 43*, they argued the Governor-General had no power to make a law or regulation which shall in any way affect any prerogative of the Crown. L.P., 27 December 1850.

[4] 'At Bombay it appears to be entirely repudiated; the journal of that Presidency can see no one virtue in it, and every variety of viciousness; and it seems to be the general opinion there, that no joint stock association can avail itself of the provisions of the Act without losing caste and character.' F.O.I., a leading Calcutta daily paper, leading article, 30 January 1851.

[5] S.T.B.I. Not until the company law was changed in 1857 did companies begin to get registered outside Bengal.

In English law (on which most Indian measures were modelled) registration was compulsory and there is no evidence to show why a different course was adopted in India.[1] Whether the influence of *laissez-faire* was the cause, or undue optimism that the power of public opinion would suffice, the result was that the Act was a dead letter, as had been feared in some circles.[2] The Act required the accounts of a company to be audited at least twice a year by two or more auditors, who must not be directors or officers of the company, to be chosen at a general meeting of the shareholders. A copy of the auditors' report (if any) together with a copy of the balance sheet and a separate profit and loss account, and a capital account showing the amount of capital invested and the manner of its investment with the estimated value thereof verified by an affidavit of the auditors all had to be filed in court. The auditors were given full powers to examine any employee of the company and had access to all documents.

Such auditors as were appointed were generally shareholders of the company as there were no professional auditors at this time. Occasional audits were done, even before they were provided for in the Act, in cases where continued losses gave rise to grave doubts in shareholders' minds. Though the profession of auditing was not well developed its implications were well understood and the job of auditor was looked at as much more than merely checking the accuracy of accounts with vouchers.[3]

There was some controversy as to whether it would not be more advisable to appoint a public officer as auditor. This had been suggested by a section of the business world, but the government turned it down on the grounds that such a step would throw unnecessary responsibility on the government and might mislead the public into thinking that it had guaranteed the accuracy of the accounts.

The provision to prepare a capital account, showing the amount, value and manner of disposal of investments was unique. It is not clear from the Proceedings whether the 'value' of the investments was meant to be their book-value or whether they were required to be revalued at current prices.

[1] Contrary to the general belief that the Indian Act was a reproduction of English Law, it deviated materially and unwisely from it in some ways.

[2] See, for instance, the letter of the Remembrancer for Legal Affairs, Bombay. L.P., 27 December 1850.

[3] *Ibid.*

The Act prohibited a company from dealing in its own shares, except when they were forfeited and reissued on account of unpaid calls, and from making any advance on them. This did not mean that a company could not reduce its capital. It was still possible to cancel part of the shares by a resolution of a general meeting. These provisions were welcomed on all sides, though not without some misgivings.[1] It was very common for companies to buy and sell their own shares at this time. When capital was reduced, it was generally not so much because the equivalent assets were lost but to return surplus funds which could not usefully be invested. The freedom to buy and sell shares had, however, been abused and had led to a great deal of stock jobbery.

The Act put a prohibition on loans to directors from the company funds, except in the case of banks, where, in submission to the great pressure of public opinion, the government conceded that the directors and registered officers could borrow up to the limit fixed by the deed of settlement or by a general meeting of the shareholders. Such loans had to be reported to the general meetings, with the name of the persons concerned in each case and details of the securities behind them and breach of the regulations was punishable by transportation for life. Even this concession was found unsatisfactory, the disclosure of these dealings being held to violate 'the almost sacred regard had to private credit in every civilised community'.[2]

There was intense opposition to this measure in both commercial and non-commercial circles, on the grounds that such dealings were an internal matter of the company; and that under these restrictions people of the right standing and quality would be

[1] For instance, the *Bombay Times*, a leading daily paper of that province, observed that the Act erred in prohibiting a company from buying up its own shares at a discount. It illustrated the remark by an allusion to the Bombay Steam Navigation Company, a numerous body, the stock of which had for some time been selling at one third of its face value. 'Why should the company', it asked, 'be precluded in this case from buying up its own shares at so enormous a discount, if the wealthy portion of the shareholders think that on this they can realise sufficient return?' This was obviously a misinterpretation of the Act. It never precluded the shareholders from buying up shares individually. It could not have done so. Quotation from F.O.I., 30 January 1851.

[2] Some such provisions were incorporated in the deed of settlement even before the passage of this Act. For example, clause 28 of the deed of settlement of the Oriental Bank of Bombay restricted loans to directors without suretyship or collateral security. They were, however, seldom observed. L.P., 27 December 1850.

unwilling to accept office. It had in fact become rather difficult at this time to find suitable people to manage companies.

The Act incorporated the provisions of the two winding-up Acts passed in England in 1848 and 1849. Companies committing an act of forfeiture were subject to the jurisdiction of an insolvents' court. An adjudication of insolvency vested the property of the company in the official assignee to realise the assets of the company and equalise the shareholders' contribution. An act of forfeiture was committed either when the directors had declared the company unable to meet its engagements by an ordinary resolution in the general meeting or when a company failed to satisfy a decree against it for Rs.500 or upwards within two months. Although the Act, like its British prototypes, did not prevent the court from dissolving companies in the exercise of its original jurisdiction, it still regarded the shareholders as partners, liable for the debts of the company to their last shilling; liable, moreover, to be singled out and sued individually by creditors; and as a winding-up under the Act could not be instituted by a creditor, it amounted merely to a proceeding on behalf of the shareholders to equalise their contributions for payment of debts, and to suit on behalf of creditors for compelling payment of their debts from an insolvent company.[1]

In the petition for the company's registration, the Act required that the amount of working capital, if separately provided for by the company, should be stated along with the number of shares into which it was divided. Such a distinction may seem unusual, but several jute companies were found to follow this practice, as late as the 1870's and '80's, impractical though this may seem.

The Act also required registered companies to hold general meetings of the shareholders bi-annually and an extraordinary general meeting if seven members requested it. Lastly, transfers of shares were to be registered at the company's office.

The press showed little awareness of business matters at this time. In Calcutta and Bombay, the centres of joint stock companies in India, editorial comment on the Act makes very sad reading. The press in Calcutta supported the Government absolutely, while in Bombay it could see only the interests of the businessmen; neither made any constructive criticism of the provisions of the Act and both, especially the Bombay press,

[1] Stokes, Preface.

44

misinterpreted it in parts; neither mentioned the key failure to compel registration, and in Calcutta the *Friend of India* greeted the continuance of unlimited liability for shareholders with great satisfaction.[1]

The Indian Companies Act of 1850 was highly significant in that it marked the first stage in the development of a body of law to regulate joint stock enterprise. This was also the first time that the government in India had taken a legal interest in commercial institutions. The provisions of the Act were sound and are still found in company law all over the world, but the failure to make registration compulsory rendered the Act largely ineffective. The complete omission of any reference to company prospectuses is also strange as the Act was supposed to be based on the English Act of 1844. Moreover, the framers of the Act showed a lack of courage as regards limited liability in failing to make any innovations not already a part of the law of England.

[1] F.O.I., 30 January 1851.

CHAPTER 4

GROWTH OF THE CORPORATE
SECTOR, 1851–1860

According to official records, the New Oriental Life Insurance Company was the first to be registered under the Act of 1850 on 16 June 1851 in Bengal,[1] but it was only from January 1859 that companies outside Bengal began to be registered.[2] By December 1860 companies had been registered in Bombay, North-West Provinces, and Madras. Some of these companies registered were already in existence prior to 1851 and were registered to take advantage of the Companies Act of 1850,[3] although others preferred to remain outside the domain of the law.[4] Their industrial classification was as follows:

Table 1

Industrial Classification of Companies Registered 1851–60

Banking	7	Miscellaneous:	
Insurance	5	Printing	4
Tea	10	Reclaiming waste land	3
Cotton Mills	5	Forming Bazaars	1
Jute Mills	1	Manufacturing	8
Screwing and Pressing		Trading	5
Cotton and Jute Bales	1		
Navigation	8		
Coal	2		
		Total .. 60	

Of the sixty companies listed in table 1 as many as twelve had been wound-up by 1860, but in some cases the winding-up was merely a formality so that these companies could re-register under an Act passed in 1857 which permitted limited liability to com-

---

[1] It had a nominal capital of Rs.1,000,000 and a paid-up capital of Rs.250,000.
[2] This statement is based on the list of joint stock companies found in the S.T.B.I., 1883, p. 64.
[3] For example, India General Steam Navigation Co., Bengal Coal Co.
[4] For example, Apollo Press Co., Colaba Co.

panies other than banking and insurance. The industrial breakdown of companies in this category was as follows:

Table 2

Industrial Classification of Companies wound-up, 1851–60

	Re-registered	Wound-up
Banking	2	
Coal	1	
Navigation	2	
Cotton Mills	–	1
Tea	–	1
	5	2

Unascertained .. 5   Total .. 12

Thus it will be seen that only forty-eight companies were actually operating at the end of 1860, showing the limited progress of joint stock enterprises during the period. Four of the eight British Indian provinces had as yet no registered companies.

The following table shows the trend of development over the years:

Table 3

Number of Companies in Operation at the end of each year 1851–60

Year	Banking	Tea	Cotton Mills	Jute & Cotton Presses	Cotton Shipping (Navigation)	Others	Total
1851					1	1	2
1852	2				1	1	4
1853	2				2	3	7
1854	4				2	5	11
1855	4				2	5	11
1856	4				2	6	12
1857	4				2	10	16
1858	4	1		1	2	14	22
1859	4	6	2	1	6	19	38
1860	5	9	4	1	6	23	48

In studying the trend of development some of the significant events in the economy of the country should be taken into account.

In the first two years of the fifties the country was just emerging from the commercial crisis of 1845–7. During these years no

E   47

important company was registered which had not been in existence prior to 1850. 1853 marked the opening of the first railway line in India, but many years had to elapse before a network of railways could be built. In the meantime transport difficulties were bound to deter entrepreneurs from starting industrial ventures. The year 1854 saw the beginning of the first truly industrial enterprise in the country. The significance of the floating of a cotton mill venture in that year cannot be exaggerated. In 1855, Auckland and Sen in Calcutta started India's first jute mill. By the middle fifties the idea of establishing cotton and jute mills had begun to stir in the minds of Indian merchants and capitalists, and the Act of 1857 permitting limited liability to joint stock companies provided further impetus; but more development was arrested for a time by the outbreak of the 'Sepoy Rebellion'. The Rebellion made traffic with the North-West impossible, and even in Bengal there was a sense of insecurity which made capitalists 'grip eagerly all they could collect'.[1] By the end of February 1858, the panic was over; the roads were re-opened and the general feeling was that money would soon be a drug in Calcutta. As trade revived, about half a dozen companies of various kinds: an omnibus company, a printing company, a bridge company, an auction company, a weaving company and a Sunderbund (agriculture) company were formed, but this development was thought to be rather unwarranted at the time.[2]

1859 was also an important year in that it saw the revival of interest in tea and the beginning of Indian companies in this industry. Navigation companies also increased from two to six in this year. Plans to run steamers on the rivers to open up the country had been very much in vogue throughout the preceding years of the decade after the formation of the 'India General', the 'Calcutta Burma', and a few towing associations. This development was the result of the very rich harvest reaped by the companies during the 'Sepoy Rebellion' when the Government requisitioned their steamers. The profits were so large that in 1858 one of the companies was 'threatening' to declare a dividend of 50%.[3] 'There are facts widely known about our river communication', wrote the *Friend of India*, 'which reported of any Continental river would throw London into a fever of speculation.'[4] There was

---

[1] F.O.I., 25 February 1858.
[2] *Ibid.*   [3] *Ibid.*   [4] *Ibid.*

no doubt that prospects of earning a handsome dividend in navigation were bright, but they were overshadowed in contemporary opinion by fear of competition from an extending railway system.[1]

India continued to make some progress in 1860; the number of companies operating at the end of the year increased by ten to forty-eight. This was the last normal year before the outbreak of the American Civil War started speculation.

The overall development during this decade, however, must be regarded as very limited. Among the direct causes were the lack of adequate transport facilities and financial institutions, absence of technical knowledge and the difficulties of creating an industrial labour force.

Today, the transport problems of an industry arise mainly in connection with the movement of raw materials or finished products. But in the middle of the last century, the difficulties and therefore the risk involved in bringing technicians and machinery from England and getting a supply of labour from the distant parts of the country were more serious.

In 1858, when Ranchhodlal was trying to set up a cotton mill in Ahmedabad, the first consignment of machinery from Lancashire was lost at sea. When a fresh consignment arrived at Bombay, the nearest port to Ahmedabad, Ranchhodlal had to personally supervise both its unloading from the ship and the loading on the country bullock-carts. The machinery took another four months to reach Ahmedabad.[2]

In Assam, the seat of the tea industry, the only means of transport were country boats, elephants, elephant carts and palanquins. One of the first things the tea companies had to do was to acquire boats and elephants of their own.[3] Rivers were difficult to navigate and boats were generally towed along, when going upstream. Time was generally reckoned in months. It was only in 1860 that the India General Steam Navigation Company arranged to send a steamer to Dibrugarh once every six weeks during the cold weather.[4]

Until 1855, the only means of conveying coal to Calcutta from the Ranigunj fields was by 'shallow and unsafe' boats used

[1] F.O.I., 25 February 1858.
[2] S. D. Mehta, *The Cotton Mills of India, 1854–1954*, 1954, p. 23.
[3] H. A. Antrobus, *A History of the Jorehaut Tea Co. Ltd., 1859–1946*, 1948, p. 67.
[4] A. Brame, *The India General Steam Navigation Company*, 1900, pp. 66–7.

during the monsoons on the Damodar River. Until 1895, the Jharia coal fields, about fifty miles away, were not worked because there was no railway connection.[1]

The want of technical knowledge in the country complicated the problem still further. Not only the machines but nearly all the technicians had to be brought from Britain. Recruiting qualified technicians was difficult. From the employers' viewpoint the risks inherent in this situation were particularly heavy; the incompetence or death of an important technician could easily result in many idle months before the vacancy could be suitably filled.[2] As late as 1895 Daniel Buchanan noted that 42·4% of the managers and mechanical engineers in the Bombay cotton mills were Europeans[3] though only six out of seventy mills were under European managing agencies.[4] This suggests that the employers in particular did not take any vigorous steps to rectify the situation.

No less serious was the problem of ensuring an adequate supply of skilled labour. Training local recruits in industrial processes must have been slow, at least in the earlier period, since understanding between a British technician and an Indian labourer could only be reached little by little because of the language barrier.[5] On-the-job remained virtually the only method of training. As new mills were started, trained hands had to be tempted away from the existing mills. The demand for skilled labour exceeded the supply throughout the last century.[6]

Seldom, in discussing the issue of labour supply, has any clear distinction been made between the skilled and the raw labour, and the question of labour turnover and discipline.[7] The general belief has been that India's industrialisation has suffered from a shortage

---

[1] *Report of the Coal Mining Committee*, 1937, pp. 9–10.
[2] S. D. Mehta, pp. 23, 101.
[3] D. H. Buchanan, p. 135.
[4] See Table 21, p. 241.
[5] S. D. Mehta, pp. 116–17.
[6] *Report of the Commissioners Appointed by the Governor of Bombay in Council to Inquire into the Condition of the Operatives in the Bombay Factories, and the necessity or otherwise for the passing of a Factory Act*, 1875, p. 82. *Report and Proceedings of the Commission Appointed to Consider the Working of Factories in the Bombay Presidency*, 1885, p. 27 (Testimony of Inspector Jones) and p. 132 (Testimony of G. Jugmohandas). *Bombay Millowners Association, Annual Report, 1907*, pp. ix., xiii. The issue is discussed in Morris D. Morris, 'Some Comments on the Supply of Labour to the Bombay Cotton Textile Industry, 1854–1951' IEJ, October 1953, pp. 138–52.
[7] *Ibid.*

of labour[1] because labour mobility was low. The latter, in turn, was partly due to the lack of transport facilities and partly the result of such factors as kinship, caste, and the village which served as bonds to keep people on the land. The labourer went to work in the towns only temporarily because the various claims of the village society operated as powerful forces to bring him back.[2] The use of foreman-jobbers to hire and discipline workers resulted in a still higher turnover and indiscipline[3] since they took bribes.[4]

It now seems that the Bombay mills never faced any serious shortage of raw labour.[5] After 1850, surplus labour from the villages went to the towns to work[6] and over time the mills recruited an increasing proportion of their labour force from the permanent residents of Bombay.[7] The supply was so plentiful that the mill owners paid only a subsistence wage and could not have cared less about the living and working conditions of their employees.[8] Further, Morris's study has shown that the hiring-in wage rates were remarkably stable over time and that there was no marked shift towards using capital intensive methods, whereas the expected profits were high, wages were only a small proportion of the total costs, and the labour force expanded steadily.[9] For this to happen, the labour supply must have been sufficient since wage rates were responsive to market forces.[10]

Labour turnover, however, was high, even if not anywhere as high as the 50% or 75% claimed by Thorner.[11] Morris agrees that, to all intents, the labour force was casual[12] but he says that the statistical evidence does not support the claim of an enormous

[1] S. D. Mehta, pp. 114–16. Also *Report of the Indian Factory Labour Commission*, 1908, Vol. I. p. 19 and *Report of the Royal Commission on Labour in India*, 1931, p. 21.

[2] C. A. Myres, *Labour Problems in the Industrialisation of India, 1958*, pp. 43–54.

[3] *Ibid.*   [4] See p. 233.

[5] Except during such unusual periods as the plague of 1896 and 1897. See Bombay Millowners Association, Report, 1896, pp. 1, 135, 147–8. *Annual Factory Report of the Presidency of Bombay, 1897*, pp. 7–9, Bombay Millowners Association, Report, 1897, p. 2.

[6] Morris, IEJ, I, No. 2, October 1953, pp. 139–44. Also the Thorners, *Land and Labour*, p. 60.

[7] Morris, *Emergence of a Labour Force*, p. 200.

[8] The Thorners, *Land and Labour*, p. 60.

[9] Morris, *Emergence of a Labour Force*, p. 199.   [10] *Ibid.*

[11] The Thorners, *Land and Labour*, p. 60.

[12] Morris, *Emergence of a Labour Force*, p. 204.

seasonal swing in absenteeism associated with agricultural requirements of rural sectors'[1] and further, his view is that 'a very large part if not most of the labour turnover involved a movement of workers between mills rather than from mills to the countryside'.[2] One would like to know why labour moved from one mill to another. In Morris' scheme conditions of work including wages could not account for any significant proportion of the labour movement among mills. The conclusion must then be that the jobbers deliberately terminated the services of a large part of the labour force regularly for personal gains. This redundant labour was, so to say, forced to find employment in the other mills at the going wage rate. But why did the mill owner accept this labour jobbery when it is easy to see that an employer would prefer a stable over an unstable labour force. Morris says, 'for the bulk of its career the Bombay textile industry required workers who needed only very casual training and the most limited sort of supervision' and therefore 'the stability of an individual worker was of no fundamental concern to employers'.[3] His view is difficult to reconcile with the constant complaints of the mill owners about shortage of trained hands.

In another passage Morris says that differences in work force behaviour (including worker stability), if any, resulted from employer policy rather than any substantial difference in the psychology of the recruit or the dissimilarities in the traditional environment from which the workers came.[4] 'The necessities imposed by industrial technology and markets', he argues, 'required employers to select different systems of discipline, and these determined the way labour would work.'[5] No doubt the degree of training and supervision would vary with the technology used, but between a stable and unstable labour force any employer would still prefer the former situation unless, of course, any extra cost outweighs the advantage. Since the wages were highly stable and only very limited supervision was needed, the inference that the cost of substituting the jobber system would have been relatively higher does not seem very convincing. Perhaps the jobbers were necessary after all to ensure a sufficient supply of

---

[1] Morris, *Emergence of a Labour Force*, p. 200.
[2] *Ibid.*, p. 209, cf. The Thorners, *Land and Labour*, p. 60.
[3] *Ibid.*   [4] *Ibid.*, p. 210.
[5] *Ibid.*

labour. More must be known about the role of a jobber before one could safely reject the traditional hypothesis.

Morris's finding that 'whenever and wherever industrial functioning required the disruption of traditional distinctions (castes, sub-castes), they were apparently swept away with ease'[1] does, however, show that the traditional emphasis on the inhibiting influences of these factors is likely to have been exaggerated.

From what has been said it would appear that the Bombay mills did not find it particularly difficult to create an industrial labour force, but it would be unwise, on this basis, to generalise for all the other industries of India. The stupendous efforts made by the Assam Company to secure a supply of labour from the Gangetic plains, which resulted in the loss of hundreds of lives, is just one example of the enormous difficulties which faced the tea industry in its formative years.[2] No doubt the problem of distance was aggravated by the callous attitude of the employers who failed to make proper arrangements for the transportation and rehabilitation of workers.[3] It does show that the situation varied between one industry and another. Until labour problems have been studied in some of the other industries such as coal mining, railways, jute, paper and sugar mills which varied in the type of labour quality required, as well as the questions of management and location, no valid generalisations can be made for the whole of India.

The supply of capital for industry does not only depend on the savings made in a country, even if they are adequate. Much depends on what kind of risks the owners of capital are prepared to take and the methods of raising capital. It requires systematic effort and a network of financial institutions to tap large amounts of savings and channel this into productive investment. Although the number of commercial banks in India had increased slightly,[4] the facilities for financing companies did not really improve during the period.[5] It is doubtful whether enough capital could have been mobilised from indigenous sources to match the demand even if greater facilities had existed.

The general inadequacy in the availability of capital is indicated in various ways. The poverty of the masses is obvious and perhaps

---

[1] Morris, *Emergence of a Labour Force*, p. 201.
[2] *Papers regarding the Tea Industry in Bengal*, 1873, p. 34. See also Antrobus, *Assam*, pp. 385–90, and *Jorehaut*, pp. 50–1.
[3] See p. 100.   [4] See Tables 1 and 3.
[5] Cooke, pp. 77–8.

the best example, but there are others. Up to 1875 about £95 million were invested by British companies in Indian guaranteed railways.[1] By contrast, the total paid-up rupee capital of all Indian companies working at the end of March 1901 amounted to a mere £25 million.[2] British ownership in Indian companies apart, five-sixths of the total investment in the tea industry at the end of last century was in sterling.[3] A similar situation prevailed in the jute industry.[4] For the most part, these industries paid handsome dividends,[5] and it is therefore difficult to resist the conclusion that the amount of capital in the hands of Indians willing to take risks was very small.

The fact was that the annual per capita income in India was low.[6] Institutions to tap small savings in the rural areas were lacking. As a result, it is said, much of whatever small savings

[1] W. J. Macpherson, 'Investment in Indian Railways, 1845–1875' EHR December 1955, pp. 177–86.
For a general outline of the railway history see N. Sanyal, *Development of Indian Railways*, 1930. See also N. B. Mehta, *Indian Railways*, 1927; R. D. Tiwari, *Railways in Modern India*, 1941, and Amba Prasad, *Indian Railways*, 1960.

[2] Converted at 16d. to the rupee. See Appendix 18. Moreover in 1870 there were only 368 Indian shareholders as against 51,519 British shareholders in Indian Railways. See *Report on the Working of the Indian Railways*, 1875, p. 15. Also D. H. Buchanan, p. 152. It is therefore doubtful if the Indian merchants could have found the money to build the Indian railways. Even the British merchants of Calcutta shied away (see Macpherson, *op. cit*). It was, however, entirely possible for the Government of India to raise the necessary finance. After all it did own about one-half of the total railway investment at the end of the last century. Even if we assume that the finance necessary for railway building could have been raised from private Indian sources, there remains the slight possibility that the payment for imports for railway building and rolling stock might have adversely affected the Indian rate of exchange *vis à vis* sterling. Moreover, the cost of internal capital was likely to be greater than was the case in borrowing it from Britain although the long run effects on the balance of payments, the development of a local capital market, and the growth of industry would have been substantially different. But the organisational problem involved in such an effort could have easily delayed railway development for a long time.

[3] S.T.B.I. 1896.

[4] S.T.B.I., 1902 and 1906. D. R. Wallace, *The Romance of Jute*, 1909 and the *Jute Mills of Bengal described by the Special Correspondent of the Dundee Advertiser in Calcutta*, 1880. These sources provide figures for capital investment at various dates.

[5] Antrobus, *Jorehaut*, pp. 47–9 and *Assam*, pp. 406–8; N. Z. Ahmed, *Some Aspects of the History of British Investment in the Private Sector of the Indian Economy, 1874–1914*. M.Sc. (Econ.) (London, 1955), unpublished thesis, p. 215.

[6] Estimates vary between Rs.20 and 40. For a critical assessment of the estimates for this period see D. Thorner, 'Long-term Trends in Output in India' in Kuznets *et al.* (Eds.) pp. 103–28, and M. Mukherjee, 'A Preliminary

could be made was hoarded in the form of gold and silver ornaments as a store of value to tide over difficult times.[1] It was, so to speak, an involuntary, second-best choice. But it is doubtful if saving in the form of ornaments was entirely involuntary; they were also bought primarily for use as ornaments—at least by the middle-class people. The rajahs, maharajahs, nawabs and *zamindars*, who also hoarded large quantities of precious metals,[2] could not be said to have done so because investment opportunities were lacking. Occasionally these people did invest small amounts in industrial ventures,[3] but this seems to have been a weak motive for them. On the other hand, they indulged in conspicuous consumption on a huge scale. Conspicuous consumption was a feature of the Indian society as a whole. Fear of social sanction obliged almost every head of a family to celebrate births, marriages, deaths and other such occasions in a grand style. This further accentuated the high propensity to consume associated with low income.

Until about the middle of the last century the village trader occupied only a subordinate place in the rural economy. His capital resources were small and money lending was only a casual aspect of his business. For a variety of reasons the peasant increasingly changed over to growing commercial crops in the latter half of the nineteenth century. To produce crops for the market he needed credit. The moneylending operations as well as the buying and selling of crops made the local trader very important.[4] As Thorner says, 'the new form of landholding, land revenue systems,

Study of the Growth of National Income in India, 1857–1957', in *Asian Studies in Income and Wealth*, 1965.

[1] D. H. Buchanan, pp. 148–52. Anstey, 1952, pp. 57, 331, 332, 403, 419. G. B. Jather and S. G. Beri, *Indian Economics*, 9th Edn., 1952, pp. 358, 361 (Vol. II).

[2] *Ibid*. See also Findlay Shirras, 'Gold and British Capital in India', EJ. December 1929, pp. 629–36. India's hoard of gold and silver was probably second only to the U.S.A. India imported about 20% of the annual gold production of the world between 1919–20 and 1928–9, most of which was hoarded. *Ibid*., p. 630. Cf. P. P. Pillai, *Economic Conditions in India*, 1925, pp. 200, 270–2. For annual average quinquennium figures for net import of treasure from 1868–9 see Anstey, Fig. VI, p. 330. For the period 1868–9 to 1898–9, the average of the above mentioned quinquennial averages amounts to an annual net import of Rs.110 million. For a discussion of hoarding in modern context, particularly in relation to form of taxation, see N. Kaldor, *Indian Tax Reform*, 1956, pp. 107–9, 115–20.

[3] Especially the Maharaja of Gwalior, the Gaekwar of Baroda and the Nizam of Hyderabad. D. H. Buchanan, p. 152.

[4] The Thorners, *Land and Labour*, pp. 54–7.

legal procedures and commercial agriculture . . . opened up a golden age for the moneylender'.[1] They grew in number and wealth and were sure of a good return on all their capital without dabbling in any new and uncertain industrial enterprises.[2]

In the urban areas those professional men and salaried officials who had savings to invest found it attractive to put most of it in landed property since with the development of transport and communication, land values began to rise rapidly from the middle of the last century.[3] Although they also invested in industries, the magnitude of the total was not significant enough to make any appreciable impact.

Company promotion and finance before 1850 owed a great deal to the servants of the East India Company.[4] They were imbued with a spirit of adventure which was not quite conditioned by mercantile discipline, but they gradually receded into the background during the fifties.

The small increase in numbers of companies during the period was the result of the capital invested by merchants, whether Indian or British, living principally in Bombay and Calcutta; their number in Madras was small and the amount of inter-regional investment was negligible. The vision of a merchant is, generally, limited by the discipline of his class. Immediate gain and a quick turnover of capital are two attributes of such a discipline, and as such the criteria he uses for investment are essentially different from those used by an industrialist, who must cast his glances long into the future and expect his capital to be sunk for a number of years and profits to increase only slowly. Merchants, therefore, developed and supported only such industries as led to immediate success. Industries which presented technical or other problems were pursued by a very few and the support they received from the mercantile community can at best be described as half-hearted. As a result they were either abandoned or failed to become the nucleus for further development.[5] Mercantile discipline does not provide the right kind of thrust to break through difficult barriers,

---

[1] The Thorners, *Land and Labour*, p. 55.

[2] D. H. Buchanan, pp. 148–52.   [3] Ibid., p. 152.

[4] See Chapter 2 and also D. Thorner, *Investment in Empire, 1825–1849,* 1950, pp. 96–9.

[5] Brown, pp. 64–6. J. Coggin-Brown, *Iron and Steel Industry of India* (articles reprinted from the *Mining Magazine* for June and July, 1921) pp. 5–6. S. D. Mehta, pp. 4–5 regarding the difficulties of establishing a paper mill.

inasmuch as merchants tend to lack tenacity of purpose, the *sine qua non* of a true entrepreneur. Yet, in the Indian conditions, it is difficult to imagine who else could have provided it, and as the number of sufficiently enterprising merchants was very small and grew only slowly, until a sufficient number of them had graduated into industrialists, the growth of the corporate sector was bound to be slow.

During the fifties the mercantile community underwent changes of great significance. Three such changes were: the growing ascendancy of the Parsees in Bombay, the decline of the Bengali merchants in Calcutta, and a change in the outlook of the European houses.

The Parsees had risen rapidly from the 'humble status of the tillers of the soil'[1] to merchant princes who had spread through India to China on the one side and to London on the other. By acting as a community and adopting a policy of compromise and mutual toleration they steadily managed to ingratiate themselves into the favour and confidence of Hindu Rajahs, Moghul Nawabs, the Maharatta Peshwas and the British Government, and always lived on terms of peace and unity with the numerous races among whom their lot was cast. They traded in close association with the European merchants in cotton and opium which enabled them to amass considerable wealth.

Some Parsees were already trading with China even before the close of the eighteenth century. By 1812 many were regarded as 'opulent' and there was hardly any European agency house in Bombay which did not associate a Parsee merchant in 'most of its foreign speculations'.[2] The trade in cotton and opium with China was a particular Parsee speciality. Jamshedji Jeejibhoy (the first Parsee baronet), Khurshedjee Rustomjee Cama (the founder of the first Indian business house in London in 1855), Nusserwanji and Jamshedji Tata (the founders of the famous industrial house), all started their tutelage in Bombay or Calcutta, went to China, opened a branch in Hongkong, Shangai or Canton and spread to other parts of the world.[3] Many less eminent Parsee merchants and brokers came up the same way.

---

[1] From a review in the T.O.I., 13 June 1879 (overland and weekly edition) of *Parsi Prakash*, by Bomanjee Bramjee Patell.

[2] Millburn, *Oriental Commerce*, quoted in S. K. Sen, *Economic Policy*, p. 54.

[3] *Ibid.*, pp. 54–7. See also Cooverjee Sorabjee Nazir, *First Parsee Baronet*,

A typical Parsee pioneer started by being apprenticed as a boy to a European agency house, where, after gaining sufficient knowledge, he was allowed to act as a broker for the firm. Finally, he established a firm, either on his own or in partnership with another Parsee or European. Thus the Parsees who floated banks, started cotton pressing companies and pioneered cotton mills in Bombay, all had considerable resources of their own and enjoyed a reputation for experience, knowledge and integrity: the ingredients of good credit.[1]

Bengali merchants on the other hand traded mostly in jute, rice, seed and such other commodities.[2] During the eighteenth century they were important middlemen for the British private trade. Gokul Ghosal, Baranashi Ghosh, 'Hidram' Mukherjee, Maharaja Naba Krishna, Gangagovind Singh, Krishna Kanta Nandi were some of the millionaire *banias* of the second half of the eighteenth century.[3] Even during the first half of the nineteenth century the Bengalis of Calcutta played a significant part in promoting joint stock enterprises in association with Europeans.[4] The leading spirit of this community during this period was undoubtedly the great philanthropist Dwarka Nath Tagore. He built up a fortune as a *zamindar* and Head Dewan of the East India Company's Salt and Opium Department. Later he established indigo factories, cultivated sugar and founded the famous house, Carr, Tagore & Company. There was hardly any company which did not owe him a debt of gratitude for its existence. Tagore was a promoter and a large shareholder in the Union Bank (1829), the Steam Tug Association (1837), the Bengal Tea Association (1839), the India General Steam Navigation Company (1844) and the Bengal Coal Company (1843). The combined capital of these companies ran into many millions of rupees in 1845. 'India General' and 'Bengal Coal' survive to this day and are the foremost companies in their respective fields. Before the East India Railway Company was formed, he had promised to raise one-third of the required capital

1866; S. M. Edwardes, *K. R. Cama (1831–1909)*, 1923; also by the same author, *The Rise of Bombay*, 1902; and F. R. Harris, *J. N. Tata*, 1958.

[1] S. D. Mehta, pp. 3–25.

[2] Proceedings of the Annual General Meeting, *Report of the Bengal National Chamber of Commerce*, 1887, quoted in S. K. Sen, *Economic Policy*, p. 58.

[3] N. K. Sinha, pp. 90–6.

[4] H. Banerjee, *The House of the Tagores*, 1965. See also Cooke, p. 77–8; Thorner, *Investment in Empire*, pp. 44–53.

for the Calcutta-Ranigunj line. The firm of Carr, Tagore & Company collapsed in 1851, following the commercial crisis of the mid-forties which produced widespread failures.[1] For the same reason, perhaps, other prominent Bengalis also disappeared from the annals of commerce and industry in Bengal.

While the commercial crisis had been causing considerable reshuffling in the ranks of the European agency houses in Calcutta, the economic climate in the country was undergoing a change in other directions. Steamships, railways and the telegraph were promising a new deal. Auckland and Sen had successfully established a jute mill in Calcutta. The Assam Tea Company, which had long been moribund, had started again to pay dividends.[2] British capitalists were looking for profitable investments abroad. The importance of this changed outlook was not lost on the British merchants in Calcutta. They seized the opportunity eagerly, investing in industries themselves and persuading capitalists in England to do the same. The managing agency system, to a certain extent already a feature of management in India, provided the necessary link.[3]

The raising of capital was very much a matter of individual effort. The days of public meetings in connection with the launching of corporate enterprises were over.[4] The schemes were now hatched out in the premises of agency houses. Here the pioneer met his close business associates, decided upon the project and floated the enterprise. The prospectus, applications, and allotments were issued and money received at these premises.[5]

Only ordinary shares were used in financing companies. Seventy to eighty per cent of the authorised capital was generally paid-up soon after the enterprise had come into existence.[6] If the capital required was small, it was divided into a small number of shares with a high face-value, and was generally subscribed by a limited number of wealthy merchants.[7] On the other hand, if the sum

[1] Brame, p. 31 fn.
[2] Antrobus, *Assam*, pp. 406–7 (Company's statistics). Also, *Papers regarding the tea industry in Bengal, op. cit.* Mr Edgar's letter, p. VII.
[3] See Chapter 12.
[4] H. Sinha, for an account of the General Bank of India. Cooke, for an account of the Commercial Bank of India. Thorner, *Investment in Empire*, for an account of the history of the Great Western Railway.
[5] Cooke, for an account of various banks. S. D. Mehta, for an account of Petit Mill.
[6] *Ibid.*   [7] *Ibid.*

required was large, the face-value of the shares was kept relatively small in order to attract a large number of investors.[1]

As observed earlier, promoters in Bombay had considerable resources of their own and good credit in the market. As a result, there was a quick response from the public to their appeals for funds and it was not unusual for an issue to be oversubscribed.[2] But the difficulty of raising even a small amount of capital outside Bombay was very great indeed. The efforts of Ranchhodlal, a Brahmin, to raise capital for a cotton mill in Ahmedabad, a town not far from Bombay, illustrates this. In 1848, he published his plan and estimates for a cotton mill in the *Ahmedabad Samachar* to enlist the support of local capitalists; he was not successful. Later, he found an Englishman, James Landon, who shared his ideal and they decided to raise Rs.500,000 each to make up the total capital required. The Ruler of Rajpipla and Gourishankar Oza, a politician from Bhavnagar, were among those whom Ranchhodlal had persuaded to take up shares in his enterprise. But the scheme did not bear fruit, because of the timidity of the Indian shareholders who doubted James Landon's ability to perform his part of the agreement. Only in 1858 was Ranchhodlal able to float a small mill company, with a capital of Rs.100,000 divided into twenty shares which were taken up only gradually. Among the earliest shareholders were Ranchhodlal himself and Rao Bahadur Magandas Karamchand, taking two shares each, Rao Premabhai, Huthee Singh, Keshar Singh and White, a good friend of Ranchhodlal.[3]

The lack of confidence shown by the Indians did not daunt the daring spirit of James Landon, who, in 1854, launched the first successful Indian cotton mill with the help of Lackie & Sons of Bombay, even though he had to transfer his very profitable oil mill to the company in return. The capital of this new company, the Broach Cotton Mill, was divided into 80 shares of Rs.5,000 each, of which 20 were issued as fully paid-up to this great pioneer in return for his undertaking to proceed to London at his own expense to arrange for the construction of factory buildings, and the purchase and erection of machinery.[4]

The picture in Calcutta was slightly different. There the com-

---

[1] Cooke, for an account of the Mercantile Bank and the Central Bank.
[2] S. D. Mehta, *op. cit.* Thorner, *Investment in Empire, passim.*
[3] S. D. Mehta, pp. 22–3.   [4] *Ibid.*, pp. 12–13.

panies were pioneered by the British merchants as opposed to the Bombay Parsees. This was not merely a difference in nationality, for whereas the influence of the Parsees was limited to the capital market in Bombay, the British merchants had access to capital markets in Britain as well as in India.

Thus, when William Mackinnon obtained the government contract to carry mails between Calcutta and Rangoon, on behalf of his young mercantile firm, Mackinnon, Mackenzie & Company, he went home and in London and Glasgow raised the money to establish the Calcutta and Burmah Steam Navigation Company, Limited, registered as such on 24 September 1856. The capital was what would now be regarded as the paltry sum of £35,000 in 700 shares. The largest individual subscriber was one J. Halliday, who took 80 shares worth £4,000. Mackinnon, for himself and his firm, took only £3,000 worth and shrewdly reserved, as was the fashion of the day, shares to the value of £7,500 'for sale in India to parties interested in Trade'.[1]

Similarly, William Roberts and Henry Burkinyoung, on their retirement from the Assam (Tea) Company came home and laid the foundations of the Jorehaut Tea Company, Limited, registered in London on 29 June 1859, with a capital of £60,000 divided into 3,000 shares of £20 each. This was the fourth tea company in India and the second to be registered in London.[2]

The firm of George Henderson & Company provides an example of the pioneering role of the managing agency house, through a partner, George Henderson, senior. During his visit to Calcutta in 1857 he met Auckland, the jute mill pioneer, and was impressed by the prospects of the jute industry. On his return home, he persuaded the Borneo Company, for which his Calcutta firm were agents, and which had then a huge amount of idle capital on its hands, to invest a few lakhs in a jute mill. The Borneo Jute Company, which started work in 1859, was the first sterling company in the Indian jute industry.[3]

The aggregate paid-up capital and the average paid-up capital of companies registered in the various parts of India, up to 1860, suggest, as is shown in the following table, that the supply of capital was much higher in Bengal than in any other part.[4]

[1] G. Blake, *B.I. Centenary (1856-1956)*, 1956, pp. 24-5.
[2] Antrobus, *Jorehaut*, pp. 13-36.
[3] Wallace, pp. 17-18.　　　　[4] S.T.B.I., 1883.

Table 4

Regional distribution of Companies and their paid-up capital to 1860

Region	No. of Co.'s	Capital (in rupees)			% of Total
		Nominal	*Paid-up*	*Average Paid-up*	
Bengal	34	35,943,000	24,722,000	727,118	87·0
Bombay	5	3,975,000	3,459,000	691,800	12·2
Rest of India	2	203,000	203,000	101,500	0·8
	41	40,121,000	28,384,000	692,293	100·0

Nearly 75% of the total capital in Bengal was accounted for by the companies which were floated prior to 1851;[1] even discounting this, the aggregate capital there was still the highest in India.

The situation in Madras was much worse than one would have imagined. Only one company had been registered there by the end of 1860 and even this company, the Mail Coach Carrying Company, Limited, registered on 7 December 1860 with a nominal capital of Rs.50,000 to carry mail and passengers, never commenced business.[2] The only other known company of any significance, the East India Iron Company, was founded in 1850 by a body of Madras businessmen with a capital of £40,000 to take over the old Porto Novo Iron and Steel Company, but it repeatedly ran into technical and financial difficulties and was never registered under the Indian Companies Act.[3] This decline in the importance of Madras, once a great centre of commerce, has already been noted elsewhere.[4]

Despite the slow growth of the corporate sector, the period was characterised by many important developments. A large inflow of sterling capital through the medium of corporate enterprises registered and administered from abroad was one of them. The following table sets out the number and industrial classification of such companies as were found to exist prior to or at the end of 1860.

[1] Apart from jute and tea companies, nearly all the other companies were floated prior to 1851. The capital of the jute and tea companies amounted to only Rs. 3,100,000.
[2] S.T.B.I., 1883 (Company No. 816), p. 91.
[3] This company also had a large loan from the Government and was several times reconstructed. Brown, pp. 61–6; J. Coggin-Brown, pp. 5–6.
[4] See p. 26.

Growth of the Corporate Sector, 1851–60

Table 5[a]

Number of Companies operating exclusively in India but incorporated in Britain

Railways	6
Navigation	1
Jute Mills	1
Tea	2
Total	**10**

Number of Foreign Companies operating in India as well as elsewhere

Banking[b]	7
Life Insurance[c]	8
Navigation[d]	1

(The exact number of marine insurance companies which operated only in India could not be ascertained and they are therefore not included.)

[a] Sources: *London Stock Exchange Year Books:* Anstey (1952 edition); Blake, *op. cit.*; *Jute Mills by a Dundee Correspondent*; Gow, Wilson & Stanton, *Tea Producing Companies of India and Ceylon*, 1897; Antrobus, *Jorehaut*.

[b] D. S. Savkar, *Joint Stock Banking in India*, 1938, pp. 53–4.

[c] R. M. Ray, *Life Insurance in India*.

[d] This is the Peninsular & Oriental Company; for an account of its formation, see Thorner, *Investment in Empire*.

From the viewpoint of the economic development and growth of corporate enterprises, the railway companies were the most important of all foreign companies.[1] The formation of these companies, which were pioneered by R. M. Stephenson,[2] was preceded by years of controversy, lobbying, and negotiations. Eventually it was decided that the railways should be built by private enterprise and not by the State, and that the Government should guarantee a minimum return of 5% on their capital, in a contract which included many other terms regarding the control, supervision, grant of land, purchase and surrender of railways by or to the Government. By the summer of 1857, a sum of £14 million had already been raised in the London capital market.[3]

The growth of trade between India, China, and Australia resulting from the progress of steam communication, made the business of exchange and remittance[4] very attractive. A number

[1] Tiwari, *op. cit.* See the chapter on the Evolution of the Railway System.

[2] Thorner, *Investment in Empire*, on R. M. Stephenson.

[3] L. H. Jenks, p. 206.

[4] Cooke, pp. 368–9. See Prospectus of the Chartered Bank of India, Australia and China.

of banks, known as the 'exchange banks' were established in London. These banks had large capital resources and they did a considerable portion of their business in India. The Comptoir National d'Escompte de Paris was the only foreign bank with offices in India which did not originate in England.[1]

Englishmen retiring from a career in India played an important part in the formation of these banks. Their names added great weight to the boards of directors and easily drew large subscriptions from the public. Some of these banks were actually started in India and only subsequently were their headquarters transferred to London.[2] The control and management of these banks led to frequent disputes between the shareholders in London and those in India.[3] The effect of these banks on the development of Indian banking companies, however, has been a subject of great controversy during the present century, but since this question is bound up with the much larger question of the British influence in the external trade of India and since no case has come to light where an Indian bank failed to develop on this account during the period under discussion, the issue is not considered further.

The life insurance companies which were working in India were generally the agencies of sterling companies. Their business extended only to Europeans, but even so it was estimated by a contemporary authority at five million pounds.[4] During the Sepoy Rebellion alone, considerably more than a quarter of a million pounds, a sum not far short of the Indian Relief Fund at that time, was paid by life assurance offices, in respect of policies taken out by persons whose lives were lost in this period. Of such companies, easily the most important from the standpoint of the amount of business transacted in India were the 'Albert' and the 'European', which achieved this ascendancy by amalgamations and by takeovers of Indian and other foreign companies.[5]

The change in company law was another important development during the period. By an Act of 1857, all companies, other than banking and insurance, were permitted to be formed on the basis of limited liability.[6]

---

[1] Savkar, pp. 53–4.
[2] Cooke, see accounts of the Oriental Bank Corporation, pp. 141–51, and Chartered Mercantile Bank of India, London, etc.   [3] See Chapter 12.
[4] D. M. Slater, *Rise and Progress of Native Life Assurance in India*, 1897, p. 4.
[5] R. M. Ray, *op. cit.*
[6] *Act XIX of 1857* of the Government of India.

Today, limited liability is taken for granted but not much more than a hundred years ago it was a matter for great debate. For a number of reasons, the demand for it in India dates back only to 1849. Firstly, the first commercial company of any significance, the Union Bank, was started only in 1829, and in the next twenty years there were too few companies to make a great impact on the public mind.[1] Secondly, until the failure of the Union and the Benares banks in 1848, the companies had an easy passage, which made the shareholders complacent regarding the dangers of unlimited companies. Thirdly, the shareholders were insulated by a feeling of security arising from an ingenious safety clause generally incorporated by companies in the articles, which provided that, if the company shall at any time appear to lose one-third of its capital, the business shall immediately cease and its affairs be wound-up.[2] This clause, if fully implemented, would have secured what amounts to a form of limited liability, but as there was no legal sanction behind it, the shareholders were dependent upon their directors to carry out this trust. They failed to appreciate, however, that it was unrealistic to expect a director to wind-up a going concern. There were, no doubt, provisions for auditing, but, here again, the persons elected to do the job were neither particularly well qualified nor under a legal duty, nor was their independence always unquestionable. The accounts presented to the shareholders were, therefore, often 'window-dressing' and particularly in difficult times when vigilance was most needed.[3] Thus, a shareholder never knew the true state of a company until it was already effectively bankrupt. It was the failure of the Union Bank which shook the confidence of shareholders in their security device. The entire loss of paid-up capital amounting to one million pounds and the outstanding claims of depositors and other creditors of the Bank[4] brought home to them the risks of an unlimited corporate body, as nothing else could have done. The

---

[1] As early as 1786, the General Bank of India had claimed limited liability for its shareholders. It incorporated a clause to that effect in its Articles and gave public notice of the fact; whether such a claim based on the principle of 'notice' could be sustained in a court of law was never decided. But this was, at any rate, a solitary instance. The debate in India began only after the failure of the Union Bank, in 1848.

[2] See the memorial of the United Services Bank in papers connected with *Act LXIII, 1850*, in L.P., 27 December 1850.

[3] Cooke, account of the Union Bank.

[4] *Ibid.*

shareholders of the leading banks in Bombay, Calcutta and elsewhere pressed their boards of directors to appeal to the Government for an Act of limited liability.[1]

The ensuing discussions made it clear that it was an illusion to regard unlimited liability as a safeguard for creditors.[2] The legal treatment of a company as a partnership requiring every shareholder to be joined in a suit, made nonsense of this concept, the more so, in the Indian context, since a large proportion of the shareholders in an Indian company came from the ranks of British merchants or servants of the East India Company, who were only temporarily resident in India, and in the course of three or four years, as many as half of them might have gone to Singapore, Hongkong or Britain, either in pursuit of new business or in retirement.[3] Moreover, it was not unusual for Europeans to leave India at the first sign of distress, which added to the plight of their Indian counterparts.[4] Again, Europeans in India did not generally own any real property and, therefore, even if a court judgement was obtained against them, there was nothing on which to execute it.[5] It was also argued that unlimited liability had an adverse effect on the investment of capital, as in many cases, Europeans, on retirement, sold their shares and repatriated the capital, whereas if conditions in India had been more favourable, they might have left it behind.[6]

In addition, it was pointed out by four *mofussil* banks in a joint memorandum to the Legislative Council, that 'unlimited liability was liable to be abused', and 'it could be applied by the managing body against their co-partners oppressively, and in a manner extremely alarming and contrary to equity',[7] as the experience of India had shown. This was probably a reference to the action of the directors of the Benares Bank, who had cancelled a large part of their own shares when the Bank was on the verge of bankruptcy, without proportionately cancelling the shares held by others.[8]

From the viewpoint of corporate finance, there were two further disadvantages in retaining unlimited liability. Securities with

---

[1] L.P., 27 December 1850.   [2] *Ibid.*   [3] *Ibid.*
[4] See, for instance, the cases of the promoters of Tremayne and Company in the chapter on 'The Gold Rush in Southern India' and the Bengal Trust and Loan Company in Chapter 10.
[5] L.P., 27 December 1850.   [6] *Ibid.*   [7] *Ibid.*
[8] Cooke, see the account of the Benares Bank.

limited rights of participation, e.g. preferential shares, could not be issued, whilst holders of equity could not reduce their risks of loss by spreading their investments over a large number of companies.[1] Both of these factors impede investment in companies, but since these drawbacks do not seem to have been raised in discussion at the time, they can be of academic interest only.

It is interesting to note here, strange as it may seem, that the directors of the Agra and United Services Bank did not favour the idea of limited liability. They argued, against the wishes of their shareholders, that 'the public rightly had and should always retain the fullest protection' afforded by the unlimited liability of the shareholders, on the ground that 'the public cannot control or even watch the business of the Bank . . .' and as such it was 'only proper that the proprietory which can, must attend to the application of their funds, the conduct of affairs and the choice of a proper executive, whom if they trust too far and too long, the penalty of their over-confidence or indifference, must be paid by themselves alone and not allowed to reach or ruin others'. Further, they feared that the attention 'already rare and unsatisfactory of the proprietors to the mode in which their affairs was conducted . . . would be . . . further impaired . . .' and the 'directors will not feel the responsibility to the same extent or of the same nature . . .'[2] under limited liability.

This was the only case where company directors opposed limited liability. It does show, however, the sincerity, apprehensions and misconceptions with which the issue was being debated in India.

Two ideas seem to have been popular regarding the method of limiting the liability of shareholders. The first was that it should be limited to the amount subscribed by a shareholder, or, in case the Government found this insufficient, to twice that sum, in which case, it was suggested that each shareholder should give a promissory note, equivalent in value to the stock he held, payable on demand in part or in full, as required by the directors. 'Notes of this description', the memorialists observed, 'would be considerably far greater protection to creditors than mere limited liability'.[3] Whatever may be the merit of this suggestion, and it certainly had some, its novelty cannot be denied.

---

[1] F. W. Paish, *Business Finance*, 1957, pp. 41–2.
[2] L.P., 27 December 1850.   [3] *Ibid.*

The second proposition was to fix a time limit on the liability of shareholders. Two suggestions of this type were made: that the liability of a shareholder should cease one year after he had sold out his interest in the company,[1] or that the liability of a shareholder should be limited to the debts incurred by a company during the period of his holding.[2]

But the Government of India rejected the idea of the introduction of limited liability altogether, under the influence of sharply divided, and, on the whole, unfavourable expert opinion in Britain[3] and of similar opinion held by many important Government officials in different provinces of India[4] preferring the interests of the creditors. The issue was, therefore, shelved at the time of the Companies Act of 1850.

No further steps were taken in this direction until the climate of opinion had changed in Britain. In 1856, the British Parliament passed an Act (*19 and 20 Vic. c. 47*) allowing companies, excepting banking and insurance, to be formed on the principle of limited liability and their example was followed in the next year by the Indian Legislature. The reason given for this dependency on the British Parliament, unsatisfactory as it may seem, was that it was desirable that 'the law of England and the law of India should be . . . alike . . ., so that the persons forming themselves into partnerships on the principle of limited liability in England, and desirous of carrying on either the whole or a portion of their business in India, might know that the law in both countries was substantially the same, and that they would incur no greater risks in India than they would in England'.[5]

The significance of this Act is not limited to the concession of

---

[1] Since a shareholder was legally regarded as a partner, his liability did not automatically cease when he sold his holding; the justification of this rule was that when a company was known to be on the verge of bankruptcy, a wealthy shareholder could make a fraudulent sale to escape liability.

[2] L.P., 27 December 1850.

[3] For instance, Mr Bethune, who prepared the 1850 Act, quoted with approval the opinion of Mr Jervis Lloyd, a celebrated London banker, who had stated before the House of Commons Committee on Company Law Reforms that 'the only check on the proceedings of directors, and even that proves a very insufficient one, is that they should be watched by a body of proprietors whose whole fortunes were at stake. With responsibility limited only to the nominal amount of shares, the public might be plundered with comparative immunity.' L.P., 27 December 1850.   [4] *Ibid.*

[5] See the speech of Mr Peacock in the *Abstract of Proceedings of the Legislative Council*, p. 603.

limited liability alone. It was the first Act to take a comprehensive view of the joint stock enterprise, regulating it at birth, as a going concern, and on liquidation. The following are some of the important changes and other provisions introduced by this Act.[1]

Registration of companies had hitherto been optional. The new Act divided companies into four categories for the purpose of registration:

(a) If a company with more than twenty shareholders desired to limit its liability, it had to be registered;

(b) Registration remained optional for companies with shareholders between seven and twenty, but it is not clear whether such companies could limit their liability; as the privilege of limited liability was conferred by the Act, it would be reasonable to think that only companies registered under it were entitled to its benefits;

(c) Companies with less than seven shareholders were not eligible for registration; and

(d) Companies in the first two categories existing prior to the new Act could only be registered if three-quarters of the shareholders voted for it. But such registration did not affect the liabilities already incurred by a company.

Dividends could be paid only out of profits and if paid otherwise, the directors consenting in doing so were made severally liable for the whole debts of the company. But the Act did not define the word 'profit'.[2]

The Government could appoint inspectors on the application of one-fifth of the shareholders.[3]

In addition, it provided for the audit of accounts, filing of balance-sheets and annual list of shareholders with the Registrar of Companies, transfer of shares, calling of general meetings and winding-up by the court, in addition to voluntary winding-up.

It abolished the requirement for a minimum subscription under the 1850 Act so that companies need not call up more money than they could use initially.[4]

In comparing the Indian Act with its British prototype two differences of great significance stand out. First, on a matter of

---

[1] *Act XIX, 1857.*
[2] *Ibid.* See sections 12 and 34.
[3] *Ibid.*, section 48.
[4] *Abstract of Proceedings*, p. 605.

principle the Indian Legislature made it compulsory for all registered companies to file copies of their balance-sheets with the Registrar of Companies. Under the British Act this was optional.[1] This emphasis on publicity and disclosure of details of accounts has remained a feature of Indian company legislation ever since. The other difference concerned a matter of expediency. Under the British Act, if the number of shareholders of a company fell below seven and if the company continued as a going concern, all the shareholders were made personally responsible for the debts of the company. Under the Indian Act, only the directors were made responsible in such circumstances, since it was thought undesirable that the British shareholders in Indian companies should keep watching the fluctuating list of shareholders.[2]

The one great defect of this Act was that it made no provision for the issue of a prospectus.

The Act gave a great impetus to the formation of companies.[3] But banking and insurance companies could not yet be registered on the basis of limited liability. Mr Peacock, who had drafted the Indian Act, himself confessed the propriety 'of preventing Banking and Insurance companies from dealing on the principle of limited liability if others were willing to deal with them on that principle'. But, in the same breath, he observed that 'inasmuch as the point had been abandoned in England, . . . it would be better, at least until the new law of limited liability had been tested and was more fully understood than at present, to follow the same course here . . .'.[4] One can read between the lines the timidity of the Indian Legislature.

Following the English Act of 1858, the Government of India passed another Act in 1860,[5] which extended the privilege of limited liability to banking companies, but the position of insurance companies remained unchanged.

To enable us to appreciate adequately the significance of this period, it must be emphasised, in conclusion, that the developments during this period set a pattern, in almost all matters, that was to remain for the rest of the century.

The railway tracks and the tariff policy determined the type, location and pace of development of industries; the first jute and

---

[1] *Abstracts of Proceedings*, pp. 607-8.   [2] *Ibid.* pp. 606-7.
[3] See Table 3.   [4] *Abstract of Proceedings*, pp. 608-9.
[5] *Act VII of 1860.*

cotton mills became the corner stone of India's economy; the revived interest in the tea industry was to grow even more throughout the period; and the limited liability acceded to the banking companies was to become an instrument in developing the wildest share mania in the corporate history of the century.

CHAPTER 5

THE AMERICAN CIVIL WAR AND THE BANKING INFLATION IN BOMBAY, 1861–1865

Between June 1864 and March 1865, the South Sea Bubble, the Mississippi Scheme of John Law, and the Railway mania of 1846 found a successor in Bombay, and a new chapter was written in mass delusion. The great wealth suddenly produced by the rise in the price of cotton shortly after the beginning of the American Civil War,[1] coupled with the absence of opportunities for legitimate investment,[2] or lack of enterprise in the community,[3] produced as its natural result the development of excessive speculation.

The Civil War in America began on 12 April 1861, and cut off cotton supplies to Lancashire mills. India alone could save Lancashire from total disruption and as a result, the price of Indian cotton soared to an unprecedented level. Demand was so great that even cotton mattresses are said to have been requisitioned and what was previously sold for 2·7 annas fetched 11·5 annas at the height of the boom.[4]

---

[1] 'In four years Bombay has received 82·5 million pounds of sterling for what, but for the American Civil War, would have given her only a quarter of that sum.' F.O.I., 4 January 1866 (Weekly Edition), S. D. Mehta estimated this to be £80 million; see also D. E. Wacha, *A Financial Chapter in the History of Bombay City*, 1900, p. 12; and S.T.B.I., 1883.

[2] *Report of the Commission on the Failure of the Bank of Bombay*, p. 11, P.P., XV, 1868–9.

[3] *Bombay Chamber of Commerce Report*, quoted in Wacha, *A Financial Chapter*.

[4] PRICE OF INDIAN COTTON IN ANNAS PER LB.

1859	1860	1861	1862	1863	1864	1865	1866
2·7	3·7	4·2	5·5	10·5	11·5	7·1	6·2

Source: D. R. Gadgil, *The Industrial Evolution of India in Recent Times*, 4th Edn., 1954, p. 15. Cf. Wacha, *A Financial Chapter*, p. 12.

IMPORTS OF RAW COTTON INTO THE U.K. FROM INDIA (IN BALES)

1859	1860	1861	1862	1863	1864	1865
509,695	562,738	986,280	1,071,768	1,229,984	1,399,514	1,266,513

Source: the article on Cotton (Gossypium) in G. Watt, *Dictionary of Economic Products of India*, quoted in Gadgil, 1954, p. 15. Gadgil also quotes figures for the extension of cotton cultivation in the Central Provinces from the Annual Report of the Cotton Commissioner for C.P. and Berar for the year 1867–8,

But company promotion in Bombay remained remarkably unaffected during the first two years of the Civil War. From 1 January 1861 to 31 December 1862 only nine new companies were registered in the Presidency,[1] but in the following year, presumably because the belief in a prolonged war became established, the feeling of hesitancy died out, whilst the wealth pouring into the Presidency accumulated and spread throughout the community. As a result, the first spate of company promotions started and within a year forty-six new companies were incorporated compared with only four in the preceding year. Most of these companies fell into the following categories: cotton presses (12); steam navigation (9); banking (6); marine insurance (4); and shipping agencies (3).[2] Marine insurance companies were the first to arrive. These were immediately followed by cotton pressing companies, and later in the year, as the spirit of the entrepreneur became bolder still, some huge banking and steam navigation companies were launched.

Symptoms of over-speculation had begun to appear towards the end of the year, but the economy was as yet in no danger. The sudden crop of companies, large and unprecedented as it was, should be viewed as fulfilling the legitimate needs of the Presidency resulting from the greatly increased export trade in cotton which must have been a great strain on the existing commercial, financial and industrial institutions.

By this time, orthodox banking had come to be regarded as too timid, almost an anachronism.[3] The Financial Association of India and China, formed on 22 June 1864, with a capital of Rs.10,000,000 by some of the most prominent citizens, was the first institution which sought to provide a new departure in banking methods.[4] Its aim was revolutionary and apart from trading there was nothing it

---

p. 132, which show that the acreage under cotton cultivation increased from 375,623 acres in 1861–2 to 691,198 in 1864–5 and after a slight fall in the next two years, to 750,875 acres in 1868–9. Gadgil, *Industrial Evolution* 1954, p. 16.

The figures quoted by Morris, *Emergence of a Labour Force*, p. 18 fn., from the *Statistical Tables Relating to Indian Cotton, 1889*, Table 29, p. 59 to show that the export of cotton from Bombay in 1861 amounting to one million bales was not exceeded until 1865, when 1·1 million bales were exported, are thus not corroborated. And the extension of acreage provides independent evidence to show that the supply was not only not amazingly 'inelastic' but highly responsive.

[1] See list of companies in S.T.B.I., 1882.
[2] *Ibid.*   [3] Wacha, *A Financial Chapter*, p. 170.   [4] *Ibid.*

did not purport to do.[1] Another giant, the Bombay Reclamation Company (commonly called the Back Bay Company), followed within a month. Its promotors were also prominent people and in addition it had the blessing of the Government of Bombay, which originally intended to take four hundred shares in the Company, but later, in obedience to the orders of the Government of India, abandoned the idea.

These companies were not bubble companies and 'might have run a successful course in quieter times',[2] but they provided a great impetus to speculation as they were immediately welcomed by the public and applications for their shares poured in from all quarters.

The tide of speculation increased immediately after the 400 shares of the Back Bay Company, abandoned by the Government of Bombay, were put up for public auction on 6 July 1864, when, for a paid-up value of Rs.200,000 they realised Rs.10,500,000. This transaction intensified the hope of quick gains among speculators. Bombay became 'wild with the spirit of speculation'.[3] During the remainder of 1864 and the beginning of 1865, there was an enormous increase in the number of projects. After the Back Bay auction sale, those who understood the tendency of the share market saw a chance of swindling the gullible public. Soon, a group of unscrupulous promoters emerged and companies were started for every imaginable purpose, banks and financial associations, land reclamation, trading, cotton cleaning, pressing and spinning, coffee planting, livery stables and the manufacture of

---

[1] 'The Association will make advances repayable with interest at fixed terms or by instalments upon security . . .

1st—of Landed Estates, first class House property and Real Property, of all descriptions and tenures.

2nd—of Rates, Dues, Assessments, etc., imposed under sufficient legal authority.

3rd—of Government Stocks, Railway Debentures, Shares of Public Companies, etc.

The Association effects purchase and sale of stocks and shares on commission, on behalf of residents in Bombay, up-country, or in England and undertakes the safe custody of . . . Deposits received for fixed periods. . . .

Four months—5% per annum

Six months—7% per annum

Twelve months—8% per annum'

(T.O.I., 11 August 1864, advertisement.)

It will be noticed that this was not a bank but a complementary financial institution, inasmuch as it did not negotiate bills or open current accounts.

[2] P.P. XV, 1868–9, p. 11.   [3] *Ibid.*

bricks and tiles. Promotions had become extravagant and reckless.[1]

It was, however, the financial mechanisms adopted by the banks, the 'financials' and the *khados* (land reclamation companies) which really provided the opportunities for speculation. The various miscellaneous companies might have been a nuisance but they did not present any real danger to the economy. During the eleven months following the launching of the Financial Association of India and China (popularly known as the 'Old Financial'), forty-eight other banks and financial companies and three more *khados* were registered in the Bombay Presidency. The aggregate paid-up capital of companies registered between 1863 and 1865 amounted to Rs.206,000,000. Of this large sum 94·4% belonged to the banks, financials and *khados*.[2] Moreover, companies existing prior to 1861 increased their capital during the mania and a few other companies, although local concerns, were registered in London. The combined paid-up capital of all companies in existence just before the crash in 1865 amounted to approximately £30 million, of which 96·5% was accounted for by the banks, financials and *khados*.[3]

In 1864, when the speculative fever really began, banking companies were the first to be formed; next came the financials and then the *khados*, the most formidable and ambitious of them all. As Wacha rightly observed, 'it practically became the fashion among the prominent financiers of the day that the most influential bank should have at its elbow an equally influential financial and that as a corollary or appendix to both, there should be a powerful reclamation company'.[4] He also gave some examples of the so-called 'first class' triangulated concerns which were closely related or affiliated to others with almost identical boards of directors.[5]

Asiatic Bank–Old Financial–Back Bay
Credit Mobilier–Old Financial–Port Canning
Alliance Bank–Alliance Financial–Mazagon

[1] For a list of companies with objects and capital, see S.T.B.I., part XIV, 1883.
[2] Wacha, *A Financial Chapter*, pp. 26–32, figures adjusted by reference to list of companies in S.T.B.I., 1883.
[3] *Ibid.*   [4] *Ibid.*, pp. 34–5.
[5] *Ibid.*, p. 36.

Central Bank–Joint Stock Financial–Colaba land
City Bank–Asiatic Financial–Frere land

The *modus operandi* was simple enough. When a financial was started the bank helped to promote its speculation by advancing on its shares. When the financial in turn launched the reclamation company, it fed the speculation jointly with the bank.[1]

At the height of the frenzy, a sum of no less than £35 million was quoted as the premium on the aggregate paid-up capital of about £30 million.[2] The figures are large enough to give an idea of the folly and irresponsible speculation that had developed during the ten months between June 1864 and March 1865. The basis of this large-scale speculation was built on the credit freely granted by the numerous banks and financials who were themselves involved in the speculation. The fact that there was no legitimate outlet immediately open for their large capital left no alternative. Once the game had started it became of vital importance for a bank and financial to support it as their entire assets consisted of shares in each other.

The speculation might not have assumed such large proportions but for the introduction of the use of 'time bargains' into the share market. Time bargains were already a feature of the future's market in produce, particularly in cotton from which they percolated into the share market. A time bargain in shares can be defined as a contract whereby one party agrees to sell to the other party a certain number of shares of a certain company, to be delivered on a certain date in the future at a price agreed at the time of making the contract. The essence of such a contract, from a legal standpoint, was the delivery of shares, or else, in the eye of the law, it was no more than a mere wagering contract, or *satta* as it would be called India. As it turned out, almost the whole fabric of this speculation came to be woven on *satta*,[3] as people were only interested in realising the difference of price or 'premiums' on the contracts. In many cases these contracts amounted to many times more than the number of scrips available for any particular company. Those who held shares seldom wanted

---

[1] Wacha, *A Financial Chapter*, p. 37.
[2] *Ibid.*, pp. 24–5.
[3] See the judgement of Mr. Justice Anstey, in the case, *Bhimji Girdhar*, T.O.I. (Overland edition) 8 to 23 August 1865.

to part with them so that delivery became a physical impossibility.[1]

Enormous credit facilities, immediately realisable premiums, and the very small sum required as earnest money to make a time bargain contract produced a spate of transactions involving many sections of the community.[2] First they bought, then they hedged, with the result that the premiums went on increasing at every point in a vicious circle whose growth was further facilitated by the long period for which these time bargains were generally made. In principle, the time was three to six months but in reality it seems that they were all made for settlement on 1 July 1865. It is not clear from a study of contemporary newspapers or Wacha whether any interim settlements were made but if they were it would be reasonable to presume that while speculation was still rife no actual delivery was made and only the difference in price passed. It is hardly surprising then that these hundred and fifty odd companies, barely a few months old and without a single dividend to their credit, were able to command a premium which was out of all proportion to their real worth.

The lead to the speculation was given by the Asiatic Bank, which 'pioneered' advancing on shares by lending on the Back Bay shares, and by the Bank of Bombay, established a long time previously with the avowed purpose of regulating and upholding the credit of the Presidency, which opened its coffers unreservedly to virtually anyone, regardless of their financial backing, under the corrupting influence of Premchand Roychand.

The Asiatic Bank, with a capital of Rs.5,000,000 which was soon doubled, was started mainly to profit from exchange operations. It had a very influential board of directors, each of whom enjoyed a high measure of esteem among the financial and mercantile community of the city.[3] When the Back Bay was launched in the

---

[1] 'Time Bargain', *Bombay Gazette*, 18 May 1865.

[2] 'To hear of nothing but shares and premiums must be nauseating . . . as for the ladies, it must be intolerable, unless, indeed, like Lady Bertie and Bellair—they do a little business in the share market themselves.' T.O.I., 19 January 1865.

'We will not be far out if we say that nearly two-thirds of the officers [military] in this Presidency have dabbled in the share market, more or less.' *Bombay Saturday Review* quoted in T.O.I., 2 August 1865.

[3] Promotors of the Asiatic Bank: Michael Scott of Ritchie Stuart & Co.; Gavin Steel of Grey & Co.; Cowasji Jehangir—'an independent gentleman of large means'. As observed earlier, these giant companies were generally promo-

middle of 1864, it attracted deposits amounting to nearly Rs. 20,000,000 at a high rate of interest. The result was that the coffers of the Asiatic were swelled and the only way in which this huge capital could be made to pay was to advance it on the high rate of interest obtainable only on money required for speculation in cotton and shares for which, of course, there was a great demand at the time. So it began by advancing on the shares of the Back Bay Company and the Bank of Bombay, thus turning its cash into share certificates. The Old Financial with common directors, did the same thing. Soon they started advancing on each other's shares as well as their own and on the personal security of virtually anyone. The example was quickly taken up by others and in no time the practice became universal.[1]

The Bank of Bombay adhered to a policy of strictly orthodox banking until 1863, when a significant change was introduced in its constitution by taking power to advance on the shares of public companies. Due to the extreme laxity of the directors, the real power to make loans passed into the hands of its Secretary, Blair, a person of feeble mind.

Premchand Roychand, 'the largest speculator in the island' was a director of the Bank of Bombay during the critical period of its history. The intelligent Premchand soon discovered the weakness of Blair and in a very subtle way, by lending him large sums of money through his father, procuring him allotments of large numbers of shares on which a large premium was immediately realisable, and by buying and selling shares for him without charging any brokerage, quickly acquired 'great influence over him' and his subordinates who had complete command of the Bank's funds. The result was, in the words of the Bank of Bombay Commission that 'the Bank became Premchand's'.[2] He had simply to write: that Mr. So-and-So is good for so much and the money was immediately made available.[3]

It was this reckless use of the enormous funds of the Bank of

---

ted by very prominent people, e.g. the Old Financial had the following directors: Andrew Grant, of Campbell, Mitchell & Co.; Richard Willis of Forbes & Co.; A. F. Wallace of Wallace & Co.; John L. Scott of Finlay, Clark & Co.; Samuel L. Acland, solicitor; Cowasje Jehangier; and E. D. Sassoon of E.D. Sassoon & Co.— T.O.I., 11 August 1864. Andrew Grant was the reputed pioneer of financials.

[1] Wacha, *A Financial Chapter*, p. 173.

[2] P.P. *op. cit., passim*, in particular pp. 14–15.

[3] Exhibits A40 and A44 in Appendix with Index to Evidence pp. 31–2, P.P XV., 1868–9.

Bombay which intensified the speculation to such an extent that it was eventually to lead to 'universal demoralisation'[1] and ruin for many. For, as Wacha rightly observed, 'in such matters the gregarious nature of community asserts itself'.[2] What the first class merchants and capitalists did the first day, the second class merchants and traders did the second day and so on in a descending scale.

In fact, the degree of credit prevailing in Bombay was almost unique at this time. Banking facilities were enormous; brokers were all private bankers, the business in cotton was rapidly increasing, and bullion from the country districts was flowing in daily, 'a million a week'.[3] These facts, naturally, encouraged even men of straw to combine and form all kinds of associations hoping for the aid of established firms, and looking round for some reputed capitalist to back them up, privately or openly. On occasion these names were alleged to have been bought for ten or twenty lakhs a piece. As soon as the preliminaries were performed, the plans came out and such was the madness of the times that 'before the newspapers were half-glanced-at, the shares were applied for'.[4] No matter what the association, applications for shares would arrive in thousands, for it was well known that even to get one share, at least a hundred had to be applied for. The increasing tempo of the share market can be judged from the fact that 'shares were actually sold before allotted, before even the allotment papers were printed and when the allotments really came out they might be at forty or fifty (per cent premium on the nominal value) in a day'.[5]

The financial game of 'battle-dore and shuttle cock' began as soon as the allotments were over and the company formally established. The speculators would start by 'selling at forty or fifty, then attempt to depreciate, then buy at twenty, then tell who was behind the scenes and then sell again at, perhaps, one or two hundred'.[6] But this was not the end. They would then 'get up another company to purchase the old company'—at least 'old' here, where months did the work of years for a time, 'then propose another company to purchase that, and what was sold once for a lakh would become worth a crore'.[7] The stability of the concern was rarely

[1] F.O.I. (weekly), 3 January 1867.   [2] Wacha, *A Financial Chapter*, p. 39.
[3] T.O.I., 19 January 1865.   [4] *Ibid.*
[5] *Ibid.*, 6 January 1865.   [6] *Ibid.*, 19 January 1865.   [7] *Ibid.*

G   79

considered and the long memorandum which the shareholders had to sign was read still more rarely. The mood of the public, in the words of *Times of India*, was such that 'if the man in the moon obtained the names of two or three distinguished capitalists in Bombay he could start a scheme which would enable him to retire with a crore' the next day.[1]

It was considered inadvisable to employ intelligent managers because of the fear of their knowing too much.[2] In fact, there were not as many suitable managers and accountants as there were banks and financial houses. As a result, assistants in merchant houses or persons holding obscure situations (below the rank of deputy manager and deputy accountant) in old established banks were eagerly sought by the new class of promoters. The bait of becoming the manager of a big bank, no doubt newly established, upon a salary two or three times larger was tempting enough for them to leave their former employers.[3] But having got the managership, they did not remain contented—it would have been remarkable if they had. At a time when the whole city was involved in a speculative boom and the directors themselves were misusing the funds of the institution, it was natural that they should want to speculate as well. They overdrew their accounts at will, borrowed large sums from other institutions, whose managers they accommodated in the same way, and bought large numbers of shares without considering the cost or the consequences. Until the day of reckoning came, these millionaires 'lived well on the Malabar Hills, kept several horses and drank simpskin instead of beer'.[4] The broker, the lawyer, the newspaper proprietor were also among those who made large gains from the extravagant promotions and excessive speculation. Market rigging was an integral part of the scheme for successful launching of an ephemeral concern. The broker gifted in the art of raising the price of shares was, therefore, in great demand and was well paid for his services. Very often his payment took the form of a large allotment of shares in the new company,[5] which provided an added incentive to the broker to push up the price of shares.

A lawyer would charge anything from Rs.5,000 to Rs.10,000 for

---

[1] T.O.I. 6 January 1865.
[2] *Ibid.*, Overland Weekly, 8–28 August 1865.
[3] *Ibid.*   [4] *Ibid.*
[5] Wacha, *A Financial Chapter*, p. 40.

preparing the memoranda and articles of association. Company law, for the most part, was not understood by the promoters, and consequently his advice had to be taken on every matter, large or small. The attendance fee was of the order of Rs.100 an hour but as was the fashion of the day, he also received his remuneration mostly in the allotments of shares and not infrequently was also offered a seat on the board of directors.[1]

Company advertisements occupied more space in the newspapers than ever before. Prospectuses, call notices, announcements of meetings, forfeitures and commencement of business filled many pages. Even full-page advertisements were seen as sometimes appear in *The Times* when a new issue is announced.

The moving spirit behind the speculation was Premchand Roychand, regarded by many as all-powerful[2] and possessing great financial skill.[3] Sir Bartle Frere, then Governor of Bombay, observed in his evidence before the Bank of Bombay Commission, 'his position was like nothing that he had ever seen or heard of in any other community'.[4] Thirty-four years of age and lithe of limb, Premchand was a short, dapper Hindu of fair complexion, sweet temper, engaging manners and free from the pride of riches. Following in the footsteps of his father, Deepchund Roychund, he began his career as a broker and was doing a moderate business before the civil war broke out. He rapidly amassed a large fortune in the cotton speculation and at the time of the share mania, 'he was in such a position', reported the Bank of Bombay Commission, 'that his name and influence were considered essential to the safe launching of the ephemeral schemes of the day'.[5] No matter whether he was a promoter or not, he was always allotted a large number of shares. He was consulted by the promoters and was invited to participate in the distribution of shares. Shares were allotted so as to establish a company on the broadest possible basis but without losing sight of individual interests for, at this time, the shares of all companies were at a premium which was at once realisable.[6] Nobody could do this job better than Premchand, who, observed the Commission, 'judiciously distributed them,

[1] Watcha, *A Financial Chapter* p. 41.
[2] T.O.I. Overland Weekly, 8–23 August 1865, 'The Unveiled Prophet of Bombay'.
[3] Wacha, *A Financial Chapter*, pp. 47–8.
[4] P.P., XV., 1868–9, *Minutes of Evidence taken in England*, Question 6773.
[5] *Ibid.*, Report, p. 14.   [6] *Ibid.*

first among the managers of the Banks, and, secondly, to the friends of the promoters and himself and to other persons who might be useful to them or to the undertaking'.[1] In fact his every stroke was masterly. Intensely shrewd, he scrupulously avoided having his name involved with the affairs of any company. And although he received large allotments of shares in almost every company launched, his name was not to be found on the register of any of them. All those allotted to him were in the names of his *munims* (accountants, cashiers), servants, distant relatives and other such men of straw.

The secret of Premchand's wide influence lay in his power over the treasury of the Bank of Bombay to which he was a 'trusted adviser'.[2] The manner in which Premchand abused his position *vis-à-vis* the Bank is brought out very clearly in the following extract from the Commission's report.:[3]

If Premchand had a friend to oblige, who wanted money, he recommended him for a loan. If Premchand had shares to sell, he would suggest to an acquaintance that he should buy, offering at the same time to 'finance' the purchase money, by procuring him a loan from the Bank of Bombay. If Premchand wanted money for speculation, he would suggest to some friend to join him in it, and then procure a loan in his friend's name for the money required. His influence was felt not only at the Head Office but at the branches also, the agents at Kalbadevi, Broach, and Surat all receiving instructions to consult Premchand or his agents respecting advances.[4]

His own debts to the Bank, at the end, totalled upwards of forty-two lakhs (Rs.4·2 million) of rupees. For others who applied the money to purchase shares from himself, he procured a sum of Rs.6,690,000. In addition, he obtained Rs.2,958,938 for his partners in speculation and for his own purposes besides, recommending many other loans to a large amount and of the last mentioned, two sums of Rs.4,345,478 and Rs.1,302,408 were irrecoverably lost.[5]

In the end, 'it is no exaggeration to say', to quote Wacha, 'that his financial acumen was such that had his luck carried him to the seat of wealth in London, he would have proved no mean a match for the Rothschilds, the Barings. Till the day of his death his head was so clear, his financial sagacity so keen, and his mental and

[1] P.P., XV, 1868–9, Report, p. 14.   [2] *Ibid.*, Report, p. 40.
[3] *Ibid.*, pp. 14–15.   [4] *Ibid.*   [5] *Ibid.*

physical energy so unimpaired, that he would rival the most towering monetary individual in Lombard Street or on the Bourses of Berlin and Paris.'[1] And although he failed in 1866 for upwards of ten million pounds[2] 'such was his optimism, his confidence and his business courage and such his inveterate love of speculation, that he was able to accumulate again a handsome fortune . . . which popular account reckons at a quarter million sterling'.[3]

Next to Premchand Roychand, the name of Pestonji Cursetji Shroff was, perhaps, the most familiar. Originally an obscure clerk, he made some money by speculation in cotton and shares. At the time of the share mania, he came into touch with Premchand who introduced him to the promoters of the Eastern Financial, the Company with which he was most identified. Shroff was allotted a thousand shares in this institution, which was on the verge of bankruptcy at this time, and was also made one of its directors. With his thousand shares, Shroff rigged the share market in such a way that the price soon reached a premium of 40%. When the other directors of the Financial took the opportunity of unloading their holdings, Shroff bought them and thus acquired complete control over the affairs of the company.[4] Details of the way in which he misused the money of the Financial, interesting as they are, fall beyond the scope of this book, but the following example shows his skill in financial manoeuvring.

At the close of 1864, Shroff called a general meeting of the shareholders in which he announced that the estimated profits of the Company for the year were likely to be Rs.2 million. On the basis of this assurance, the meeting was asked to vote for an interim dividend of 22%, which it did. As soon as the news reached the share market the premium on the Financial's shares began to rise until they reached 168%. Pestonji Cursetji followed his ruse by making a further call of Rs.50 on the shares which the shareholders, blinded by the declared dividend, soon paid up. But Pestonji did not stop here. Encouraged by his success, he next moved to make a new issue of 25,000 shares, half of which he reserved, following the example of Back Bay, for sale by public auction. At the auction, he

---

[1] Wacha, *A Financial Chapter*, pp. 52–3.
[2] F.O.I. (weekly), 3 January 1867.
[3] Wacha, *A Financial Chapter*, pp. 52–3.
[4] *Ibid.*, pp. 62–3.

himself bought a large number of shares in an effort to boost up the premiums. But he had nothing to lose. He debited the entire purchase amounting to Rs.2,700,000 to the accounts of the Financial and passed an I.O.U.[1]

At times Pestonji Cursetji Shroff tried to rival Premchand Roychand but he was no match for the genius of the latter; when the crash came, Pestonji fell and unlike Premchand he fell for ever.[2]

Other leading figures who may be mentioned include Dr Diver, a medical man; Atmaram Madhevji, a broker; and George Taylor, a lawyer; popularly known as the 'Gunpowder Trio'. They were best known in connection with the Mazagon Reclamation Company and the Alliance Financial, which had a paid-up capital of one million pounds each. Initially the right to reclaim land at Mazagon, not worth more than Rs.500,000, was purchased by Premchand in partnership with Michael Scott of the great merchant house of Ritchie, Stuart and Company. The price paid was Rs.4,000,000, but Premchand, characteristically, soon managed to sell it to Dr Diver for Rs.6,000,0co, clearing a profit of Rs. 2,000,000 in a day. In fact, if anything, the story of the 'trio' serves to show what even the uninformed can do in such times. They had absolutely no financial skill and the result was that they became tools of Jamnadass and Devidass, a well-known firm of brokers, through their stooge Atmaram Madhevji. This firm made a clean sweep of the resources of the two institutions[3] and when the final crash came, Dr Diver, who had risen to the highest rank of English society and purchased such properties as Government House at Dapoorie, 'had to escape from his creditors, leaving behind an umbrella as his sole asset'.[4]

It must not, however, be thought that the whole picture was painted black. Even in such unbalanced times there were merchants and capitalists like Sir Cowasji Readymoney Jehangir and John Fleming and brokers like Choonilal Motilal who, although drawn into the vortex, tried to stem the tide of speculation and maintained their credit unsullied. Details of their activities are beyond the scope of this book but a word must be said here about John Fleming, a shrewd, sturdy and honest Scot. He was a partner in the famous firm of W. Nicol, who were the promoters and also

[1] Watcha, *A Financial Chapter*, p. 65.   [2] *Ibid.*, p. 66.
[3] *Ibid.*, p. 79.   [4] F.O.I. (weekly), 3 January 1867.

'secretary and treasurer' of the first land reclamation company to have been established in Bombay in 1859.[1] He went to India during the Civil War and left soon after it was over. At the time of the mania, it was inevitable that the Elphinston Company should become an object of speculation. Its shares of Rs.36,000 each were bulled by B. H. Cama, so that they reached a premium of Rs. 100,000. Later, Dr Diver and a few others, with Premchand Roychand as their moving spirit, formed a syndicate with the object of amalgamating the Mazagon, the Frere and the Elphinston into one super reclamation company. The syndicate offered three million pounds to M. Nicol and Sons, but John Fleming intervened and successfully stifled the attempts of the speculators in the two general meetings of the shareholders requisitioned by the syndicate, openly denouncing the 'gambling spirit' of the day.[2] But this did not prevent the speculators from making large gains from their take-over manoeuvres. It had created such a 'furore' in the market that the price of an Elphinston share had reached a premium of Rs.175,000 by the time the syndicate secretly unloaded its holding.[3]

THE CRASH AND THE AFTERMATH

The warning that 'the termination of the American Civil War would leave England inundated with inferior 'surats' [a variety of Indian cotton] and the article will stink in the structurals [*sic*] of English manufacturers'[4] was sounded by the *Times of India* of early as March 1862. It was repeated again and again in the following years but the newspapers wrote 'on sand in face of a flowing tide'.[5]

The apprehension of a permanent fall in the price of cotton had been felt in some degree since September 1864, but the speculation continued as before. The reaction set in early in January 1865, and the price of Indian cotton in the Liverpool market began to fall off gradually until towards the end of March it came down to the low figure of 10d. a lb.[6] Simultaneously, the share market also showed

[1] Extraordinary General Meeting held on 14 January 1865, T.O.I. (Overland), 13–28 January 1865.
[2] *Ibid.*   [3] Wacha, *A Financial Chapter*, pp. 190–200.
[4] S. D. Mehta, quoted in p. 30.
[5] T.O.I. (Overland), 28 April–13 May 1865.
[6] *Bombay Gazette*, see 'Special Telegrams' from January–March 1865.

an unmistakable bearish tendency and by March the share prices had fallen off considerably. The fall in cotton prices was thought due mainly to large quantities of stocks held in England. The speculation was still continuing. The uncertain prospects of the American War failed to end the hopes of revival in Bombay. As late as March 1865, Sir Charles Trevelyan, the Finance Minister of India, sounded a note of optimism in his Budget speech.[1]

The victory of the Northerners in the spring of 1865, however, meant the end of the speculative boom and ended the prosperity of Bombay. The price of 'Fair Dhollera' touched $9\frac{1}{4}$d. a lb. for a time. It became difficult for the traders to meet their commitments. The price of shares fell heavily and the panic was so severe that a meeting of the sharebrokers held on 21 April 1865, unanimously decided to close the share market.[2] Dealings in shares were resumed after about a week but transactions were very limited. Despite the 'gloom and confusion', 'despair and anxiety', people in Bombay maintained their optimism. The situation was further aggravated by the policy adopted by the old established exchange banks in the city which refused to advance even on the security of merchandise.[3] But a general sense of 'forbearance' prevailed among the merchants and capitalists which helped to prevent any precipitation of the crisis,[4] and various schemes were proposed to circumscribe and alleviate it. In principle, they attempted to tackle the problem from two ends: firstly, by rescuing such banks and financials as could still be saved and amalgamating them on a true appraisal of their net assets; and, secondly, by bringing about a settlement through compromise of the time-bargains due on the first of July. These were not mere plans on paper: a *Panchayet*, or a committee of five Indians to which two Europeans were later added, was in fact appointed to settle the impending time-bargains.[5]

On 2 May 1865, the newspapers in Bombay announced news of the surrender of General Lee's army. Within a fortnight came the

---

[1] 'The year has been distinguished for a remarkable development of the principle of municipal administration and private enterprise. The extensive plans of reclamation . . . (in) . . . Bombay and Calcutta and the numerous companies . . . show that the future growth of India will not be limited by the standard of the means and action of the Government . . .' T.O.I., 1 April 1865.

[2] See share market report in *Bombay Gazette*, 22 April 1865 and later.

[3] T.O.I., 13 May 1865.   [4] *Ibid.*, 23 May 1865.

[5] *Ibid.*, 23 May; 19 May (A Letter by a Merchant); 13 May 1865.

Banking Inflation in Bombay, 1861–65

first large-scale failure, of the House of B. H. Cama, one of the largest shippers of cotton, which suspended payment with liability amounting to Rs.33,000,000. The news precipitated a ruinous fall in the price of shares,[1] making any kind of settlement impossible and the plans were abandoned.[2] Henceforth, many merchants and traders closed their doors to their creditors. The intensity of the panic increased every day until the nadir of depression was reached on 1 July 1865, as time-bargains amounting to £8 and £9 million fell due.[3] The general stagnation of business rendered the 'Fort' as quiet as at holiday times so that the day passed with outward quietness. All the excitement was transferred to the offices of brokers, speculating capitalists, solicitors and financial associations, where lawyers were the masters of the situation. Money changed hands only in the case of a few of the smaller time-bargain contracts, where the scale of compromise adopted ranged from five to ten shillings in the pound. In cases where regular mercantile business transactions were mixed up with share transactions, debtors earnestly requested postponement, but the deficits were generally very large in proportion to the assets, and creditors were, therefore, very reluctant to accede to these requests.

Very careful measures were taken, both by buyers and sellers, in order, on the one hand, to test, and on the other, to ensure the strict legality of tender of shares. Attorney's clerks, 'impelled by expected perquisites, found themselves running from one place to another with an energy which surprised none more than themselves'.[4] The number of notices served was variously estimated at from 300 to 700 from each office, and as the charge was stated to have been Rs.15 for serving them in the 'Fort' and Rs.30 outside, the solicitors must have done very well. Many speculators took careful note of the numbers of shares presented for settlement to see that the numbers were in accordance with those contracted for, and that the same shares were not tendered in respect of other bargains, since it was a well-known fact that more shares had been contracted for than actually existed, particularly in some companies, such as the Back Bay. In many cases, where shares were tendered, merchants asserted that their contracts had not been

---

[1] Wacha, *A Financial Chapter*, p. 212.
[2] T.O.I., 13 May 1865.
[3] Wacha, *A Financial Chapter*, p. 212.
[4] T.O.I. (Overland), 3–18 July 1865.

fulfilled as the transfers had not been registered with the companies concerned. This was a technical loop-hole since in many cases the companies had kept no records so that compliance with legal requirements was impossible, rendering most of these contracts invalid as *sattas*.

As demands for differences were pressed, more and more insolvencies were declared, and auctions of shares, which had already been taking place for some time, became more frequent. The ordinary machinery of the insolvency court was jammed, and the Government of Bombay, receiving an urgent memorial from the mercantile community,[1] immediately passed an Act,[2] by which the trustees of estates whose liability exceeded five lakhs were empowered to liquidate. But this Act had unforeseen results, in that fraudulent debtors, to take the benefit of the Act, swelled their liabilities by buying worthless shares when the market was utterly depressed and entering them in their books at a previous date when the price was higher; and as transfer books had not been kept by the majority of joint stock companies, it was impossible to verify the date of purchase. Act XXVIII of 1865 became a 'by-word of reproach'.[3]

As the public realised that most of the assets of the financial and other associations consisted of shares and local bills, which had become worthless, there was no alternative but to wind them up. One after another companies went into liquidation. The Back Bay and the Mazagon, which had paid sums of half a million pounds for swamps to reclaim and for hills to throw into them, were wound up with nothing to show for the money that had been spent beyond a few acres of earth at useless places.

The verbatim reports of the meetings held to put the companies into voluntary liquidation, in the newspapers, read much like a series of selections from *Punch* after the Railway Mania of 1846. Noisy shareholders hurled abuse, books and papers into the faces of their directors and other officers. Shareholders, registered and unregistered, lawyers and even members of the public crowded these meetings. The directors frequently sought the assistance of the police to keep order. Penetrating questions put by local shareholders brought forth confessions from the directors which revealed complete disregard of shareholders' interests, flagrant

---

[1] T.O.I., 8 July 1865.   [2] *Act XXVIII of 1865.*
[3] Wacha, *A Financial Chapter*, p. 221.

breaches of company law and of the most rudimentary principles of business, misappropriation of companies' money by their directors and officers, and pitiable ignorance of the provisions of company law, and of the memoranda and articles of association of the companies.[1] In some cases, indignant shareholders took their directors to court, and in others, criminal proceedings were taken against them. One such proceeding against the directors of the Commercial Finance and Stock Exchange Company ended in their conviction. The judge, Mr Justice Anstey, made a stern example of them by escheating their property to the Crown and transporting them for life.[2] This decision alarmed the whole city, with the result that directors of other companies preferred to settle out of court at any cost and knowing that they were open to serious charges, tried to put their companies quietly into voluntary liquidation; but this only led to the emergence of 'a tribe of voluble and noisy blackmailers'[3] who extorted money by threatening to prosecute them.

The improved prospects for cotton and a slight increase in its price early in July 1865, revived in some a hope of a return to the past. A sudden advance took place in some local stocks and the clamour at the corner of Meadow Street was renewed. The *Times of India* wrote:

The maxim that a burnt child dreads the fire does not hold good in the case of those with whom speculation has become a vice in their blood. Rather are they like the foolish moth which nothing but total destruction will cause to cease from folly.[4]

The warning, once more, went unheeded and Bombay took another 'gallop through the mire' although this time not quite at the same speed. In the month of September there was a rise in the value of all shares which continued till the end of the year.[5] But from the second week in January of the next year, the trend reversed unmistakably. The price of shares fell off gradually until the end of April when the fall became steeper. By the end of June 1866, the collapse was complete.[6] The appearance of the mirage, as

---

[1] T.O.I. *passim*, May, June and July, 1865 (particularly 23 June–8 July).

[2] Wacha, *A Financial Chapter*, p. 218.   [3] *Ibid.*, p. 217.

[4] T.O.I., 14 July 1865.

[5] P.P., XV, 1868–9, *Minutes of Evidence taken in England*, p. 116, Question 3827.

[6] See share market quotations, *Times of India Calendar and Directory*, 1867.

Mehta wrote, 'only served to intensify the shock and the severity of the impending disaster'.[1] Over sixty merchants failed for more than a million rupees each.[2] The liabilities of twenty-four bankruptcies alone amounted to Rs.19 crores, and of the others, to Rs.7 crores.[3]

By the end of 1866, of the hundreds of companies projected during the boom fostered by the American War, only a dozen had survived and even these were waiting final liquidation in the insolvency court, for 'no one would pay the more than eight millions sterling of calls on their shares'.[4] The liquidation of estates and companies continued up to 1872. The average rate of distribution of the insolvents' estates ranged from 1% to 5%, which clearly shows the extent of over-trading indulged in by them during the mania. Premchand's estate paid only $1\frac{1}{2}\%$ and the estate of B. H. Cama alone returned a little over 10 annas in the rupee. In the case of compromises effected outside the court, the dividends paid were much better, ranging from 2s. 6d. to 5s. in the pound. The Bank of Bombay returned only about Rs.100 on a fully paid share of Rs.5,000. Of more than sixty banks and financials, a few returned a minute fraction of their capital to the shareholders, while many paid nothing. The shareholders of the Back Bay Company received only Rs.1,750 for a share on which Rs.5,200 had been paid-up and which was contracted for Rs.55,000 for 1 July.[5]

There had been commercial speculation elsewhere but probably no community ever took it to the lengths that Bombay did in 1864. The collapse of a mania is a certain result of the nature of the mania. It does not need an external force to destroy it, although this often helps, but it dies of its own accord, 'by the sudden substitution of the real difficulty of making money for the supposed facility of making it', as the *Economist* rightly observed.[6] Thus the

---

[1] S. D. Mehta, pp. 31–2.
[2] T.O.I. *Calendar*, 1868; also S. D. Mehta, *Ibid*.
[3] Wacha, *A Financial Chapter*, p. 223.
[4] F.O.I. (weekly) 31 January 1867. This does not mean that there were no tangible benefits from the Civil War speculation. In fact, a significant portion of modern Bombay's physical plan is known to date from the period 1864–72. See S. M. Edwardes, *Rise of Bombay*, 1902, pp. 279–300; D. E. Wacha, *The Rise and Growth of Bombay Municipal Government*, pp. 88–9, 1913; Morris, *Emergence of a Labour Force*, pp. 19–20.
[5] Wacha, *A Financial Chapter*, pp. 215–24, *passim*.
[6] Quoted in T.O.I., 14 July 1865.

collapse in Bombay was due not to the close of the American War or the fall in cotton prices, but to share prices falling of their own weight. Even in normal times, unbounded optimism in business expectations may gradually push up the price of shares to an unrealistic level, resulting in a sudden collapse. In periods of intense speculation, this whole process is merely accelerated. For a full appreciation, the Civil War speculation must be viewed in relation to the past economic expansion of Bombay.

Bombay had been a port for very long and as far back as 1735 there was a shipyard there.[1] From about the time of the defeat of the Marathas in 1818, it was increasingly used as the nearest port of call by the ocean-going vessels. Even the goods traditionally shipped from west coast ports such as Surat and Broach were diverted to Bombay for transhipment overseas.[3] A major roadway through the Western Ghats sharply reduced the internal transport charges after 1830.[2] The charter revisions of the East India Company further boosted the international trade of India. The following table shows the growth of international trade at Bombay.

Table 6

Commodity Foreign Trade Moving Through Bombay 1809–10 to 1870–1 (In millions of Rupees)

(*Annual Average for Decade ending*	*Imports*	*Exports*	*Total*
1809–10	7·3	9·8	17·1
1819–20	9·3	10·7	20·0
1829–30	14·9	20·4	35·3
1839–40	19·5	35·1	54·6
1849–50	32·4	49·9	82·3
1859–60	53·9	91·7	145·6

Table taken from Morris, *Emergence of a Labour Force*, p. 14. (His source: Edwardes, *Gazetteer* I., p. 148.)

Profitable business investment and worker employment opportunities increased *pari passu* with the expansion of international trade. After the British authority had been established over

[1] R. A. Wadia, *The Bombay Dockyard and the Wadia Master Builders*, 1955, p. 176.

[2] Morris, *Emergence of a Labour Force*, p. 15.

[3] J. M. Maclean, *A Guide to Bombay*, 1877, p. 68; also C. W. Grant, *Bombay Cotton and Indian Railways*, 1850, p. 149.

Western India, Bombay also became the seat of the Provincial Government. The East India Company set up an ordnance factory there which employed nearly 1,000 workers in its gun carriage section in 1823.[1] Among its other direct beneficiaries was the shipyard which built ships for the navy. In 1847 the shipyard gave employment to about 2,000 people.[2] Port and dockyard facilities were continuously increased and land had to be reclaimed to provide for new offices and residential accommodation.

In 1836 some Indian and British merchants founded the Bombay Chamber of Commerce. The first modern bank—the Bank of Bombay—was established in 1840. Two more banks had been started by 1845. In 1847, nine steamers were plying from Bombay. The Bombay Steam Navigation Company, a numerous body, alone operated five of them between Karachi, Colombo and Surat. By 1851 there were twenty-five insurance offices seeking business in Bombay and of the cotton bale screwing and pressing firms, one was so large that it employed nearly 1,000 persons.[3]

By 1855 telegraph lines had been opened between Calcutta and Bombay and some other cities.[4] Postal services had been organised on the present system[5] and the first twenty-three miles of railway linking Thana and Bombay had by 1860 been extended far enough to cover the cotton fields of Gujerat and Central India.

The character of Bombay had begun to change, from the second half of the last century, from a commercial to an industrial city. Its

[1] H. A. Young, *The East India Company's Arsenals and Manufactories*, 1937, p. 202.

[2] From 1829 the shipyard also built iron steamships from imported materials and in 1851, it built an eighty-ton steamer entirely from locally manufactured components, see Wadia, pp. 269-89 and 322.

[3] *The Bombay Times Calendar of 1855*, p. 99.

[4] After prolonged experiments Dr W. B. O'Shaughnessy, Professor of Chemistry in the Medical College at Calcutta, obtained the sanction of the Government in 1851 to construct experimental lines from Calcutta to Diamond Harbour. In 1852, the Governor-General, Lord Dalhousie, obtained the sanction of the Court of Directors to the extension of the services by the construction of lines between Calcutta and Agra, Agra and Bombay, Agra and Peshawar, Bombay and Madras. These lines extended over 3,050 miles. They were opened from 1 February 1855. S.T.B.I., 1901, p. XXXVI.

[5] Until 1837 no general system of postal services existed in India. Certain services instituted by the Government were also used by the public. In 1837 a public post was established as a Government monopoly. The system of postage stamps and prescribed rates for conveyance of letters irrespective of distance was introduced for the first time following the *Act XVII* of 1854. Until then it used to cost one rupee per *tola* to send a letter from Bombay to Calcutta. S.T.B.I., 1901, p. XXXVIII.

economic expansion was remarkable, not only for its size and variety, but also for its rapidity. In the early 1850's the population of Bombay was very likely in the neighbourhood of 500,000. By the time of the share mania in 1864 it had increased to about 816,000.[1] Yet it would be wrong to characterise the development prior to the outbreak of the Civil War as 'economic ebullience'.[2] It should be recalled that it took nearly two years of even the American War to warm up the Bombay economy to a point where signs of speculation began to be visible and the point of ebullience was not reached until a year afterwards.[3] On the other hand the past economic history of Bombay does show that neither the spirit of enterprise nor the opportunities for investment were lacking in such a large measure that they could be blamed for the resulting banking inflation.[4]

The census figures show that Bombay had lost about 21% of its population between 1864 and 1872.[5] It was, however, still the most populous city in India—more populated than either Calcutta or Madras.

---

[1] These figures should be used with caution. See Morris, *Emergence of a Labour Force*, pp. 13, 19, and Table III on p. 20.
[2] *Ibid.*, p. 18.   [3] See pp. 72–4.   [4] See p. 72.
[5] Morris, *Emergence of a Labour Force*, p. 20.

CHAPTER 6

THE BOOM IN THE
TEA INDUSTRY

Bombay was not the only city to undergo a period of wild speculation, for Calcutta underwent the same experience, although on a
smaller scale.

As in Bombay, the stock market in Calcutta generally remained
remarkably quiet in the first two years of the 1860's except in the
case of the tea companies. The impetus given to the trade by the
American Civil War was first felt in Calcutta towards the end of
March 1863, and during the following six months, the speculative
fever on the stock market developed into what seemed to contemporary observers to be a 'dangerous epidemic'.[1] Traders who had
found it 'difficult to make a fortune out of their shops began to
launch them on the share market'[2] as limited companies. Like
Bombay, the unsound nature of the undertakings was concealed
by associating them with the names of respectable merchants or
firms who intended to 'pocket large premiums'[3] before the boom
ended. The development was characterised by an 'uneasy and
anxious' desire for wealth on the part of people who had not the
personal capabilities necessary for long-term success in this field.
How widespread the infection was may be judged from the
following extract from the *Friend of India*:[4]

... When we see Doctors of Divinity prominently announced in the
newspapers as attending meetings of companies ... that grave fathers
of families, innocent of all familiarity with the money market, spend
sleepless nights as they ruminate over selling out of this limited company and buying into that, it is time to repeat our words of warning.

The reason why the idea of converting a trading business into a
limited company was so much more popular in Calcutta than elsewhere in India lies in the racial composition of the mercantile
community there which included more Europeans than in the

[1] F.O.I., 8 October 1863.   [2] *Ibid.*
[3] *Ibid.*   [4] *Ibid.*

other cities, as is revealed in the local trade directories of the time.[1] Since these Europeans must have been better acquainted with the advantages of the corporate organisation, it was quite natural that they should have sought its benefits.

By October 1863, however, most of these trading companies had collapsed or were on the verge of collapsing. In fact, the shares of these converted businesses had become unsaleable so quickly that in some cases even the speculators had burnt their fingers, and had been left with the shares before they could unload them on to others.[2]

It must not, however, be inferred from this that trading companies had disappeared altogether. It would have been surprising if, with the continued prosperity in the country, some of the traders had not continued to think of expanding their businesses by taking advantage of company organisation, but the pace of development slowed down as the purely speculative element disappeared, or, perhaps, transferred its attention to the more profitable field of tea shares. Interest revived again in 1865, and the number of miscellaneous trading companies registered in that year rose to eight, after a drop from twelve in 1863 to three in 1864.[3]

These developments were, however, only a minor aspect of the speculative boom which had started in 1863, and they were overshadowed by the more significant events taking place simultaneously in the tea industry.

In 1858, there was only one company in the tea industry, the Assam Company, incorporated in Britain. By 1865, as many as sixty-two companies had been registered in India, in addition to thirty sterling companies.[4] To understand this sudden and unprecedented development, it is necessary first to trace the history of tea cultivation in India.

Before the advent of the British rule in India, two adventurous Scots of the name of Bruce had settled in Assam. It is not clear which of them actually discovered the plant, but the credit for proclaiming the discovery goes to the younger Bruce.

No advantage, however, was taken of the discovery until after the monopoly of the East India Company of the tea trade with China had ceased in 1833. In the following year, the Company

---

[1] See e.g. Directory published by Thacker's.
[2] F.O.I., 8 October 1863.
[3] Table 9. [4] See Appendices 6 and 8.

appointed a commission to enquire into the possibility of introducing the cultivation of tea into India. In 1837, after some trial and error, a sample consignment of tea from the Government experimental gardens in Assam fetched such a high price in London that it immediately drew the attention of some capitalists in Britain and India.[1] As a result, two companies were formed, the Bengal Tea Association of Calcutta and the Assam Company of London, to take over the Government experimental gardens and the cultivation of tea in Assam, but as prospects were limited and there were better facilities for raising large amounts of capital in London, the Indian company was persuaded to amalgamate with the Assam Company in 1839. The Assam Company then acquired two-thirds of the Government experimental gardens,[2] and took a vigorous interest in its affairs. For a time matters seemed to be developing well, but in a few years gross mismanagement, inexperience in tea cultivation and lavish expenditure led to such a depressed state that the shares of the concern, once worth £20, could not be sold for half a crown apiece.[3] It was revived, however, in 1852, by better management and within the next seven years the area under its cultivation reached 4,000 acres, with an annual turnout of 760,000 lbs. of tea.[4] By 1859, all its factories were in full swing and its shares were quoted at a high premium.[5]

Meanwhile, in 1849, the Government of India had sold the remaining third of its experimental garden to a Chinese employee,[6] so that the further development of the tea industry was left entirely to private enterprise.

Other competition had sprung up. In 1855, tea was also found to grow naturally in Cachar. Sylhet also entered the market but a considerable time elapsed before an attempt was made at cultivation there. It was really the success of Colonel Hannay which encouraged private enterprise. He owned a private tea garden in Dibrugarh about 1850. In 1853 there were only nine such gardens; by 1859, there were no fewer than fifty-one.[7] Apart from the Assam Company, the Hope Town Association, Limited, registered in Calcutta on 6 February 1858, with a paid-up capital of Rs.305,950, was the only other corporate body engaged in the

[1] *Papers Regarding the Tea Industry in Bengal.* See Edgar's letter.
[2] Antrobus, *Assam.*   [3] This was in 1846. *Ibid.*, pp. 413–15.
[4] F.O.I., 9 June 1874.
[5] In 1859, the highest quotation reached was £31 5s. 0d.; Antrobus, *Assam*, p. 415.   [6] F.O.I., 9 June 1874.   [7] *Ibid.*, F.O.I.

cultivation of tea. It is a little surprising to find no reference to this company during this period, except in the official statistics.[1]

The number of new companies registered in Britain and in India up to the end of 1862 was as follows:

Year	India	Britain
1857 and before	–	1
1858	1	–
1859	5	2
1860	4	–
1861	9	2
1862	5	5
Total	24	10

The rapid progress of the tea industry gave rise to hopes of high profits. Developments up to the end of 1862 were healthy,[2] and the operations of these companies, which took over private gardens by purchase, were marked by prudence with the result that they held their ground even during the crisis in the industry in 1866.

From 1863 to 1865, however, there was a thoughtless rush for the waste lands. When the land was barely scratched a speculator set about forming a company which was to 'start by buying the lands he had scarcely finished clearing as accomplished tea gardens and what still remained of undeniable waste, at a cost out of all proportion . . . to what it was worth'.[3] The sudden rush was, no doubt, caused by the liberal rules for the purchase of waste land promulgated by Lord Canning which were still more liberally administered by the officials. These tempted many speculators in Calcutta to enter immediately upon what the *Friend of India* called the 'delicate task' of company promotion.[4] The following figures reveal the increase in the pace of development:

Year	Number of Companies Registered in	
	India[a]	Britain[b]
1863	23	9
1864	10	6
1865	5	5
Total	38	20

[a] S.T.B.I., 1883.   [b] See Appendix 6.

[1] S.T.B.I., 1883.   [2] F.O.I., 9 June 1874.   [3] *Ibid.*   [4] *Ibid.*

In fairness to the promoters of these companies, however, it must be said that they were often misled by their agents on the spot, who lumped together one or two really good gardens with three or four inferior jungly tracts and sold the lot to a company at prices twice or three times their true value. These promoters and their agents, even when, as was usually the case, their intentions were honourable, lacked the professional knowledge necessary to say what was good soil for tea and what were the best plants for the soil. Companies were thus floated on the London and Calcutta markets, and many of the fortunate sellers departed for England with their purchase money.[1]

Every day the mania increased and the more daring adventurers began to persuade the public to invest in 'gardens' that actually had no existence. For instance, 'an estate in Nowgong was sold in two divisions, one division for £80,000. This purported to be a garden of 1,000 acres under cultivation of two year old plants. At the time the sale was effected in London, there were only small patches of cultivation in existence. A telegram was sent out from London to the manager in India to have the requisite acreage cleared and planted by a certain date. The company carried on for two seasons, under the Board of Directors, of which one of the vendors was the chairman. After that the estate was wound up.'[2] J. W. Edgar, Secretary to the Government of India, Department of Agriculture, etc., records that the Cachar planters had a saying to the effect that it was very doubtful whether the making of tea would pay, but that there was no uncertainty about the making of gardens, which, in fact, were made for sale and not for cultivation.[3]

The *modus operandi* was to purchase for a mere trifle a piece of waste land, plant it with tea and sell it at a price which often gave the vendor a thousand per cent profit upon his expenditure. E. Money, in his 'Essay on Tea' which received the Grant Gold Medal in 1872, remarked that in those days a small garden of forty acres was sold to a bewitched body of money-seekers as one of two hundred. 'I am not joking,' he said, 'it was done over and over again. The price paid, moreover, was quite out of proportion to even the supposed area. Two or three lakhs of rupees have often

[1] F.O.I., 17 May 1866.
[2] See the evidence of J. W. Jamieson, pp. vii to ix in Appendix A of the *Report of the Commissioners Appointed to Enquire into the State and Prospects of Tea Cultivation in Assam, Cachar and Sylhet, 1868.*
[3] *Papers regarding the tea industry, op. cit.*

been paid for such gardens when not more than two years old, and forty per cent of the existing areas vacancies [*sic*].'[1] Consideration was not paid always in the form of cash. In at least one case, and there must have been many more, the entire purchase money was paid in debentures.[2]

The following extract from the *Friend of India* gives another account of the confusion and the reckless manner in which companies were promoted:

Land was roughly cleared without reference to its quality, elevation or requirements of tea cultivation. . . . The property was represented in London or Calcutta markets as being of 'virgin soil, carefully selected, within thirty-six hours of Calcutta, reduceable to four and twenty . . . specimens of tea, collected anywhere, left no doubt of its excellence. . . ' Men of mark and position, if not high character, countenanced the falsehood and supported the speculators. . . . The Great Cheetam Tea Company Limited, one of many similar instances, was soon launched, after paying to the late owner of that magnificent estate a consideration varying from £20,000 to £30,000.[3]

This was not all. Highly-paid managers with large subordinate staffs were immediately sent to superintend properties which had no real existence.[4] Directors sought to satisfy the shareholders by making one tea bush do the work of half a dozen, as they demanded the production of more and more tea. The managers, driven to reckless behaviour by their false position, 'pulled every leaf and would have chopped up the tea wood itself had it been practicable'.[5] Their object was simply to collect so many tons of coarse leaf and sticks and indifferently brand them 'Flowery Pekoe' or 'Bohea', although resembling, as the *Friend of India* put it, 'either of these teas as closely as ground peas resembled the finest 'Mokha' coffee.'[6] Naturally, not only did the tea fall in value until it was scarcely worth the carriage, but the plants were all but destroyed by over-picking.[7]

These ill-based companies soon produced a multitude of evils. When the collapse came, many Englishmen, sent out to manage the concerns, found themselves stranded, without even the means of subsistence. Some died, and others literally begged their way out

---

[1] *Papers Regarding the tea industry, op. cit.*

[2] *Report of the Commissioners*, etc., Appendix A. p. xxix, evidence of Revd. E. H. Higgs., *op. cit.*

[3] F.O.I., 18 July 1867.   [4] *Ibid.*   [5] *Ibid.*   [6] *Ibid.*   [7] *Ibid.*

of Assam. Local labour was diverted and the *bona fide* tea firms had to import hands from Bengal at a ruinous cost, which, however, was somewhat counterbalanced by the profits realised from an increase in the price of seed. But this latter source of profit soon came to an end while the labour situation remained as before. The demand for labour was very great.[1] The Calcutta recruiters, wrote the *Friend of India*, 'drained the purlieus of the city to supply the demand. The lame, the blind, the insane, the diseased, no matter what so that they could crawl, were drafted off to Assam, whose gardens began to look more like open air hospitals than thriving plantations.'[2] But it was not only the tea companies that suffered; the misery of the poor coolies defies any description. 'On the voyage to their new homes the miserable creatures died like flies, the sturdiest alone reaching a haven. Even these then succumbed',[3] and in one instance, wrote the *Friend of India*, 'the mortality was so great on a certain estate that the manager fled, leaving behind him heaps of unburned dead and scores of dying ceatures unattended by medical aid of any kind'.[4] On the same subject, the Commission on Tea Cultivation in Assam reported that 'practically the supply of labour was regarded as an ordinary commercial transaction between a native supplier and the planter, all parties considering their duty and responsibility discharged when the living were landed and the cost of the dead adjusted'.[5]

At the beginning of the speculative fever the prospects seemed very bright so that the directors of the newly formed tea companies were liberal with the companies' finances, with the result that while the greater part of the estates was still uncleared or was under young plants, on the analogy of an unfinished railway line, dividends were paid out of capital, ranging from 5% in the case of sterling companies to the 15% which was considered necessary to satisfy the Indian shareholders. But in this way the capital became exhausted. Wages were rising and inferior soils were being trenched upon by inferior agents. A crisis became inevitable.[6] It was precipitated by an unprecedented scarcity of money. In the beginning of 1866, with trade generally more active and the demand for money higher in the markets of London, Paris,

---

[1] *Report of the Commissioners*, etc., *passim*.
[2] F.O.I., 9 June 1874.   [3] *Ibid.*   [4] *Ibid.*
[5] *Report of the Commissioners*, etc., p. 25.
[6] F.O.I., 17 May 1866.

Calcutta and Bombay, the Bank of Bengal rate of discount in Calcutta rose on 17 April 1866, to 15%, the highest ever known in the history of India.[1] The failure of the Agra Bank in that year aggravated the monetary situation still further.

It became impossible, therefore, with money borrowed at 16%, when it could be borrowed at all, to import coolies into Assam at £10 per head. Land under tea began to relapse into jungle and in some cases gardens had to be closed. A few of the speculators were forced by the circumstances to surrender their gains, or were involved in lawsuits which rendered a compromise advisable. The South Cachar Company, which realised only a sixth of its original capital, gives an idea of the depression; and this was neither the first, nor the worst case of its kind. Earlier, the older companies, foreseeing the impending crisis, closed their capital accounts in the hope that if their shareholders exercised a little patience, they would be able to resume operations profitably.[2]

The tea industry collapsed in May 1866, and the shareholders, lacking confidence, sold their holdings quickly at whatever price they could get, and thus deepened the crisis. On 12 July 1866, of the shares of the seventy-five companies of various kinds listed in the newspapers, seven only were at a premium, ten at par, and no less than fifty-eight at a discount. The aggregate paid-up value of one share in each company under the head 'commercial', excluding such as were 'in liquidation' was Rs.13,113, while their value on that day amounted to Rs.10,117, or, in other words, they were quoted, on average, at a discount of 33%. Similarly, the total cost of one of each of the 'tea' shares in the same list, excluding those whose value was 'nominal' came to Rs.6,637, while their current value was Rs.5,496; i.e. they showed a fall of 17% on the paid-up capital.[3] Compared with the crisis in Bombay, and taking into account the reckless manner in which the tea companies were promoted and managed, the crisis, as revealed by the fall in the value of shares, would seem to have been remarkably mild.

The trend of share prices over a number of years provided a better picture of the gains and losses, and of the course of the speculative boom. In the following table three tea companies have been selected to give a representative view. Of these, the Assam Company had the best reputation and was established in 1839,

---

[1] *Ibid.*, 3 January 1867.   [2] *Ibid.*, 17 May 1866.
[3] F.O.I., 12 July 1866.

while the remaining two were started in May 1863. The prices are for the middle of May and November.

Table 7[a]
Prices of tea shares of three companies, 1863–7

	Name of Company		
	Assam	*Central Cachar*	*Bishwanath*
Paid-up in rupees	200	200	200
Market value			
1863 November	520	370	260
1864 May	530	300	235
November	530	310	230
1865 May	528	250	250
November	585	240	225
1866 May	490	200	190
November	390	130	130
1867 May	300	85	112
November	150	55	80
Percentage of paid-up value			
Highest	292	185	130
Lowest	75	27	40
In November 1866	190	65	65

[a] *Ibid.*, share market reports, *passim*.

The boom reached its peak only in the third quarter of 1863. In 1864, the prices had come down a little, but, nevertheless, prices were high throughout 1864 and 1865. In May, 1866, the market had sagged but it did not reach its lowest point for a long time. The slight deviation from the general trend in the case of the Assam Company, noticeable in November 1865, resulted from a dividend of 25% declared by that company in the latter half of that year. But the market failed to anticipate correctly the prospects for the following year. The continued high price of the Assam Company shares, in spite of a general fall, reflect that the share market was still hoping for a good dividend. But when the Company passed its dividend in 1867, the value of its shares fell sharply, as seen in its November quotation.[1]

The dividend payments, besides fairly picturing the seriousness of the crisis, are also indicative of the high profit level maintained by the established concerns. The Jorehaut, the second sterling

---

[1] Antrobus, *Assam*, Chapter on Company's Statistics.

company to be established in 1859, paid dividends of 36% in 1864 and 34% in 1865.[1] On the other hand, so severe was the crisis that both the Assam and the Jorehaut failed to declare any dividend in 1867, the first year after the beginning of the crisis.[2] The Assam Company could not pay a dividend for several years[3] and the position of the smaller companies was correspondingly worse.

The number of companies which went into liquidation and their share capital provide another index of the losses sustained by the investors as the result of the collapse of the tea boom.

Up to the end of 1866, sixty-five companies were registered in India. By the end of 1870, thirty-three of these had to be wound-up. Nine others were liquidated by 1881. The paid-up capital of these companies for which figures are available are set out in the following table:

Table 8[a]

Capital of tea companies registered in India up to 1866 but wound-up before 1882

Companies for which figures are available	Number	Capital in Rs.(000's)	
		Paid-up	Nominal
Registered up to 1866	56	21,884	34,181
Wound-up by 1870	25	7,599	15,900
Wound-up, 1871–81	8	3,004	4,692

a S.T.B.I., 1883.

The table clearly shows that nearly half the total capital invested had been lost. In addition, the paid-up capital of the eight sterling companies which went into liquidation by 1869 aggregated about £485,907.[4] Thus, over one million pounds were lost by investors in India and Britain within about five years. These figures, moreover, are bound to be on the lower side as they are taken from the official statistics which were compiled from the returns submitted by companies to the Registrars of Companies and do not include, in many cases, the amount of capital paid up by shareholders subsequent to the filing of the first returns.[5]

Rs.200,000 was regarded as sufficient to open a tea garden of

---

[1] F.O.I., see share market reports.　　[2] *Ibid.*

[3] Antrobus, *Assam*, Chapter on Company's Statistics.

[4] See Appendix 6.

[5] Compare, for instance, the figures of companies in Appendix 6, with P.P., LVI, 1868–9 (104–1), pp. 1–60, and P.P., LVIII, (1864) pp. 513–52.

about 400 acres,[1] but the average paid-up capital of companies formed during 1861–5 in Bengal was actually over Rs.450,000.[2] It is, however, a general characteristic of a period of speculation that the public invests eagerly in everything that is promoted, and calls on shares are paid-up immediately (73·8% of the nominal capital of tea companies formed in Bengal during 1861–5 was paid-up)[3] which naturally encouraged promoters to form large companies. In normal times, with such large financial bases, these companies should have fared well, but in the circumstances, payments of large considerations to vendors and of dividends to shareholders exhausted their capital.

A further aspect of the boom in Calcutta was the attempt to launch giant reclamation companies which were then very much in fashion in Bombay. They did not, however, assume the proportions reached in Bombay and their number in Calcutta was limited to three. The largest of them all was the Port Canning Land Investment, Reclamation and Dock Company Limited, with a capital of Rs.12,000,000 in 6,000 shares of Rs.2,000 each.[4] Its prospectus appeared on 23 January 1865, in the *Englishman,* and its promoters included some of the best-known names in Calcutta and Bombay. In fact, this was the only project in which many shares were subscribed by the people in Bombay, acting, no doubt, under the influence of Premchand Roychand, who took a great interest in the scheme.[5]

Two of the leading financial companies, the Credit Mobilier of Calcutta, and the Old Financial of Bombay,[6] supported the Company with the result that its shares became the centre of speculation. There were other reasons, of course, which inspired confidence in the public. As with the Back Bay scheme in Bombay, the Government of India showed considerable interest in the project, and consequently, even when the speculative boom was coming to an end in late May 1865, speculators were able to manoeuvre a recovery in its shares from par to a premium of Rs.1,000.[7] But the project languished, and despite various attempts to retrieve it, the Company ceased to exist as a legal entity in Calcutta on 16 September 1871. It continued to exist,

---

[1] *Report of the Commissioners*, etc., p. 7.
[2] S.T.B.I.   [3] See Table 9.   [4] S.T.B.I., 1883.
[5] See Premchand Roychand's evidence in the *Report of the Commission on he Failure of the Bank of Bombay*, P.P.
[6] See p. 75.   [7] T.O.I. (Overland), 13–23 May 1865.

however, for many years afterwards in Bombay, where it obtained a separate registration on 2 August 1870. It was reconstructed on 13 January 1871 when its original capital was reduced to Rs. 6,000,000 and its objects were modified to include the erection of factories for the spinning and weaving of cotton.[1]

The Salt Water Lakes Reclamation and Irrigation Company Limited, registered on 22 March 1865, with a capital of Rs. 6,000,000, divided into 3,000 shares of Rs.2,000 each,[2] with the object of reclaiming and irrigating the plain partially submerged by the Salt Water Lake, within $2\frac{1}{2}$ miles of Calcutta,[3] and the utilisation of sewage, stable refuse, manure and night soil,[4] was the second such company. It achieved great notoriety and the following incident relating to it, mentioned by the financial reporter of the *Times of India*, provides an amusing and instructive instance of the undesirable tactics practised by speculators in those days. 'A telegram was published professing to quote the shares at from Rs.2,000 to Rs.3,000 premium in Bombay, when apparently they had never been placed in the market. . . .'[5] In consequence, however, of the refusal of the India Office in London to sanction the concession granted by the Viceroy, the Salt Water Lakes Company soon fell in the public estimation,[6] and was dissolved on 17 March 1866.[7]

The Sunderbund Company, the last of the three reclamation companies, was promoted with the object of reclaiming and cultivating the sunderbands, but it came out too late in the day and was withdrawn even before it was registered. The moving influence behind this scheme was a European called Schiller, who achieved a reputation similar to that of Dr Diver in Bombay. After the Salt Water Lakes Company had fallen from popular favour, it was not expected to succeed and the promotors were, therefore, obliged to return the money deposited with the applications for shares.[8]

In fact, many other schemes of various kinds were reported in the newspapers, but never matured. As the *Times of India* put it, 'like the storm's evil will . . . [they] died in their birth'.[9] Some were still-born and others, like the East India Timber Company and the Imperial Finance Association, had but a short existence.[10]

[1] S.T.B.I., 1883. [2] *Ibid.* [3] T.O.I., 24 February, 1865.
[4] S.T.B.I., 1883. [5] T.O.I. (Overland), 13–23 May 1865.
[6] *Ibid.*, 13 May 1865. [7] S.T.B.I., 1883.
[8] T.O.I., 13–23 May 1865. [9] *Ibid.* [10] *Ibid.*

Finally, to put things into their proper perspective, it is interesting to summarise the overall development in the corporate sector in Bengal.

Table 9[1]

Number and Capital of Companies Registered in Bengal, 1861–5

Type of Co.	1861	1862	1863	1864	1865	Total	a	Capital in Rs.(000's)	
								Nominal	Paid-up
Tea	8	4	23	9	4	48	41	25,805	18,529
Navigation	1	–	4	2	–	7	6	4,800	3,024
Banking	–	–	1	1	3	5	4	55,200	6,976
Jute Mills	–	1	–	–	–	1	1	1,200	1,200
Jute Press	1	–	2	3	–	6	5	1,770	1,216
Coal	1	–	2	–	–	3	3	2,360	2,295
Shipping Agency	–	–	1	1	–	2	2	500	341
Miscellaneous:							37	34,898	19,295
Manufacturing	1	2	9	3	5	20			
Trading	–	1	12	3	8	24			
	12	8	54	22	20	116	99	126,533	52,876

a (Number of companies for which figures of both nominal and paid-up capital were available.)

A comparison of the figures relating to companies registered during 1861–5 with those relating to companies wound-up during 1861–9, i.e. the period of the boom and the following crisis, reveal some significant facts.

Table 10*a*

Number and Capital of Companies wound-up in Bengal during 1861–9

Details of companies wound-up	1861–4	1865	1866	1867	1868	1869	Total
Number	10	8	10	11	18	9	66
Capital in Rs.(000's):							
No. of Cos. for which figures are available	8	5	7	10	18	9	57
Nominal	7,005	2,450	8,760	29,275	8,100	12,670	68,260
Paid-up	1,913	1,443	2,876	8,121	6,151	4,197	24,701

[1] S.T.B.I., 1883. *a* S.T.B.I., 1883.

The Boom in the Tea Industry

An analysis of the two preceding tables shows that 57% of the companies registered in the first half of the sixties were wound-up within the next four years, but the amount of capital lost was only 46·7% which indicates that the companies wound-up were slightly weaker financially than those which survived. The difference between the average paid-up capital of a company registered up to 1865 and one wound-up by 1869 was Rs.97,000. Further, 41·8% of the aggregate nominal capital was paid-up in the case of companies registered up to 1865, but only 36·2% was paid-up in the case of those wound-up by 1869, which again shows the financial weakness of the companies in the latter group. This may, however, have been due to the failure of the shareholders of these companies to pay calls on their shares after the crisis which must have shaken their confidence.[1]

It is perhaps convenient at this point to look back at the developments of the past and fix our bearings.

The conditions which had favoured the growth of companies in the West after the industrial revolution, e.g. canal and railway construction, the development of industry and finance, etc., were largely absent in India, where, before 1830, the people had been mainly engaged in trading and agriculture, and the growth of such conditions was hindered by lack of technical knowledge, occupational immobility and widespread political unrest.

Europeans were the first to take an interest in the development of modern industries in India, e.g. coal mining, iron and steel, cotton textiles, banking, shipping, etc., but the success of their efforts was limited. By 1850, a number of banks and shipping companies had been started, which provided some modern facilities for trading, and by 1860 the situation had changed in many ways. The rule of law had been established, construction of railways had been undertaken, merchants in India, particularly the Parsees, had adopted a European outlook and Western methods of business organisation. As a result a few cotton mills and jute mills had been started but the facilities for industrial enterprises were still few and limited.

During the first five years of the 1860's, the intense speculation in Bombay and Calcutta, described above, led to the promotion of hundreds of companies and although many of them came to a sad end, they left behind benefits of permanent value. For the first

---

[1] *Report of the Commissioners*, etc., p. 16, para 28.

time a large part of the population of the two cities, especially the Indian merchants, had a taste of the joint stock company, formerly the province of the European agency houses; the sudden prominence of the share markets attracted many into the business of share broking, the number of share brokers in Bombay increasing from 60 to 250 between 1860 and 1865. The share market became an important factor, and joint stock companies, which hitherto had been few, isolated and esoteric, became an integral part of the economic life of the cities. When, by the beginning of the 70's, conditions became more favourable for starting industrial concerns, these developments of the speculative period had an important influence on the supply of capital. The growth of joint stock companies after 1865 is discussed in the following chapter.

CHAPTER 7

GROWTH OF THE CORPORATE
SECTOR, 1866–1882

The period begins in 1866 with the lull in the tempo of economic
activity created by the crash that followed the share market boom,
and ends with the close of the gold rush in 1882 in South India. It
is proposed here, first, to make a quantitative survey of the number
and capital of companies formed in this period in the various fields
of enterprise. The development will be examined in the wider
economic setting of India afterwards.

A total of 776 companies were registered throughout India
between January 1866 and March 1882.[1] In other words, on
average, between forty-five and forty-six companies were launched
every year. Compared with this, only between twenty-four and
twenty-five companies were formed each year during 1851–65.
Thus the rate of new registrations had almost doubled in the
period 1866–82. By contrast, the average paid-up capital of a
company registered between 1866 and 1882 had declined by
nearly 46%.[2] This weakening of the overall strength resulted from
the registration of a large number of small savings and loan
companies from 1869 in Madras and Mysore. Another reason for
the fall in average capital was that, after the year 1867, the giant
banking, financial and reclamation companies promoted during
the Civil War speculation had gone out of fashion.

Of the 1,149 companies registered in India during the entire
period of 32 years, from 1851 to 1882, only 503 survived to the end
of March 1882.[3] Thus, 646, or 56·2% of those registered had been
wound-up. An analysis of the unsuccessful companies shows that
246 (37·8% of the total) were registered from 1863 to 1865, the
period of share market speculations in Bombay and Calcutta.[4]

---

[1] S.T.B.I., 1883. See Appendix 7. Throughout this chapter, unless otherwise
mentioned, the period 1882 relates to the first three months of the year only.

[2] See Table 13, p. 113.

[3] See Appendix 8 for a table of the number of companies registered and
wound-up in various industries.

[4] See Appendix 9 for a table of the frequency distribution by age and size of
companies formed 1863–5.

Another twenty-seven, or 4·2% had been dissolved as the result of reconstruction or amalgamation. Approximately 100 of the 200 or more mutual loan societies registered up to 1882 had also gone into liquidation. If the foregoing 373 companies are, however, excluded from those dissolved on the grounds that they were exceptional in nature, it would be found that only one in every four or five companies formed between 1851 and 1882 had proved to be a failure. The result of an analysis of the rate of mortality in relation to the size of the capital of companies is incorporated in the following table:

Table 11

Frequency Distribution by Paid-Up Capital of Companies Registered and Wound-Up in India, 1851–82

Capital in Rs.(000's)	Companies Registered		Companies Wound-up		
	Number	% of Total	Number	% of Total	[a]
Not specified	314	27·3	251	39	80
1–5	72	6·3	38	5·9	53
6–10	56	4·9	30	4·6	53·5
11–25	93	8·2	40	6·2	43
26–50	74	6·4	31	4·9	42
51–100	96	8·3	45	6·9	47
101–500	290	25·2	138	21·2	47·5
501–1000	84	7·3	38	5·9	45
1,001–2,500	52	4·5	24	3·7	46
2,501–5,000	10	0·9	6	0·9	60
5,001–10,000	5	0·4	3	0·5	60
10,001–25,000	3	0·3	2	0·3	66·6
	1149	100·0	646	100·0	56·2

[a] Companies wound-up as a percentage of those registered in each group.

It will be seen from the above table that over 50% of the total registered companies fall under two capital groups, first (not specified) and seventh (101,000–500,000). These same groups were also responsible for 60% of the total number of companies wound-up, but whereas one can see some causal relationship between the registrations and liquidations in the first group of companies, such a relation is not obvious in the case of the seventh group. The rate of mortality in the latter group was 47·5%. The lowest rate of liquidation in any group was 42%. Relatively speaking, therefore, the mortality in the seventh group does not seem to be particularly high, especially when sixty-three or 45.6% of the companies in this group were found to have been formed during the three exceptional years, 1863–5.[1] Their demise, therefore, does not call for any special explanation. A word must be said, however, about the first group of companies.

Altogether, there were 314 companies in this group. Over 300 of these were shown without any paid-up capital in the official register of companies, but it would be wrong to presume that they did not have any paid-up capital. A more likely explanation would be that the information about their paid-up capital was not furnished to the Registrar of Companies. Moreover, some of them were limited by guarantee,[2] and had, therefore, no actual paid-up capital, but their number could not be ascertained. It would be true to say, however, that most of the companies in this group were weaklings, since 80% of the total companies registered had gone out of existence by the end of 1882. No less than 131 were formed during the stormy years of 1863–65, of which only sixty-seven survived beyond five years, although two of them had a life span of between sixteen and twenty years.[3] Of all the companies whose capital was unspecified only sixty-three were working at the end of March 1882, but fifty-one of these had been formed in the preceding two years. It is also interesting to note here that 58% of the total number of companies wound up in this group were registered in Bombay and only 16% in Bengal. The classification of the objects for which they were formed shows that 36·6% had trading and other miscellaneous activities in view; 22·7% were banking companies formed mainly in Bombay during the Civil War speculations; 12·8% were for screwing and pressing jute or cotton bales; 7·2% had coastal and river navigation in mind; and of the rest, 6% were doing insurance business of various kinds.

It will also have been noticed in the preceding table that the mortality rate among the giant companies, i.e. those with a paid-up capital of over 2·5 million rupees, was rather high. Most of these companies were formed during the period of speculation in Bombay, and collapsed after the speculations ended. Some of them, however, were reconstructed and, therefore, the figures for

---

[1] See Appendix 9.
[2] Companies limited by guarantee of shareholders were allowed by Sec. 9. of the Companies Act of 1866 (Act X).
[3] See Appendix 9.

winding-up do not really mean that they had actually been finally dissolved.

A double frequency distribution by the age and the size of the paid-up capital of the 1,149 companies formed between 1851 and 1882, shows that six to ten years was the most prevalent life span for the companies in the period,[1] there being 362 companies in this category. The next largest group had a life span of two years. Of the 362 companies in the 6–10 year group, 204 had been wound-up and only 158 were working at the end of March 1882. Similarly, in the two-year age group, sixty-eight had gone out of existence by 1882.[2] Statistically, the largest single group of companies was found in the age group of 6–10 years and the capital group of Rs.101,000–500,000. The total number of companies formed in this group was ninety-seven[3] of which thirty-six had been wound-up by 1882.[4]

Interesting changes can also be noticed in the pattern of regional growth of companies during the years 1866 to 1882 over that of 1851 to 1865. The changes are best seen in the following table:

Table 12

Number of Companies Registered in Different Regions, 1851–82

Regions	1851–65		1866–82		1851–82		% change
	No.	% of Total	No.	% of Total	No.	% of Total	1866–82 over 1851–65
Bombay	163	43·6	207	26·7	370	32·1	−16·9
Bengal	161	42·9	219	28·2	380	33·1	−14·7
Madras	22	6·0	193	24·8	215	18·7	+18·8
Others	27	7·5	157	20·3	184	16·1	+12·8
	373	100·0	776	100·0	1149	100·0	00·0

In terms of mere numbers, it is at once apparent from the table that the growth between 1866 and 1882 was more balanced over the different parts of India than between 1851 and 1865. For one thing, Madras would seem to have regained its pride of place as the third major city in India. But the number of companies alone is of very little significance as is clearly evident from the following analysis of the paid-up capital of companies.

---

[1] See table in Appendix 10.   [2] See table in Appendix 11.
[3] See Appendix 10.   [4] See Appendix 11.

Table 13

Capital of Companies by Regions, 1851–82

Regions	1851–65			1866–82			1851–82		
	No. of Cos.	Capital[a] Total	Average	No. of Cos.	Capital[a] Total	Average	No. of Cos.	Capital[a] Total	Average
Bombay	56	41,639	742·0	150	132,950	886·0	206	174,589	846·0
Bengal	133	77,598	584·0	180	58,008	332·0	313	135,606	433·0
Madras	12	3,302	275·0	172	10,753	62·5	184	14,055	76·4
Others	13	7,531	580·0	119	7,376	61·8	132	14,907	112·0
India	214	130,070	606·0	621	209,087	336·0	835	339,157	406·0

[a] Figures for capital in Rs.ooo's.

(The percentage of total companies registered, for which figures of paid-up capital were available in the three periods were respectively 63%, 80·4% and 72·6%.)

The table unmistakably shows a sharp fall in the average paid-up capital per company in Madras and in 'others'. In Madras it resulted from the growth of numerous small mutual loan companies. In 'others' it was due to the increasing tendency to launch small shops and other trading concerns as joint stock companies. The only province which had steadily gained in strength was Bombay. This was primarily due to the fact that the cotton mills of Bombay had a large capital base. The decline in Bengal was due to the growth of smaller tea companies. A tea company generally required only about 25% as much capital as a cotton or jute mill.

The foregoing tables do not, however, tell us anything about the sectors of the economy responsible for growth or their relative importance. An analysis of the industrial pattern of the companies formed during 1866–82 shows that 246, or 21·5% of a total of 776 were registered as banking companies.[1] No single development would have been of greater significance had these companies really been banking concerns. The truth, however, is that only eleven or so companies were doing proper banking business, and nine even of these were *mofussil* banks, medium-sized concerns with their headquarters in the interior centres of trade and commerce. Their aggregate paid-up capital amounted to Rs.4,600,000. Seven of these *mofussil* banks were registered in the North-West Provinces and two in the Punjab.

[1] See Appendix 8.

Of the other two banking companies, one, the Oriental Loan Association, was registered in Bombay in 1876 with a paid-up capital of Rs.100,000, and though still working at the end of March 1882, could hardly have fulfilled the banking needs of a metropolis such as Bombay. It is a little surprising that the banks and financial companies which were so popular in Bombay during the speculative period should have been so completely ignored.

The remaining banking company was registered in Bengal. This was the Hongkong and Shanghai Banking Corporation Limited, the only company whose capital was registered in India in a foreign currency. The official equivalent of its dollar capital was stated to be Rs.11,250,000, the largest capital possessed by any company in India. But this bank can hardly be called an 'Indian' bank: it was a subsidiary of a Hongkong bank and its principal business was in foreign trade and foreign remittances. Such a bank is known as an 'exchange bank'. There were nine other exchange banks operating in India at this time, four of which originated in India, but their headquarters were transferred to England subsequently when the bulk of their shareholders retired there. By any standards, these banks were very important commercial institutions in India. They had large capital resources, were responsible for the entire foreign exchange business of the country, received deposits there and financed the short-term commercial needs of the three major cities, Bombay, Calcutta, and Madras, in which their branches were found.

The country had as yet no banks to finance either its agricultural or its industrial needs. The many financial companies launched in Bombay during the period of Civil War speculation whose objects included, *inter alia*, financing of agriculture and industries, might, had they been formed during a more auspicious period, have met one of the greatest needs of the country, but both in Bombay and Calcutta, entrepreneurs failed to show any interest in the promotion of banking companies.[1]

The remaining 235 companies listed under the heading 'banking' were a mixture of small savings, loan, moneylending and building societies. Nearly 200 of these were registered in the state of Mysore and the city of Madras, and fifteen in the Mymensing, Jessore, Fareedpore, Barrisal and Dacca districts of Bengal. Only sixteen of those in Madras and Mysore had a paid-up capital of

[1] See Chapters 5 and 10.

over Rs.100,000. The average paid-up capital of the rest was between Rs.20,000 and Rs.21,000. The small cost of registration and the lack of a separate statute for the registration of friendly societies were the reason for their registration under the Companies Act. As the societies had more or less the same objectives, once a memorandum and articles of association had been drafted by one of these companies, all formalities of registration under the company law could be smoothly completed simply by copying these documents and paying a small fee. From 1869, when these companies first began to be registered, until the end of the century, the statistics of the growth of companies in India became subject to great fluctuations on their account.

COTTON, TEA AND JUTE

Cotton, tea and jute were the three major industries of India. The following table depicts their overall growth:

Table 14

Growth of Cotton, Tea and Jute Companies, 1851–82

	Registered 1851–82			Registered 1866–82			Working 31.3.82		
	No.[a]	PUC.[c]	No.[b]	No.[a]	PUC.[c]	No.[b]	No.[a]	PUC.[c]	No.[b]
Cotton[d]	101	72·4	76	88	65·1	68	59	47·8	48
Tea	168	39·4	144	106	17·7	91	113	27·6	101
Jute	16	12·8	15	14	11·0	13	8	7·5	8
All industries	1149	339·1	835	776	209·1	621	503	156·7	440

[a] Number of companies registered or working as the case may be.
[b] Number of companies for which figures of both the nominal and paid-up capital were available.
[c] Paid-up capital of companies in millions of rupees.
[d] Includes companies reported separately in the official statistics under the heading 'Mills for cotton, jute, wool, silk, hemp, etc.' Companies manufacturing non-cotton textiles have, however, been excluded from the above figures. See Appendix 17 and note (b) in Appendix 8.

Some significant facts emerge from the table. Not only that cotton, tea and jute together accounted for more than half of the aggregate paid-up capital in the corporate sector at the end of March 1882, but these companies were also bigger and survived better. But their importance was, however, not only because of a better rate of survival, they also attracted a much greater proportion of the new capital.

As between cotton, tea and jute companies, cotton was by far the most important from the viewpoint of capital employed though in the number of companies, tea was easily the first; jute lagged behind both by a big margin. But whereas cotton and jute companies employed just under a million rupees of capital each, tea companies employed only about a quarter of this sum. In other words, one jute or cotton company was equal to about four tea companies. Owing to dissolutions of companies during the period 1851–1882, cotton, tea and jute between them lost one-third of their paid-up capital. The jute industry lost the largest proportion of its capital but tea did better than the cotton mills.

Between 1866 and 1882, cotton attracted over 31% of the total new capital to be invested in the corporate sector. The annual rate of increase in capital was also the largest in the cotton industry, closely followed by jute, with tea far behind. Compared with 1851–65, the rate of new capital inflow in tea actually declined. In judging the relative importance of cotton, tea and jute companies one must not, however, forget that there were also 113 tea companies working in India in 1882, which were registered in Britain. Their aggregate capital amounted to about £2·5 million.[1] There was no difference between a sterling and a rupee tea company in terms of size or capital employed. Just like tea, ten out of twenty jute mills in 1880 were owned by sterling companies. As if by design, the ownership of jute and tea industries was divided into two equal halves between the sterling and rupee companies. Tea thus emerges as the largest single industry, closely followed by cotton.

TREND OF DEVELOPMENT

From 1867 to 1875 there was a net increase in the paid-up capital of the corporate sector. In the following period, 1876–82, the aggregate capital kept on declining.[2] After the peak of 1864 new registrations dwindled rapidly. Recovery started from 1869, at first slowly, but rapidly after 1871. The largest increase in capital took place in 1874.[3]

Although there was a net increase in the corporate capital during 1875, registration had actually declined, and for the next two years

---

[1] Ahmed, p. 73a.   [2] See graph in Appendix 22.
[3] See graphs in Appendices 21 and 23.

fewer and fewer companies were formed. From 1878 new registrations picked up again. In particular many companies were formed during 1880 and 1881. The steep decline in corporate capital between 1880 and 1881 was not, therefore, the result of a lack of new investment; it was mainly due to the dissolution of companies between 1878 and 1882.[1]

The cotton industry followed more or less the same pattern and was the single most important factor in influencing the course of overall development. During 1873 and 1874 there was a net increase in the capital of cotton mills to the tune of 23 million rupees and the capital continued to increase in the next two years. A good deal of this rapid development was the result of the lure provided by the managing agency system.

One of the great contemporary industrialists and philanthropists, Sorabji Sapruji Bengali, described this as 'an evil system of men starting joint stock companies with the stipulation that they are to act as and remain agents for life or in perpetual succession when the agents consist of a firm, the members of which form a family group. In these cases, the commission payable to the agents is generally fixed, not according to the actual profits, but on the quantities manufactured, whatever the results thereof to the shareholders. These companies are started mainly by the capital subscribed by the agents and their friends, but after paying some good dividends, the shares are floated successfully upon the market.'[2]

Whatever the other advantages or disadvantages of the system, it certainly produced in the minds of many businessmen the vision of a permanent source of large income.[3] Many companies were thus formed without much regard to the conditions of demand and supply. By the time the companies formed in 1873 and 1874 had put up factories and were ready to produce at full scale, large parts of the country were in the grip of famine, which seriously impaired still further the low purchasing power of the masses.[4] As the price of foodstuffs went up, people must have

[1] In general there was a time lag of about 2 years between the time a company was put into dissolution and actually wound-up and removed from the Register of Companies. See Appendices 21 and 23.

[2] J.P., 1882, Departmental No. 212.   [3] See Chapter 12.

[4] There was a famine in Madras in 1865, in Orissa and Bihar in 1866, in the North-West Provinces, the Punjab and Rajasthan in 1868, in Bengal in 1874, again in Madras in 1877 and in the N.W. Provinces in 1878. For a study of

been forced to cut down their consumption of cloth. But, regardless, the managing agents continued to produce to the full capacity of their mills. This was only natural as their commission was based on production—not on the profits to the shareholders—with the result that the shareholders fought many battles with the managing agents of their mills.[1] In this way the managing agents were forced to try to find new markets for the stock which was piling up in the mills.

Tea was an exception to the general trend: the demand for tea was almost entirely for export. It was therefore not subject to the internal demand conditions as was the case with cotton. Tea was not able to recover from the earlier crisis until 1869. During this period the aggregate capital declined. The opening of the Suez Canal in 1869 gave a lift to the industry, though general economic conditions had also improved at this time. From 1870 to 1880 there was a slow but steady increase in the aggregate capital of tea companies.

The story of the jute industry is told very simply. Until 1873 there was only one jute company in Bengal with rupee capital. The demand for jute also came largely from the foreign markets, but unlike tea it had to contend with serious competition from the Dundee manufacturers. By contrast, tea offered a more attractive field of investment to the European investor in the earlier years. It was probably for these reasons that the development of the jute industry was delayed until 1873.[2]

MISCELLANEOUS

The number of manufacturing companies of various kinds such as paper mills, breweries, sugar mills, etc., increased by 305 during 1866–82. Nearly two-thirds of these companies had collapsed by 1882. At this date they accounted for only 18.5% of the reported paid-up capital of all existing companies.[3] Most of these companies were located beyond Bombay and Calcutta, the main centres of joint stock companies in India.

---

famines, see B. M. Bhatia, *Famines in India*, 1962. See also George Rosen, 'A Case of Aborted Growth: India, 1860–1900, Some Suggestions for Research'. EW, 11 August 1962, pp. 1299–1302.
[1] For a detailed account, see Chapter 12.
[2] For number of co.mpanies annually registered in various industries, see graphs in Appendix 13.   [3] See Appendices 8 and 12.

An entirely new and short-lived development in this period was the rush for gold mining in Madras and the State of Mysore, but an account of the circumstances of the rise and fall of the gold mining mania must be postponed to a later chapter.[1]

In the 1870's, for the first time, business corporations had come to occupy an important position in the country's economy. Almost all the tea factories, jute and cotton mills were organised on a joint stock basis; twenty-two out of thirty-three coal mines in the year 1881–2 were owned by six companies[2] and the two woollen mills in the country were also worked by companies. The joint stock form of organisation had become the *sine qua non* for the launching of industrial enterprises. An indication of its popularity can be gathered from its use for many small trading companies. It was also in this period that stock exchanges were organised, and individuals and firms started to specialise as auditors and brokers.[3] This development was the result of various favourable circumstances, some of which have already been noted.[4]

By 1850, the East India Company had conquered and brought under its rule almost the whole of India, and with the battles for annexation ended[5] the country was enjoying peace and security. In 1858 the Crown assumed direct rule and in the following years its administrative mechanism developed a certain degree of cohesiveness between the various regions. Apart from the two years of the Sepoy Rebellion the conditions remained conducive to the growth of trade and commerce. The country also witnessed a growing awareness in the fields of social, economic and political matters. Universities had reached the twenty-five year mark by this time and the extension of English education and the presence of Englishmen and their methods and activities were producing changes in the habits and thinking of people close to such influences.[6] By the seventies, the country had also acquired an industrial labour force which, although not yet of any high technical order, was, at least, oriented towards the atmosphere in the mills and factories of India and was developing an aptitude for

---

[1] See Chapter 8.
[2] Two mines not included in the total were worked by the Government, S.T.B.I., 1901.
[3] See the various trade directories of the time and Chapter 11.
[4] See pp. 107–8.
[5] The last such battle was fought in 1849 when Punjab was annexed.
[6] Moreland and Chatterjee, pp. 376–412.

mechanical matters. At times, one also heard of Indians whose engineering abilities and inventive bent were held as second to none.[1]

Developments in the fields of transport and communications directly influenced the promotion of trade, commerce and industry. A great deal of progress had been made during this period both in internal and external communications. Externally the opening of the Suez Canal in 1869 marked the beginning of a new era in foreign trade; within the country, the Government had revised its railway policy and had undertaken to build railways directly. For the first time it had become possible to travel between Bombay, Calcutta, Madras and Delhi by rail.[2] Some progress was also made in building roads and telegraph lines, and through telegraphic communication was established between India and Europe.[3]

All these developments naturally reduced the cost, time and risk of damage in transit, making transport and communication cheaper, faster and safer than ever before. But although distances had been abridged, the progress must be viewed in relation to the size of the country and its needs. It was still possible for crops in one part of the country to rot and for people to starve in another.[4]

[1] One such person was N. N. Wadia, for some time engineer of the Petit mills. See an obituary in T.O.I., 27 August 1889.

[2] Indian Railway Board: *Indian Railways—One Hundred Years, 1853–1953*, 1953, pp. 12–15. By 1882, 10,069 miles of rails had been laid in the country. Only 3,363 miles of this had been built prior to 1866. The total investment (Capital at charge) in 1882, amounted to Rs.1,432,400,000; of this, the investment made prior to 1866 was Rs.630,000,000. S.T.B.I. 1901. Between 1861 and 1867 the Indian Government did not sanction any new railways due to the financial stringency following the Sepoy Rebellion. The mileage added through State construction between 1869–81 totalled only 3,297. Sanyal, p. 113.

[3] It was not . . . till 1845 that systematic construction of roads in any part of India was commenced. The Chamber has been unable to ascertain the exact length of roads which have since been constructed in India, but it believes that the total length in the whole of British India probably does not exceed 50,000 miles, while England, with an area of 50,000 sq. miles, has perhaps 130,000 miles of public highways and macadamised roads. *Memo. by the Bombay Chamber of Commerce to the Famine Commission*, T.O.I., 12 May 1879.

The first telegraph line between Europe and India was established in 1866. S.T.B.I., 1901, pp. xxvi–xxvii.

[4] The Chamber believes that this state of things [very underdeveloped state of trade] is chiefly, if not entirely, attributable to the lamentably defective state of the internal communications of the country. *Memo. by the Bombay Chamber of Commerce, op. cit.* The value of the export and import trade per head of the population of the U.K. compared with that of India will occasion little surprise when the comparative position of India in regard to railways and roads is

Whereas coal was sold at about Rs.4 per ton in Calcutta, Bombay still found it cheaper to import it from Britain at a landed cost of Rs.15–16 per ton.[1] Despite the extension of the railways during this period, little, if any, emphasis was put on its relation to the development of industries and commerce of the country. The predominant considerations were political strategies, foreign trade and famine relief,[2] while, in its result, the railway tariff policy was also somewhat unfavourable to the development of the internal trade and industry.[3] Lack of attention to feeder lines reduced the

considered. The U.K., with an area of 122,550 sq. miles, has 16,872 miles of railway open for traffic and the country throughout is intersected with roads. British India, on the other hand, with an area of 1,481,866 sq. miles, has only 7,326 miles of railway, and is so destitute of roads that many thousands of tons of produce are allowed to rot yearly in the fields, there being no way by which they can be brought to market. Nevertheless, the exports and imports of British India taken together, and including treasure, have increased from £38,422,100 in 1853, when the construction of railways in India commenced to £113,919,018 in 1877. *Memo. by the Bombay Chamber of Commerce, op. cit.*

While Rajputana was stricken with a terrible famine [the famine of 1869, in Rajputana resulted in the loss of about one and a half million lives from starvation; and the loss of cattle was so great that the Governor-General's Agent estimated that one half of the usual area could not be sown], wheat, jowar and other food grains abounded in Gujerat, but were almost wholly unavailable, there being no means of transporting them speedily to the suffering districts. *Ibid.*

[1] T.O.I., 22 March 1875; 29 April 1878.

[2] 'Interacting social, political, strategic, commercial and financial factors determined the actions of the Indian Government. Sometimes defence, apparently, had priority in railway policy; at other times the Government's concern was cotton or famine; always the extent of aid to the railways was limited by budgetry problems.' W. J. Macpherson, 'Investment in Indian Railways, 1845–1875', EHR, December 1955, p. 180.

The Government wanted railways for social, economic and, perhaps, mainly military reasons. To some extent, also it was influenced by [British] commercial and manufacturing interests'. *Ibid., p.* 186. See also Tiwari, pp. 66–7 and Amba Prasad, *Indian Railways*, 1960, pp. 46–7 and 402.

[3] Firstly, the rates were high. 'In 1867, the E.I.R., in response to many requests slashed its rates, and similar steps were taken by the G.I.P.R. in 1871 to meet the reasonable expectations of the Bombay merchants.' Macpherson, p. 185. But in spite of these successful pressures, the railways continued to charge high rates.

The Bombay Chamber of Commerce in reply to the Famine Commission's memorandum, wrote: 'Satisfactory, however, as the annual progress has been in the export and import trade of India, with the limited lengths of line open, the development has been most marked in those provinces where, under a liberal system of management, the railway charges have been made sufficiently low to encourage trade. One of the principal objects of the Government in sanctioning the construction of railways in India was the multiplication of produce, and the consequent increase in the national wealth, but this beneficent object is defeated if the railway rates for the carriage of goods are fixed on a high

utility of the railways still further. These were great handicaps to the railways playing their proper part in the economic growth of the country.

In the matter of river and coastal navigation, many attempts were made by entrepreneurs in India and Britain to launch steamship companies, but nearly all of them proved unsuccessful. On the Ganges and the Brahmaputra, the impetus to form such enterprises was given first, by the Sepoy Rebellion in the fifties, second,

---

scale. The only through communication which we have had with Northern India is that which the G.I.P. Railway affords; but the high rates for the conveyance of goods have prevented W. India from reaping all the benefits which were reasonably expected to flow from the introduction of the G.I.P. system into this Presidency.' *op. cit.*

In 1880 long distance freight rates were higher than in the United States, where one ton of wheat could be hauled 450 miles for $2.50; the same mileage in India cost $5.50. P.P., 1921, cmd. 1512, pp. 53–4 mentioned by D. H. Buchanan, pp. 186–7.

Secondly, special rates were quoted for goods to and from the ports which, it was said, favoured the import of foreign goods, and discouraged the industrial development of the country. The charge of discrimination against the Indian industries continued to be brought until as late as 1946.

The issue was debated again and again in the Imperial Legislative Council and the views expressed by several Commissions showed that the complaints were not without foundation. The following is one example of such rates:

	Per maund		Pies per maund
	As.	P.	per mile
From Jubbalpore to Bombay (616 miles)	9	0	·18
„ „ „ Calcutta (733 miles)	14	8	·24
„ „ „ Kanpur (314 miles)	9	7	·37

(Amba Prasad, *op cit.*, p. 238)

In fact, prior to the Railways Act, 1890, no railway carrier in India was under any statutory obligation to treat all customers equally, and provision against undue preference was not incorporated in any contract before 1882. The 1890 Act, however, failed to provide any effective machinery to hear complaints of undue preference. See Amba Prasad, pp. 232–44 and 262–3. Also Tiwari, pp. 66–7.

N. B. Mehta, *Indian Railways, Rates and Regulations*, 1927, Chs. IV & V.

F. P. Antia, *Inland Transport Costs*, 1932, pp. 133, 137, ff.

J. N. Thadani, 'Transport and Location of Industries in India', IER, August, 1952.

Report of the Indian Industrial Commission, 1916–18, Ch. XIX.

Imperial Legislative Proceedings, Vols. 50 (1 March 1912) and 53 (24 March 1915).

Holland Commission Report, para. 149.

Indian Fiscal Commission Report, para. 149.

Wedgewood Committee Report, para 130.

H. Bell, *Railway Policy in India*, 1894.

H. E. Trevor, *Railways in British India*, 1891.

N. Sanyal, *Development of Indian Railways*, 1930.

by the tea industry in Assam in the sixties, and third, by the jute trade with the eastern districts of Bengal in the early seventies. The important steamship companies in this part of the country, the India General, the Ganges, the Bengal Rivers, the Commercial and the three sterling companies, the British India, the Oriental and the Rivers Steamship, were either wholly European owned or very largely so.

There were some Indian companies as well but they had not achieved any significant position; most of the Indian shipping at this time was owned by unincorporated firms. These companies were, except for the India General and the British India, small, and therefore their capacity to sustain any loss was also very limited, and as they were not always sufficiently insured, and the supply of new ships took a long time, the loss of ships by such natural calamities as the cyclone of 1864, or during navigation on hazardous rivers, seriously impaired their position.[1] The main reason for the failure of most of these companies was their own competition to attract custom by freight war. Naturally, only the strongest survived. The India General quickly absorbed nearly all, or bought their flats and steamers as they became weaker.[2] The British India, which operated in international waters, also played a very important part in the coastal shipping of India. From a humble beginning about the middle of the century it had grown 'massive' by 1881, and, as the *Friend of India* observed, was 'chiefly responsible for the "clean sweep" . . . of the native shipping, and of the considerable industry connected therewith'.[3]

On the western coast of India, the opportunity to start steam-ship companies was taken as money became cheaper and the trade

---

[1] Between 1880–2, the losses sustained by the India General alone were as follows:
1880 Flat *Patna*, sunk in Manikhola river.
1880 Flat *Jumma*, burnt out at Gauhati.
1881 Flat *Delta*, sunk in Athara Banka river.
1882 Steamer *Naga*, sunk in Debroo river.
1882 Steamer *Goalpara*, sunk in Kaikalmari river.
(Brame, p. 144.)

[2] 'There was not enough business to go round among the horde of starving companies, and as each one succumbed, they bought them in at starvation prices. Those that held out, like the Bengal Rivers, were induced to join forces, and were gradually assimilated'. Brame, p. 79. Between 1865 and 1869, the India General 'swallowed' the Oriental, the Commercial, the Bengal Rivers, and the Ganges. *Ibid.*, pp. 74–9.

[3] 2 May 1881.

in cotton increased on the outbreak of the American Civil War. Such was the mood of the entrepreneurs in Bombay that in the short span of three years, 1863–5, no less than fourteen new companies were started.[1] The hasty formation of so many companies naturally led to 'violent' competition, the challenge of which they were not equipped to face.[2] The management lacked foresight, and the shareholders were impatient, with the result that when the boom ended, they were obliged to go into voluntary liquidation. This marked the end of an opportunity which comes but seldom in the life of a nation.

In the sixties, the British shipping companies do not seem to have been very strong. From the eighties, the British shipping interest in India had become consolidated and from this period onwards, they fiercely resisted any attempt by Indians to enter the shipping business. The ruthlessness with which the P. & O. frustrated the efforts of J. N. Tata to ship goods to the Far East through a Japanese line illustrates this.[3] Lack of experience, bad management and insufficient capital have been blamed by some for the disappearance of many shipping companies launched by Indians, whereas others have laid the blame entirely at the doors of the Government of India. The truth would seem to lie somewhere between these two points of view. The reasons for the absence of Indian interest in the shipping industry are complex and begin early in the nineteenth century.[4]

Another major factor which held back the advance of industrialisation in India was her agricultural sector. In a predominantly agricultural society, as Professor Rostow rightly observed, 'the rate of increase in output in agriculture may set the limit within which the transition to modernisation proceeds'.[5] In such a society, according to him, agriculture has three distinctly important roles to play: (*a*) in supplying the resources to feed an increasing population and to meet the cost of urbanisation and the foreign exchange requirements for fixed and working capital for, in the

---

[1] See Appendix 8. Details can be seen in S.T.B.I., 1883.

[2] Two of the shipping companies formed in Bombay had as large a capital as the British India, but they had to retire after violent competition as there was not enough trade. T.O.I., 30 May 1882.

[3] P. & O. brought down the freight per cubic ton to Hongkong and Shanghai, to the nominal rate of one rupee, from Rs.13 and Rs.19 respectively. This event took place in 1885. For details see S. D. Mehta, pp. 60–1.

[4] See a note on the shipping industry in Appendix 15.

[5] W. W. Rostow, *The Stages of Economic Growth*, 1960. Paperback, p. 23.

transitional period, industry is not likely to have established a sufficiently large and productive base to earn enough foreign exchange; (*b*) in supplying an effective demand or tax revenues where the transition to industrialisation is based on consumer goods industries, for it is from the rising rural income that increased taxes of one sort or another—necessary to finance the Government's functions in the transition—can be drawn without imposing either starvation on the peasants or inflation on the urban population; and (*c*) in yielding a substantial part of its surplus income to the modern sector, for surplus income derived from the ownership of land must, somehow, be transferred from the hands of those who would sterilise it in conspicuous consumption, into the hands of those who would invest it in the modern sector and then regularly plough back their profits as output and productivity rise.[1]

A study of the agricultural situation in India in the latter half of the last century leaves little doubt that the major portion of the nation's bill for the social overhead capital and administrative charges of the Government during this period was met by the agricultural sector, both in payments of taxes and in earning foreign exchange by the export of agricultural products. To the extent, therefore, that the Government's powers of discharging its functions in the transition by creating social overheads were limited by the size of its revenue and of the foreign earnings which arose mainly in the agricultural sector, it can be said that the agricultural sector set the limit within which the modernisation could proceed.

Land revenue, which provided between $33 \cdot 24\%$ and $23 \cdot 54\%$ of the total revenue of the Government of India during 1875–1900, did not increase rapidly as it was settled at a permanently fixed rate in Bengal and some other areas, and for terms of years everywhere else.[2] Landlords rather than the cultivators benefited from the land revenue system, and there is no evidence to suggest that the former took any significant interest in improving the productivity of land.

The problem of agricultural development is many-sided; in the contemporary opinion, the reasons for the backwardness of Indian agriculture lay firstly in the lack of transport and communication

---

[1] For a detailed discussion, *ibid.*, pp. 17–31.
[2] S.T.B.I., 1901, p. xix.

facilities, which limited the marketability of the crops raised;[1] secondly, in the insecure tenancy rights of the farmers which removed the important incentives which must lie behind any improvement in the methods of cultivation and eagerness to increase the production of crops;[2] thirdly, in the fragmentation of holdings due both to some increase in the pressure of population and to the laws of inheritance, particularly the absence of primogeniture principle;[3] and, fourthly, in the difficulty of providing the cultivator with better know-how and the capital necessary for the adoption of improved methods.[4]

Rising rural income rooted in productivity through land reform schemes was precisely what Japan, Russia and many other nations achieved during the transition in the nineteenth century in an effort to increase the supply of capital for social overheads and other essential modernising processes.[5]

Agricultural output in India seems to have increased during the latter half of the nineteenth century, particularly from 1891, from which date alone reliable statistics are available. Between 1891–2 and 1900–1, the area under cultivation went up from 168 to 181 million acres or 0·87% per year. Acreage under food grains increased from 140 to 151 million acres, while the non-food grain acreage increased only by two million acres from 27·9 to 29·9

[1] The chairman of the Bombay Chamber of Commerce, M. Mowat (who was a partner of Ritchie, Stuart & Co.) in his memorandum to the President of the Famine Commission, stated:

'So long as we find it stated, with regard to the great producing districts of Central India, that but little more than a third of the land is under cultivation, that even under such circumstances, in years of abundance, the more perishable description of produce cease to have almost any value, indeed are often left to perish on the field, from the want of outlet by roads, we can look for but little progress in this direction. So long as such a state of things is permitted to exist, it is impossible for the *ryot* to better his condition; he must remain as at present without incentive to exertion and with difficulty able to provide the scanty means of supporting existence from day to day.' Memo., *op. cit.*

[2] See also T.O.I., 15 October 1877; 27 January 1879, and F.O.I., 18 July, 1867, also Moreland and Chatterjee, pp. 380–90 and 419–20.

[3] Regarding the increase in population, the early census requires very careful interpretation, as the area of the census subsequently increased, but it would be reasonable to suggest that except for years of famine and epidemics the population increase amounted to about 0·4% annually. See K. Davis, *The Population of India and Pakistan*, 1951, pp. 26–9.

[4] Anstey, p. 157; also Moreland and Chatterjee, pp. 381–6. A discussion of the increasing indebtedness of the peasants during the period 1860–80 can be found here. See also Irfan Habib, *The Agrarian System of Mughal India*, 1963.

[5] Rostow, *Stages of Economic Growth*, p. 24.

million.[1] All crop output increased at the rate of 0·97% per year. There was also an increase in the overall crop yield per acre during this period, which rose at the rate of 0·87% per year. The increase was largest in the non-food grain crops; 2·06% per year. But the increase in the case of food grains, which occupied six times the area of non-food grain crops, amounted to only 0·64% per year.[2]

An overall annual increase in the yield of only 0·87% could hardly be regarded as satisfactory. Failure to raise agricultural productivity substantially may well have set the limit to India's attempts at modernisation.

There were other unfavourable developments during the period which hindered growth of the country's economy in one way or another. Factors such as an increase in the 'home charges' and the burden of the cost of military adventures beyond the frontiers of India on the revenue of the country, added to the amount of unproductive debt that was raised by the Government of India in Britain.[3] The fall in the gold price of silver which gradually became worse aggravated the situation, as the servicing of the growing sterling debt required larger revenues to offset the depreciation in currency.[4] Moreover, as the value of the rupee became an uncertain quantity, the foreign investors grew chary of sending

[1] George Blyn, *Agricultural Trends in India, 1891–1947: Output, Availability and Productivity*, 1966, Appendix Table 4c,, p. 316.

[2] *Ibid.* Appendix Table 5A, pp. 327–30.

[3] The cost of wars and famines in the last few years, wrote the *Pioneer Mail* on 26 April 1882, alone had amounted to £13 million. The total borrowings of the Government of India in 1880–1 amounted to £250 million, of which 100 millions were for guaranteed railways. The servicing of this debt amounted to £6,096,212. The revenue yielded by these debts came to:

Public works	£2,160,132
Interest on loans to Native States	844,850
Total Deficit	3,091,230

The debt was used in the following manner:

Railways (10,000 miles)	£124·5	million
Irrigation (10,000 acres of land)	17·75	million
Loans to Native States, Municipalities, etc.	8·0	million
Reserve for Paper Currency	6·0	million
Employed in 'administrative objects'	90·0	million
	£246·25	million

'Productive works and the Public Debt', *The Pioneer Mail*, 26 April 1882.

[4] The value of the Indian currency had fallen from an average of about 2s. per rupee in 1870 to 1s. 7·895d. in 1881–2 and stood at 1s. 1·100d. in 1894–5,

or leaving their money in India.[1] All these developments were bound to affect adversely the availability of capital for the industries of India, to increase the burden of taxation on the people, and to delay the creation of 'social overheads' in the country.[2]

No discussion of industrial development in India could be adequate without some reference to the impact of the doctrine of *laissez-faire*.[3] A steadfast adherence by the British rulers of India to the 'free trade' policy did much to retard the industrial development of the country. The people of India had no illusions as to the effects of such a policy on the growth of her industries, but were helpless in the matter. The implications of the free trade

---

its lowest level. *Index Number of Indian Prices, 1861–1918*, 1919, p. 18. The rise in the government borrowing, on the other hand, was as follows:

Registered Rupee Debt (00,000's)	Year	Registered Sterling Debt (000,000's)
681·1	1870–1	37·6
886·5	1881–2	68·2

(S.T.B.I., 1901.)

[1] 'So long as the value of the rupee is an unknown quantity, the flow of capital into India will be checked. Let the value of the rupee be fixed and money which is a drug on the London Money Market at 3¼%, will be available in India in abundance.' Evidence of W. C. Bell-Irving of Messrs. Jardine, Skinner and Co., P.P. LXV. 1893–4, p. 191.

[2] 'Simply deplorable' was the term the *Times of India* used to describe the policy of the Government of India regarding Public Works in the country. 5 September 1879.

[3] The discussion is intended to be brief. The purpose here is to show the nfluence of *laissez-faire* policy in impeding the development of one of India's basic or heavy industries, iron and steel. Great importance was attached to this industry in the contemporary thinking because of its crucial role (on account of linkage effects) in the process of economic growth; a view strikingly similar to the one behind India's Five Year Plans.

For a brief discussion of the British mercantilist policies which discriminated against Indian goods and shipping, see Helen B. Lamb, 'The "State" and Economic Development in India', *op cit.* Also, S. K. Sen, *Studies in Economic Policy and Development of India*, 1966, Ch. VII. *Laissez-faire* truimphed in the 1870's and was pursued in India until the early 1920's. For a summary, see Anstey, pp. 345–58. See also Michael Kidron, *Foreign Investments in India*, 1965, pp. 12–14; H. B. Lees-Smith, *India and the Tariff Problem*, 1909; M. G. Ranade, *Essays on Indian Economics*, 1906, and for the well-known case of duty on cotton textiles, S. D. Mehta, *op cit.* See also bibliography under Habakkuk, Harnetty and Moore.

After the *Report of the Indian Fiscal Commission*, 1921–2, Cmd. 1724 of 1922 the policy of discriminating protection was adopted. Apart from the various reports of the Indian Tariff Board, the interested reader can usefully consult, among many others, H. L. Dey, *The Indian Tariff Problem*, 1933, and B. N. Adarkar, *The Indian Tariff Problem*, 1936. For a general appraisal, see S. Bhattacharya, 'Laissez-faire in India', IESHR, January 1965.

policy have generally been discussed in relation to the decay of the handloom and the growth of the cotton mills in India, but it had a far wider and more significant effect on the progress of industries in the country.

In 1882 the Government of India in its Finance Resolution described India as 'a country of unbounded material resources', 'capable of producing almost every article required for the use of man.'[1] In 1879 the Famine Commission had expressed the view that 'in dealing with the question, how famine can best be prevented and alleviated, the development of trade and the possibilities of new industries must occupy a prominent place'.[2] The memorandum of the President of this Commission to the Bombay Chamber of Commerce enquiring 'whether there are any trades which, though possibly not strong enough to grow of themselves, might be fostered by the Government into a lusty youth, as has been the case with the railways'[3] leaves no doubt as to which way the wind of responsible opinion in the country was blowing. The issue naturally assumed the appearance of a discussion between a policy of free trade and protection, but, as Morarji Gockuldas pointed out, that question was irrelevant, for, as he observed, 'the principle of political economy pre-supposes certain conditions before they can be applied to a given state of society or country; and where these conditions do not exist, a deviation from the principle of political economy is not necessarily their violation, and is, therefore, justifiable'. 'Moreover', he said, 'laws are to be followed as a means to an end, that end being the public welfare, not to be revered for their own sake.'[4] The construction of railways in India by the Government, as much an industry as any other, was a proof of its recognition that conditions in the two countries—Britain and India—were different.

Nobody expected the Government to adopt a policy of protection. What was suggested was that, if the Government accepted the view that it ought to help the growth of industries in the country, then there were ways, other than protection by tariff, in which it could do so. For instance, the State was a large buyer of stores which were required for its civil and military establishments. At this time, 'every item of these stores, from the biggest machinery

---

[1] Quoted by the President of the Bombay Chamber of Commerce in his memo. to the Famine Commission, *op. cit.*
[2] *Ibid.*   [3] *Ibid.*   [4] T.O.I., 12 May 1879.

to the smallest door nail'[1] was imported from Britain. It was suggested that if the Government had only held out promises to intending manufacturers to purchase on the spot, some consumer industries, e.g. shoes, soap, candles, ink, glass, tiles, paper, etc. could easily have flourished.[2] With protection it was possible to save India another seventeen million sterling in the imports of textiles,[3] but the industries whose development was most in the minds of the people and which Morarji emphasised, were iron and steel, and coal mining.[4] 'These and other like industries', wrote Morarji, 'if helped into a "lusty youth" may be expected fairly to stand on their own legs in due course, and their success would call into existence many subsidiary industries, which might be expected further to develop the resources of the country.'[5]

The Indian correspondent of the *Economist* in an article published in that journal on 2 April 1881, echoed Morarji's view. The *Times of India* wrote in still stronger terms.[6] For a time it seemed that even the Government of India had come round to the same view. In 1881–2, Lord Ripon's Government seemed determined to encourage private enterprise in India, and chose the iron and steel industry to further this policy. The *Gazette of India* for 5 August 1882, contained the first series of papers on the iron and coal resources of the country. Still more important, it contained a resolution passed in the Finance Department in which the Government outlined the advantages and the possibilities of developing an iron and steel industry in the country. In the opening paragraph, the resolution stated:

The Government of India have, for some time past, had under special consideration the importance of developing the iron and steel industry in India. The advantages which such development would afford to both the State and the public—by cheapening the cost of railway construction and maintenance, and of works for improving the water supply; by substituting metal for more perishable materials in Buildings; by reducing the home charges and their concomitant loss by exchange; by creating for the population non-agricultural employment; and by increasing the means for profitable investment for capital—are too well-known to require exposition.

The Government further stated that of 'the capabilities of the Indian

---

[1] T.O.I., 12 May 1879. For a detailed study of the policy with regard to purchase of stores, see S. K. Sen, *Economic Policy*, Ch. II.
[2] T.O.I., 12 May 1879. [3] *Ibid.*
[4] *Ibid.* [5] *Ibid.* [6] See pp. 133–4.

iron measures to fulfil all that is required of them, no doubt can reasonably be entertained. In quality the ores are mostly found to be extremely pure. Moreover, they lie, for the most part, in convenient proximity to either ample supplies of coal or forests available for use in the preparation of the ore. . . .' 'Under the circumstances', the resolution continued, 'it may be accepted as proved that India possesses the means of supplying all her wants in respect of cast iron, wrought iron, and steel and that such supply could be produced remuneratively on a strictly commercial basis.' Here, a few supplementary details may be of value.

In 1880–1 the value of wrought iron imported by the State exceeded one million sterling, while more than two million sterling worth was imported on private account. Altogether, the total imports of iron and steel amounted to £3,300,000.[1] Two out of the three most essential factors for a profitable iron and steel industry existed, therefore, and only capital was required to connect a large supply of raw material with a considerable market for steel and wrought iron. Lord Ripon entrusted the task of encouraging private enterprise and the flow of capital in this direction to his able colleague, Hope, whom the Indian correspondent of the *Economist* described as 'a sort of avtar [incarnation] of enterprise and thoroughness'.[2]

The first step taken by the Government to induce the capitalists to invest in this industry was rightly the publication of full information on the subject. But the Government also took a more substantial step by guaranteeing 'to take annually for ten years, at fixed prices to be previously agreed upon, equal to the landed cost in India of imported material, not less than a certain weight' from any firm which was willing to set up such works in India. The Government's own view was that at least four iron and steel works in four different localities should be founded.[3]

But, as was to be expected, the policy of the Government soon came in for heavy criticism in Britain. The *Economist* wrote:

So long as the Indian Government confines itself to the work of collecting and disseminating information regarding the resources and the requirements of the country, it will do good. When it goes beyond this it is travelling beyond its province.

[1] *The Economist*, 11 November 1882.   [2] *Ibid.*
[3] Government Resolution in the *Gazette of India*, 5 August 1882.

This was on 11 November 1882. The attack continued in the following week:

The latest developments of the commercial policy of the Indian Government will have to be very closely watched. A great zeal for the encouragement of private enterprise seems to have taken possession of them, and to be fast hurrying them on to very slippery ground. ... State patronage being employed as a cork jacket to float over the difficulties attending their initiation, enterprises which promise to promote native industries. And where are schemes of this kind to end? Of course, no such policy will be tolerated. The Home Government may be trusted not to permit the interest of India and of this country to be so imperilled.

Indeed, replying to a question in the House of Commons, Lord Hartington, the Secretary of State for India, on 16 November 1882, intimated that although proposals of the kind mentioned in the *Economist* had been submitted by the Indian Government, they had not met with the approval of the Home Authorities, and that the Indian Government had been informed of our 'serious objections' to them.

One wonders if the proposals of the Indian Government were really inconsistent with the contemporary economic thinking. Indian thinking on the subject, of which the proposals of the Government were only an outcome, has been described earlier, and if the Government proposals are contrasted with the policies pursued by the contemporary national Governments of other countries,[1] they do not amount to more than a 'mild yearning' to foster the industrialisation of the country; the price policy of the Government made it abundantly clear that it was not thinking of granting any protection by tariff or subsidy. In the opinion of Professor Knowles, the 'reason for the enormous industrial development' of Russia in the nineteenth century, 'was to be found in the great railway construction. Great quantities of rails were

---

[1] Germany, Austria, France, Italy and Russia almost simultaneously returned to protective tariffs between 1878 and 1882. See H. Heaton, *Economic History of Europe*, 1948, pp. 636–48. In 1864 the *average* level of duties in the U.S.A. was 47 per cent. During the next twenty-five years minor reductions were made but the structure of duties remained heavily protective. The McKinlay tariff of 1890 and the Dingley Act of 1897 between them raised the average to almost 60 per cent. See Ross M. Robertson, *History of the American Economy*, 1955, pp. 328–30.
Canada also adopted protectionist policy in 1879, S. K. Sen. *Economic Policy*, p. 115. On the history of tariff, see P. Ashley, *Modern Tariff History*, 1910.

needed and the Government made it a condition of obtaining orders that the works should be set up in the country itself'.[1]

It is not the intention here to judge the issue from hindsight, but in the light of purely contemporary opinion it seems very doubtful whether the British Government was right in taking the attitude it did, even in the self-interest of Britain. The Bombay correspondent of the *Economist* had this to say:[2]

With respect to iron, I believe that there will for many years be ample demand for a home industry, as well as foreign importations. One industry begets another, and the manufacturing history of the millions of India is only in its infancy, if, indeed, it can be said to have yet struggled into life. Visitations of famines suspend agricultural industry and, by consequence, commerce. The creation of industries that apply labour to a task, which drought and locust cannot arrest, will sustain commerce and demand even in times of recurring famine. If England wants a permanent market for English manufactures in India, she must help to establish manufacturing industry in this country. Complaints that the mother country will lose her market by teaching India to supply herself are groundless. Trade between the West and East will flow on in increased volume, though the channels may alter. English capitalists will serve themselves well if they will serve India. Fortunes may be made not in digging for gold, but converting iron and coal, or fibres and paper, into gold.

But, as Morarji Gockuldas had correctly prophesied, 'whatever its [a Government policy to aid and encourage private enterprise] benefits, economic or political, . . . it is not likely to be carried out; because arrayed against it are potent interests and influences which from their very position are unable to comprehend its eminently beneficial character.'[3] More than three years later, in 1882, the *Times of India* re-echoed Morarji's view in the following words:[4]

In these days of remorseless free trade and survival of the fittest, it is a relief to the human mind to find that a liberal statesman still exists willing to believe that something ought to be fostered; and one or two ways of carrying out the principle will at once suggest themselves. The most direct and statesman-like way, of course, would be to levy an import duty on all imported goods which compete with those native productions which it is desirable to foster. If the Viceroy, with all his

[1] L. C. A. Knowles, *Economic Development in the 19th Century*, 1948, p. 185.
[2] *The Economist*, 11 November 1882.
[3] T.O.I., 12 May 1879.   [4] 12 September 1882.

courage, shrinks from legislation on such a subject, a little might be effected by procuring all stores required by the Government in this country instead of from Europe. Government is such an extensive consumer that if all its wants were supplied in the open market here, Indian trade and industry at least would be fostered, and even Indian manufactures would share in the boom, so far as they could compete with imported productions. But no. It would seem that one of the dearest privileges of the Secretary of State for India is to go shopping on behalf of his dependencies: the Viceroy dared not interfere with this. If he hinted at such a thing, he would be reminded that the merchant's profits, the insurance company's charges, and the agents' commission were all by this means gathered into the coffers of the State. This seems to explain the ridiculous side of Lord Ripon's movement for the encouragement of native manufactures: for when he expressed his desire to encourage the local purchase of stores, if it could be confined to articles of Indian manufacture, he in the same breath warned all departments against supplying their own requirements as regarded [*sic*] European goods: that is to say, he appeared at one and the same time anxious to patronize Indian manufactures and to guard jealously against giving anything to Indian trade.

In the light of what has been said above, it is easy to understand why the Home Government threw cold water on the proposals of the Indian Government. What is surprising indeed is how Lord Ripon felt he could make these proposals. The attitude of the British authorities held back the development of this industry by nearly three decades and although it was a great blow to entre-preneurs, they continued their efforts undismayed. The growing importance of the Belgian iron and steel in the Indian market seems to have been responsible for the subsequent change in the Government's attitude and Lord Curzon's efforts to encourage this industry.[1]

The industrial problems of India have been discussed at some-what greater length than is required by the strict limits of this work, but as the question of corporate development is intimately bound up with industrial growth, this was to some extent un-avoidable. Business corporations primarily provide a mechanism to gather together the small savings of a large number of people

[1] See A. K. Sen, 'Sociological and Economic Explanations—An Illustration from the Indian Iron and Steel Industry', EW, Annual Number, February 1963, pp. 183–6.
For a brief history of the iron and steel industry, see Appendix 5.

for the purpose of investment in trade and industry. In the absence of opportunities for the employment of capital on a large scale, business corporations can hardly flourish, although some may yet exist.[1]

In conclusion, it is difficult to escape the feeling that urban development in India showed many signs, in Professor Rostow's terms, of a society that had reached a 'stage of pre-conditions for take-off'. Had it not been for the subordination of the national interests of India to those of Britain by the Government of the country, particularly in such matters as industrialisation and transport development, and for the fact that the agricultural sector sadly lagged behind, India might well have reached the stage of 'take-off' many years earlier than it is supposed to have done. Insofar as the Government failed to support the growth of basic industries in India, the joint stock institution, which existed in a fairly developed form in the country, could not be fully utilised. The *laissez-faire* attitude of the Government was, moreover, responsible for the continued misuse of their powers by the managing agents, and the occasional abuse of the corporate institution by professional promotors. At no time during the last quarter of the nineteenth century when the Government amended the Companies Act, did it heed any cry for legal reforms to curb these abuses.[2]

---

[1] Sometimes companies are formed for reducing tax burdens, and other such reasons.

[2] See Chapters 11 and 12. See also S. K. Sen, *Economic Policy*, pp. 98–104 and 199–203.

CHAPTER 8

THE GOLD RUSH IN SOUTHERN
INDIA

Of all man's explorations the search for gold has held the most
powerful fascination. The history of India is replete with legends
of abundant gold, and the dream of discovering it cannot fade
away entirely. Its legendary abundance was witnessed by Marco
Polo and other travellers, and hundreds of old workings in the
Nilgiri Hills and in the Mysore and Wynaad districts in South
India testify, beyond doubt, to the profitability of ancient mining
and quartz-crushing ventures.

In 1792, twenty-seven years after Clive had won the battle of
Plassey, a joint commission for Bengal and Bombay, reporting on
the Province of Malabar, first drew the attention of the British
authorities to the existence of gold deposits. Many other official
reports were submitted between that date and 1874, when the
first modern gold mining company, the 'Alpha' was founded.

The district of Wynaad, whose auriferous rocks caused a gold
mania at the close of the 1870's, was an area of scenic beauty.
'Nature was undoubtedly in a poetic mood', wrote a correspondent
for the *Times of India*, 'when she conceived and evolved the
Wynaad, the country, wild and lovely in extreme, at one moment
suggesting by the impressive grandeur of its mountain masses
reminiscences of the Austrian Tyrol, at another recalling the
sweet scenery of our own beautiful Wales by the delicate sylvan
richness of its wooded valleys.'[1] Here many Europeans settled as
coffee planters, among them George Viger. This old man, living in
the eighteen sixties, had spent many years as a gold miner in
Australia and is reported to have been the first European to
suspect that the quartz in the neighbourhood was richly auriferous. In association with an old friend, George Whithers, also
from the Ballarat gold fields, Viger leased a small piece of land
from the Raja of Nellembore. Soon they were joined by two
others and the outcome of the matter was that they sublet the

[1] T.O.I., 24 July 1880.

136

rights they had acquired to a mining company, formed for that purpose in May 1874, under the name, Southern India Alpha Gold Mining Company, Ltd.

The history of this initial enterprise is not brilliant; founded on incompetence, it ended in misfortune. The whole concern was started on the grotesquely small capital of £10,000, of which, needless to say, a heavy percentage went into the pockets of the promotors, while a large portion of the balance was swallowed up by buildings and prospecting. The machinery, purchased with the paltry sum that remained in hand, was as defective in quality as in quantity, and to crown it all, the Company was incompetently managed.[1] It commenced operations in February 1875, and after crushing 779½ tons of ore, it ceased working in March 1876. The gold obtained weighed 91 oz. 12 dwts. 23 grs., being at the rate of 2 dwts. 8·43 grs. of gold per ton. The average cost of an ounce of gold produced by Alpha came to Rs.127 or three times the market price. The total value was stated to be Rs.3,037 and the total expenses had amounted to Rs.59,711. Naturally, the company went bankrupt.[2]

It says much for the faith of Whithers and Viger that they were not discouraged by this fiasco. When the Alpha expired they boldly came forward and offered to take over its machinery and demonstrate by a practical test that the failure of the enterprise could not be justly attributed to the lack of auriferous stone. On 1 June 1877, a small association called the Prince of Wales Tribute Company (never registered under company law) took over the Alpha.[3] This company crushed 322 tons of selected quartz, giving an average of 10 dwts. 12 grs. of gold per ton. The total value of the gold obtained amounted to Rs.8,132–10–8.[4] The result, though satisfactory, was not sufficient to declare a dividend and consequently the additional capital needed to continue the operation was not forthcoming, and the Company closed in February 1878.[5] Meanwhile, another small firm, the Wynaad Prospecting Company Limited, had been born on 8 February 1876. It was registered with a nominal capital of Rs.41,100, of which Rs.39,000 had been paid-up.[6] The capital fund shows how greatly its promotors, most of whom were planters, underestimated the cost of operating a gold mining enterprise. They met with misfortune, inevitably

---

[1] T.O.I., 24 July 1880. [2] Ahmed, p. 293. [3] T.O.I., 24 July 1880.
[4] Ahmed, p. 295. [5] S.T.B.I., 1883. [6] *Ibid.*

from the start, and after crushing 99 tons of quartz in eight months, with an average result of only 3 dwts. of gold per ton, operations came to a standstill for want of funds.[1]

At this time, a great mercantile firm of Bombay, conspicuous for its spirit of enterprise, got wind of what was happening in remote Wynaad, and determined to step in and reap the golden harvest. But the failure of the City of Glasgow Bank with which this firm, Nicol & Company, was intimately connected, frustrated its aims. The mining rights for which the firm was bargaining subsequently changed hands for fully half a million sterling, but before Nicol & Company suspended payment, it had quietly acquired several rights which were later transferred at a very handsome price to the Indian Gold Mining Company, a concern which once had the Governor of Madras as its chairman.[2]

While all this was going on, a member of the Viceroy's Council, called Clark, visited the district of Wynaad in the course of his tour of Madras. Like Whithers and Viger, he had some experience of Australian gold mining, and like them, was impressed by the promising character of the reefs in that district. On his return, he suggested that the Council appoint an expert to examine the area thoroughly.[3] The Council took up the suggestion only too gladly for it was hoped that the discovery of gold would relieve the country from the silver crisis, easing the financial difficulties of the Imperial exchequer.[4] R. Borough Smyth, a highly reputed engineer who had been for many years the Secretary of Mines in Victoria, Australia, was chosen for the job. Smyth's report appeared at a time when the appetite of the public had been properly whetted for a paying investment in gold mines. Although carefully worded, it was long and contained many paragraphs which would have made any investor sit up and take serious notice. As an experienced person, Smyth had noted that the establishment of the gold mining industry in India was likely to be retarded, 'not by the meagreness of the sources, which were large, but by the mistaken notion that all the care and forethought deemed requisite in other pursuits may be disregarded in conducting gold mining operations'.[5] This warning proved to be a correct forecast of the events that were to follow.

[1] Ahmed, p. 294.　　　　　[2] T.O.I., 5 September 1879; 24 July 1880.
[3] Ahmed, p. 295.　　　　　[4] T.O.I., 5 September 1879.
[5] Report, p. 62.

The Gold Rush in Southern India

Smyth's report was published in October 1879. Oddly enough, another report on a legal application in the Chancery Division of the High Court in London which must have reinforced the hopes of investors, appeared almost simultaneously. The relevant facts of this case were that under a lease, the Seeputtee Estate and other mining rights in the Madras Presidency were assigned by the trustees of the late firm of Nicol & Company, to the Indian Gold Mining Company, on the understanding that the latter should, among other things pay £10,000 sterling on completion of the assignments. It was the munificent way in which the profits were to be divided that must have made the company's creditors, and everyone else who read about the case, rub their eyes in pleasureable astonishment at the golden prospects before them. After the trifling preliminary expenses had been paid, the agreement between the vendors and the Company stated that the profits up to four million pounds were to be divided fifty-fifty between the trustees and the Company; and after the first four millions had been divided, 50% was to belong to the Company; 20% to the trustees; and 30% to the liquidators of the City of Glasgow Bank. After the liquidators had received five million pounds, the profits were to be divided equally between the trustees and the Company. Those who framed the agreement can scarcely be accused of lack of foresight in arranging for the ultimate division of profits. Timid investors might well have taken heart at the cheerful forecast, for £230,000,000 worth of gold had already been found in Australia.[1]

In India the Smyth Report was received very coolly and produced little reaction, while in London, the stock market raged with gold fever as a result of it and something like forty companies were formed in the next two years to mine gold in India.[2] Only eleven such companies were floated in the whole of India, six of these in Madras and five in Bombay.[3] The depth of Indian scepticism is demonstrated by the fact that neither the Europeans nor the Indians in Calcutta even thought of such an enterprise.

The first company in Madras, the Ooregum Gold Mining Co. Ltd., was formed on 23 December 1879, with a nominal capital of Rs. 70,000, of which Rs.57,500 had been paid-up. It intended to mine gold in the Kolar district of Mysore State.[4] As very little mention of this field had been made in the Smyth Report,

[1] T.O.I., 5 September 1879. [2] Table 15, p. 144.
[3] S.T.B.I., 1883. [4] Ibid.

139

it is doubtful whether it was formed as a result of the report. The promoter of the company was one Lavelle, who had some experience of gold mining in Australia and, like all Australian gold miners, was stirred by the presence of auriferous rocks in the area. He seems to be the first European who was attracted by the richness of these rocks and attempted to work them. He took out a lease from the Government in the early seventies, but made over the concession to Arbuthnot and Co. of Madras after unsatisfactory results. Under the supervision of an Australian miner, John Munday, Arbuthnot and Co. spent a sum of Rs.130,000 to install machinery and produced a total of $40\frac{1}{2}$ oz. of gold. Once again expenses had far outstripped revenue and the project was abandoned. However, the company's mining engineer, Thomas Bray, succeeded in getting the company reconstructed and undertook to work the mines at a salary of Rs.300 per month plus a commission of 2% on the profits.[1] Again the results were disappointing. Ultimately, the Company was sold to a Londoner for £45,000. It was later registered in London, in October 1880, with a capital of £125,000 in one pound fully paid-up shares.[2]

Five more companies were registered in Madras between June 1880 and October 1881. One of these, the Madras Gold Mining Company, had a capital of Rs.1,000,000 but nevertheless sold its properties to a London firm and went into voluntary liquidation. Another, the Balaghat Gold Mining Company, with a paid-up capital of Rs. 270,000 is shown on the Indian Register, on 31 March 1882, but is known to have sold its properties to a London promoter. The other three—Amarapolliem Raj Estates and Mines Co. Ltd., Wynaad Consols Ltd., Kotagiri District Estates —were registered in December 1880; May 1881; and October 1881, with capitals of Rs.218,000; Rs.20,320; and Rs.34,750 respectively. These companies were still working at the end of March 1882.[3] They were also transferred to London promoters, whose demand for gold-bearing properties in India seems at this time to have been insatiable.

Capitalists in Bombay, on the whole, paid little attention to the Smyth Report. Neither the excitement in London nor the exhortations of the *Times of India* could create such interest in Bombay. Only C. H. B. Forbes, senior partner of the firm of Forbes & Company, a leading agency house of Bombay, saw in this an oppor-

[1] T.O.I., 24 July 1880. [2] Ahmed, p. 319. [3] S.T.B.I., 1883.

tunity to make some money. In association with leading Parsee and Hindu merchants he floated two gold mining companies. The first of these, the Wynaad Gold Mining Company Limited, had a paid-up capital of Rs.210,000 and the second, the Kaiser-i-Hind Gold Mining Co. Ltd., was registered on 14 February 1881, with a paid-up capital of Rs.1,050,000. After a while it had become clear to Forbes that the prospects of striking a rich vein were dubious, but he was shrewd enough to realise that the prospects of dealing in shares and, if the worst came to the worst, selling out to some crazy Londoner, were nevertheless good. So the companies were kept going for some time by rosy speeches from the chair at the meetings of shareholders and by cables from London, sent by their own corresponding firm, offering fantastic prices for the properties. This could not last long and the shareholders, weary of waiting and seeing their capital disappear, appointed a committee of investigation. One of the members of this committee, a European shareholder who had led the attack on the management, reported very unfavourable results. Forbes tried to suppress his findings but the dissident European frustrated that attempt by placing a newspaper advertisement inviting the shareholders to view the report at his own home. Finally, like most other concerns in India, these companies ended in the hands of speculators in London.[1]

Two of the remaining three companies, Imperial Silver Lead Mining Company Limited; and the Temple Block Wynaad Gold Mining Company Limited, were outright devices to swindle the public. The first of these, registered in Bombay on 16 November 1880, with a nominal capital of Rs.600,000 was the brain child of two Englishmen who had styled themselves Tremayne and Company. Before their efforts could mature, the *Times of India* scotched their scheme, describing the board of directors as 'an unknown band of promotors' which included such persons as a music seller, a bank clerk, and a hotel waiter, who, of course, had been described in glowing terms in the prospectus. After this untimely exposure, Tremayne and Company secretly retired to Calcutta. Here, they took the precaution of avoiding newspaper publicity and laboriously collected the addresses of many shareholders in various companies, sending them prospectuses by post.

[1] T.O.I., January 1881; 12 May 1881; 19 May 1881; 31 May 1881; 26 May 1882; 18 July 1882 and also S.T.B.I., 1883.

They thus gulled many innocents and collected a tidy sum. Soon afterwards, the whole thing came to light but before the aggrieved public could take court proceedings, the chief perpetrator of this fraudulent scheme was already on the high seas. One of the intesting things that emerged during the hearing of the case was that the provisions in the articles of association of this company gave the managing agents, who were none other than Tremayne and Company, such powers as to make them responsible to no one. Not even the board of directors could legally ask them to render an account or deposit the money received on account of calls in a bank until, in fact, they had retired to England.[1]

The Temple Block Company was floated in Bombay on 21 May 1881, with a nominal capital of Rs.400,000 by the remaining partner of Tremayne and Company, who, perhaps, hoped to escape the notice of the press. But once again, the *Times of India* hit hard and the venture failed.[2]

The remaining company, called the Ripon Gold Mining Company Limited, was registered on 18 October 1880, and had a paid-up capital of Rs.179,400.[3] Details of this company are not available except that it was reported as working at the end of March 1882,[4] but one can surmise that it also passed into the hands of British speculators.

It is apparent from the foregoing account of the development in India that it was far from being a mania. There are two probable reasons for this. Firstly, many efforts by such leading agency houses as Parry & Co., and Arbuthnot & Co. of Madras, who were close to the scene, had ended in failure. A certain amount of scepticism with regard to the Smyth Report was therefore bound to prevail. Secondly, the leading newspapers of the country were watching developments in this field very keenly and it was consequently difficult for fraudulent ventures to have widespread effects. This, however, does not mean that Indians failed to reap any benefit from the gold mining craze in the country. Speculators in land, engineers, both genuine and fake, and agency houses, among others, all made their share of money during the 'rush' that developed in London. It is interesting to note here that of the forty or so companies promoted in London, Arbuthnot & Co. alone had

[1] T.O.I., 4 September 1880; 10 February 1881; 14 April 1881; 14 June 1881; 28 June, 1881.
[2] T.O.I., 28 June 1881.　　　[3] S.T.B.I., 1883.　　　[4] *Ibid.*

the managing agency for seven.[1] Moreover, the prospects of gold mining in South India increased inter-regional investment, which, although still very small, was found most often to come from Bombay, starting from the Port Canning Scheme.[2]

In London, on the other hand, the publication of the Smyth Report caused great excitement and what amounted to a 'rush' developed immediately. It is necessary that we should look into the history of the London money market to understand this reaction.

In 1875, the disclosures before the Select Committee on Foreign Loans and the fear of a European war in the following year, made investors in Britain very suspicious about foreign securities. The profit margins in commercial, manufacturing, and mining undertakings in England had been narrowed by the Russo-Turkish war and the depression in trade. In July of 1878 the Berlin Congress gave a temporary impetus to the British economy, but even that was abruptly halted by the bankruptcy of the City of Glasgow Bank in October of the same year. In 1879, the price of Consols reached its highest peak for a quarter of a century and in the autumn trade which had been almost continuously depressed since 1873, recovered in a remarkable manner. Grains first, manufactured goods afterwards, rapidly advanced in value, and all descriptions of securities participated in the improvement.[3] In the meantime, certain events aroused special interest in gold mining projects: the adoption of a gold standard, first by Germany, then by Holland and the Scandinavian countries; and the absorption of large quantities of gold by the United States, beginning in 1879, led to a belief in the scarcity of gold, and made its search particularly attractive.

The opportunity was thus provided to bring the Indian gold mines before British investors. Speculation in Britain in gold mines was by no means confined to India alone. As a matter of fact, of the total of ninety-two companies formed in Britain during the two years 1880 and 1881, for the purpose of prospecting and mining gold, only forty-four were carrying on explorations in South India. The course of the gold mining rush for India, as developed in England, may be examined in the following table.[4]

---

[1] Brown, p. 127.   [2] See Chapter 5.
[3] D. E. W. Leighton, *The Indian Gold Mining Industry*, 1883, p. 2.
[4] *Statist*, 12 November 1881.

Table 15

Indian Gold Mining Companies, Sterling Issues: 1879–81

Date of Issue	Number of Companies	Capital (£)
December 1879	1	100,000
January 1880	1	100,000
February 1880	1	140,000
March 1880	1	100,000
April 1880	2	280,000
May 1880	–	—
June 1880	1	200,000
July 1880	1	135,000
August 1880	2	225,000
September 1880	1	80,000
October 1880	4	500,000
November 1880	5	630,000
December 1880	1	75,000
January 1881	3	360,000
February 1881	2	310,000
March 1881	4	550,000
April 1881	1	100,000
May 1881	3	400,000
June 1881	7	1,000,000
	41	5,285,000

The table, however, cannot reveal the scramble that actually took place to obtain the shares. Applications for shares almost always greatly exceeded the amount of issues. In the case of the Indian Glenrock Company, the unsuccessful applicants became so excited that they threatened the directors with legal proceedings on the ground of undue preference to the successful allottees.[1] It was not unusual, therefore, for the shares of these companies to be quoted at a premium of 100 to 200%.[2] It was a long time since new investments had offered a chance of large profits. In fact, in one or two cases where companies had reserved a portion of their shares for allotment in India, they did not offer them there, as the demand in England exhausted the whole issue.[3] Thirty-one of the forty-one companies floated during the course of a year and a half were 'at once' successful in obtaining the required capital, and the ten remaining concerns, which offered an aggregate capital of

[1] *Statist*, 27 March 1880. [2] *Ibid.*, 25 September 1880.
[3] T.O.I., 3 April 1880.

£155,000 did not proceed with the allotment and returned the subscriptions.[1]

The companies liberally selected the colourful paragraphs from the Smyth Report, ignoring all statements that cautioned and warned, and their prospectuses drew rosy pictures of the chances of large gains held out by the Indian gold fields. The hopes of investors were raised further by reference to the prospectuses of other companies which contained reports of quack engineers out in India, in whom the discovery of a few specks of gold in the quartz aroused wild excitement, sending them running to the nearest telegraph station. Such sensational telegrams as 'Grand discovery, Needlerock reef turning out very rich, heavy gold', or 'the leader in the tea plantation has been uncovered and has opened out into 4 ft. of magnificent reef, exceedingly rich in gold' intensified the fever of speculation in the shares of Indian gold mines.[2] The directors of these companies added further fuel to the fire by declaring dividends out of capital which were termed 'estimated profits' and were based on the reports of these quack engineers. As *The Times* wrote: 'The shareholders have been feeding themselves, like a pelican its young, with blood or money from their own chests.' This, however, should not sound very surprising if we take into account the quality of the Boards of these companies.

An analysis of 175 directors on the boards of thirty-three companies, as originally formed, shows that thirty-three of them were directly concerned in the sale of land to their companies and had received a sum of no less than £1,140,000 in shares alone as a part payment of the full consideration for their land.[3] The maintenance of the price of their shares was, therefore, of vital interest to them. But those directors, who were actuated by a high degree of self-interest, would not have been able to pursue their harmful activities had they not camouflaged themselves behind the names of respected people, also sitting on the same boards, who, however, were no more than figureheads and whose only interest lay in receiving handsome fees. Even this deception would not have been possible except for the prevailing optimism. The constitution of these boards was also characterised by the addition of people possessing 'local experience': the presence of British Civil Servants

---

[1] *Statist*, 12 November 1881.   [2] Ahmed, pp. 307–8.   [3] Leighton, p. 14.

retired from India, who had some money to spare and were glad to get the occupation and excitement which the office of a director offered them, blinded the British investors.[1] The fact that the governorship of Madras or the directorship of the Famine Relief Fund in India bore no relationship to the qualifications necessary for the job of a director in a gold mining company, was completely ignored. For that matter, the warnings sounded by the financial journals in England, particularly regarding the great transport difficulties in the districts of Wynaad and Kolar and the shortage of immediately available qualified technicians, also went unheeded. The result was that the mania continued with only a slight depression in the prices of shares towards the end of May and early June of 1881. In the meantime the money of the shareholders was squandered in the purchase of land right and left in the area reputed to bear gold reefs, on the reports of half-baked engineers, either already in India hoping to share in the gains, or despatched there by various companies. It was not only that plots of land, which existed only in the imagination of the vendors, had changed hands, but the prices paid could be justified only if gold-bearing reefs in sufficient quantity had really existed. Moreover, these so-called engineers ordered machinery which was, in some cases, the most modern and expensive available and, in others, the most inefficient, and erected it as if the place 'was going to be a showroom in London',[2] that is to say, in places where it could not be properly used. The only people who benefited from the confusion were the professional promoters, vendors of land, engineers, the governments of Madras and the State of Mysore and their officers,[3] and the agency houses in India. As much as half the capital raised had gone into the pockets of the vendors. Most of it, however, was in the form of shares and, had it not been for the rule of the London Stock Exchange which restricted the payment of consideration to vendors to a third of the total share capital of a company, the vendors would have taken the whole of the sale money in shares.[4] Thus, much of the five million pounds issued in London was simply business on paper and very little hard cash had gone into India.

---

[1] Ahmed, pp. 308–11.
[2] W. Wanliss, *A Three Months Prospecting Trip to the Indian Gold Fields*, 1881, quoted in Ahmed, p. 307.
[3] Ahmed, *passim*.   [4] *Ibid.*, pp. 321–3.

The mania ended as suddenly as it had started. On 5 July 1881 the Indian Gold Mines Company of Glasgow received at its London office a telegram from its manager in India explaining an error in a previous message. This was to the effect that the yield of 4 oz. of gold was from the crushing of the first ton of quartz only and the subsequent 19 tons had yielded 2 oz. in all and not 2 oz. per ton as was at first understood.[1] This news tolled the death knell of speculation. Prices fell heavily and within a few months, most shares were quoted at a discount.[2] The situation was aggravated by heavy unloading by the vendors who, in many cases, were prohibited from selling their shares in the first year of their holding. In the next two years many companies disappeared for ever and the shares of the remaining companies could not be sold for as many shillings as could once be obtained for them in pounds.

The mood of the investors can well be judged from the fact that news in August 1882, about an Indian gold mine striking quartz bearing 20 oz. to a ton, did not cause any excitement in the market and the price of shares of this particular company moved up only slightly.[3] The exhaustion of the funds of the companies for the various reasons already stated, accelerated the downward trend and soon brought about the closing of all but a few companies. Those which had some money left and were still hopeful, continued their operations.

The gold, it was later found, was concentrated in a few richly auriferous rocks. All the others were only slightly gold-bearing and did not offer any basis for work. It was the lucky strike at the mines of the Mysore Company, which, in fact, 'galvanised the whole list of mines throughout the world into life'.[4] The company had taken the decision to sink deeper with only a few thousand pounds left in its coffers and had rocks rich in gold not been found 20 or 30 feet lower, as, incredibly, they were, who knows what the history of gold mining in India would have been.

The success of the Mysore Company in 1884 revived the speculation which began in 1885 and continued in 1886, but this time it was confined to a small number of investors and to properties in the vicinity of the Mysore mine. In the meantime, there had been no further promotion of companies and at the time of the

---

[1] *Statist*, 26 August 1882. [2] *Ibid.*, 12 November 1881.
[3] *Ibid.*, 26 August 1882. [4] *Ibid.*, 15 May 1886.

revival of the speculation the companies in existence were as follows:[1]

1. Kaiser-i-Hind
2. Balaghat
3. Ooregum
4. Nundydoorg
5. Mysore
6. Nine Reefs
7. Kolar
8. The Great Southern Mysore
9. The Madras

In 1886 new mining companies were again prominent; in May 1886, the speculation subsided for a time[2] but it soon revived and by October the market was under a 'sharp attack of yellow fever'.[3] Between January and November 1886, some nine companies were promoted with an aggregate capital of £2,445,000, of which one, the Indian Mysore with a capital of £1,000,000 was subsequently withdrawn. By the end of the year the gold mining industry in Mysore had finally come out of the mire of speculation. In 1887 the *Statist* reported that the 'evidence at all events in the Mysore district, shows that there is every reason to look hopefully to the future',[4] and that 'the prospects of the Indian mines were never so favourable as now'.[5] From this period onwards the Mysore gold mining companies made steady progress. After this period of speculation the flow of British capital for gold mining in India was reduced to a trickle. Between 1887 and 1900 only three more companies—the Champion Reef (1889), the Oriental Gold (1895) and the Indian and Colonial Goldfields (1896)—with capitals of £200,000, £137,500, and £500,000 respectively were formed. Only five companies, the Balaghat, Champion, Mysore, Ooregum and Nundydoorg, proved really successful and paid handsome dividends.[6]

Although the gold mining rush in Southern India proved to be a 'Giant Despair', its outcome was not wholly without benefits since it led to the development of the only gold mining region in India.

---

[1] Companies numbers 1 and 2 were not known in the London Market and companies numbers 7, 8 and 9 amalgamated to form the Indian Consolidated Mines. *Statist*, 7 November 1885.
[2] *Statist*, 15 May 1886.   [3] *Ibid.*, 30 October 1886.
[4] *Ibid.*, 6 August 1887.   [5] *Ibid.*, 12 November 1887.   [6] See Appendix 16.

CHAPTER 9

GROWTH OF THE CORPORATE
SECTOR, 1882–1900

1882 to 1901 were years of great development for corporate enterprise in India. During these nineteen years 2,692 companies were registered as compared with only 1,149 in the preceding thirty-five years. On an average, annual registrations had increased fourfold, but these figures must be considered with care because 50% of these new companies were shady and/or small and weak, adding very little to the productive capacity of the nation. For this reason as many as 1,831 companies became extinct during this period. Three important factors which led to the development of these weaklings—the Bengal gold mining mania of 1890, the growth of assessment insurance companies, and the creation of savings and loan companies—will be dealt with elsewhere.[1] In its net effect the increase in the number of companies amounted to a mere 861.

In an earlier chapter it was noted that the development of corporate enterprise in India was heavily concentrated in two provinces—Bengal and Bombay.[2] There was no significant change in the pattern of regional growth in the period now under consideration. Table 16 (p. 150) shows the share of the various regions at the end of March 1901.

In terms of the number of companies, the three major areas— Bombay, Bengal, and Madras—were fairly balanced, but in terms of paid-up capital, Bombay and Bengal still possessed nearly 84% of the total. The reason why Madras had such a large number of small companies will be found in the growth of numerous mutual loan and savings societies which were registered under the Companies Act.[3] The table also shows that Bengal had the largest number of companies, but on an average their paid-up capital was lower than companies in Bombay. This was due to a mushroom growth of small loan companies and the assessment insurance companies during the eighties and nineties.[4]

---

[1] See Chapter 10.   [2] See pp. 112–13.
[3] See Chapter 10.   [4] See Chapter 10.

Table 16

Regional Distribution of Companies, March 1901

Regions	Number	Paid-up Capital (Rs.)
Bombay	342	15,60,33,551
Bengal	398	15,47,11,734
Madras	361	2,43,56,104
Mysore	88	28,25,249
Berar	3	1,45,000
C.P.	12	30,59,058
Punjab	50	72,55,752
Ajmer-Merwar	9	9,98,275
N.W.P. & Oudh	75	1,71,97,630
Assam	6	1,90,433
Burma	22	38,57,100
	1,366	37,06,29,886

CAPITAL FORMATION

The aggregate paid-up capital of all companies at the end of March 1882 stood at Rs.156,817,560. During the next nineteen years, it went up by Rs.213,812,316 or 4·5% annually. In interpreting the amount of capital formation, it should be borne in mind that, in addition, a sum equal to about 50% of the equity capital was generally raised in the form of loans.[1] The following figures show the trend in capital formation:

Years	Companies at work	Paid-up Capital in Rs. (000's)	% Change over previous year
1881–2	505	156,817	–
1882–3	547	170,959	9
4	649	187,506	9·8
5	694	206,358	10
6	806	210,025	2
7	886	213,804	2
8	910	223,261	4
9	895	229,975	3

[1] This is a conservative estimate. In fact, in the cotton industry, which was responsible for nearly a third of the total paid-up capital in the corporate sector in 1900–1, the total of reserves and loan capital would exceed the paid-up capital. It would be reasonable to assume similar conditions in the tea and jute industries, but companies outside these categories only occasionally issued debentures. On the whole, an estimate of 50% for the entire corporate sector will, therefore, seem appropriate.

Growth of the Corporate Sector, 1882–1900

Years	Companies at work	Paid-up Capitol in Rs. (ooo's)	% Change over previous year
1889–1890	886	236,842	3
1	928	244,584	3
2	950	265,854	9
3	956	267,931	0·8
4	1,065	275,100	2·7
5	1,204	276,687	0·6
6	1,309	293,872	6
7	1,596	311,565	6
8	1,572	331,233	6·3
9	1,417	355,989	7·5
1899–1900	1,340	354,387	−0·4
1	1,366	370,629	4·6

The figures in the preceding table need some explanation, particularly for the years 1891–2 to 1894–5 and 1899–1900. The great increase in the investment in the year 1891–2 was the result of a very large increase in the capital of the Hongkong and Shanghai Bank and the formation of many gold mining companies during the Bengal gold mania of 1890.[1] The following three years were marked by great uncertainty in respect of the exchange rate of the rupee and as a result new investment was held back.[2] The disinvestment during the year 1899–1900 had been used by some leading authorities to prove that this was a bad year.[3] In reality, however, the disinvestment was the result of the transfer of the giant India General Steam Navigation Company Limited from the Indian to the British register of companies involving a sum of Rs.9,750,000, and the removal of some twenty defunct gold mining companies with an aggregate paid-up capital of about four million rupees from the Register of Companies. But for these technical reasons the trend in capital formation was still positive.

Capital formation at an annual rate of 4·5% was by no means small, but judged by the standard of industrially more advanced nations, the absolute amount of capital formed during the nineteen years by the companies in India would seem very low. In Britain, for instance, new registrations amounted in 1888 to £333 millions; in 1889 to £241 millions, and in 1890 to £238 millions.[4] Thus, even

[1] See Appendix 17 and Chapter 10.   [2] See pp. 154–6 and 184–6.
[3] See for instance Muranjan, *op. cit.*
[4] Levy, p. 118. According to P. Sargant Florence, the total paid-up capital of English and Scottish joint stock companies in 1885 amounted to £495 million. See his *Ownership, Control and Success of Large Companies*, 1961, p. 2.

if only ten per cent was paid-up on the nominal capital in any oi these years, it will more or less match the total amount of capital formed in the nineteen years in India. It is natural to ask, therefore, if there was scope for further expansion of the corporate sector in India. To get an answer to this question it is necessary, first, to examine the factors which determined the growth of industries in India. The following table depicts the overall view of the share of the various industries in the increase in the rupee paid-up capital between 1882 and 1901.

Industry	Increase in Paid-up Capital in Rs. (ooo's)	1882–1901 % of Total
Cotton Mills	85,106	40·0
Railways	27,881	13·1
Banking	24,227	11·4
Jute Mills	22,863	10·7
Trading	21,598	10·1
Coal	10,106	4·7
Tea	5,624	2·6
Others	16,407	7·4
Total	213,812	100·0

In the following pages the task will be to look more closely into the process of growth in particular industries.

BOMBAY COTTON MILL INDUSTRY

The cotton mill industry was the single most important element in the growth of the corporate sector as far as the rupee investment was concerned. Not only that the cotton mills contributed two-fifths of the total increase in the paid-up capital but its share of the total rupee investment at the end of the century amounted to 34·4% compared with only 30·47% in 1882. The rate of annual capital formation was 6%. The number of companies increased from 59 in 1882 to 179 in 1900–1, but the ratio of cotton mill companies to all companies in 1900–1 came to only 13·9% showing that an average cotton mill company employed more than three times as much equity capital as the rest of them.

The tremendous development of the cotton mill industry and its rapid spread in many parts of the country during the last two decades of the century can be quickly seen from the following table.

Table 17

Number and Nominal Capital of Cotton Mills working on dates shown

Area	Capital in Rs. (000's)					
	1880–1		1890–1		1900–1	
	No.	Capital	No.	Capital	No.	Capital
Bengal	7	5,525	7	9,275	10	15,475
Agra	—	—	1		2	1,500
Cawnpore	2	500	4		4	8,600
Ajmer-Merwar	—	—	—	—	1	700
Indore	1	—	1	—	1	—
Punjab	—	—	—	—	5	3,604
Bombay Island	32	30,159	60		84	75,765
Ahmedabad	4	1,804	7		30	17,717
Others in Bombay Province	10	10,572	15	73,502	24	16,336
C.P.	2	1,500	3		7	8,751
Berar	—	—	—	—	1	550
Hyderabad	1	700	3		3	3,100
Madras City	3	1,575	4		4	2,700
Others in Madras Province	—	—	4	5,100	7	4,550
Bangalore	—	—	2		2	1,300
Pondicherry	—	—	2	Fr. 5 million	4	3,455
Travancore	—	—	1		1	1,200
	62[a]	52,335	114	101,578[b] Fr. 5 million	190	165,303[c]

[a] Of the 62 mills, 9 were private mills and their capitals were not known. They were situated as follows: Bombay Island—2, Ahmedabad—1, Others in Bombay Province—1, Bengal—2, C.P.—1, Indore—1, and Cawnpore—1.

[b] The difference of Rs.13,701(000) in the total capital is accounted for by the 13 mills in Agra, Cawnpore, C.P., Hyderabad and Bangalore.

[c] The capitals of the mill in Indore and another in Morvi in the Province of Bombay were not known.

The expansion of the cotton mills, as can be gathered, was much faster in the eighties than in the nineties with this difference that Ahmedabad attracted nearly as many cotton mills in the nineties as did Bombay. Further, mills were opened in Amritsar, Lahore and Delhi in the Punjab.

In considering the growth of the cotton mill industry, it is necessary to remember that its progress in the 1870's had already indicated that the mills in India could successfully compete with Lancashire mills in the production of yarn and cloth of up to count 20 for sale in the Far East and the Near East by using home-grown cotton, indigenous labour and imported machines and technicians. In the eighties and nineties this pattern did not change except in so far as one or two mills tried to spin finer counts.

Monetary Conditions[1]

The natural advantages enjoyed by the Indian mills were further reinforced by a considerable depreciation of the rupee during the period under study. The depreciation of the rupee was in effect analogous to the levy of an import duty on Lancashire goods consumed in countries on the silver standard. By the time the rupee reached its lowest value, Lancashire goods imported into countries on the silver standard could cost over 25% more than when the rupee was still at 2s. But even this drastic fall in the value of the rupee does not seem to have made it profitable to import long-staple cotton for the manufacture of finer cotton goods in India. It is therefore doubtful if the cotton mills really derived any benefit from the depreciation of the rupee, except that it made the Lancashire competition completely ineffective within count

---

[1] The discussion on exchange rate, monetary conditions, transport and communications, fiscal measures, etc., is intended to be brief. The purpose here is only to show the more important effects of these factors on the growth of industry and cotton mills in particular. For further information on currency and related problems, the following books may be usefully consulted:

B. R. Ambedkar, *The Problem of the Rupee*, 1932.
B. G. Bhatnagar, *Currency and Exchange in India*, 1924.
H. L. Chablani, *Indian Currency and Exchange*, 1925.
H. F. Howard, *India and the Gold Standard*, 1911.
H. S. Jevons, *Money, Banking and Exchange in India*, 1922.
J. M. Keynes, *Indian Currency and Finance*, 1913.
B. F. Madon, *India's Exchange Problem*, 1925 (2 vols).
K. T. Shah, *Sixty Years of Indian Finance*, 1921.
G. Findlay Shirras, *Indian Finance and Banking*, 1920.
H. B. Turle, *An Outline of Indian Currency*, 1927.
C. N. Vakil and S. K. Muranjan, *Currency and Prices in India*, 1927.
P. A. Wadia and G. N. Joshi, *Money and the Money Markets in India*, 1926.
B. P. Adarkar, *The Indian Monetary Policy*, 1939.
L. C. Jain, *Monetary Problems of India*, 1933.
D. K. Malhotra, *History and Problems of Indian Currency, 1835–1943*, 1944.
M. D. Joshi, 'Currency' in V. B. Singh (Ed.), *The Economic History of India, 1857–1956*, 1965, pp. 375–88.
Report of the Herschell Committee on Indian Currency, 1893.
Report of the Fowler Committee on Indian Currency, 1898.

twenty; as a result the Indian mills could safely expand their production.

A further effect of the fall in exchange was a moderate inflation in the country which was particularly noticeable from 1886 to 1896 as the imported silver was coined into money. The inflation could only have been moderate because wages remained almost stationary and because part of the increased money supply was absorbed by the increase in the transactions demand for money. A study of the movements in the general price level shows that it moved continually upwards from 1886 to 1897[1] but the increase was due to the rise in food-grain prices[2] which, in the Indian set-up, meant mainly an increase in the income of middlemen rather than the farmers. What was, however, most extraordinary about the movements in prices was that at a time when the exchange rate of the rupee was falling greatly *vis-à-vis* the sterling pound, the terms of trade remained favourable.[3] The period coincided roughly with a depression in England during 1890–6 which was produced by an 'extreme abundance of gold and an extreme ease of credit'.[4] In contrast, a similar situation in India led to a boom in investment. Monetary conditions remained unusually easy during most of the period and in 1891–2 short term interest rates fell below the long term trend. The result of these developments—easy credit, and high profits—was that the investment in the corporate sector increased at a very rapid rate.

Among the adverse effects of the fall in the exchange rate, three must be mentioned. Firstly, occasional, rapid and serious fluctuations in the rate of exchange paralysed business and made the entrepreneurs apprehensive. This was particularly noticeable during the period of speculation connected with the passing of the Sherman Act in the U.S.A., which raised the value of the rupee and produced very quick and violent changes in the exchange rate. Secondly, connected with this, the Government of India in 1893 took the decision to close the mints for the free coinage of rupees and to fix its value at 1s. 4d. The speculation in the market prior to this move, the measure itself, and the apprehension of an import duty on silver, subsequently had the effect of 'seriously disturbing and paralysing'[5] the markets in China for Indian yarn. The export

---

[1] See *Index Numbers of Prices, 1861–1931*, 1953.   [2] *Ibid.*
[3] *Ibid.*   [4] S. K. Muranjan, *Modern Banking in India*, 1940, p. 44.
[5] T.O.I., 6 January 1894.

of yarn fell by 23% and that of cloth declined by more than one-half within one year.[1] The losses incurred by the cotton mills to the end of 1893, after the currency scheme had been introduced in the Legislature in June of that year, were roughly estimated at over Rs.7,500,000.[2] The share prices fell heavily on the Bombay stock market.[3] But the fall in exports and the depression in the share market were only temporary; the result of a panic.

The closing of the mints did not become effective until about 1897. In fact, the exchange rate declined still further in the following years and the level of exports was actually higher in 1895 than in 1892. In 1897, although delayed, the closing of the mints produced results. Money became extremely tight and interest rates reached levels only equalled in the crisis of 1866. The Bank of Bengal found difficulty in meeting the demand for loans even at 18%.[4] The reappearance of famine, which was widespread and acute in the North in 1897, and in the South and the Centre in 1900, considerably increased the financial strain on the Government, which had already been badly hit by the fall in value of the rupee and the need to meet its sterling obligations and the costs of frontier wars. Between 1896–9 the Government borrowed Rs.100,000,000 in India and intensified the tightness in the money market.[5] All this naturally slowed down investment during this period.

Finally, during the last four years of the century, the adverse movement of the exchange rate of the rupee *vis-à-vis* the Japanese yen and the Chinese dollar (these countries were still on the silver standard) facilitated the growth of cotton mills in those countries, intensified the competition from Japan in the Chinese markets,[6] and brought to an end two decades of easy profits for the Indian mills.

Transport and Communications

During the period under consideration 16,000 miles of new railway lines were opened for traffic in India at an average rate of 600 miles a year. There was a great extension of post offices and telegraph stations. The construction of short telegraph lines to

[1] S. D. Mehta, pp. 65–6.   [2] T.O.I., 6 January 1894.
[3] *Ibid.* See issue of 28 June 1895 for quotations of shares of Bombay cotton mills for the years 1893–5.
[4] Muranjan, pp. 47–8.   [5] *Ibid.*   [6] S. D. Mehta, pp. 77–80.

select outlying post offices started in 1883 and by the end of the century the telegraph had fully come into its own. On 31 March 1900, the Telegraph Department maintained 60,000 miles of wire and cables and the Postal Department was working 1,612 telegraph offices in the country. In 1885 the rates for overseas telegrams were reduced by half a franc per word. The value of these developments for commercial purposes can be judged from the fact that during the last decade of the century both the inland and overseas messages sent on private account had nearly doubled.[1] Telephones were also being used to aid and ease communication, but their use grew slowly and their range was limited.[2] There were also improvements in the shipping and port facilities.

While the growth of transport and communications increased the demand for goods at home, new ports were opened in China and expansion of railways there made more of her interior accessible to Indian textiles and yarn. On the supply side, the improved transport facilities helped in locating the cotton mills in the interior parts of India since it was mainly from the resources supplied from Bombay, the nucleus of this industry, that the mills in the up-country, central and south India were successfully started. To be successful, the remote control of distantly located enterprises depended on the facilities for quick transmission of news, views and decisions between the centre of production, markets, and the seat of management, and this was gradually achieved by the growth of facilities mentioned earlier. Further, the improvement in shipping and communication made expatriate staff more willing to come out in the 1880's and 90's than previously.

Initial Capital and Cost of Production

According to Mehta, in the 1860's, the construction of a cotton mill in Bombay used to cost three times as much as its equivalent in Lancashire. In the 80's and 90's it cost only a third more.[3] Moreover, specialised agencies began to supply machinery and to

---

[1] S.T.B.I., pp. xxxiv–xl.

[2] From the report of the Bombay Telephone Company in the T.O.I. of 12 January 1883, we find that the calls per week during the previous year had gone up from 470 to 1,000 and the Company was intending to extend its operations to Poona and Hyderabad. 'Madras had been very go-ahead in the matter of telephones and it had enjoyed a Telephone Company as far back as 1881; but now in 1893, the . . . Company rose to its first directory. It included 75 lines. . . .' Brown, p. 135.

[3] S. D. Mehta, p. 49.

erect mills which made it easier both to start new mills and to expand the old. These agencies saved the promoters much of the time spent in negotiations with overseas firms and frequently supplied credit facilities to promote sales of their particular machines. Meanwhile, mechanical innovations were reducing costs of production and though this did not give the Indian mills any absolute advantage over Lancashire, it did have the effect of increasing the profit margin and/or the demand for home-produced goods.

Electricity, first used in the cotton industry around the mid-nineties, made it possible for the mills to run extra shifts and work longer hours. Overhead costs could now be spread over a larger production and the capital employed could turn over more quickly. The significance of these developments in increasing investment in the cotton industry can hardly be exaggerated.

The Capital Market

The Bombay share market was first organised in 1875, when a committee of sharebrokers was appointed to regulate the admission of brokers and to supervise dealings in the market. There was as yet no provision for the control of stocks and shares dealt in on the market, which meant that an increase in the number of companies automatically increased the volume of business in the market. The number of brokers had increased greatly in the late seventies, resulting in a pressure to transact more business. Brokers frequently went out canvassing to place shares of new companies, thus bringing new members of the public within the fold of the market. The new class of share owners definitely came from a lower income group, as is evidenced by the necessity forced upon the old companies to split their shares to lower unit-prices. Shares of high face value had only a limited market which depressed their prices unduly. Surprisingly, however, the companies did not issue bonus shares to lower prices, probably because the public were prejudiced against the word 'discount'. The practice of dealing in 'futures', added to the relatively high tendency for speculation in the Indian business community, and made dull times rare in the market. Further, the practice of private borrowing was being gradually discarded in favour of issuing debentures.[1] A great increase also took place in the rupee loans raised by the Govern-

---

[1] See pp. 204–5.

ment.[1] The last two elements added to the volume of business in the market and helped it to grow. The increased facilities for marketing shares naturally made it easier to raise capital for industry.

The Managing Agency

The managing agency, particularly the system of a quarter anna commission on output, provided another powerful incentive in attracting entrepreneurs to promote cotton mills, especially those who were already connected with the industry in some way. The reduction in the capital required to start a mill and the increase in the facilities to raise it combined to widen the ranks of the entrepreneurs. Engineering services offered by specialised agencies removed the impediment of a lack of technical know-how. Thus merchants, technicians, machinery agents, financiers and speculators were all enabled to start cotton mills. The lure of a share in the managing agency commission was so great that even a lawyer like Sir Pheroz Shah Mehta became a partner in a firm of managing agents.[2]

The profits earned during this period were so high that, despite the large amount of money siphoned away by the managing agents, enough remained to satisfy the shareholders. Dividends generally ranged between 10% and 15% which accounts for the willingness of the otherwise reluctant shareholders to invest in the mills run by managing agents on the old system of a quarter-anna commission.[3] What these shareholders did not realise was that the figures for profits were mostly arrived at either without providing any depreciation of assets or else after providing only very inadequate depreciation. The profits were further inflated by the manipulation of stocks. Audit was of very dubious value and in many

[1] The following figures show the Registered Debt of India in millions of rupees: 1881-2—886·5; 1892-3—1029·4; 1900-1—1153·3. The debt increased by Rs. 266·8 million between 1882 and 1901. Moreover, Indians held 42% of the rupee loan in 1900 compared with only 23·7% in 1868, which shows a remarkable shift in their attitude. S.T.B.I., 1901, pp. 284-5.

[2] On 5 August 1899, the T.O.I. reported that, by a special resolution passed at an extraordinary meeting of the shareholders, the managing agents of the Star Mills, Visran Ebrahim & Company, first appointed in 1893 in place of K. N. Heermandeek & Company, were removed from their office for sharing their commission with one of the directors, P. M. Mehta.

[3] See Appendix 14 for details of difference in the standard of working in the cotton mills.

cases it was a complete farce,[1] since the appointment of an auditor was dependent on the support of the managing agent. Moreover, the word profit was nowhere defined in law, and consequently there was much scope for the window-dressing of final accounts.

One of the leading managing agents, Greaves, Cotton & Company, seems to have been the first to introduce the practices of allowing for depreciation on assets, building up reserves and declaring steady and uniform dividends.[2] But this firm worked for a commission of 10% on net profits and therefore had a very strong interest in the long term development of companies they managed. Repeated comments in the press further impressed the advantages of these practices, in stabilising dividends and financing renewals and expansion, on the minds of the investing public.[3] Nevertheless, these practices grew very slowly because the managing agents who charged a quarter-anna commission feared that the acceptance of these accounting methods would considerably diminish the distributable profits and further expose them to the attacks of shareholders.

Hitherto a firm of managing agents had generally managed only one cotton mill. During the period under review many managing agents acquired the agencies of up to four or five mills, which led to the practice of inter-company financing. And although this brought relief in times of financial difficulty, the practice was not altogether without evil consequences, as the case of Kessowji Naik amply illustrated.[4]

Fiscal and Other Influences

Between 1894 and 1896 the cotton mill industry was faced with the imposition of an excise duty on Indian cotton manufactures which were supposed to compete with Lancashire goods. Earlier, the Government had to impose an import duty on the cotton manufactures to tide over financial difficulties, and the excise duty was levied as a countervailing measure. The direct economic consequence of the excise duty was little but it significantly affected the political situation in the country.[5]

---

[1] See articles in the T.O.I., 10 November 1894; 17 November 1894; and 1 December 1894.
[2] See for instance the editorials in the T.O.I., 4 January 1884; 2 January 1885; and 8 January 1886.
[3] Chapter 11.   [4] See pp. 234–6.
[5] Moreland and Chatterji, pp. 416–17.

Among other temporary influences may be mentioned the depressing effects on business resulting from the fears of 'Franco-Chinese wars' in 1884–5[1] and the 'Russian scare in connection with the Panjdeh affair'[2] on the Indian frontiers. For a time in 1895 the outbreak of communal riots in Bombay city brought the mills to a standstill.[3] The greatest danger to production, however, came in 1896 with the violent epidemic of plague which broke out in Bombay and spread rapidly to other parts of the country, claiming over a million lives within the period under review.[4] Mill-hands died in large numbers or fled from the cities for safety. Capitalists sought refuge, labour and capital markets were completely disorganised, and production suffered heavily.[5] The famines, mentioned earlier,[6] further hit the industry by reducing the demand for its products.

THE LIMIT OF EXPANSION: THE DEMAND FOR GOODS

The most important limit to the growth of capacity in the cotton mill industry came from the size of the market and not from a lack of investment. From the 1870's onwards the Indian mills, with the exception of one or two, depended for their prosperity on the markets of China and Japan, mainly the former. Although new ports were opened in China and in Africa and the quantity exported increased greatly during the period under study, the growth of the market was relatively slower, and so smaller than the growth in the capacity of the industry. At times, therefore, when production exceeded off-take, surpluses were accumulated which could be liquidated only at a very low price. This naturally halted further increases in the capacity until the demand caught up.

This view is amply supported by the repeated reports in the Indian newspaper about the market situation in China, movement of prices, fluctuations in the volume of exports, and the efforts of the Mill-owners' Association to control production. For instance, in 1888–9 several new mills contemplated earlier, started production, while others were formed during the year.[7] The result was that the following year the Chinese market was glutted with stock

---

[1] T.O.I., 4 January 1884.   [2] *Ibid.* Also 2 January 1885; 8 January 1886.
[3] S. D. Mehta, p. 64.
[4] The Bombay Share Market in 1898: T.O.I., 7 January 1899; Commercial Affairs in Bengal: *Ibid.* Also S. D. Mehta, Chapter on Crises.
[5] *Ibid.*   [6] See p. 156.   [7] T.O.I., 4 January 1889.

and this, combined with an adverse movement of the foreign exchange rate, reduced the fortnightly off-take of bales by nearly two-thirds to two or three thousand.[1] This situation continued until, in the middle of 1890, the arrangement to close the mills visibly reduced the stocks in China.[2] In 1890–1 the situation repeated itself when the number of mills suddenly jumped from 114 to 125. Again the mills had to be closed for two days a week.[3]

In spite of the limited demand for coarse cotton goods, the investment could have been increased if finer varieties had been manufactured. For doing so, the Indian mills possessed two advantages over Lancashire mills: a large home market and a supply of cheap labour. Against these had to be set, however, the higher charges for imported cotton, machinery, technical staff and managerial remuneration. J. N. Tata was the first industrialist to believe that such a course of action would be profitable.[4] He demonstrated this by starting a mill for the manufacture of finer yarn and cloth, and by running it successfully; but his example was not followed. The reason was simple: Tata charged only a commission of 10% on net profits for the management of the mill, whereas the other managing agents would not have been satisfied with anything less than a quarter-anna commission on the output.

Imposing a protective tariff remained, perhaps, the only major possibility which could have induced the entrepreneurs to undertake the manufacture of finer cotton goods, but the Government of India could not adopt this policy since Britain was still under the strong influence of the *laissez-faire* philosophy. Even so, the *Times of India* advocated, the industry could have made more vigorous attempts to open new channels of demand to reduce the risk of having to depend on a single market. Also it could have produced more of other textiles like wool and silk, and finally, the investment could have been channelled into entirely new fields to prevent the cotton industry from being overdone as well as to add to the productive powers of the nation.[5] But this timely advice of the *Times of India* went practically unheeded until the crises in the closing years of the century shook the entrepreneurs out of their slumbers.

[1] T.O.I., 3 January 1890.   [2] *Ibid.*, 3 January 1891.
[3] *Ibid.*, 2 January 1892.
[4] See a letter by J. N. Tata in the T.O.I. of 17 August 1886.
[5] T.O.I., 2 January 1892. See also issues of 3 January in 1890 and 1891.

Growth of the Corporate Sector, 1882–1900

THE GROWTH OF INDUSTRIES IN BENGAL

The industrial development in Bengal differed fundamentally from Bombay in one respect: whereas the most important industry of Bombay—the cotton mills—was largely pioneered by the Parsees whom the Hindus subsequently followed, the rupee investment in the important industries of Bengal—jute, tea and coal—came mainly from British people. Our immediate task, therefore, is to try and understand the reasons why the Indians in Bengal did not take to the promotion of corporate enterprises.

Characteristics of the Indian Entrepreneurship in Bengal

Trade, as an occupation among the Hindus, who constituted nearly 80% of the population of India, was related to caste, though not entirely limited by it.[1] Not everyone in the minority entitled to trade showed a taste for it. In Bengal, the Bengalis, who predominated in the region, seem to have been mainly concerned with investment in land, and finding employment in the civil services, particularly between 1850 and 1880. As political consciousness grew during the last two decades of the century, however, they became more and more aware of the importance of developing industries. Industrial conferences were held to emphasise this point and the use of joint stock organisation was advocated to overcome the scarcity of capital.[2] The Bengali-edited newspapers

[1] The emphasis here is not on religion but on the social structure and traditions. On the relationship between caste and trading occupation see Mrs D. P. Pandit, 'Creative Response in Indian Economy—A Regional Analysis', EW, 23 February 1957, pp. 283–6, and 2 March 1957, pp. 315–17.

Mrs Hemlata Acharya, 'Creative Response in Indian Economy—A Comment', EW, 27 April 1957, pp. 547–9. See also Gadgil, *Origin of the Modern Indian Business Class, op. cit.*

Helen B. Lamb, 'The Development of Modern Business Communities in India', *Proceedings of the Conference on Human Resources and Labour Relations in Under Developed Countries*, 1954. P. S. Lokanathan, 'Entrepreneurship: Supply of Entrepreneurs and Technologists with Special Reference to India', in K. Berrill (Ed.), *Economic Development with Special Reference to East Asia*, 1964. M. V. Namjoshi, *The Development of the Large-Scale Private Sector in India*, (Thesis submitted to the Gokhle Institute of Politics and Economics, 1956). G. C. Ghurye, *Caste and Class in India*, 1957.

[2] See proceedings of the *Industrial Conference* held at Poona, in the T.O.I., 8 September 1893 and 2 September 1894. See also the report of the *Bengal Industrial Conference* in The *Statesman* of 7 November 1891. The Conference President, P. M. Bose, speaking on the agenda: 'How Best to Promote the Joint Stock System in This Country in Connection With The Feasibility of Joint Stock Organisation', remarked as follows:

exhorted their fellow countrymen to promote industries, but these efforts did not lead to any spectacular change. An examination of the names of the shareholders who attended the general meetings of companies or sent proxies did, however, indicate a small and gradual increase in Bengali names.[1] The Bengalis were also successful in launching at least one glass manufacturing company,[2] but their infiltration into the industrial sphere remained, on the whole, very small.

The Muslims, another large group in Bengal, though free from the trammels of the caste system, did not show any great aptitude for industry. The Bohras and Memons, originally Hindus and later converted to Islam, were two prominent trading communities but they operated largely on the West coast.[3] The traditional explanation for a lack of business interest in the Sunni Muslims of India was that before the advent of the British Rule in India they had been either a *rentier* class who had not, as yet, been reconciled to the changed political situation, or, as was the case in Bengal, they were poor farmers. Whatever the reason, in neither case were they much concerned with trade or industry and they did not make any significant contribution in this regard.

Bengal, particularly Calcutta, also contained a small element of Parsees, Kutchees, Gujaratis, Jews, Armenians, and Marwaris. Of these, the Marwaris, though not very large in number, were the most prominent trading community.

'No industry is nowadays likely to be remunerative unless started on a large scale; and that means large outlay and it is of no use to give technical education unless such industries be started. Ours is a very poor country. Still by joint stock organisation sufficient capital could be raised for the successful starting of many large industries. A beginning has already been made in this direction. The recent establishment of a glass-manufacturing company and of a cotton weaving company in Bengal is a very helpful sign.'

[1] See, for instance, the list of shareholders present by proxy at a General Meeting of the Fortgloster Jute Company. Of the 27 proxies the following were Indians and those *in italics* were definitely Bengalis:
1. B. Jutia. 2. H. Mammoji. 3. S. Daga. 4. *S. N. Ghose.* 5. N. D. Sarawgee. 6. N. Sonee. 7. L. Sonee. 8. *J. Seal.* 9. *G. Chakraborty.* 10. *N. Roy.* 11. Paladas Bansidhar. 12. *R. C. Ghose.* 13. *K. L. Mullick.* 14. N. Dobay. *Englishman,* Daily, 12 September 1890. Nos. 1, 3 and 5 at least were Marwaris.

[2] This was the Pioneer Glass Manufacturing Company registered on 22 February 1890 with a nominal capital of Rs.300,000 of which Rs.223,380 was paid up. The Consular-General for Sweden and Norway, Voigt, was its managing agent.

[3] The emphasis, again, is not on religion. The Muslims of Lebanon, for instance, are well known businessmen. So are the Jains of India, the Buddhists of Japan and the Zoroastrian Parsees.

Growth of the Corporate Sector, 1882–1900

The Marwaris: The Business Magnates of Today

The Marwaris were an inward looking community, restricted in their social contacts with other communities by their dietary and marital habits. They came from Rajasthan and traded in food-grains and textiles, besides lending money.[1] Their business was organised around the 'joint-family system' in which the grandfather, father, son, his son and so on worked and lived together and shared the properties, until a family row separated them, when they set up independently on the same pattern. The system had various advantages, but there was a limit to which business organised in this way could grow. It certainly could not compete with the almost limitless expansion possible under a joint-stock organisation. Though there was nothing to stop a joint family from promoting corporate enterprises, it offered a large enough scope to satisfy the ambitions of most ordinary individuals, particularly those with a limited vision of life.

Unlike the Parsees, their close trading relationship with the Europeans had little influence on either their business or social

[1] Marwari means people of Marwar or Rajasthan, and not only Mewar, which is only a part of Rajasthan. The term here does not include all Marwaris but only the *banias*. A Jain can also be a Marwari—many are. Within the Marwari community there are also further groups such as Mahesari, Bikaneri, Bagri, Bhihani, etc. Though Marwari is a regional concept the emphasis here is not on geographical origin. Mrs Pandit's very large claims about the Gujaratis has so far only proved the futility of this approach (see her articles and Mrs Acharya's reply, *op. cit.*). *Banias* were the trading community among the Hindus all over India. Nobody in Rajasthan calls a person known in Calcutta as marwari, a Marwari; he is called a *bania*. The terms Marwari, Sindhi, Gujarati, as a business class, were attached to the *banias* in other parts where some of the *banias* settled to do business. The reason why some *banias* from certain parts became well known should be sought more in the type of economic opportunities available in the region of their settlement rather than any other factor.

Why did not the Bombay or Ahmedabad Gujaratis invest in jute mills or coal mines or tea companies but only in cotton mills till the end of last century? Why did the earlier influence of the Chettis of South India, or *banias* of Bengal decline or, for that matter, why did not the British invest largely in the Bombay or Ahmedabad cotton mills? The Marwari *banias* seem to have been the more mobile within India and even they did not go to the jungles of Assam to start tea gardens (but this may be partly because tea did not have an internal market). Technology certainly was not an important obstacle; with more than 200 tea gardens in 1881, there could hardly be any secret about how tea was produced. As regards investment in other industries such as iron and steel, paper, etc., it was not only a question of technology and demand conditions, but also of governmental attitude. Cultural traditions are certainly important; mainly so in determining the stresses and strains involved in institutional changes. See pp. 165–7.

165

habits, because in the case of the Marwari apprentice, the focus of attention was not how the Europeans conducted their trade, but how his master conducted his trade with the Europeans. Naturally he could not get out of the traditional framework. Nevertheless, visible changes in their business outlook did begin to take place from the eighties onwards. They gained control of a number of jute pressing and baling companies and became increasingly influential as shareholders. By the nineties they wielded such great influence that when plague broke out, the Calcutta stock market was almost completely disorganised because so many of them had left the city. In two decades the Marwaris had come to be the mainstay of the share market in Calcutta, important both as brokers[1] and speculators. But as no study of the Marwaris has been made as yet, the reasons for the changes in the pattern of their behaviour can only be surmised.

Brokerage was one of their traditional occupations, but their importance as shareholders can be traced to their proverbial love for speculation. This would account for the prevalence of 'forward contracts' in the Calcutta share market and the 'forced sales' during periods of monetary stringency. In the art of 'options', they were masters. With their ears to the ground, they always received the news affecting the share market first, and were unsurpassed in spreading rumours and confusing the market. In the early nineties when the Calcutta market was wild with the speculation in gold mining companies, even the Europeans were surprised by their skill in getting the best out of the market.[2]

Their interest in the long-term investment, however, extended only slowly and gradually, since they preferred the assured earnings from trade and moneylending to an uncertain dividend. Investment in jute mill shares provided the first stepping stone in this direction, as was only logical since they were already well established in the jute trade as brokers, balers and exporters. Some of them became important shareholders in jute mills. This was, perhaps, why the jute mill shares were the main interest in the Calcutta market despite the fact that the share capital of the tea companies exceeded the capital of the jute companies by as much

---

[1] The list of 'Native sharebrokers' in *Thacker's Bengal Directory for 1875* mentions names which were nearly all Bengalis. So, it seems that the Marwaris had not entered this field till then.

[2] The *Englishman*, 1 September 1890. Also see Chapter 10.

as twenty million rupees at the end of March 1882, and was always higher until the end of the century.

The Marwaris, with one exception,[1] never promoted any company up to the end of the century: firstly, because they lacked technical knowledge and secondly, because they had no patience to wait for profits arising long after the initial investment. Moreover, the scope for establishing jute mills, which was their particular interest, was limited. Between 1882–3 and 1900–1 the number of jute mills increased by nine only, and, further, it would have been pretty difficult to break into this field because the Europeans were firmly entrenched from the days they pioneered it. Other industries such as tea and coal were situated in distant places and therefore could not be developed as a side line. Apart from these techno-economic reasons there were probably some socio-psychological reasons such as an aversion to sharing the true profits of a venture, since partnerships are not very popular among them, or a prejudice against the system of elaborate business organisation with many divisions of labour, since they regard the European method of business organisation as extravagant. In the circumstances it would have been out of character for them to have promoted many industrial companies. We can now turn to the growth of ndividual industries in Bengal.

THE JUTE MILLS

On 1 April 1882, there were only eight jute companies with an aggregate paid-up capital of Rs.7,464,000. By 31 March 1901, their number had increased to 21 and their capital to Rs. 30,327,800.The rate of growth works out at 7·5% annually which was quite large. In April 1882, the average paid-up capital of a jute company was Rs.933,000. By March 1901, it had increased by 1½ times. The increase in the size of companies absorbed about half of the increase in investment during this period. There was no increase in the average paid-up capital employed by a cotton mill in this period, which shows that a European-owned company tended to become bigger. But the aggregate rupee investment in jute companies was only 8·2% of the total investment in all rupee com-

---

[1] They promoted a cotton mill in Calcutta which was exclusively Indian both in ownership and management. The capital invested in this mill was the least per loom in this region and it made the best profit. See pp. 250–1.

panies at the end of March 1901, as compared with 34% in cotton mills. Even if we were to add the sterling investment in jute companies which was of the order of Rs.20 million at the end of the century,[1] the rupee investment in the cotton mills would work out to be 2½ times larger.[2] Why was, one may ask, the total investment in the jute industry so little? The main limiting factor seems to have been the demand for jute products, as will be clear from the following analysis of the trend of the growth of jute companies.

From the second half of 1880 to the end of 1883, the jute industry enjoyed modest prosperity. In 1882–3, the first year of the period under study, four new companies were started which increased the paid-up capital by Rs.1·3 million. No new company was registered in the next year but the calls increased the capital by another Rs.1·3 million. From 1884–5 the industry ran into difficulties. The market could not absorb the increased production. Only four mills were able to show any profit and one company went into liquidation. The following year all companies were in trouble and one more wound-up. The situation became so desperate that in November 1885, a conference of the millowners decided to fix minimum prices for all jute manufactures and to maintain these prices by judiciously curtailing output. For five years from February 1886 the mills worked only 4 to 4½ days a week instead of seven.[3] As a result companies were able to declare a dividend in 1887 and increase it steadily thereafter.[4] But no new investment took place up to the end of March 1890.

By 1891 the situation had changed radically,[5] although the industry suffered losses in 1892 as a result of a wrong forecast of the jute crop by the Government. The demand was so good from 1893 that there was a great rush to increase the output. In 1894 many mills installed electric light and worked 14 to 15 hours a day,

---

[1] The investment is estimated at the exchange rate of 1s. 4d., the official rate at the end of the century. Even otherwise, the actual rate, on the average, was not far out during most of the period under study.

[2] The sterling investment in the cotton mills was negligible.

[3] Ahmed, p. 190.

[4] See a table of dividends in W. van Delden, *Studien uber die Indische Jute industrie*, 1915, quoted in Ahmed, p. 215.

[5] 'The jute manufacturing industry has every reason to gratefully remember 1891. Jute mills have earned enormous profits, shareholders have received large dividends and considerable sums have been placed to reserve. The market value of most jute mill shares was therefore higher at the end than at the beginning of 1891.' The price quotations show gains of up to Rs.20—T.O.I., 'Commercial Affairs in Bengal', 9 January 1892.

while two mills used small lamps and candles to increase their production. The increase in the productive capacity resulting from electricity was estimated by the *Economist* at one-sixth in November 1895.[1] At the end of March 1895, the jute companies numbered only thirteen and their aggregate paid-up capital amounted to Rs.14,634,760. Within a year the number of companies increased to nineteen and the paid-up capital went up by about Rs.2·6 million. The calls made in the following year further increased it by Rs.4·05 million. At the height of the boom, on 31 August 1896, the shares of jute companies were quoted at between Rs.30 to 75 higher than on the same day the previous year.[2]

From the latter part of 1896 the industry was adversely hit by a set of temporary circumstances. First, the forecast of the jute crop made by the Government of India turned out to be wrong which upset all forward contracts for buying and selling. Secondly, an earthquake in 1897 destroyed the Serajgunj Mill and damaged some others. Thirdly, an occurrence of plague caused exodus of labour. And, finally, the great increase in the output during the boom led to an excess of supply over demand which brought down the prices. The industry, however, continued to make moderate progress until the end of the century despite these difficulties.

The scope of this book does not permit an analysis of the world demand situation, but there can be no doubt about the nature of the problem faced by the investors in India. They were two: firstly, the world demand for jute manufactures was very limited and rose only slowly; secondly, much of the world market was already in the hands of the Dundee jute manufacturers, whose techniques of production were, if anything, superior to their counterparts in India. In these circumstances the investment in the Indian jute industry could increase only to the extent the British entrepreneurs there were able to wrest the markets from Dundee. This they did throughout the period under study; first in the coarser variety, and then in the finer.[3] It is doubtful if they could have pushed out the Dundee manufacturers more than they actually did.

Not only were the British managing agents able to dislodge the Dundee jute manufacturers from a good deal of the world market, but they also showed a greater sensitiveness to public opinion than

---

[1] *The Economist*, 23 November 1895.
[2] *Idid.*, 14 December 1895.   [3] Ahmed, pp. 246–56.

the Indian managing agents of the cotton mills in Bombay. In the beginning the managing agents of the mills, just like their counterparts in the Bombay cotton mills, did not either allow for depreciation on assets or create general reserves for fear of reducing distributable profits. After, however, the *Friend of India* had directed a tirade of criticisms exposing the hollowness of the balance sheets issued by jute companies, the managing agents accepted the inevitable and changed their methods.[1] In doing so they were nearly a decade ahead of the managing agents in Bombay. The issuing of debentures and preference shares by the jute mills also preceded their use by the Bombay cotton mills by about the same length of time.

THE TEA COMPANIES

The rupee paid-up capital of all tea companies at the end of March 1901, amounted to only about 8% of the total paid-up capital of all rupee companies. Thus it was of the same order as the investment in the jute industry, but the proportion was more than twice as high on 1 April 1882. In considering these figures, however, one must remember that towards the latter part of the nineties many rupee companies were converted into sterling companies, since the depreciation of the rupee gave a higher capitalised value in sterling. Nonetheless, between April 1882 and March 1901, the rupee capital increased by 5·6 million. For a total picture of the investments in the tea industry, account must be taken of the investments by the sterling companies, which have been stimated at various dates as follows: [2]

Year of Estimate	In Million £s.[a]	In Million Rs.[b]
1881–2	2·5	37·5
1892–3	5·0	75·0
1896–7	8·0	120·0

[a] Includes equity, preference and debenture capital.
[b] Sterling converted @ 1s. 4d. Official rate in 1900.

The sterling and rupee investment, taken together, amounted to 46% of the total paid-up capital of all rupee companies at the end

---

[1] These articles appeared in the *Friend of India* between 1877 and 1882 under the head, 'Our Jute Mill Finances' and 'Our Jute Mills'. See, for instance, 9 November, 5 October, 30 June, etc., in 1877 and 16 January 1882.

[2] The figures for sterling investment are from Ahmed, p. 73a.

of March 1901. Thus viewed, the investment in the tea indnstry was unmatched by any other sector except the railways.

The tea industry made only modest progress during the first eleven years from 1882, mainly because the market was limited. Further, communications with the tea districts in the early part of the eighties were still very slow and hazardous, and the price of tea fluctuated a great deal as a result of the fluctuations in the exchange rate, particularly around 1890. As pointed out, the flow of investment was determined primarily by the rate of growth of the market. This was also the responsible contemporary opinion: 'It is within the experience of your memorialist', wrote the Darjeeling and Terai Planters Association to the Viceroy of India, 'that whatever difficulties they meet with in procuring financial assistance from capitalists resident in England are . . . attributable to over-production of tea, and not to any deterrent effects produced upon English capitalists by the fluctuations in Exchange.'[1]

The tea industry enjoyed an extraordinary prosperity between 1892 and 1896. During this period 88,000 acres of land were planted in Bengal and Assam, about fifty new rupee companies were formed, more than thirty rupee companies were reconstructed or absorbed, and the sterling investment increased by three million pounds. In 1894, forty-six sterling companies paid an average dividend of $7 \cdot 9\%$ as compared with only $5 \cdot 2\%$ in 1888[2] and in 1895 the yield on capital employed by fifty-six sterling companies was calculated to be $155 \cdot 7$s. $\%$[3] This boom was brought about by a combination of favourable circumstances. The demand for Indian tea increased enormously; the exports went up, on an average, by ten million pounds a year for the rest of the century. In 1895 the price index for tea jumped by eighteen points.[4] The profit margin increased still further as a result of the increase in productivity, improvement in the quality of the tea and the drop in freight charges.

Wages, a very important item in the cost of production, remained stationary throughout the period,[5] while famine conditions

---

[1] P.P., Vol. LXV, 1893–4, Appendix I.
[2] Ahmed, p. 154; 1888 figures relate to 26 companies only.
[3] Gow, Wilson and Stanton, Preface.
[4] *Index Numbers etc., op. cit.*, p. II.
[5] See Index of real and money wages in *Report on the Enquiry into . . . Prices in India*: Government of India, Finance Department, 1914. Also see a letter dated 24 June 1892, P.P. Vol. LXV, 1893–4, p. 151 from which the following

in India increased the labour supply, which removed the greatest obstacle in the way of expansion. The depression in the late eighties had revealed that great profits were to be made by amalgamating and reconstructing the small and relatively uneconomic gardens which were many at this time. The climate was especially favourable for attracting sterling capital since trade was still stagnant and the money supply easy in Britain, while the rupee had touched its lowest value in terms of sterling and a further fall was very unlikely in view of the currency measures of 1893. Sterling could, therefore, buy more of the factors of production whose money cost did not rise. A tea planter aptly described the effect of all these influences in the following words:[1]

> While the jungle, forest, bamboo, sunn and okra grass was being cut to make room for tea plants, agency houses in London, Glasgow and Calcutta were busy turning land syndicates into gardens, established gardens into companies, and companies into still bigger companies. The bones of the industry were stirring with a vengeance.

The fortunes of the tea industry began to turn from 1897. An earthquake in that year caused some damage to the gardens in Assam. The earlier expansion caused over-production in 1898, which became a more serious problem in the next two years as young plantations matured. Prices fell very low and as a financial columnist put it, 'the gardens could be picked up for a song'.

THE COAL MINING INDUSTRY

The coal mining industry received its first impetus in the middle of the fifties when the East India Railway passed through the Ranigunj coal fields. At the same time the railways and the river steamers shifted part of their demand for fuel to these fields. But as late as 1880 the annual output of coal fluctuated around one million tons and was less than three at the end of 1893. From 1896

---

extract of a speech by J. L. Mackay, partner, Mackinnon, Mackenzie and Company, delivered as the chairman of a public meeting held in Calcutta on 25 August 1892 is taken: '. . . while those of us who are engaged in jute and cotton manufacturing, in tea planting and other industries, may see advantages in still being able to pay our labour in the depreciated metal, we feel that there must be a limit to the gullibility of the coolie, and that the impossibility of filling their stomachs with their wages must eventually lead to a readjustment'.
[1] *Recollections of a Tea Planter*, p. 25, quoted in Ahmed, p. 67.

the industry entered into an era of unprecedented growth as the following figures will show.

Year (Ending March)	Number of Companies Operating	Paid-up capital in Rs.(000,000's)	Output (Calendar[a] Year) In Tons (000's)
1881–2	6	39·0	997
1890–1	10	52·3	2,168
1891–2	11	61·7	2,328
1892–3	14	64·8	2,537
1893–4	16	79·5	2,562
1894–5	20	79·8	2,823
1895–6	28	96·7	3,540
1896–7	34	102·8	3,863
1897–8	—	114·8	4,066
1898–9	—	127·5	4,608
1899–1900	—	133·0	5,093
1900–1	34	140·0	6,118

[a]S.T.B.I., 1901, p. 36.

As the figures show, the paid-up capital of coal companies more than doubled during the seven years after March 1893, and if the investment by non-corporate bodies were to be included, the figure would probably have trebled. Why was, one might ask, the flow of investment delayed until 1894? There were ample resources; the quality was not as good as the best Welsh, but it was good enough for industrial purposes; it was found near the surface; labour, though untrained, was cheap and in plentiful supply; and the railways had been running through Ranigunj for at least forty years. The causes must be traced either to scarcity of capital and/or technical knowledge or to demand conditions. Lack of sufficient demand seems to have been the decisive factor.

Coal is, in a major sense, a subsidiary industry, depending for its use on the development of other industries. In India it was used mainly by railways,[1] steamers, and cotton mills, since other industries which would normally depend upon coal such as iron and steel and to a lesser extent engineering, were rare until the end of the century. The demand for coal from railways, steamships, and manufacturing industries was large enough for the industry to assume respectable proportions, but its growth became limited to

[1] At the end of 1900, the railways used as much as 31% of the total output of over six million tons. S.T.B.I., 1901, 'Summary of Contents and Explanatory Memoranda'. See also Chapter 13.

the quantity of coal consumed in Bengal, where the mines were located, because freight rates were so high that it was cheaper elsewhere to use imported coal even at four or five times the Calcutta price. Between the 1870's and 1890's, India imported between 600,000 and 900,000 tons of coal annually, excluding the coal used by ships plying between India and other nations.

It has been suggested that lack of sterling investment held back the growth of the coal mining industry. The sterling investment stood at £1 million at the end of March 1886, and it did not increase by more than £159,000 up to the end of the century. Information about the size of non-Indian investment in rupee enterprises is not available but it was probably not more than one-half of the total investment, including the investment by unincorporated firms, which accounted for between one-fourth and one-fifth of the total.[1] The reason why more sterling capital did not flow into this industry, it is further said, was the instability of the Indian currency, because profits would have arisen entirely in India and would have been affected by the falling exchange rate when transferred to Britain.[2] The argument would have been valid had there been a good demand for Indian coal and if the possible margin of profits was unlikely to cover the probable fall in the value of the rupee.

We have already seen that the demand was rather poor for much of the period under consideration, and there is no reason to believe that the profit margin was small. Actually the development of the coal industry at this time did not require either any large unit of capital or any particular technical knowledge because the coal deposits occurred near the surface. From the viewpoint of the cost of production, companies with large capital had only a small advantage over small entrepreneurs. In fact, right from the start, owners of small mines had operated them successfully alongside the large companies and, though their relative importance gradually declined, they were responsible for a significant proportion of the total output till the end of the century, varying from a third to between a fourth and a fifth.[3]

There were two reasons for the sudden change in the fortunes of the coal industry. Firstly, the price of imported coal rose steeply;

[1] Ahmed, pp. 260–6. Also S.T.B.I., 1901, pp. 364–7.
[2] Ahmed, pp. 410–11.
[3] *Ibid.*, pp. 260–6. Also S.T.B.I., 1901, pp. 364–7.

in 1900 imported coal in Bombay cost nearly ten times more than the Bengal coal delivered to Calcutta. It became cheaper, therefore, to obtain coal from Calcutta by means of coastal transport. Secondly, the shifts in demand from imported to home-produced coal coincided with the extension, in 1894, of the railway to the rich Jharia coal fields (now in Bihar) which had remained unworked for lack of transport facilities. Coal from these fields was sent to other parts of the country which had previously been dependent on imports. It also became competitive in nearby countries to the east and west of India to which it was supplied in increasing quantities. At the end of the century, the coal industry had not only come out of its moribund state, but it was on the verge of a great boom.

The discussion that follows concerns industries which operated on an all-India basis, unlike the cotton, jute, coal and tea industries which were largely located in particular provinces.

THE RAILWAYS

At the end of 1900 the capital expenditure on the Indian railways amounted to Rs.2,942 million, representing, at the exchange of 16d. per rupee, £196 million, but a great proportion of the capital was raised and expended when the rupee was worth much more than 16d.[1] The sterling capital invested at the end of 1893 amounted to £100.3 million, of which only £13.1 million had been invested since 1880. In the case of the railways, it was quite true that the British capitalists were deterred from investing by the instability of the Indian currency during this period, because the yield on capital employed was small.

In 1893, the Government of India, unwilling to increase its sterling liabilities which it thought were partly responsible for the depreciation of the rupee, proposed to invite capital on a rupee basis for the construction of feeder or branch lines. It offered an indirect subsidy by giving rebates on earnings of the railways in place of the onerous guarantee but the terms were not sufficiently attractive and so there was no significant increase in rupee investment. The Government revised its policy in 1896 and offered an absolute guarantee of 3% plus a rebate, to the full extent of the

[1] S.T.B.I., 1901, 'Summary of Contents and Explanatory Memoranda'.

main line's net earnings, making a total of $3\frac{1}{4}\%$ on capital outlay.[1]
This had an immediately favourable result on the growth of rupee
investment: whereas at the end of March 1896, the rupee capital
invested in the railways amounted to only about 5 millions,[2] it
stood at over 31 millions at the end of the century. The near
stability in the value of the rupee reached at this time must have
contributed towards this relatively large flow of capital.

BANKING

The banking statistics published by the Government of India were
highly confusing because they included hundreds of companies
which were no more than small savings and loan societies. For
example, the figures for 1895–6 show 299 'banking and loan'
companies with a paid-up capital of Rs.40,466,720 but on analysis
only the following companies could properly be classified as banks:

Name	Registered in Province	Year	Paid-up Capital in Rs.(000's)
1. Hongkong & Shanghai Bank	Bengal	1869	22,500
2. Bank of Upper India	N.W.P.	1863	1,000
3. Allahabad Bank	N.W.P.	1865	400
4. Oudh Commercial Bank	N.W.P.	1881	200
5. Alliance Bank of India	Punjab	1874	1,000
6. Punjab Banking Company	Punjab	1885	117
7. Comm. & Land Mortgage Bank	Madras	1885	2,445
8. Bangalore Bank	Bangalore	1868	434

Rs.28,096

To these banks could perhaps be added the Ajodhia Bank, the
Gorakhpore Bank, the Bangalore Mercantile Bank and the Punjab

---

[1] R. D. Tiwari, pp. 74–5.

[2] The following are the particulars of the railway companies:

Name of Companies	Date Registered	Paid-up Capital (Rs.)
1. Darjeeling-Himalayan Rly.	1879	1,750,000
2. Deoghar	1882	275,000
3. Tarkeshwar Rly.	1884	1,750,000
4. Dehradun Rly. Promotion Co.	1887	13,070
5. Indian Rly. Feeder Co.	1887	98,250
6. Bengal Provincial Rly.	1890	790,280
7. Jaigunj Rly.	1895	—
8. Ahmedabad-Prantej Rly.	1896	—

(S.T.B.I., 1897, p. 481.)

National Bank whose individual paid-up capital was very small.[1] On the other hand, the Hongkong and Shanghai Banking Corporation could not be properly regarded as an Indian joint stock bank since its Head Office was situated outside India and its paid-up capital was registered in Hongkong dollars. The exclusion of this bank would reduce the aggregate paid-up capital of the remaining Indian banks to Rs.5,596,180, an extremely modest sum. In contrast, the aggregate paid-up capital of the 280 or so mutual savings and loan societies, nearly all of which were located in Madras and Mysore, amounted to over Rs.12 million. Between April 1896 and March 1901, the aggregate paid-up capital of 'banking and loan companies' together went up by Rs.4,690,802. At the same time the number of these companies increased by 131 which shows that much of the increase in capital resulted from the growth of loan companies rather than the banks. Why was the growth of banking so poor?

The following figures show the progress of banking in India between 1870 and 1900:

	No.	Capital and Reserves Rs. mn.	£'s mn.	Deposits[a] Rs. mn.
1870				
Presidency Banks	3	36·1		63·9*
Exchange Banks	3		6·1*	5·2
Indian Joint Stock Banks	2	1·1		1·3*
1880				
Presidency Banks	3	40·5		84·9*
Exchange Banks	4		7·3*	33·9*
Indian Joint Stock Banks	4	2·1		6·3*
1890				
Presidency Banks	3	44·7		147·6*
Exchange Banks	5		8·9*	75·3*
Indian Joint Stock Banks	5	5·1		27·0*
1900				
Presidency Banks	3	55·9		122·8
Exchange Banks	8		15·7	105·0
Indian Joint Stock Banks	9	12·7		80·7

[a] The figures marked * are taken from S.T.B.I., 1901, Part XII. The other figures are taken from Muranjan, p. 7. The deposits of the Presidency banks are on private accounts only and those of the exchange banks relate to deposits in India only.

[1] These banks were registered between 1894 and 1895. Of these, the Punjab National Bank actually became very important by 1900.

The Presidency banks were semi-government institutions and the exchange banks, which occupied a predominant position in the international trade of India, were owned by foreigners. The Indian joint stock banks, which were owned mainly by Indians, concerned themselves primarily with internal trade. The statistics indicating the progress of these institutions were collected by the Government for the first time around 1899 and they are, therefore, limited to banks actually in existence at that time.

The omission of banks which had passed out of existence or ceased to do business in India necessarily makes the increase of capital and deposits in 1900 over former years seem larger than they really were. Even so, it cannot be denied that the Indian joint stock banks, which were almost absent in the seventies, gained both in number and size during the eighties and made substantial advances in attracting deposits during the nineties. The gain in deposits requires particular attention since during the nineties the Indian joint stock banks were able to increase their deposits by Rs.53 million compared with an increase of only Rs.30 million in the deposits of exchange banks, while deposits of Presidency banks decreased by nearly Rs.20 million. The fall in deposits at the Presidency banks was probably because they closed the Savings Accounts in 1896–7.[1] The growth of deposits at the Indian joint stock banks, on the other hand, resulted mainly from the easy monetary conditions which prevailed up to 1896. But there were other conditions as well.

These banks paid a higher rate of interest on deposits than others, which is why most of their deposits consisted of 'time deposits'; moreover, there was better demand for banking facilities in places where offices of these banks were located because of the increase in the volume of trade and industrial output. The increase in the issues of bonds and shares, and the volume of their turnover further created a demand for short-term funds which made it easier for the banks to invest their excess cash.[2] Even competent students of Indian banking have ignored these facts in explaining the relatively faster growth of Indian banks in the last

[1] S.T.B.I., 1901, Part XIII, see footnote to Table 1 on savings banks.
[2] The cash balance held by the Presidency banks and the Indian joint stock banks as a percentage of deposits at the end of various years was as follows: 1870—83%; 1880—74%; 1890—64% 1899—29%. (S.T.B.I., 1901, Part XII.)

two decades of the nineteenth century.[1] Similarly, no convincing explanation has been offered for the lack of sufficient growth in the earlier period. Jain, for example, put the blame on the instability of the exchange rate without showing how it really affected the growth of Indian banks.[2] Muranjan, on the other hand, dismissed this as the main or even a substantial cause, on the ground that the techniques for covering against adverse movements in the exchange rate were not less known then, than they are today.[3] But both of them seem to have missed the point.

The instability of the exchange rate was surely the most important factor in the last three decades of the nineteenth century. As Mr Geoffrey Tyson had rightly observed, 'the whole period was one of considerable financial nervousness'.[4] The possibility of loss on account of fluctuations in the exchange rate could undoubtedly have been covered, and to that extent banks were not necessarily helpless, but expansion in a period of anxiety is a different matter altogether. Moreover, there is no suggestion anywhere that the external trade suffered as a result of insufficient banking facilities in this period. The reason why the Indian banks did not enter the field of financing external trade has to be found not in the instability of the exchange rate but in the fact that the external trade, apart from the imports and exports of cotton goods, was primarily in the hands of Europeans who could not have been easily persuaded to divert custom to Indian banks which were not well known in foreign countries. The possibility of hedging against fluctuations in the exchange rate is, therefore, irrelevant to the development of Indian banks, which were mainly concerned with the internal trade.

What has to be emphasised is that the risk shouldered by these banks was only indirectly connected with the fluctuations in the exchange rate; the risk arising from the bankruptcy of traders who had been given advances by banks. This risk was indeed great. There were many failures of Indian importers in both Calcutta and Bombay arising not only from the vagaries of the exchange rate in conducting the legitimate business of imports, but as the

---

[1] See, for example, Muranjan, or L. C. Jain: *Indigenous Banking in India*, 1929.
[2] *Ibid.*, pp. 149–51.
[3] Muranjan, pp. 5–6.
[4] Geoffrey Tyson, *The Bengal Chamber of Commerce and Industry, 1853–1953, A Centenary Survey*, 1952, p. 93.

result of indulging in large-scale speculation.[1] The extreme care with which advances had to be made in this period was not conducive to the growth of banking institutions.

In Muranjan's view the 'almost stationary economic conditions of the latter half of the nineteenth century'[2] were actually responsible for the slow growth of banks in India. In making this point he further observes:[3]

The prices of indigenous manufactures with which the city-located banks were most directly concerned continued low and falling from 1866 to 1886, recovered appreciably between 1888 and 1895 and fell heavily thereafter till 1899. Such a course of events was obviously ill-suited to stimulate growth of deposits and banking in a backward country like India.

This is a somewhat strange argument because economic conditions, particularly in the cities, were not stationary during the period. In fact, the growth of the cotton mills, the jute mills, the tea companies, besides a host of isolated enterprises in other fields was remarkable. Moreover, the low and falling prices of indigenous manufactures, in the twenty years mentioned, in itself, cannot be said to have any relation with the bank deposits or banking. What matters surely is the state of industry which depends on profit margins which in turn depend on the difference between the cost of production and the selling price, and one must assume that the cost of production in the period under review fell faster than the selling price, otherwise the growth of industries during this period cannot be explained.

Moreover, the cash balances maintained by the Indian banks show that the problem before the banks was not how to attract deposits, but how to invest their funds. In 1870 these banks held over 83% of their deposits in cash.[4] In 1899, this percentage had fallen to a little over 29%.[5] In 1899 the cash balance of the exchange banks amounted to only 17.9%,[6] which goes to prove not only that the cash balances as large as those held by the Indian banks were unnecessary, but that the exchange banks were able to utilise their funds better. This view is further

---

[1] T.O.I., 2 January 1892. Leading article.
[2] Muranjan, p. 6.   [3] *Ibid.*, pp. 6–7.
[4] See p. 178, note 2.   [5] *Ibid.*
[6] S.T.B.I., 1901, Part XII, Table 2.

confirmed by the opinions expressed in contemporary news-papers.[1]

The question still remains, why the banks did not move into the interior parts of India. Here, the growth of pure commercial banking, unaccompanied by trading, on British lines would have required a certain concentration of demand for funds with risk conditions acceptable to a bank. There is no evidence to suggest that such a demand existed. The business of banking was certainly very profitable, as is indicated by the amount of income-tax paid by indigenous bankers and money lenders; whereas the income-tax paid by the entire corporate sector in the two years, 1895–6 and 1899–1900, came to Rs.1,144,670 and Rs.1,329,586 respectively, the corresponding figures for unincorporated banking and money lending alone amounted to Rs.3,594,570 and Rs.3,821,430.[2] The scope of this book does not allow a more detailed discussion of the subject, but the short analysis presented here, it is hoped, will help to dispel some of the clouds surrounding the growth of banks in India.

INSURANCE

The government statistics concerning insurance companies are no less confused than the banking statistics. This confusion has been caused because these statistics include hundreds of small and short-lived companies which were once started on the principle of assessment insurance.[3] Insurance companies on modern lines were hardly in evidence towards the end of the last century. There was only one grand period for Indian insurance: many companies were formed during the period of the cotton boom in Bombay, but they collapsed when the boom ended.[4] At the end of March 1896, the latest date for which details were available, there were 183 insurance companies registered in India, and their total paid-up capital amounted to Rs.899,010.[5] On scrutiny it was found that only those listed in the table on p. 181 could properly be described as insurance companies.

[1] T.O.I., 2 January 1892.
[2] S.T.B.I., 1901, pp. 142–9.
[3] See Chapter 10.
[4] Between 1863 and 1876, 33 insurance companies were registered in Bombay alone. Most of these were formed during the boom. S.T.B.I., 1877.
[5] S.T.B.I., 1897.

Business Corporations in India, 1851–1900

Name of Company	Business	No.	Capital (Paid)	Place & Year (started)
Triton Insurance Co.	Marine	1	Rs.450,000	Bengal, 1850[a]
Indian Guarantee & Suretyship Assoc.	Guarantee	1	50,000	Bombay, 1872
Oriental Govt. Security Life Assoc.	Life	1	150,000	Bombay, 1874
Indian Life Assoc. Co.	Life	1	60,140	Bombay, 1892
—	Life	3	101,100	Mysore, —
		—	Rs.811,240	

[a] The name of Triton does not appear in the list of companies mentioned in India up to the end of March, 1882. But it is mentioned as having originated in 1850, by R. P. F. Smallwood, in his article, 'The Nature and Structure of Insurance Markets in the Far East,' *Journal of the Chartered Insurance Institute*, Vol. 59, p. 84. The company is still operating. See also 'Transacting Fire Business in India and Pakistan', JCII, Vol. 46, 1957–8. Later in 1896 one more company was registered. This was the Bharat Insurance Company, Limited, which is still operating. Smallwood, *op. cit.*

These details fairly depict the state of Indian insurance business. There were three main reasons which held back the growth of insurance companies in India. These were: (*a*) lack of knowledge of the principles of modern insurance among the Indian entrepreneurs; (*b*) the poverty of the people coupled with the security of the kind provided by insurance inherent in the joint-family system; and (*c*) the 'invasion' by numerous insurance companies of all kinds from other parts of the world which solicited business in the country through European agency houses. Business done on behalf of foreign companies was mainly in the fields of marine and fire insurance. There was a great increase in such business during the last three decades of the nineteenth century. The tie-up of external trade with lucrative insurance business in the hands of European agency houses removed the impetus which these houses would have otherwise had in developing these lines independently, signs of which were most strongly in evidence during the 1860's.[1]

[1] Of the thirty-three companies mentioned in p. 181, note 4, twenty-nine were marine insurance companies.

MISCELLANEOUS

Apart from the companies already dealt with in the preceding pages, at the end of March 1901, there were a further 516 companies in existence. Their industrial classification appears below:

	Number	*Capital (Paid)*
Navigation	9	Rs.26,26,102
Co-operative Association	28	6,32,938
Shipping, Landing & Warehousing	5	15,04,100
Printing, Publishing & Stationery	30	5,15,372
Miscellaneous Trading	190	3,27,11,225
Cotton & Jute Screws & Presses	116	1,64,85,374
Paper Mills	7	52,49,620
Rice Mills	3	1,23,766
Flour Mills	20	30,49,738
Saw & Timber Mills	3	4,05,000
Misc. Mills & Presses	19	5,79,017
Coffee & Chinchona	4	1,57,570
Misc. Planting	12	12,12,472
Gold Mining	9	21,27,699
Misc. Mining	15	16,16,682
Land & Building	5	65,59,100
Breweries	4	17,00,000
Ice Mfg.	10	15,97,537
Sugar	10	36,66,651
Others	17	43,09,965
	516	8,68,29,928

Together, these companies constituted 37·7% of the total number of companies registered in India at this time, but in terms of paid-up capital, their share was only 23·4%. It is not possible to deal separately with all the categories of companies listed above. A few comments on some of them may, however, prove helpful in understanding the trend of their development, which is shown in Appendix 17.

Co-operative Associations

Until late in the first decade of the present century there was no separate statute for the registration of these associations and, therefore, they were of necessity registered under the Companies Act.

Miscellaneous Trading Companies

They form the largest single group of companies in the preceding table. A considerable proportion of the sum invested in these companies was for the purpose of retail stores in Bombay and Calcutta.[1]

Miscellaneous Mining Companies

Most of these companies were in the business of stone quarrying in Bengal.

Sugar Companies

The sugar industry tended to expand rapidly towards the end of last century. From the very beginning, the expansion of this industry was bound up with the question of tariffs. In the nineties there was a sudden increase in the imports of the bounty-fed continental beet sugar into the country. This led to a considerable agitation and as a result countervailing duties were imposed which helped this industry to grow rapidly.

CONCLUSIONS

Earlier in this chapter the question was raised: 'Was there any scope for further expansion of the corporate sector in India?' The question has already been partly answered in the preceding pages: capitalists were willing to invest funds in such industries as by now had become established, e.g. jute, tea, and cotton textiles, but the output of these industries could not be increased any further on account of the limited demand. The limitations imposed by the nature of Indian entrepreneurship further restricted the mobility of capital from one region to another. The flow of foreign investments into industries other than jute, tea, railways and coal was adversely affected by the uncertainties created by the fall in the exchange rate and government policy with regard to industrial development.

The devaluation of a currency at long intervals, in itself, is no bar to the investment of foreign capital. An unpegged currency, if fairly stable, is again no obstacle to such investment. But if the value of a currency involves a large element of uncertainty, a foreign capitalist must think very seriously before he invests. His

---

[1] See the Explanatory Memoranda in S.T.B.I., 1897.

anxieties arise from his inability to calculate the likely depreciation of his capital if he wished to repatriate it at a later date. Similarly, he must also be able to form some judgement about the loss on the transfer of his profits. If he thinks that the income from investment will outweigh the likely depreciation of currency, he can be expected to invest. But the fall in the exchange rate had become very uncertain during the period under study and therefore such calculations were not possible. In the circumstances the margin of profit had to be very high indeed for any capitalist to take the risk of investing in India.

In the case of the tea and jute industries in which sterling investment was very prominent, the situation was a little different in that they had become fairly well established before the depreciation of the rupee became really serious, and, most important of all, the income from these industries arose mainly outside India. Investment in other fields, if made, would have produced income mainly in India; besides, the management of companies sponsored in England had, of necessity, to be done through the managing agency houses whose charges were high. Moreover, the control of the Government of India, directly or indirectly, over the whole question of industrial development was bound to make foreign investors chary of the prospects. Its vacillatory policy regarding the development of the iron and steel industry is a case in point. The Government was the largest single buyer in this field but there was no significant change in the 'shopping habits' of the Secretary of State for India who continued to buy nearly all stores in England to the end of the century.

The investment in industries such as coal mining was inhibited firstly by a lack of demand which depended on the development of primary industries like iron and steel, and secondly, by inadequate transport facilities as evidenced by the delay in the development of the Jharia coal fields, and imports of foreign coal by industries situated on the west coast. The government expenditure on 'social overheads' was, of course, tied up, among other things, with its ability to raise revenue. Every year the Government of India had to remit a large sum of money to England from the revenues of India to meet the 'home charges', payment of interest on sterling loans, and the railway guarantees. The depreciation of the rupee during the last three decades of the nineteenth century not only greatly increased the existing burden, but as the British investors, quite legitimately, would not touch the rupee loans of the Government, the latter had no alternative but to go on increasing its sterling liabilities.

The frontier wars and natural calamities added further to the creation of unproductive debts. Consequently not only had the building of social overheads to suffer (because the Government could not find money to finance such projects) but old taxes had to be increased and new taxes levied on trade, industry and incomes to meet these bills. This has been a sore point for such a long time to the Indian historians and the arguments are so well known that it is not necessary to repeat them here.

The growth of a large number of assessment insurance companies, savings and mutual loan societies, and the gold mining craze in Bengal referred to earlier, is discussed in the following chapter.

CHAPTER 10

SAVINGS, INSURANCE, AND THE GOLD MINING COMPANIES

As mentioned earlier,[1] during the eighties and nineties of the past century a large number of mutual savings and loan companies, assessment insurance companies and gold mining companies were formed in different parts of India. Together they accounted for just over two-fifths of the total registrations during 1851–1901 and 44% of all dissolutions. Of these, the mutual savings and loan companies were the most numerous.

MUTUAL SAVINGS AND LOAN COMPANIES

According to official records, 1,126 companies were registered under the heading 'Banking and Loan Companies' during the fifty years from 1851. 1,025 of these were merely mutual savings and loan societies or *nidhis* as they are called in India.

About 1850 a 'Sudder Court Fund' was started to enable the officials in Madras to borrow money in case of need at a reasonable rate of interest and to save them from usury.[2] The Fund was modelled on the English Building Society though no particular reason can be traced for doing so. At first it was a terminating fund established for six months at the end of which members were paid back at the rate of Rs.102$\frac{1}{2}$ for a monthly subscription of one rupee. The Fund lent on $6\frac{1}{4}$% per annum but charged penalties on overdue accounts. Subsequently branches were opened and the Fund was made permanent.[3]

The idea spread rapidly and many funds were started in no time. In some the periodic collection was put up to a Dutch auction; the member offering the biggest discount getting the loan. Others charged fixed but higher rates of interest varying from

---

[1] See pp. 176–7.
[2] *Report of the Madras Provincial Banking Enquiry Committee*, Vol. I, 1930, p. 33, para. 72.
[3] *Ibid.*

10 to 15%. In 1872, the Madras High Court held that these societies had no legal existence since they were not registered under the Companies Act and, therefore, could not institute any money suit. The result was that many debtors refused to pay and the societies collapsed. Their losses amounted to an estimated 2,000,000 rupees.[1] The societies were thus forced to register. In Madras alone thirteen *nidhis* were registered in 1872 compared with only one each in 1869 and 1870 and none in 1871. By the end of March 1901 total registrations in Madras had reached 741. The idea of these societies was also very popular in the neighbouring state of Mysore which accounted for 191 registrations. Fifty-three companies were formed in the eastern district of Bengal and of the total of 1,025 companies, the remaining forty were located in the Punjab, the North-West Provinces and Bombay.

In all 605 companies were wound up by the end of March 1901. Many of those liquidated were fraudulent, formed only to benefit their promotors, and therefore disappeared after a short and hectic life. Many others were dissolved because they were formed only for a term of years. But as far back as 1872 some companies were already being formed on a permanent instead of a terminating basis.[2] The trend towards permanent societies was further accelerated by a High Court decision by which all members who had completed their subscriptions, received the money back and left the *nidhi*, were still considered liable for the debts of the *nidhi*, because such a withdrawal was regarded as a reduction of share capital without the approval of the court.[3] Many societies founded during the last century were highly successful and some continue to prosper even to this day. Table 18 shows the large financial resources of these companies. They had in addition built up sizeable reserves and, like banks, received deposits and opened branches.

The *nidhis* have sometimes been confused with another South Indian institution of very old origin called the 'Chitfund'.[4] Although a Chitfund is distinct from a *nidhi*, it is not always easy

---

[1] *Report of the Madras Provincial Banking Enquiry Committee*, Vol. 1, 1930 p. 33, para. 72.

[2] See S.T.B.I., 1883. This is suggested by the use of the word 'permanent' n the names of companies.

[3] *Report of the Madras Provincial Banking Enquiry Committee*, p. 196.

[4] Sir F. Nicholson grouped the Chitfunds and the *nidhis* together in his *Report on the Possibility of Introducing Land Banks into India*, 1895–8.

Savings Companies

Table 18

Frequency Distribution of the Savings & Loan Companies Registered from January 1869 to March 1882

Region	Size of Paid-up Capital in Rs.(000's)			
	10–50	50 + 1 − 100	100 + 1 − OVER	TOTAL
Madras	59	16	19	94
Mysore	36	2	4	42
Bengal	8	2	—	10
	103	20	23	146[a]

[a] Out of a total of 236 registered during the period.

to distinguish the two. This is how an Indian Judge described a Chitfund in the eighties:[1]

In this Presidency, Madras, and especially in the Presidency Town, numerous companies are formed under the designation of 'Chit-Fund'. Some twenty-five persons (more or less) club together and agree to subscribe, each a certain sum, say Rs.25, by instalments of one rupee a month. Each subscriber in his turn, which is determined by lot once for all, receives the total amount of a month's subscription, 25 rupees, on the understanding that he shall continue to pay his monthly subscriptions regularly up to the end of the prescribed period (twenty-five months). One of the subscribers is appointed an agent, who collects the subscriptions each month, pays the same to the subscriber who gets the prize in that month, upon his executing a promissory note in favour of the agent, or the company itself for the difference between the amount of subscriptions which he has already paid and that which will have to be paid till the termination of the fund.

In fact they were operated in a variety of ways, not always fair.[2] And despite legal difficulties[3] and malpractices they continued to be formed in large numbers.

[1] See a Memorandum by P. Sreenevas Rao, Judge, Court of Small Causes, Madras, J.P., 1882, Departmental No. 125.

[2] For details see *Report of the Madras Provincial Banking Enquiry Committee*, pp. 228–35.

[3] Not until 1863 was it clear whether Chitfunds were not a form of lottery which was illegal in India. See *Kamakshi vs. Appavu Pillay*, I, *Madras High Courts Reports*, 448. For other legal problems see several cases cited in 8, *Madras High Court Report*, 193.

Both the Chitfunds and the *nidhis* were formed with the aim to enable poor people to save small sums regularly which could be used to buy land or jewellery, to pay old debts or expenses on ceremonial occasions such as marriages. In other words, the Chitfunds were primarily adapted for people living together in a village before communications and other credit institutions were developed, and they still retain their rural character. The *nidhis* on the other hand are found only in towns and over time they have functioned more like a bank, except that they do not open current accounts. The Chitfunds have remained an association in which members subscribe and lend the subscriptions to themselves though occasionally surpluses are lent out as temporary investments.[1] The Companies Act Amendment Committee realised that the *nidhis* suffered many difficulties from having to comply with the requirements of the Companies Acts, and recommended that they be excluded from its operation and be covered by more appropriate State legislation.[2]

ASSESSMENT INSURANCE COMPANIES[3]

The term 'assessment insurance' is applied to a system of mutual insurance in which on the death of a member every surviving member has to contribute a fixed sum which is then paid to the beneficiary of the deceased. This is a fallacious substitute for the life insurance system in which an annual premium based on past mortality experience at the respective attained ages is collected from each member in advance.

Assessment insurance started in India in 1894 with the formation of sixty-four companies in a single year. Progress was remarkable. In 1897, the peak year, as many as 215 assessment companies were registered, a figure exceeding even the total number of

---

[1] *Report of the Madras Provincial Banking Enquiry Committee*, pp. 212–14 and 228–35.

[2] Report, 1957, pp. 184–5.

[3] The statistics of Indian assessment insurance companies are derived from the various issues of S.T.B.I. All other information and quotations are taken from the following issues of the T.O.I.:

1894—27 July and 10 August
1895—28 June and 16 November
1898—24 September
1899—16 September

companies formed in any other year during the nineteenth century. The official statistics of this period show these companies grouped somewhat misleadingly under 'insurance'. They should therefore be used with some caution.

India borrowed the system of assessment insurance from the western world. It seems to have flourished in the United States of America at about the same time and most probably spread to other countries from there. One hundred and thirty-one assessment companies were reported working in the State of New York in 1890. Hundreds had already come to grief; their average life being about nine years. The scheme of assessment insurance had also been tried in Britain, where, as in other places, it had both spread and failed. Leading newspapers, journals and insurance authorities frequently attacked the system which shows how widespread the evil must have been.

According to the *Times of India*, a Mr Scott, then the Deputy Collector of Ratnagiri in the province of Bombay, first introduced this system to India. He founded the Ratnagiri Provident Association in 1887 for the benefit of government employees but they were a bit sceptical of the scheme, so the Association was opened to the public. At the close of 1893 it had 939 members. Typical of its kind, it will serve to illustrate the assessment insurance system.

Anybody waiting to join the Association had to pay an entrance fee of a few annas for every year of his age. The entrance fee was increased by one anna annually while at the same time the maximum age of admission was reduced by one year. This was done with the object of keeping old people out of the society. When a member died, a 'death-call' of one rupee was made on those surviving, which amount was then paid over to the heir of the deceased.

The working of the system is revealed by a report of the Ratnagiri Provident Association issued in 1893. During the seven years of its life, a total of thirty-five members had died. To put the matter in life insurance terms the result was that for a monthly premium of about eight annas, the members had secured to themselves a possible benefit of Rs.1,000. In the eleven cases cited in the report, the members had received Rs.6,931 for an outlay of only Rs.315, or, as the report put it, the members had secured a 'net profit of Rs.6,616'. The report further revealed that in 1893 the total income of the Association amounted to Rs.27,000, while the total expenditure was only Rs.7,000. The prospects which these societies thus held out naturally attracted many people to become their members.

If the assessments payable by the respective persons insured under an assessment plan were to be determined proportionately to the actual death rates at the several attained ages of the members during each year, the resulting cost would work out about the same as under a modern yearly-renewable-term plan. There cannot be a fundamental difference between them. Theoretically an assessment scheme might therefore be worked indefinitely. In practice, however, assessments were not graded properly by attained age although it was realised that a member's assessment ought to bear some relation to his age. Generally, all members were assessed equally, irrespective of age, in the mistaken belief that all that was needed was to ensure a continuous inflow of young members to keep the average age of the whole group nearly the same. But the assumption that if the average age of all members does not increase, the total death rate will not increase is fallacious. As the earlier members reach higher ages, assessments increase in frequency which must adversely affect the ability to secure and retain new and young members. Therefore with the decrease in the number of members the sum assured at death also diminished in proportion until each of the last half dozen surviving members who had paid out most money had a prospect of receiving only five rupees instead of a possible thousand, which made it impracticable for such organisations to remain viable for long.

Very likely, the initial promoters of assessment schemes honestly believed that subscribers would benefit, but the popularity of these schemes soon attracted many unscrupulous operators concerned only with gaining 5% managing agency commission for their own pockets. The spread of these companies was attacked by both the local and English language newspapers. New registrations declined considerably in 1895 but the following year brought a fresh spate. Promoters tried to counter hostile press criticism by making worthless modifications in company constitutions and emphasising the honesty and professional qualifications of people managing the companies. But, as the *Times of India* rightly pointed out, no amount of honesty and professional expertise could ever make a silk purse out of a sow's ear.

The clamour of press criticism led clever minds to devising new forms of assessment companies and the Indian society provided a grand field for their operation. Their activities centred on the eastern districts of Bengal. According to the report of the Commissioner of the Presidency Division for the year ending March 1895, the new type of assessment company originated in Beckergunj whence it spread to the eastern sub-divisions of the district. Companies registered in the year of the report included:

Death Companies	85
Marriage Companies	15
Birth Companies	3
Fever Companies	1
Pilgrimage Companies	1
	105

Promoted by Indians, these companies possessed no share capital in the ordinary sense of the word and had no investments. The number of shares in each company was usually fixed: generally a share cost only one rupee and often less. There was an entrance fee of a few annas. In the case of smaller companies, the preliminary expenses such as the cost of registration, establishment, postage and printing absorbed most of the money received for these 'shares'.

As mentioned earlier, in a death company each shareholder was allowed to hold only one share and could nominate his beneficiary. On the death of a shareholder, the directors called up (from each surviving shareholder) a sum, generally equivalent to the face value of the share held by the deceased. The amount collected was paid to the nominee.

Marriage and birth companies operated on similar lines, the only difference being that the nominee had to be a female who was entitled on marriage or on the birth of a child to a sum collected in the same manner. The object of the fever company was to provide fever-stricken members with funds for treatment out of a regular monthly subscription of six pies collected by the company. It ceased operations in 1895. The Pilgrimage Provident Fund had a share capital divided into 2,000 shares. Members had to contribute a sum 'not exceeding Rs.2 per month' and they were entitled to receive a certain sum in cash while on pilgrimage; this right passed on to the nominee in case of premature death.

The growth of these new assessment companies was not entirely confined to the eastern districts of Bengal. In western India, Guzerat provided a happy hunting ground for their promoters. According to the *Times of India* in Ahmedabad alone no fewer than twenty-six companies were registered in the year ending 31 March 1899, while twenty-six more were formed in Nadiad and many others in even such small towns as Kaira, Umerath and Thasra. However, all these companies collapsed soon after they were started, for the reasons already discussed.

The desire for economic security is deeply rooted in human beings. Insurance companies (as we understand the term) had been working in India for a long time but it is very doubtful whether they could satisfy the desire for security among the mass of Indians without going bankrupt: the cost of issuing policies for very small sums would have been prohibitive. Friendly societies on the British pattern might well have provided the answer but would not, of course, have proved profitable to promoters. Shares in assessment companies were offered as a cheap bargain and cheapness always has an attraction for the poor. Press criticisms in rural areas where these companies were most popular could not have been effective because of both poverty and illiteracy. The trend of registration reversed in 1898 when it fell to twenty-eight companies from the height of 215 attained in the previous year. By the end of 1900 the idea appears to have been so thoroughly discredited that new registrations had ceased altogether. In all, 450 assessment companies were formed in India from 1894 to 1900 and excepting a few, all had been dissolved. Only thirty-one companies were reported operating at the end of March 1901. Many of these were engaged in genuine insurance business and the confusion had largely gone out of these statistics.

BENGAL GOLD CRAZE[1]

Surprising though it may seem, about the middle of 1890 the Calcutta stock market was seized by a gold mining mania. Not

[1] Adapted from my article in the IESHR, Vol. III, No. 1., March, 1966, pp. 53–64 by permission of the Editor. The statistics of gold mining companies are derived from the various issues of the S.T.B.I. For other information, the sources are:
  (a) Weekly Money Market Report in *Englishman* from 5 August 1890 to 30 September 1891.

even those living in those times could have been aware of how the whole thing began, but in the light of available evidence it seems that three factors contributed to its development; the reputed existence of gold both in the form of quartz reef and alluvial deposits in the Chhotanagpur area; the extension of a railway line to the area; and the prevalence of easy monetary conditions. The second and the third factors account for the encouragement of speculation at that particular time.

About June 1890 somebody had the brilliant idea of forming a 'gold syndicate', the 'Kharswan', registered with a nominal capital of Rs.200,000 of which Rs.160,000 had been paid-up. The idea soon attracted the leading agency houses. In July a few more syndicates and companies were formed. It was alleged that the Kharswan had acquired its property for Rs.80,000 and had sold only a portion of it for as much as Rs.3,500,000. This feat naturally fired the imagination of others who immediately formed syndicates to acquire mining rights and launch new gold mining companies. These syndicates issued what were known as 'founders' shares'[1] which could be exchanged for ten or twenty fully paid ordinary shares of any company which such a syndicate might form in future for the purpose of prospecting and/or mining of gold. The face value of these shares was fixed at only a rupee each and they passed by delivery. The whole arrangement was pregnant with mischief. The possibilities it offered for speculation by people of petty means were immense. Whether or not the originators of the scheme were impelled by any sinister idea cannot be known, but that they had planned their success well cannot be doubted. All companies with two or three exceptions had the same capital structure. By the end of July 1890, the City was well on its way to fall into a whirlpool of speculation. On 5 August, in its weekly share market report, the *Englishman*, a leading daily, wrote:

(b) *Englishman* (weekly) from January 1891 to December 1892.

(c) *Statesman and F.O.I.* (weekly) 6 and 13 September 1890 and 26 September 1891.

(d) *Englishman*, leading article, 10 September 1890.

(e) T.O.I., 12 September, and 18 October 1890 and 7 and 21 August and 5 December 1891.

[1] This was not a new idea. Founders' shares were first introduced in India towards the end of the 1870's by a sterling company which opened a cotton mill in India, the first such company to do so. Part of its share capital was offered for subscription in India. In general, founders' share carried a disproportionate voting and/or dividend right.

The first half was comparatively dull and lifeless if we except the transactions in the Manbhoom and the Singbhoom Gold companies, commonly called the 'twins'. Gold companies are being floated in all directions, and as they are mostly shares of only a rupee paid-up, they afford a grand field for speculation. The gold fever too has got such a strong hold on the Calcutta market that these shares soon rise to a premium and an advance of 25% for several consecutive days is no uncommon occurrence.

During the following week whatever cautious attitudes there may have been in the market had given way to considerable excitement and speculation. Several thousand shares of a new company, the Karo, were dealt in at a premium of 150% to 175% within twenty-four hours of allotment. One of the other companies, the Bengal Gold Syndicate, had declared a dividend of 25% 'for the month of July' and the accompanying statement by the management declared that the profits already made would admit of rich dividends for some months to come, without, however, any suggestion of the source whence the profits were derived. In the following week, the Sonapet Gold Syndicate formed itself into a limited liability company with a capital of Rs.1,724,000. Each of the 'original certificates' of the Syndicate, that is, its shares, could be exchanged for ten shares in the new company. The new shares immediately changed hands at a premium of 50% to 60%. The Sonapet was the brain child of F. W. Heilgers & Company, a leading agency house in Calcutta. The conversion of a syndicate into a limited company was a device to enrich the members of the former without in any way benefiting the latter, since the issue of ten fully paid shares in the new company for every one in the syndicate did not add anything to the assets passed on to the new company by the syndicate, whose members reaped much more on their shares than the original certificate in the syndicate had been worth.

The gold fever had got such a hold on the market that during the months of July and August 1890 almost all other business was neglected. Company after company was floated and the existing companies increased their capital. Following the example of the Sonapet, the Chhotanagpur increased its capital from a mere Rs.200,000 to Rs.1,500,000. On September 2, the fever reached its peak. Transactions in some of the leading shares were reported at the following prices:

Gold Mining Companies

Bengal Gold	Rs.	11, $11\frac{1}{4}$, $11\frac{1}{2}$		
Chhotanagpur		12, $12\frac{1}{2}$, 13, 14		
Manbhoom		6, $6\frac{1}{4}$, $6\frac{3}{4}$, $6\frac{1}{2}$, $6\frac{1}{4}$		
Sonapet		$1\frac{15}{16}$, $1\frac{7}{8}$		

There was a mad rush for shares in all gold companies and an enormous number changed hands. According to newspaper reports the share market was the scene of intense and wild excitement passing all expectations. The launching of the Pat Pat Gold Company under the managing agency of Kilburn & Company, one of the oldest and most influential houses, added fuel to the fire. The office of the managing agents was 'literally besieged by an excited crowd eager to get in their tenders for the shares at par'. The week after business in gold shares was still brisk, but the wild excitement had subsided considerably. The announcement of a new company with enormous capital and rumours of others with equally large capital proved an effective antidote to the raging fever. The public had become suspicious of the numerous gold companies and had begun to discriminate between them; some companies were still quoted at the previous high level but others were at a discount. During the following week the market assumed an even tenor but this was merely the lull before the storm. A few days later, another burst of wild excitement outdid even the earlier frenzy. The City Editor of the *Englishman* reported on 24 September:

All classes are dabbling more or less in gold shares, but the Marwarees, whose love for gambling is proverbial, have taken to these shares with a zest never before witnessed, the share market is a perfect Babel of Confusion.

Prices again advanced rapidly. Some companies regarding which 'some exceptionally good things' had transpired made considerable gains; others advanced at a more steady rate. The largest rise was recorded in the 'Ranchis', having been freely offered at Rs.$1\frac{3}{4}$ on the first day, they rose to Rs.15 by the weekend on the news that the company had acquired 'a most important and very valuable concession'. The market opened next week with the same firmness but prices eased slightly towards the end.

Then the inevitable happened. The signs of weakness observed at the close of the previous week were symptomatic of what was to follow, but nobody seems to have anticipated the panic which actually set in almost immediately, leading to a complete collapse of prices. The cause of this crisis, in the opinion of the financial editor of the *Englishman*, was the rapidity with which company had followed company with share issues, and the consequent inability of a large number of speculators (principally Indians, who had bought largely for settlement) to meet their obligations. The true reason is that the bubble had burst.

Market movement had been the product of rumours; the rise or fall in share prices cannot be attributed to anything but to various 'good' or 'bad' reports or, as the *Englishman* put it, the 'successful manipulation of concessions and companies'. Reports on the analysis of the gold content in quartz, authenticated by responsible and disinterested parties, had never been put before the public. Moreover, the leading newspapers of the country, who had been watching these developments but had remained rather quiet, were suddenly aroused by the mania of early September, and vigorously attacked what was going on. The *Englishman* issued the following warning on 10 September 1890:

It is estimated that a crore of rupees has changed hands during the past week or two . . . it is to be feared that several of the Catchpenny companies of today will be a matter of unpleasant reminiscence at no distant past. [But people] do not view the 'gold rush' more seriously than if it were a gigantic Derby Sweep. The fascination of the game has even reached the Durwans [hall porters] of Calcutta, who are known to have taken a rather sporting part in the lively proceedings of the past few weeks.

More than a thousand miles away in Bombay, the *Times of India* wrote in the same vein:[1]

It scarcely needs a Sibyl to prophesy the outcome of the Bengal Gold Craze. Tea, jute, cotton, all have given way to a craze as wild and reckless as anything that has been known in the financial world since the days of the South Sea Bubble. . . . Gambling it is, pure and simple; none of the gold has been seen, no responsible person has had courage enough to vouch for the wonderful discoveries reported almost daily. . . . The fate of the speculators will be classic.

The warning by the financial writer of the *Statesman and Friend of India* evoked much public interest.[2]

---

[1] 12 September 1890.
[2] See a letter to the Editor by 'An Old Merchant', F.O.I., (weekly), 6 September 1890.

Gold Mining Companies

The panic had some beneficial effects by nipping in the bud many fresh ventures on the eve of their blossoming. The heavy fall in the prices brought forward some buyers towards the end of the week and the market rallied again but only moderately. Thereafter, the market became irregular and selective. By the end of 1890, the shares of even the popular companies were selling at 50% below face value. A good deal of interest in gold shares subsisted, however, and new companies continued to be formed. The market hardened a little at the beginning of 1891 and in some instances prices doubled again.

This favourable turn had some very slender roots—attributed to the excellent results obtained from an experimental crushing of two tons of quartz from the Pat Pat mines, under the managing agency of Kilburn & Company. The market eased after about two weeks and continued irregular with a downward trend, with the Marwaris selling and the Europeans buying. About the middle of May 1891, the 'discovery of a nugget on the Sonapet property (managing agents—F. W. Heilgers & Company) as also several pieces of reef gold and a favourable opinion from the Company's manager' gave the gold market a fresh impetus. Prices rose rapidly until they stopped just short of Rs.2. For nearly another month fairly large parcels of shares changed hands but the marked lacked buoyancy. Indian speculators had begun to take all the 'good news' with a pinch of salt and believed in taking quick profits. The Marwari speculators found the prospects held by the Sonapet to be far from bright, which brought on a heavy drop in prices in the last week of August. This event surprised the Europeans. To quote the financial editor of the *Englishman*:

... the calculations of the wisest are frequently upset, and in this, as in former instances, the Marwari has proved one too many for the general public. It is difficult to ascertain the sources whence he derives his information, but that it is correct in nine cases out of ten, and that he has it before anyone else, is a fact which cannot be contradicted.

In the following weeks prices fell further still and the market became altogether crippled. There were to be no more recoveries. After being quoted at one or two annas for a few more months, gold shares were to be found no more in share market reports. In the newspapers, legal proceedings and rowdy shareholders' meetings replaced them. Some companies had gone into voluntary liquidation after selling their 'valuable' mining rights; some were brought to the courts with great difficulty; some settled their affairs outside the court for fear of conviction; many others simply lingered on the Register of Companies to be finally struck off at the end of the century.

Nearly all the leading houses were inexorably implicated in perhaps the worst kind of fraud. The two cases which drew most attention were those of the Jut Put Company under the manging agency of Posner & Company, and the Dhadka under Vansittart. The disclosures in the Dhadka case were startling. The agency of this company had been offered in the first instance to Jardine, Skinner & Company, who had refused it. F. W. Heilgers & Company, who took up the agency, seemingly failed to exercise control by continuing to leave the Dhadka Company in the hands of C. G. Vansittart, the *pro tem* managing director. Vansittart withdrew the whole capital of the Company from the Bank of Bengal and deposited it with the Bengal Trust and Loan Company. The shares of the latter company stood in the name of Vansittart and his wife except for five lots of ten shares each, registered in the name of his employees or nominees. One of them was Critchley who acted for Vansittart when the latter left for England. Critchley thus represented both the debtor and the creditor companies. The Dhadka shareholders approached Critchley to produce the capital of the Company, amounting to Rs.330,000. He told them that he could not do so, and declined to say what had become of the money. Mr Agnew of Macneil & Company and Siddens of Place, Siddens and Gough then offered to receive subscriptions from the shareholders to start legal proceedings. A shareholders' meeting was held later to consider whether to take steps to recover the Dhadka capital and/or wind up the company. However, by then the atmosphere had changed, inasmuch as the European shareholders appeared to have made common front which gave rise to some racial tension among the shareholders, as appears from this report in the *Englishman*:[1]

The meeting was numerously attended, and at one time threatened to become very disorderly owing to the manner in which Mr Critchley attempted to 'sit upon' a wealthy native shareholder. Mr Vansittart's friends mustered in force, and from the very outset it was obvious they would have things their own way. The first Resolution proposed . . .

[1] 21 August 1891.

that 'the opinion of the Hon'ble Mr Evans (solicitor) be adopted and steps taken to inforce recovery and replacement in the Bank of Bengal of the capital monies of the company withdrawn by the managing director'.

One would have thought that Mr Vansittart's friends would have agreed to this resolution, in their own interest, as shareholders; their money has disappeared, but, as the result showed, they seemed quite content to let it go. This is not the usual conduct of ordinary prudent businessmen, and considering their position, simply as shareholders, their action is incomprehensible.

When the above resolution was carried by a show of hands . . . Mr Vansittart's friends immediately demanded a poll, which Mr Agnew, the chairman of the meeting, settled should be taken at once. As there is a clause in the Articles of Association to the effect that no person, as bearer of a share warrant, shall be entitled to vote at a meeting without producing a share warrant, and some people present had forgotten to bring their warrants, the decision of the chairman to take the poll at once caused a moment's confusion . . . Mr Vansittart's party rejected the Resolution polling 125,000 votes while those in favour . . . polled 100,800. . . . The Resolution to wind up the Company was also defeated.

Within a year from June 1890, thirty-five gold companies had been registered with a paid-up capital aggregating about Rs. 8,000,000 but the amount of money that really changed hands in payment to the vendors and in the share market in fact ran into hundreds of millions. None of these companies had been promoted by Indians.

It is therefore a little surprising that although almost every European managing agency house in Calcutta was involved in these promotions, they either did not try or failed in their attempts to persuade investors at home to launch even a single sterling company. If Indians gambled heavily in gold shares, they did this with their eyes wide open, but it was the weight of the European agency houses which gave the impetus and kept the ball rolling for so long. Their conduct was severely criticised as early as 6 September 1890 in a letter to the Editor of the *Statesman and Friend of India*:

What seems to me most surprising is that mercantile firms of respectability and long-standing in this city such as Messrs Gillanders, Arbuthnot and Co., and others, should have so far forgotten what they owe to themselves as to lend their names to the support of projects which are wanting in all the elements of fair and reasonable speculation.

A project (Tamar Gold Prospecting Company) more monstrous has not as far as I am aware been broached before the mercantile world within the present generation . . . And I must say that I had thought that a firm like Messrs Kilburn & Co. would have been alone chaperoning an enterprise which men without any credit or reputation to lose would have been ashamed to identify themselves with. . . .

However, these criticisms do not seem to have affected the course these agency houses had embarked upon. In some cases their principals in London had reproved them but that was all. When the first panic seized the market and the confidence of the public in the reports issued or leaked by these houses was rudely shaken, they resorted to other methods, such as bringing gold mining experts from famous British firms, or involving others like Bosworth Smith, who was well known for his Australian experience. After a while, even the statements by these gentlemen ceased to have any effect on the public and the life finally went out of the gold speculation.

The episode of the Bengal gold craze is important for several reasons. It showed the conduct of the European managing agencies not to have been above reproach since they alone promoted the shady gold mining companies. The manner in which they conducted the meeting of the shareholders of the Dhadka lays them open to even more serious charges. The gold craze also brought the share market in Calcutta into the limelight and demonstrated the necessity for a formal organisation to protect the public from unscrupulous sharebrokers and fraudulent companies.

So far this book has been concerned with details of the growth of the corporate sector between 1851 and 1900. The two following chapters examine the overall trends in the field of financing and managing business corporations, and the final chapter discusses whether the economic growth in India was aborted in the second half of last century.

TRENDS IN CORPORATE FINANCING AND LEGAL DEVELOPMENTS

The experience of industrial entrepreneurs with joint stock companies between 1850 and 1870 significantly changed their ideas about the capital structure of a company, that is, about a proper nominal value of ordinary shares, the methods of raising loan capital, and its relationship with the equity capital.

With the passage of time, the number of corporations increased greatly. The promoters of new companies were obliged, therefore, to reach a wider public in an effort to raise capital. The public had, in the meantime, become better acquainted with the workings of companies and their willingness to invest in them naturally increased. Thus the class of investing public widened gradually, bringing into its fold many whose means were definitely limited.

In the fifties and the sixties it was quite usual to have shares of the denomination of Rs.5,000 and Rs.2,500, as they were generally taken up by wealthy merchants or occasionally by the rulers of Indian states and rich landlords. But as the demand for capital grew and the composition of the investors changed, the shares of high face value became difficult to negotiate. It was said that the reason why the shares of the Royal Cotton Mills of Bombay were selling at a discount of Rs.400 to Rs.500 in 1873 was that the high face value of these shares made it difficult for many people to invest in them.[1] It was realised that the unit value of the shares needed to be drastically reduced but there were some legal difficulties in doing so. Strictly speaking, the face value of the shares could not be legally reduced without first going into voluntary liquidation,[2] and this was the course that the Great Eastern

---

[1] T.O.I., 28 April 1873.

[2] Section XII of the *Act of 1866* reads as follows:

'Any Company limited by shares may so far modify the conditions contained in its memorandum of association, if authorised to do so by its regulations as originally framed, or as altered by Special Resolution in manner hereafter mentioned, as to increase its capital, by the issue of new shares of such amount as it thinks expedient, or to consolidate and divide its capital *into shares of larger amount than its existing shares*, or to convert its paid-up shares into stock,

Spinning and Weaving Co. Ltd., had decided to take.[1] But there seems to have been some confusion about the correct interpretation of the law on this point. The Colaba Spinning and Weaving Co. Ltd.,[2] and the India General Steam Navigation Co. Ltd.,[3] for instance, did not observe the legal niceties while changing their share value. Thus in the seventies and eighties, and even more in the years following, shares of the value of Rs.1,000, Rs.500, Rs.250 and Rs.100 were issued. An exceptional and extreme step in this direction was taken in 1890 when the Calcutta market was seized with a craze for gold mining; all the three dozen or so companies floated in that period issued only one rupee shares.[4] A gradual reduction in the nominal value of shares was certainly a correct move. The issue of one rupee shares was, however, no more than a device to attract the poor and ignorant.

Hitherto,[5] the practice had been to raise the great bulk of the working capital by private borrowing from local banks and shroffs against the hypothecation of the stores, and by mortgaging the fixed assets of the company. Loans arranged in this way had the disadvantages, first, of being relatively costly in terms of interest rates and secondly, of being subject to greater pressure from the individual lenders for repayment in times of monetary stringency or whenever the company ran into difficulties. From the company's point of view this aggravated its difficulties still further and caused much embarrassment which led, at times, to foreclosures of mortgage on its properties and its liquidation.[6]

---

but, save as aforesaid, and save as hereinafter provided in the case of a change of name, no alteration shall be made by any company in the conditions contained in its memorandum of association'.

[1] T.O.I., 28 April 1873.   [2] *Ibid.*, 1 August 1874.

[3] In 1881 the company changed the nominal value of its shares from Rs.1,000 each to Rs.100 each. 'It was considered that the larger sum was too unwieldy for the local market, other companies consisting almost wholly of Rs.100 shares, and to have retained the unit of Rs.1,000 would have handicapped dealings and made the scrip issue less accessible to small investors.' Brame, p. 132.

[4] See Chapter 10.   [5] See p. 235.

[6] Reviewing the reasons for the crisis in the cotton mill industry, James Greaves of Greaves, Cotton & Co., said: 'Another cause which has been making itself felt, is the insufficiency of the share capital invested in these undertakings. Borrowed capital is all very well in its place, and in prosperous times is a great advantage to the shareholders, but if adversity comes, the loans are called in and have to be replaced at heavy rates of interest, which I need hardly add militates against the successful working of the mills and very often leads to embarrassment'. T.O.I., April 1879. See also: T.O.I., 8 December 1879; 31 May 1881; 29 April 1878; and 17 February 1879.

A loan had, therefore, come to be regarded in the seventies as a curse and a parasite which sucks the life-blood out of a cotton or jute mill. This was certainly a very poor way of meeting the deficiency of equity capital. Press criticism enlightened the shareholders and a change followed. Both preference shares and debentures were used to replace private borrowing but only debentures can be said to have acquired a certain popularity in the remaining years of the century.[1] Criticisms in the press, particularly in periods of depression when dividends either disappeared or were declared out of capital, also did a great deal to change the concepts of the management about a proper policy towards depreciation, dividends and reserves. Almost to the end of the seventies, depreciation as an item in the profit and loss account was ignored, stocks were overvalued and dividends fluctuated. In Bombay the lead for a change of methods was given, once again, by the firm of Greaves, Cotton & Company. The mills under their management followed a consistent policy of building up a dividend equalisation reserve and declaring a steady 10% in dividends.[2] On the other hand, J. N. Tata seems to have been the first to declare his support for a policy of sufficient depreciation allowance before arriving at the net profit figure.[3] In Calcutta the change of heart began about the year 1879, after the unreserved criticisms by the *Friend of India*,[4] and it was not long afterwards that the policy of providing for depreciation became general. General reserves were also started by some companies to finance expansion and in some cases these were later capitalised by the issue of bonus shares.[5] This must have been a particularly difficult task for the management to achieve, as the pressure from the shareholders for large dividends was great, and this probably accounts in part, at least, for the reluctance of the management to build up reserves.

Another interesting experiment in the technique of financial management was the issue of bearer dividend warrants. This was obviously introduced for the purpose of facilitating the use of an already widely used practice of blank transfer of shares.[6] The

[1] See a list of debentures issued in Calcutta in T.O.I., 30 May 1880 and share market quotations in any issue of the F.O.I. or the *Englishman* in 1900.

[2] T.O.I., 4 January 1884.   [3] *Ibid.*, 17 August 1886.

[4] Various issues. See, for instance, 24 March 1880; 28 November 1881; 9 November 1877; 28 September 1877.

[5] T.O.I., 28 March 1882 (on the Empress Mill).

[6] T.O.I., 18 October 1890.

only thing the registered shareholder had to do now was to send the bearer warrant to the holder of the blank transfer.

Dealings in government securities and shares of such companies as then existed were a feature of business life in Calcutta and Bombay long before 1850. Business in these instruments of finance had become particularly important in the early sixties as a result of the speculative boom in those years. The enthusiasm generated by the boom in Calcutta was such that the European bill and share brokers of the city thought it fit to organise a stock exchange. There is a reference in the *Thacker's Bengal Directory* of 1864 to a 'Stock Exchange' at 11, Strand in Calcutta. Out of the thirty-six Europeans listed as bill and share brokers, fourteen were named as the members of this Stock Exchange. The only other information recorded about this institution was that 'a room, where leading foreign and local papers, together with the latest telegraphic despatches, were available was open to the subscribers paying Rs.5 a month'.[1] It is doubtful if this institution ever achieved anything more than providing a meeting-place and an information service.

There was, however, in existence another institution in Calcutta which was founded on 1 June 1858 at 1, Clive Row. This was a mercantile exchange and had a managing committee of nine persons, one of whom, Ramgopal Ghose, was an Indian.[2] In 1867 its offices were removed to 102, Clive Street where they remained until, in 1893, they were again shifted to the Royal Exchange Buildings. Although the institution had been variously described before 1867 as 'The Exchange' or 'The Merchants' Exchange', during the rest of the century it was always designated as 'The Brokers' Exchange'.[3] The *Friend of India* headed its share market quotations as the 'Official Quotation' and they were supplied by the 'Brokers' Exchange',[4] The management committee of the Brokers' Exchange met regularly on the first Saturday of every month. Unfortunately, our researches have not revealed any further information about this institution, though it would seem to have been an attempt to organise the share market in Calcutta.

In the sixties the Indian element in the share bazaar in Calcutta was not large, whilst the Brokers' Exchange was a purely European organisation both in its membership and management. The

---

[1] *Thacker's Bengal Directory for 1864*, p. 85.   [2] *Ibid.*
[3] *Ibid.*, for 1868.   [4] See any stock market report in 1876, 1877 and 1878.

business of dealings in shares and other securities was done under a Neem tree, where all the brokers met. When the Bengal Chamber of Commerce acquired in 1893 the buildings of the Oriental Bank and renovated and renamed them the Royal Exchange Buildings, an attempt was made to remove the share bazaar from under the Neem tree to this building, but the admission of Indians, particularly of the Marwaris, who had by now become the mainstay of the share market, led to some controversy as they were regarded as 'noisy'. It was, however, admitted that without their presence it would be useless to think of any shift in location. To resolve the dilemma, a suggestion was put forward that a partition wall might be built in the proposed hall. Nothing, however, seems to have come out of this proposal and the share market remained under the Neem tree until, in 1908, the Calcutta Stock Exchange was formally constituted.[1]

Business in the share market in the nineteenth century, it would seem, was conducted by established customs of the city rather than any formal rules, for, as late as 1927 the *Indian Year Book* reported

[1] The following books on Indian capital markets, industrial financing and the development of stock exchanges may be usefully consulted:

S. K. Basu—*Industrial Finance in India*, 1939.
K. L. Garg—*Stock Exchanges in India*, 1946.
M. A. Mulky—*New Capital Issues Market in India*, 1947.
P. C. Jain—*Industrial Finance in India* (1961 ?).
R. C. Mehta—*Capital Market in India for Planned Growth*, 1965.
Stock Exchange [London] Official Year Book
Calcutta Stock Exchange Official Year Book, 2 volumes, 1940–2.
Madras Stock Exchange Official Year Book.
Investor's India Year Book, compiled by Place, Siddons and Gough, 1st issue, 1912.
Navaroji Jamshedji Bulsara, *Guide to Indian Securities, Stocks and Currency Notes*, 1897.
A Manchester Man, *A Guide to Indian Investments*, 1861.
N. Das, *Industrial Enterprise in India*, 1938.
A. Krishnaswami,*Capital Development in India, 1860–1913*, [typescript], 1941.
I.M.F., *Financial Institutions of India*, 1950.
K. K. Sharma, *The Indian Money Market*, 1934.
V. R. Cirvante, *The Indian Capital Market*, 1956.
P. S. Lokanathan, *Industrial Organisation in India*, 1935.
M. M. Mehta, *Structure of Indian Industries*, 1955.
M. V. Namjoshi, *The Development of the Large-Scale Private Sector in India* (Thesis), Gokhle Institute of Politics and Economics, Poona, 1956.
D. R. Samant and M. A. Mulky, *Organisation and Finance of Industries in India*, 1937.
National Council of Applied Economic Research, *Capital Market in a Planned Economy*, 1966.

that 'there are no settlement days, delivery is due the second day after the contract is passed, and sales of securities are effected for the most part under blank transfer'.[1] But, without further research, one cannot feel certain that there was no formal element at all in the rules which governed the transactions of the share market. The fact that the committee of the Brokers' Exchange met once every month throws doubt on the matter. One wonders what was the purpose of this meeting so regularly held. Dealers in the stock market acted as brokers as well as dealers. Transactions were made both for ready delivery and future delivery. Contracts for future delivery were known as 'time bargains'. There was also a fairly large business in the 'margins' on borrowed money.[2]

In Bombay, on the other hand, Indians were dominant from the very beginning in the business of stocks and shares. Between 1840–50, it is said, there were no more than six share brokers in Bombay who were recognised by the banks and the merchants.[3] In 1860 the number had increased to sixty. The brokers were led by Premchand Roychand 'who gave to the stock and share brokers a standing and importance not hitherto achieved'.[4] The oubreak of the American Civil War, and the boom that followed, increased the number and popularity of the brokers on an unprecedented scale. At the height of the boom there were as many as 200 to 250 brokers in Bombay.[5] The crash on the cessation of the Civil War, however, brought in its train widespread failures and the resulting disillusionment naturally decreased both the popularity and the number of the share brokers in Bombay. The real basis for the sustained growth of the share market activities was provided by the expansion of the cotton mill industry in the early seventies. In 1877 the number of share brokers had increased to 318 and for the remaining years of the nineteenth century it remained in that neighbourhood.[6]

Originally the brokers used to meet on the Cotton Green where the Elphinston Circle is now situated and they continued to meet at this place until 1855. Afterwards, for a time, they met between the old Fort walls and the old Mercantile Bank. Finally, they found a place in Dalal Street and began to assemble there.[7] Here, for the

[1] A. K. Sur (Ed.): *The Stock Exchange—A Symposium*, 1958, p. 62.
[2] See Commercial Affairs in Bengal, T.O.I., 28 December 1874.
[3] *Report of the Bombay Stock Exchange Enquiry Committee*, 1924, pp. 3–6.
[4] *Ibid.*   [5] *Ibid.*   [6] *Ibid.*   [7] *Ibid.*

rest of the century, the brokers met and moved about hectically in sweltering heat and rain, much to the annoyance of the passers-by; moreover, they remained liable to be removed by the police for causing obstruction to the pedestrians.[1] After the brokers had organised themselves in 1875, they, together with the leading mill-owners of Bombay, endeavoured to house the share bazaar in a suitable building. To this end, D. M. Petit donated twenty-three shares of Victoria Mill which, together with other government securities and cash given by him, amounted to Rs.25,000.[2] The brokers themselves collected Rs.7,000.[3] At the end of the year 1887 the Native Share and Stock Brokers Association had some 38,000 rupees invested in the Petit Mills at 6% per annum.[4] It was then suggested that the Association should issue debentures to make up the deficiency to acquire a building, but the idea does not seem to have gained favour.[5] Three years later the funds of the Association reached a figure of Rs.50,000 and a European gentleman was appointed as the *ex-officio* member to take steps toward erecting a proper hall.[6] It was not until 1899, however, that a special hall for the Stock Exchange was actually acquired.[7]

The movement to organise and regulate the business in stocks and shares gained strength in Bombay after the shattering experiences of the crash that followed the share mania of 1863–5. The frequent resort to excessive and unhealthy speculation and the use of undesirable practices in pursuance of private gain by the unscrupulous elements among the brokers, whose later bankruptcies left many in complete destitution, stimulated a demand for bringing some order and cohesion to the 'chaotic' Dalal street. On 10 July 1875 the *Times of India* reported a meeting of the brokers held for the purpose of restricting dealings in 'differences'. On the 11th the brokers had set up a committee to draft rules for the Native Share and Stock Brokers Association which they had founded only two days before, with the object of protecting 'the character, status and interest of native share and stock brokers and for providing a hall or building for the use of the members of the Association'.[8] In fact, a little earlier than the founding of this Association, a joint stock company was promoted

---

[1] T.O.I., 11 January 1889.   [2] *Ibid.*, 7 January 1887.
[3] *Ibid.*, 6 January 1888.   [4] *Ibid.*   [5] *Ibid.*   [6] *Ibid.*
[7] *Report of the Bombay Stock Exchange, etc.*, p. 4.
[8] T.O.I., 16 July 1875.

to provide an 'Open Stock Exchange', but the scheme did not find any favour in Bombay and was dropped.[1] Twelve years after the Native Share and Stock Brokers Association had been founded it was formally constituted by an indenture dated 3 December 1887[2].

The aims of the Association, as contained in its Articles, were, among other things, 'to promote honourable practice; to suppress malpractices; to settle disputes among brokers; to decide all questions of usage and courtesy in conducting brokerage business'.[3] None but the natives of India were eligible for the membership of the Association and the admission fee as originally fixed was Rs.51 only.[4] By this time, it seems, the Association was not being properly managed, as the *Times of India* wrote that 'the present Stock Exchange, as it is, is imperfect in its constitution, and has for its members, with a few honourable exceptions, a set of disorderly and unprincipled persons'.[5] Yet, after the near-crisis situation on 24 October 1888, created by the failure of some brokers who had been making heavy forward purchases for over two years in certain mill shares and were embarrassed by the enforced closing of accounts, the same paper reported that 'the defaulters had been put out of the "Stock Exchange" and that the management had taken stringent measures to prevent a recurrence of the event in the future'. Nonetheless, the paper opined that the Board needed a change for the better and the rules of the Association also required a good deal of tightening up. The most important thing, it emphasised, was the provision of a good guarantee by the members of the Association.[6] Despite these criticisms the Association seems to have been gaining steadily in strength. By 1890 the 'Exchange Banks' in the city had recognised the Association and they did their business with only such persons as were approved by the directors of the 'Stock Exchange'.[7]

The growth of stock exchanges can be said to be a function of the growth of companies. The increase in the number of companies in its turn brings about an increase in the number of brokers to cope with the increased volume of share market business. When all and sundry start dealing in securities the standard of performance, in the absence of regulatory measures, naturally falls.

[1] T.O.I., 23 October 1874.
[2] *Report of the Bombay Stock Exchange*, etc., p. 3.
[3] *Ibid.*, p. 4.   [4] *Ibid.*   [5] T.O.I., 7 January 1887.
[6] *Ibid.*, 4 January 1899.   [7] *Ibid.*, 3 January 1891.

It is at this stage that serious-minded people who honestly depend for their income on the share market begin to take measures to secure the confidence of the investing public, to organise the share bazaar into a stock exchange which will enforce and guarantee a minimum standard of performance from its members on which the public will be able to depend. About the middle of the seventies Bombay and Calcutta had reached such a stage of development. This is further evidenced by the fact that though the brokers in Bombay had got together and taken concerted action to deal with an emergency situation almost a decade earlier,[1] it was not thought necessary to organise the market until a real and substantial increase had taken place in the number of companies.

At this stage it would be convenient to look at some of the peculiarities of the share markets in Bombay and Calcutta. In both places the share market operations were characterised by a large amount of speculative business. This was probably due to the presence of a large number of Marwaris who are generally regarded as being, by instinct, more speculative than others. The system of time bargains and absence of compulsory settlement days helped to develop and maintain this bias in the markets. Dealings in differences on borrowed money are a sure sign of speculation as well as disaster. This was clearly evident from the occasional crisis that the failure of the brokers, known already to be weak, could bring about.[2] Moreover, twice at least each year, particularly in Calcutta when the share market was closed for long periods on account of Puja and Christmas holidays, the speculators had to make forced sales as they were obliged to return the borrowed money. On these occasions shrewd people looked around for cheap bargains. False rumours were frequently resorted to as a means of making quick profits. The brokers waited eagerly for *Bilayat Ka Tar* or the telegram from London and the markets were sensitive to the news of war and peace. It must also be admitted that the brokers and dealers in shares in Bombay and Calcutta were very shrewd people—well versed in the art, the techniques, and the subtleties of stock market operations. One of their boasts was that they could teach a trick or two to even those on the London Stock Exchange in the art of making 'put' and 'call' options.[3]

---

[1] See p. 86.   [2] T.O.I., 4 January 1889.
[3] *Ibid.*

CHANGES IN COMPANY LAW

Following the English Act of 1862 a comprehensive Act was passed in India in 1866[1] for consolidating and amending 'the laws relating to the incorporation, regulation and winding up of Trading Companies and other Associations'. This Act was recast in 1882[2] embodying thirteen amendments made in English law up to that time, and thirty-two verbal changes necessitated by the decisions of the Courts in India. The other amending Acts passed in India between the years 1882 and 1900 were as follows:

Act VI of 1887 — providing for priority of debts in the winding up of a company.

Act XII of 1891 — making some verbal corrections and introducing the word 'hundi' after the word 'bill' in s.144 cl. (f) of Act VI of 1882.

Act XII of 1895 — giving power to companies to alter their objects or forms of constitution subject to confirmation by the High Court.

Act IV of 1900 — authorising certain companies to keep branch registers of members in the United Kingdom.

It is not possible to make a detailed study of the foregoing Acts within the scope of this work, although some of their more important features must be noted.

The Act of 1866 removed the disability of the insurance companies from being registered as limited liability companies. The insurance companies were the only ones suffering from this handicap at this time, and the Act had a favourable effect on the growth of these companies in India. The irony was that before this period although insurance companies registered abroad could function on the basis of limited liability in India, the Indian companies could not do so. The *Act of 1866*, however, failed to reintroduce the provision which prohibited a company from buying its own shares, a provision which the Legislature had thought fit and found necessary to introduce even in the *Act of 1850*[3] when the companies in India were still in their infancy. This provision

---

[1] *Act X of 1866.* [2] *Act VI of 1882.*
[3] See Sec. 8 of *Act LXIII of 1850.*

together with some others of a similar nature were dropped when the Act was amended in 1857, probably to give impetus to such enterprises by freeing the hands of the management or more probably in the blind adaptation of its English prototype. But its absence in the *Act of 1866* becomes particularly surprising when one remembers that the Act was passed during the crisis period and after the dreadful experiences of 1863–5.

The necessity to amend the law in 1882 arose as a result of the discovery of a loophole in Sec. 49 of the *Act of 1866*. It came to light in a case in the Province of Bombay that it was perfectly legal for a company to pass one set of accounts in the shareholders' meeting and file another with the Registrar of Joint Stock Companies.[1] The *Act of 1882* plugged this hole. Besides, in line with English law, it introduced a retrogressive principle whereby the shareholders, if they so wished, could make the liability of some of their directors unlimited.[2] This shows that the majority of the British Parliament was unable to comprehend the true nature and significance of the joint stock institution. As the Registrar of the Joint Stock Companies in Calcutta rightly observed, the provision would, at best, make the right kind of people offering themselves for directorships hesitate; at worst, it would encourage the election of dummies.[3]

As mentioned earlier, companies in India frequently did not provide for depreciation of assets.[4] Many overvalued their stocks. Some did not even deduct bad debts from their profits before declaring dividends.[5] Thus part of the dividends paid out constituted in fact a return of the invested capital.

On the other hand there were companies which could not care less about the difference between a capital and revenue expenditure, and happily charged additions to buildings and purchases of new machinery to profit and loss account.[6]

Moreover company officials indulged in the speculation of their own company's shares. Companies appointed anybody they liked as auditors, who were not required to hold any educational or other

---

[1] See the Statement of the Objects and Reasons in the Bill which became the *Act VI of 1882. Legislative Proceedings of India.* See also *The Pioneer Mail,* 18 September 1881, and T.O.I., 10 March 1882 (Editorial).

[2] *Act VI of 1882.*   [3] J.P., 1882, Departmental No. 446.

[4] See p. 205.

[5] T.O.I., 24 July 1891 on Oriental Spinning and Weaving Mills Co.

[6] F.O.I., 16 November 1877 on Gourepore Mills.

qualifications. Though firms of public accountants had emerged early in the 1870's,[1] it was not necessary to appoint them. To the non-professional often what mattered was the fee, which made auditing a farce in many cases.[2]

The 1857 Act had provided a form of balance sheet which companies, in preparing their accounts, were required to follow as near thereto as circumstances admitted. But as usually happens, the business community found in the phrase 'as near thereto as circumstances admit' an open licence to ignore the whole thing. It was for these reasons that the Press often urged the Government to appoint company auditors, or at least to make strict regulations governing the appointment of auditors, their qualifications and liability for gross misconduct or negligence, but no heed was paid to these appeals at the time the Acts were revised.[3]

What the shareholders wanted above all was a control by law of the power of the managing agents. The appointment of managing agents for life, heavy compensation payable to them in case of the loss of office, the system of quarter-anna commission per pound weight of production and the variety of ways in which a managing agent siphoned away company's profits were the main points of grievance.

But all the clamour of the Press and the enlightened public opinion in the country for strict measures to control the abuses of the managing agents had no effect on the legislators. One looks in vain to these Acts for any significant change affecting the management of companies or the protection of the rights of shareholders. In fact, the Acts provide examples of a complete disregard and an utter failure on the part of the legislators to take into account the peculiarities of conditions in India. If there is any underlying theme running through the company legislation of a full half century in India, with the *Act of 1850* somewhat excepted, it is a steadfast adherence to the policy that what was good for Britain must also be good for India. It was not that the legislators responsible for these Acts were not able men, some of them were well qualified and experienced in company affairs in India. Whitley

---

[1] See an advertisement by Swift and Farrow, Public Accountants, T.O.I., 18 October 1875.

[2] See an Editorial on Fort Gloucester Jute Mill, F.O.I., 9 November 1877.

[3] See T.O.I., 10 February 1879. Also the comments on the case of the Oriental Life Assurance Company in T.O.I., 7 November 1891, and the issue of 21 June 1895 for comments on the Himalyan Bank case.

Stokes who introduced and piloted the Bill which became the *Act of 1882* was, at least, one such person. What they seem to have lacked most was the will, rather than the wisdom, to change.

In 1913, when the Companies Act came up for amendment once more, the Secretary of the Commerce and Industry Department, R. E. Enthoven, impressed on the Government that 'to pass a Bill regulating the constitution and management of companies in India and to fail to deal with the notorious irregularities of the managing agent system would surely be to lay the Government open to serious criticism. It has to be recognised that English Company Law when imported into this country requires special modifications if it is to deal with conditions which do not exist in England'.[1] The managing agency firms in India exercised much the same functions as directors do in England.[2]

Indian law did not, as far as one can see, impose on managing agents obligations of the kind which company directors had to accept in English law.[3] The managing agents were remunerated by commission and, in addition, through their relations with the managed companies, made profits for themselves from the sale of products and the purchases made for the companies. These offered considerable scope for abuse.[4]

To quote Enthoven again, 'it is possible, and not uncommon, the managing agents, as firm, should buy a very large quantity of jute, cotton, coal or other commodity without indicating at the time the transaction is completed, whether they purchased for their firm or for one or more of the companies for which the firm acts as managing agents. Hence it may occur that, after making a large purchase of this description, if the market becomes unfavourable, the managing agents are tempted to represent the transaction as effected on behalf of one of the managed companies while, similarly, if the market improves there is nothing to prevent them treating the transaction as the property of the firm, and thus become entitled to the profit'.[5] A company director in England would not be permitted to allow his private interest to be at variance with the interest of the company.[6]

As a result, the Government made what Clark, who moved the

---

[1] For Enthoven's Note, see Commerce and Industry Department, *Companies*, Nos. 66–8, September 1913. The Note is printed in S. K. Sen, *Economic Policy*, Appendix A, pp. 199–203.

[2] *Ibid.* [3] *Ibid.* [4] *Ibid.* [5] *Ibid.* [6] *Ibid.*

Indian Companies Amendment Bill (Act of 1914), described as a 'modest beginning'[1] to regulate the unfettered freedom enjoyed by the managing agents over half a century, during which time they had consolidated their position. The Bill provided, *inter alia*, for the majority of directors to be elected independently of the managing agents (excepting in the case of private companies or where the managing agents held a majority of voting powers). Moreover, a written memorandum of the terms of contract was required where the company was an undisclosed principal. As was to be feared, the Bill came under heavy criticism. The Bengal Chamber of Commerce went so far that they 'refused to discuss' the 'vexed clauses' with Clark when he offered to come to Calcutta for the purpose, and urged the postponement of the Bill 'for a few years'.[2] The matter was raised even in the British Parliament, where Sir J. D. Rees referred to the Bill as one which 'closely concerns the interest of business firms partly or wholly domiciled in England'. 'Certain of its provisions are', he said, 'in the opinion of businessmen, likely to have injurious effects both in India and in this country, particularly those relating to directors' and he suggested that it be postponed.[3] The Government gave way, but as Kenrick, the Advocate General of Bengal, said, 'The elimination of Section 83(c) which was the keynote of the Bill, cuts directly at the whole subject of the legislation, and in my opinion, diminishes the practical utility of some of the remaining clauses almost to vanishing point'.[4] The matter was not taken up again until 1936.

CASE LAW DEVELOPMENTS

The Companies Acts are not a complete code and it would be very misleading to think that the major developments during the nineteenth century were wholly statutory. In fact, it was the courts which evolved a coherent and comprehensive body of company law. In doing so they drew on the law of partnership, the law of corporations and the statutes. 'Many of the most fundamental and statutory principles' to quote Gower, 'were worked out by the

---

[1] Quoted in S. K. Sen, *Economic Policy*, p. 113.
[2] Clark's speech in the Council, 5 March 1913, *Gazette of India*, Part vi, 1913.
[3] *Ibid.*
[4] Letter of G. H. B. Kenrick, Advocate General, Bengal, 12 February 1914. *Companies*, August 1914, quoted in S. K. Sen, *Economic Policy*, p. 104.

courts with little or no help from the statutes and their decisions constitute landmarks which later Acts have done little to obliterate.'[1] Some of the most fundamental principles were evolved in the following cases during the last quarter of the nineteenth century. Though the cases were decided in England, their authority in India was equally good.

In 1875 the House of Lords held in *Ashbury Carriage Co. vs. Riche*[2] that it was beyond the powers of a company to do acts not expressly or implicitly authorised in its memorandum of association. But the end result of the application of the *ultra vires* doctrine has been an inordinate lengthening of the 'object clause' in a company's memorandum of association to include all imaginable purposes for which a company is formed, rather than prevent them from misusing the corporate powers. In *Trevor vs. Whitworth*[3] and *Ooregum Gold Mining Co. vs. Roper*[4] their lordships laid down the principle of the raising and maintenance of capital so that some protection was afforded to the public against the abuses of limited liability.[5] They also protected the shareholders by enumerating the principle in *Erlanger vs. New Sombrero Phosphate Co.*[6] and *Gluckstein vs. Barnes*,[7] that company promoters stood in a fiduciary relationship towards their 'fledglings'[8] and must therefore observe good faith and make full disclosure of their interest to shareholders.

In *Andrews vs. Gas Meter Co.*[9] they boldly rejected the idea borrowed from partnership law that there was any implied condition for all shareholders to be on equality and thereby made it possible for a company to raise capital by issuing new preference shares. And it was not until the famous case of *Solomon vs. Solomon*[10] had been decided, towards the end of the century, that the full meaning of the principle that a company was a separate entity in the eye of the law had been really grasped. Only then it became apparent, among other things, that it was not necessary for all the seven shareholders, the minimum number required to

---

[1] L. C. B. Gower, *The Principles of Modern Company Law*, 1957, p. 51.
[2] L.R. 7 H.L. 653.   [3] (1887) 12 App. Cas. 409, H.L.
[4] (1892) A.C. 125, H.L.   [5] See Gower, Chapter 6.
[6] (1878) 3 App. Cas. 1218, H.L.   [7] (1900) A.C. 240, H.L.
[8] See *per* Lord Macnaghten in (1900) A.C. at p. 248.
[9] (1897) 1 Ch. 361, C.A., overruling *Hutton vs. Scarborough Cliff Hotel Co.* (1865) 2 Dr. 8 sm. 521.
[10] (1897) A.C. 22, H.L. for a summary of facts in this case see Gower, pp. 63–4.

form a company, to be beneficially interested in the company, e.g. some could be nominees for others, without anyone losing the benefit of limited liability. As a result, there was no longer any need for an Act of limited partnership since 'one man' and other small 'private companies' could be easily formed.[1] The situation has been well described by O. Kahn-Freund:[2]

Whereas in the eighteenth and early nineteenth centuries the law of partnership had been pressed into the service of joint stock enterprises, now the legal form of joint stock undertakings has come to annex the functions of the law of partnership. A similar reversal has taken place in the law of trusts into whose service the joint stock company is now pressed as a Trust Corporation.

But the courts were not so successful in evolving principles which could adequately protect the minority against the oppression of the majority of shareholders. The application of the Common Law principle regarding misrepresentation or misleading statements by directors in prospectuses ended in disaster.[3] Moreover, to quote Gower, 'by construing the statutory rules for public registration as implying a constructive notice to all the world of the registered data, they introduced an entirely artificial doctrine which has been fraught with complications and which has caused the basically healthy publicity principles to do almost as much harm as good'.[4]

[1] Gower, p. 51. [2] Quoted in Gower, p. 51, fn. 83.

[3] The reference is to the decision in *Derry vs. Peek* (1889), 14 App. Cas, 337, H.L. which had to be promptly modified by the legislature by the passing of the Directors' Liability Act, 1890. See Gower, p. 52.

[4] Gower, p. 52, see also Chapters 5 and 8 of his book for examples of this harm.
The following books, reports and journals may be further consulted on the subject of Indian Company legislation and case law developments.

L. P. Russell, *The Indian Companies Acts, 1882 – 1887*, 1888.

E. R. Smetham, *Indian Companies Act, 1882*, 1902.

Rama Aiyer Kodanda, *Law of Corporate Bodies and Registration*, 1903.

S. C. Bagchi, *Principles of the Law of Corporations with Special Reference to British India*, 1914.

K. M. Ghosh, *The Indian Company Law*, 11th edition, 2 volumes, 1963, is the current authority on the subject.

Seminar on Current Problems of Corporate Law, Management and Practice, Proceedings, 1964.

Proceedings of the Council of the Governor-General of India, assembled for the purpose of making laws and regulations from 1862 (Indian Office Library).

Bengal Law Reports, Digest of Cases Reported, Volumes I to XV, 1878.

Reports of Cases decided in the High Court of Bombay, 1875.

Reports of Cases decided in the High Court of Madras, 1862 to 1874, Volumes I to VII.

(Continued)

CHAPTER 12

CORPORATE MANAGEMENT: THE MANAGING AGENCY SYSTEM

The attention of students of economics was drawn to the managing agency system first during the inter-war period by the Industrial Commission[1] and the various reports of the Indian Tariff Boards.[2] This interest resulted in a number of studies of this system of which Lokanathan's is still regarded as important.[3]

Legal provisions relating to this system were made for the first time in the *Companies Act of 1936*. Since then the managing agency system has caught the attention of students in many parts of the world and has remained a subject of great controversy in India. The *Companies Act, 1956*, made very strict provisions regarding the terms of appointment of a managing agent, his duration of office, methods of remuneration and his powers and duties. The

---

[1] *Report of the Indian Industrial Commission*, 1916–18, pp. 13, 18, 39 and 349.

[2] Particularly the *Report on the Cotton Textile Industry, 1926*, and another more elaborate report on the same industry in 1932. See also *The Indian Central Banking Enquiry Committee Report, 1931–32* and the reports of the *Fiscal Commission, Planning Commission*, and the *Income Tax Investigation Commission*.

[3] P. S. Lokanathan, *Industrial Organisation in India* (1935). Other books, articles and reports which may usefully be consulted are: D. H. Buchanan, pp. 165–75. D. R. Samant and M. A. Mulky, pp. 32–7. P. Griffiths, *The British Impact on India*, 1952, pp. 453–62. *Report of the Company Law Committee*, 1952, paras, 113–14. Employers' Association, *Achievements of Managing Agency System*, 1954. A Brimmer, 'The Setting of Entrepreneurship in India', *Quarterly Journal of Economics*, Vol. LXIX, No. 4, November 1954. M. M. Mehta, *Structure of Indian Industries*, 1955. Raj K. Nigam, *Managing Agencies in India*, 1957. Charles A. Myers, 'Recent Development in Management Training', *Indian Journal of Public Administration*, April–June 1958, Vol. VI., No. 2 and Chapter VI (The Managerial Response) in his book, *Industrial Relations in India*, 1958. National Council of Applied Economic Research, *The Managing Agency System*, 1959. Geoffrey Tyson, *Managing Agency—A System of Business Organisation*, 1961. P. S. Lokanathan, Entrepreneurship: Supply of Entrepreneurs and Technologists with special reference to India, in K. Berrill (Ed.), *Economic Development with special reference to East Asia*, 1964.

Indian Law Reports, Bombay, Allahabad, Calcutta and Madras from 1876.
B. D. Bose, *A Digest of Indian Law Cases (1836–1909)*, 1912 (British Museum Library).
The Indian Law Magazine, 1878.   *Joint Stock Companies Journal*, 1936.

protagonists of the managing agents argued, as usual, that there was nothing inherently wrong in the system and it was only the behaviour of a few black sheep in the business world which brought it a bad name; that before abolishing the system Parliament would do well to remember the great services rendered by the managing agents in pioneering and developing the industries of the country in the last century; that it was still capable of performing valuable functions; that it was economical and efficient; and that instead of abolishing the system, it should be retained and strengthened especially as the private sector was being called upon to discharge its full share of a rapidly industrialising economy. Some fresh studies followed the passing of the *Companies Act,* 1956, and the argument about its usefulness continues unabated.

Even after so many studies the origin of the system remained obscure,[1] since it was regarded as 'the result of gradual evolution'.[2] Naturally, its beginning became a subject of speculation and vague generalisations. For instance, consider the following oft-quoted statement:[3] 'History, geography and economics have all combined to create and develop the managing agency system.' There is hardly any human institution which is not the result of historical, geographical and economic factors. Unless, however, we know the way in which these factors combined to produce an institution, we do not really know very much.

The purpose of this chapter is to shed some light on the circumstances surrounding the origin of this system and to trace the course of its development during the nineteenth century.

Until the beginning of the 1860's many interesting experiments were made in India in the field of corporate management. After that period and particularly from the seventies onward, the managing agency system became the most generally accepted way of running business corporations in the country. Although generally adopted, the system was by no means popular among the shareholders; and even at this early stage of its career many regarded it as the bane of the corporate institution. The remaining years of the nineteenth century witnessed great agitation from the shareholders for reforming the system.

For all practical purposes it can be said that banking enter-

---

[1] Anstey, p. 113 fn. [2] Lokanathan, p. 15.
[3] S. K. Basu, *The Managing Agency System—In Prospect and Retrospect,* 1958, p. 1.

prises were the first to develop the principle of the joint stock company in India.[1] At first the banks were local in character. The first joint stock bank, the General Bank of India, formed in Calcutta on 17 March 1786, was promoted principally by the Europeans in the service of the East India Company. The European agency houses would have nothing to do with its formation since it intruded upon one of their staple lines of business. The form of management adopted by the General Bank was typical of corporate management elsewhere in the world, that is, the board of directors directly supervised the affairs of the bank through paid officials. Its directors were primarily drawn from the ranks of the civil and military servants of the East India Company. The hostility of the European business community, perhaps, accounts for the particular structure of management adopted by this bank. After the failure of the agency houses in Calcutta following the commercial crisis in the mid-twenties, the faith of the European government servants in these houses as depositories for their savings was greatly shaken; this led them to establish joint stock banks of their own, such as the Simla and the Benares banks formed in the 1830's. The management structure adopted by these banks was similar to that of the General Bank. This new movement obliged the agency houses to partake in the management and promotion of banking companies and many new banks were formed in this era.[2]

So far as the banks remained local in character the pattern of management remained the same as before, but as soon as they began to branch out in other parts of the country, the management of the branches presented some difficulties. These were solved in various ways. In some cases, where local shareholders of high calibre could be found, a local board of directors was established to supervise the affairs of the branch.[3] In other cases, a person of repute was appointed as the manager of the branch on a fixed salary plus a commission on profits.[4] The commission on profits

[1] See Chapter 1. [2] See Chapter 1.

[3] The Agra and United Services Bank Ltd. opened an agency in Calcutta in 1838 which was 'conducted under a Committee of Shareholders resident in Calcutta; and the result . . . was favourable. Some intention existed of employing a mercantile house but objections were raised on the grounds of confliction of interest'. Cooke, p. 208.

[4] L. Carmichael transacted the business of the Calcutta agency of the Simla Bank in 1849. Subsequently the agency was taken over by John Morgan. Both were paid by a percentage on 'disbursement'. *Ibid.*, p. 293.

was to act as an incentive. Both these forms of management were also adopted by the British banking companies operating in India[1] which offered, as a rule, a third of their share capital for subscription in India.[2] The managing agency system as such was never adopted for the management of the banking companies; the payment of a commission on profits was the nearest it ever approached it. In one or two cases, however, agency houses were appointed to handle the local business of a bank.[3]

The composition of the shareholders of the banks founded in India led to a great problem in bank management. A large number of shareholders were British, who retired, in the normal course, to Britain. In some cases, they became dissatisfied with the management and formed a committee of shareholders in London to voice their protests. Soon afterwards such a committee would assume the title of a board of directors and try to dominate the properly constituted board in India, which naturally caused dissension among the shareholders. The ultimate outcome of these struggles was usually unwholesome. In the case of the Simla Bank such a dissension led to a proposal to remove the headquarters of the bank to London, and finally the schism between the shareholders resulted in the division of the capital; one-half to maintain the Simla Bank and the other half to open a new bank in London under the style of the London and Eastern Banking Corporation.[4] The struggle did not always take this form. In 1846 the Bombay shareholders of the then Oriental Bank Corporation, being dissatisfied with the expense and conduct of the London directors, resolved to put an end to that direction. But the move was somewhat premature, as no alteration in the constitution of the Bank could be made without the express consent of the British as well as the Indian shareholders.[5]

Since the banks in India never adopted the managing agency system or any other novel form of management not found elsewhere in the world, their subsequent history is of no particular interest for the purposes of this study. It is the early history of the life insurance companies in India which best illuminates the origin of the managing agency system. The business of life

---

[1] Cooke, p. 222.   [2] *Ibid.*, p. 351. See also Chapter 4.

[3] Parry & Company held the Madras Agency of the Land Mortgage Bank of India Ltd. Similarly, Hoare, Miller & Company of Calcutta were appointed the agents for Mauritius Bank—*Thacker's Bengal Directory, 1875*, pp. 368 and 370.

[4] See history of the Simla Bank in Cooke, *op. cit.*   [5] *Ibid.*, p. 142.

insurance in India was started in Calcutta by the European agency houses at the turn of the eighteenth century. They were already familiar with conducting the business of marine insurance.[1] Although the life business was organised on an all-India basis, Europeans only were insured. This greatly limited the scope of the business, the prospects for which were bound to be small in the beginning anyway. Thus it did not warrant the setting-up of separate establishments in other parts of the country for securing business. The agency houses with their close connections with the various parts of India provided a splendid way out of this difficulty.

The mechanism of starting a life insurance company was simple: the senior partner of a leading agency house invited other leading members of the business community to meet at his residence where they discussed the scheme, and if agreed, they set up a company of which these gentlemen became the first directors. The management of the company was handed over to the agency house which initiated the scheme.[2] There were obvious advantages in this arrangement: an agency house could, for a very small remuneration, run the business of an insurance company from its own establishment without adding materially to its costs. The problem of distance was similarly overcome by appointing agency houses in other parts of the country and in the Far East, as sub-agents under the principal agency house at Calcutta. But whereas the Calcutta agency house was truly and properly responsible for the management of the entire affairs of the company, the sub-agency houses were no more than insurance agents concerned only with such matters as bringing the business of the company to the prospective clients and receiving and forwarding proposals for insurance.

The terms of appointment, remuneration, powers and duties of the principal agency house in Calcutta as the 'secretaries and treasurers' of insurance companies provide us with the earliest instance of the institution which was later to become known as the managing agency system. The oldest document we have in this connection is the 'Regulations' of the 'Third Laudable Society' of Calcutta, founded on 1 February 1809. The promoters and directors of this Society were Alexander Colvin, John Palmer, Josia Dupré Alexander, John William Fulton, and John Cruttendon, all of whom were eminent merchants of Calcutta. The firm of Alexander & Company were appointed as 'secretaries and

---

[1] See Chapter 1.   [2] *The Bengal Almanac*, etc., *op. cit.*

treasurers' of the Society and by Article V of its 'Regulations' they were to be remunerated by a monthly allowance of Rs.200 which was paid 'in lieu of all other charges (excepting advertisements, printing the requisite papers for the Society and law expenses)'. In other words, all necessary expenses which were clearly incurred for the Society, were to form a direct burden on its funds. Articles VI, XI and XIII defined the powers and duties of the secretaries and treasurers. The powers were limited and the duties were of a purely managerial nature. Important functions such as the acceptance of risk and the employment of the funds and their control, were vested exclusively in the hands of the 'Committee of Directors'. The 'Regulations' did not fix any term of office for the 'secretaries and treasurers' but as the Society was formed for only six years at a time, the understanding must have been that they were to remain in office for the whole duration of the Society.[1]

An interesting and rather extraordinary feature of this Society's constitution may be noted in passing. Although the Society sought and must have had policyholders (who were also the shareholders[2]) in many parts of India, it restricted the right to manage the affairs of the Society to the shareholders resident in Bengal. This was probably done to save the expense of sending notices, etc. to other parts of the country, which would have been wasteful because the shareholders in other provinces, even if they wished to attend the meetings of the Society, would have found it almost impossible in face of the transport difficulties of those days.

The 'Regulations' of the Union Society, formed in Calcutta on 23 April 1814, show both that the volume of life insurance business had increased and that the management of these societies had become more sophisticated by this time. To save the board of directors or 'managers' as they were called in the case of this Society, the trouble of deciding daily the merits of the 'proposals' put before them, the Society appointed a sub-committee of 'managers' which included three medical men. Articles 27 and 28 of the Regulations concerned the maintenance and publication of accounts and voting procedure at the board meetings. They show that the nature of problems in managing companies were clearly understood by these early pioneers.[3]

The Union Society also took a step further in the matter of

---

[1] *The Bengal Almanac*, etc., *op. cit.*   [2] See Chapter I.
[3] *The Bengal Almanac*, etc., *op. cit.*

fixing the remuneration of its 'Agents'—Mackintosh, Fulton & McClintock. Article 26 of the Society's Regulations provided that '. . . Mackintosh, Fulton and McClintock should receive, for conducting the business of the society, and defraying the charge of an establishment for the same, including all contingencies, excepting printing and law charges, a commission of 3% on all premiums received and a further commission of 2% on all payments on account of lapses, provided, in the last case of charge on payments, that the ultimate funds of the Society shall afford, including the previous advance, 3000 rupees per share to eventual insurers'.[1]

The provisions in the Articles of the Union Society is the earliest evidence we find of a contract of a managing agency in India which is clearly complete in all essential aspects of that system except those which later led to its abuse, as, for example the appointment of a managing agent for life. It is very unlikely that the system had an earlier origin or that it began in any other field of business.

When the founding of a number of shipping, coal mining and sugar manufacturing companies ushered in the next stage of the growth of business corporations in the country, the agency houses still remained the characteristic unit of business and the means of linking up the different parts of India. In some cases where details are available, agency houses were found to hold the managing agencies of these new companies without necessarily possessing a controlling interest.[2] The shareholders of these companies came from many different walks of life; most of them were locally resident, which enabled them to keep an eye on the day to day developments of their company. Their vigil often ended in a quarrel with the management. It is because of these disputes that we know today that even in the formative years of the managing agency system a close association of a company with an agency

---

[1] *The Bengal Almanac,* etc., *op. cit.*

[2]

Companies	Agents	Source
Nischindpore Sugar Co.	Gisborne & Co.	Cooke, p. 274
Ganges Steam Navigation Co.	Richmond & Co.	*Bengal and Agra Directory and Annual Register, 1850*
Union Steam Tug Co.	Apcar & Co.	*Ibid.*
Calcutta Docking Co.	Rustomji Cowasji	Brame, p. 11
Steam Tug Association	Carr, Tagore & Co.	*Ibid.* pp. 9–10
Bengal Coal Company	Carr, Tagore & Co.	*Ibid.*

house whose business interests were many, and at times conflicting, had led to the abuse of powers, particularly when they speculated heavily in commodities. The following instance is a case in point.

In 1844, the firm of Carr, Tagore & Company who were then the 'managers' of the Steam Tug Association, a joint stock company, thought of extending the operations of the Association to include inland navigation, and accordingly sounded the shareholders on the subject. The deliberations resulted in the formation of the India General Steam Navigation Company, on 6 February 1844. Its proposed capital of Rs.2,000,000 was readily subscribed. The Company appointed Captain A. G. Mackenzie, who was then the superintendent of the Steam Tug Association, as its managing director. In June 1847, at a meeting of the shareholders, Captain Mackenzie was openly accused of subordinating the interest of 'India General' to that of the firm of Carr, Tagore & Company and the Steam Tug Association. It was alleged that he put aside the work of the 'India General' to permit that of the Association to be expedited; that bills against Carr, Tagore & Company for work done were overdue; and that the sale of plant and stores from Carr, Tagore & Company to the 'India General' was conducted wholly by Mackenzie in the interest of the vendors. The result was that Mackenzie was summarily removed and the post of managing director was also abolished. The management of the Company was then undertaken by the directors, assisted by a secretary with extensive administrative powers.[1]

In another instance, in 1850, in which the Oriental Bank Corporation sustained a loss through the failure of the firm of Richmond & Company of Bombay, T. R. Richmond, the senior partner of this firm, was the managing agent for the Ganges Steamship Navigation Company, and in that capacity, borrowed money from the bank which he stated to have been for and on account of the Ganges Company. The Company, however, repudiated the debt, alleging that the loan had not been appropriated to its purposes.[2]

The starting of manufacturing enterprises necessitated further innovation in the techniques of management. Machines and various other stores were of necessity obtained from Britain, and liaison with the manufacturers there had to be established for the correct and quick delivery of these imports. The British shareholders of

---

[1] Brame, pp. 9–25. [2] Cooke, p. 14.

companies in India who went home on retirement provided useful links between the two. A committee of shareholders formed among these persons produced a most effective, economic and efficient liaison between the Indian company and the care of its affairs conducted in Britain. This arrangement, however, was later found to sow the seeds of dissension between the shareholders in India and those in Britain as the latter, through the medium of the committee, tried to assume a position of independence and dominate the affairs conducted in India.[1]

The dawn of the railway era in India brought in its wake the development of industries. The railway companies themselves, however, were British in origin and their business in India was necessarily controlled directly by their boards in London.[2]

The beginning of the cotton mills, jute mills and tea companies in the fifties marks a new stage in the development of the managing agency system. These enterprises required relatively large capital, usually from Rs.300,000 to Rs.500,000, and were of a nature which could not only support an independent establishment of their own but actually required it for the efficient management of their affairs. Yet, from the very start, managing agents were appointed to run them. Why this should have been so seems difficult to explain. The absence of an investing class, shortage of managerial talent and lack of transport facilities do not provide all the answers. These factors certainly contributed to the development of the managing agency system but they were by no means unique to India. A natural course in such a case would have been the development of closed family corporations, and world history is full of

---

[1] 'There was also a London board of three persons, formed of shareholders whose duty it was to supervise the building of the vessels under order, placing indents for stores and representing the interests of the shareholders resident in England. The board assumed a position of independence, and repeatedly complained of the inadequate information doled out to them by their Calcutta co-directors regarding the company's affairs. The position was an anomalous one, as on one occasion, when a call was made, the home [London] board issued a circular to English shareholders, advising them not to respond until the London board was satisfied with the policy of the Calcutta directors. Thereupon the Calcutta board in general meeting, abolished the home board. The latter declined to be abolished, and internal dissension was carried to such a pitch that the opposition party in Calcutta carried a resolution not only confirming the appointment of the home board, but adding a vote of thanks for their able services in the company's interest. As the Calcutta directorate became less the prey of faction, the relative powers of the two boards were more clearly defined, until, in 1850, the London board came to be finally dissolved.' Brame, pp. 25–6.

[2] Jenks, p. 195.

such cases. Written contracts of agencies suggest something more. A possible explanation may be that in the initial stages of industrialisation the required capital for a project had to be raised from a small group of prosperous but *busy* merchants, most of whom were not related to each other through any family. Such a situation would make it desirable to place the management of a company in the hands of a person or firm possessing business reputation but willing to undertake the responsibility only if the remuneration was high and guaranteed for a long period. The use of the managing agency must have, therefore, appealed to the merchant-shareholders who were occupied in managing the affairs of their own private businesses. The managing agency agreement entered into between Parsee Cowasjee Nanabhoy Davar, the promotor of the first cotton mill in Bombay, and the shareholders of that cotton mill seems to support this view. Of the nine clauses found in this agreement, only clauses 1 and 4 are important from our point of view. They read as follows:[1]

Firstly, . . . you [Parsee Cowasjee Nanabhoy Davar] shall secure the buildings . . . here and import machineries [*sic*] from England and arrange for their erection. You shall do all things necessary for the purpose and engage men for the same. Whatever expense has to be incurred . . . may be incurred by you. The entire management of these matters is entrusted by us, of our own will and pleasure, to you, and you will continue to do so in the course of your life time.

Fourthly, we all shareholders have . . . resolved that in recompense of the trouble taken by you in the flotation of the factory, you are appointed *Arhatiya* or Broker of the said factory during your life time, that is to say, that whatever cotton is required for the said factory should be purchased by you and whatever yarn and cloth are manufactured in the said factory should also be sold by you, and whatever sales you effect on account of the said company a commission of 5% shall be taken by you in your life time, but on purchase you will not charge anything. . . . In the event of the company selling goods directly you shall be entitled to your commission of 5% on the sale proceeds in your life time.

In interpreting this contract it is important to remember that there was no board of directors in this company. The first clause, as is apparent, outlined the duties of Davar and appointed him the sole manager of the company for life. There were certainly other people in Bombay who could have filled the post of a manager for this

---

[1] S. D. Mehta, pp. 26–7.

company but Davar offered as good a choice as any, and moreover had shown an initiative and ability which surely deserved praise. There was nothing peculiar about his being appointed the sole manager. Even in securing a life managership, one cannot see in the circumstances, anything more than a desire on the part of Davar to get an assurance that he should continue to reap the benefit from the mill which was so much due to his own efforts. As to the remuneration allowed to Davar, it can be said that, in effect, he placed his services at the disposal of the company for nothing. A sole-selling-agency for the products of the mill, which is what it amounts to in fact, could not be the remuneration for the duties of a mill manager. A 5% commission on sales would be a usual incident of trade and had to be paid irrespective of the fact of Davar's being the manager of the mill. But as the commission offered a good and permanent source of income, the eagerness of Davar in undertaking all the worries of mill management can well be understood. In terms of administrative theory, the only extraordinary feature of this agreement was the vesting of control of production as well as of sales in the same person and it was here that this agreement carried dangerous germs for future generations. But then the whole agreement must be viewed in the light of the fact that nearly all the shareholders of this mill were local residents, many of them were in the cotton and piece goods trades, and would have first hand knowledge of every development in their mill and could provide a multiple, though informal check on Davar's activities. The fact that the contract did not postulate the removal of Davar in any circumstances may well be the evidence of the confidence of the shareholders in his integrity, as well as in their own watchfulness.

Joint stock organisation made the launching of industrial enterprises possible but only the mercantile community in India had the resources and the desire to form them. A cotton mill or two, or for that matter, a jute mill or a tea company, could possibly have been formed by persons outside this class, but such persons either lacked a taste for these ventures or did not command the power to inspire enough confidence in others to part with their capital. No doubt there were quite a few merchant-capitalists, at least in the cities of Bombay and Calcutta, but the marginal productivity of capital in their hands was high and, hence, only the chance of making very large profits could attract them to promote industrial enterprises. The managing agency contract provided them with just this attraction, from which they could earn a large sum of money permanently, without sinking their capital in the company for ever. A managing agent, by virtue of his contract, was made into a holding company without the need to invest in the subsidiary, or he could be said to have been cast in the image of an absolute dictator.

The managing agency system, well defined by Brimmer as 'an institutional setting . . . in which entrepreneurial decisions were made'[1] worked smoothly until about the end of the sixties in the few cotton mills, jute mills and tea companies that had been formed by that time, because of the high integrity of the managing agents of such concerns. But the system had, as yet, not been put to any extensive test. Most of the years in the sixties were taken up by the terrific share manias in both Bombay and Calcutta. The number of existing companies was small: possibilities of large profits in cotton and jute mills became apparent to the general public only from the beginning of the seventies. And in the case of the tea industry where people did realise their opportunities in the sixties, it led to such a fever of speculation that its scars were not quite wiped out at the end of that decade.[2]

During the sixties some significant changes took place in the terms of the managing agency contract. The most important of these changes was in the method of remuneration. The standard pattern now was to charge a commission of $\frac{1}{4}$ anna or $\frac{3}{8}$ of a penny per pound of yarn and/or cloth produced in the mill. The particulars of remuneration charged by tea company agents are not known in detail, but enough is known to say that it was no lower than in the cotton or jute mills. In the opinion of contemporary observers, a managing agent earned, on an average, about Rs.30,000 to Rs.40,000 annually from a single concern, and we might as well take the opportunity to refute the argument advanced by many authors that the system was productive of great economy in the management expenses and ask 'But, in whose interest?' The accountant in the office of a managing agent might cast the ledgers of four different companies but each of those companies paid an amount to the managing agent large enough to have supported a separate establishment for each.

When, at the beginning of the seventies, the business cycle took

[1] *Op. cit.*   [2] See Chapters 5, 6, and 7.

an upward turn, many people of questionable integrity were attracted to the promotion of industrial enterprises. These people saddled the managing agency contract, which had already become pregnant with possibilities of great mischief in the hands of shrewd people, with further financial burdens such as office allowances and heavy compensation in case the managing agent had to lose office as a result of amalgamations, absorptions, and reconstructions.[1] The appointment of a managing agent was incorporated in the memorandum of association so that any future change became impossible.[2] These new managing agents knew very well that what an ordinary investor cares about is his dividends, and few, if any, take the trouble to scrutinise or understand the provisions of a memorandum or articles of association. On the other hand, large profits made by the existing companies held out very good prospects of handsome dividends and that was all that was needed to gull the public. To attract investors, some of the new managing agents went so far as to make promises publicly that if their mills failed to declare a certain minimum annual dividend, they would forgo their managing agency commission. When, however, the time came to act upon these promises, they usually went back on them, leaving the shareholders with only the memory of unfulfilled hopes.[3] Not that the shareholders did not protest; they did so vigorously, but to no avail. The lesser known promotors started their companies quietly, financing them largely from their own resources and with the help of friends and relatives, and after declaring one or two large dividends, unloaded their holdings on the market with themselves firmly in the saddle of the managing agency contract.[4] These managing agents were interested only in earning their commission and had no regard for the

[1] See a report of the case between the Mandvie Spinning and Weaving Company, Limited and Rahimbhoy Alladinbhoy, its secretaries and treasurers, wherein it was stated that the secretaries and treasurers were to receive, as per the articles of the Company, Rs.50,000 as compensation if the company was wound up within 25 years of its formation. T.O.I., 10 January 1880.

[2] See report of a case—*Neriad Spinning and Weaving Company, Ltd. vs. Anundji Visram*. T.O.I., 24 January 1876.

[3] See a letter from Gokuldass Jugmohandas to the T.O.I. regarding the agents of the United Spinning and Weaving Company Ltd., 5 March 1873.

[4] See a memorandum by Sorabji Sapruji Bengali to the Government of India in J.P., 1882, Departmental No. 212. S. S. Bengali was a prominent Bombay merchant, journalist, educationist and legislator. See a short sketch of his life in S. M. Rutnagur, *Bombay Industries: The Cotton Mills*, 1927, p. 699.

welfare of the mill or the shareholders. Writing of them, the editor of the *Textile Journal* said:[1]

The directors were the friends and relatives of the agents and were nominated by them along with the auditors. The agents had full executive powers in the management of the mills and the purchase of cotton and sale of yarn, and they could be interested in any other mill in a similar capacity, or own and work a mill themselves, or deal in cotton yarn and other commodities on their own account. They attracted other large investors who were given an interest in the business in addition to the dividends. Until about the late 1880's the agents were almost exclusively drawn from the merchant classes . . . were ignorant of the machinery and processes of manufacture. The spinning and weaving was supervised by managers and overlookers from Lancashire with the help of Parsee assistants and Hindu jobbers.

The large profits were mainly due to low wages, cheap raw materials and a constant excess of demand over supply, but when, after 1874, the business cycle took a downward turn and a trade depression set in, they soon became a matter of the past. The situation was seriously aggravated by a complete disregard of the laws of supply and demand by the managing agents who, as they were only interested in earning their fat commissions, continued to produce to the full capacity of the mills, even when the demand for their goods was falling.[2] The result was that not only did the high profit vanish, but the companies began to operate at a loss.[3]

Investors soon realised the situation and the independent shareholders became resentful. By the time the business cycle hit the

[1] Rutnagur, pp. 49–51.

[2] The agents resisted all moves to cut down production, so much so that even the Millowners' Association failed to bring about an effective agreement for shorter working hours.

[3] The fall in the prices of raw cotton, T. Cloth, and yarn in Bombay from 1873 to 1882 was as follows: (Unweighted Index)

Year	Yarn (20's)	T. Cloth	Raw Cotton
1873	—	—	100
4	100	100	82
5	81	86	80
6	80	76	75
7	86	89	82
8	79	83	81
9	74	80	86
80	84	85	98
1	85	89	95
2	78	83	90

(*Index Number of Indian Prices*, *op. cit.* Table VI. p. 12.)

bottom, the meetings of the shareholders had grown highly animated and acrimonious.[1] Many of the shareholders who were locally resident and were in the cotton textile trade soon found out about the wholesale abuses of their power by the managing agents, and about the mill and office staff, who were tempted to make money in addition to their salaries by abusing their situations, made possible by the laxity and technical incompetence of the agents. The following account by Rutnagur provides a graphic picture of these abuses:[2]

It was abundantly clear that the latter [managing agents] dealt in cotton and yarn belonging to the mills and speculated in the shares of the company according to the extent of the profits or losses which they were in a position to ascertain and even modify in Balance Sheets to suit the situation. Open contracts were entered into by the Agent's firm for the supply of cotton which were complacently passed on to the mill account if the prices began to drop. Speculation remained unchecked in buying and selling on the mill account while a variety of yarn labels were kept in reserve for purposes of unfair competition and spurious imitation. Cotton was purchased by uneducated selectors who were no judges of staple or of value and whose honesty was more than doubtful; it was weighed by corrupt weighers who were bribed for excess weight. Coals were purchased which were defective in quality or weight or both and the cotton was manufactured by machinery that was loaded with surreptitious commissions and maintained with stores in which the teeth of the shark had made heavy marks. The factory pay sheet was charged with useless or fictitious employees, and the employees themselves paid *bucksheesh* [bribes] to the jobbers and overlookers. The Board of Directors was faked, the auditors were chosen for the amiability of their disposition, and lavish office expenses and lawyer's fees added dignity to the business. Every canon of honest trading and manufacturing seemed to have been turned upside down, and the whole when considered together gave one the impression that the industry existed for no other purpose than to support a gigantic system of swindling.

The shareholders naturally became indignant and put searching questions to the management which, however, only received unsatisfactory and evasive replies. The agents went so far as to seek the help of lawyers to silence the enquiring shareholders. The shareholders did not only face the baton of the managing agency

---

[1] See, for instance, T.O.I., 3 March 1873; 21 August 1874; 26 August 1877; 30 March, 1873 on the Bombay United Spg. & Wvg. Co., Ltd., the Madras Spg. & Wvg. Co. Ltd., the New Colaba Co. Ltd, and the Bhownugger Mills and Press Company, Ltd. respectively.　　　　[2] Rutnagur, pp. 50-1.

contract, but had to contend with the opposition of their fellow-investors who also had a finger in the mill pie, and who defeated any attempt to censure the management formally.[1]

Helpless, they went to court in the hope that it would set aside the contract on the plea that it was harmful to the general interests of the shareholders, but the judges could no more alter the written words than priests could change what was written in a holy book.

Though the shareholders could not do anything to stop the mis-management except by defeating, in one or two cases, the resolution to pass the annual or half-yearly accounts, the depression brought its own revenge on the managing agents, but ruined the shareholders as well in the process. The managing agents, being mercantile firms, had habitually indulged in large speculation in cotton and opium. The losses suffered in the depression brought about the failure of several firms. The agents, in feeding the speculations and in an effort to avert failure, not only used their own resources but also exhausted the funds and the borrowing powers of the mills under their management.

The most spectacular of these failures was that of Kessowji Naik & Company, who were the agents of four cotton mills in Bombay. This took place towards the end of 1878 and produced a crisis which was considered similar to the one caused by the failure of the City of Glasgow Bank in Britain. And, here, those who argue that it is always the small obscure managing agent who dis-credits the system, may pause and rethink a little: who could have doubted the reputation, integrity and ability of this firm before the failure actually took place? But despite the honour and the credit enjoyed by Kessowji Naik, all four cotton mills, from which his remuneration was stated to be no less than Rs.400,000 annually,[2] and several other concerns connected with him, went into liquidation. The shareholders of these mills lost every pie of their capital and the creditors about 50% of their claims, which later alone amounted to Rs.6,000,000.[3] When the firm of agents failed, their total liabilities came to nearly Rs.30 million.[4] The figures are staggering.

[1] See T.O.I., 28 Feburary 1871, regarding the managing agency contract between Kessowji Naik and the Bombay Royal Spg. & Wvg. Co. Ltd. See also T.O.I., 4 March 1871 and 9 March 1871.
[2] T.O.I., 30 December 1878 and 6 January 1879.
[3] See the Memorandum by S. S. Bengali, *op. cit.*
[4] T.O.I., 6 January 1879.

How was all this done ? The answer is interesting and lies in the practice of industrial finance followed in those days. As a rule, promotors of industrial concerns limited the issue of shares to the amount of capital needed for providing only fixed assets. The bulk of the working capital was raised in the form of short-term loans, as and when required, and, for this purpose, the articles of association generally empowered the directors to borrow funds from the market with or without a limit. In the case of the four mills referred to above, advantage was taken of this power far in excess of the wants of the mills, and loans from the public were arranged by the agents with the authority of the directors. But before the agents could use the funds so raised, a technical hurdle had to be overcome. The articles of association of these companies provided that the excess funds over a certain amount with the mills were to be deposited with the bankers of the companies. To avoid any appearance of illegality, the agents appointed themselves as the bankers of these companies by resolutions passed by the boards of directors, and thereby evaded the need for entries in the books of accounts, and then used the money for speculation. One of the members of the managing agent's firm was later tried and sentenced to four years of imprisonment[1] and the suit against the directors resulted in a judgement against them for nearly Rs.1,000,000.[2] This was the first case in India in which a managing agent was convicted, and it proved beyond doubt the vulnerability of the association of industrial enterprises with mercantile firms as their managing agents.

It is generally argued that the managing agents nourished the infant industries by their financial support, but any substantial evidence to establish this claim would be hard to obtain. If anything, the general clamour for investment in cotton, jute and tea industries during the seventies proves the contrary. Even if some managing agents financed their companies, this was no more than could be expected considering how much they made out of them. All the traffic was certainly not in one direction. In fact, the agents found, in the control of their companies' finances, other means of earning money: whenever an agent had excess funds he lent them to the company at high rates of interest[3] whether it

---

[1] T.O.I., 29 September 1879.   [2] *Ibid.*

[3] At a shareholders' meeting of the Madras Spg. & Wvg. Co. Ltd. it transpired that the Company had borrowed Rs.50,000 at 9% p.a. when it could have raised

needed money or not, and whenever he needed funds he borrowed them from the company at less than market rate, even if the company had to borrow at a higher rate to meet its own requirements.[1] Moreover, there was a great difference in the nature of the risks involved in the financial assistance given to and received from agents. Whereas when a company lent to its agents, the loan remained unsecured and carried the very high risk of being entirely lost in speculative ventures, the loan given by the agents had behind it such assets as land, machines, and stocks of the company watched over by the agents themselves, from which there was always a chance to recover something, if not the whole.

To return to the events of the last quarter of the nineteenth century: the disclosures in the Kessowjee case, the protests of the shareholders, the verbatim reports of the shareholders' meetings in the newspapers and journals, and their criticisms, created in Bombay an atmosphere for the reforms that followed. The shareholders of the companies that had failed also took the opportunity, while reconstructing them, to appoint more suitable persons as their managing agents, and to provide for a more equitable basis of remuneration and a reasonably limited period of office. In some cases, the reaction of the shareholders was very sharp indeed. The shareholders of the New Colaba Company fought hard to abolish the system of managing agency from their company and instead to appoint a manager under the direct supervision and control of their board of directors. Their first attempt in 1877 remained unsuccessful[2] but they achieved their objective soon afterwards. When the Madras Spinning and Weaving Company was formed, the shareholders incorporated a clause in the Articles to forbid the appointment of any managing agent[3] but within a year the directors, in contravention of this clause, appointed a firm in Bombay as their managing agents on a commission of 5% on profits plus Rs.10,000 as fixed remuneration for ten years.[4] The *Times of India* tells us further that though the managing agents of this company fought hard for their commission, they never

---

the sum from Calls. Doubts were also expressed as to the Company's really needing the money. *Ibid.*, 21 August 1874.

[1] In a suit against the Secretaries and Treasurers of the Mandvie Spg. & Wvg. Co. Ltd. it was revealed that they had, under an agreement with the Company, used its funds for which they paid only 5% p.a. in interest.

[2] Reports of the shareholders' meeting in T.O.I., 26 February 1877.

[3] *Ibid.*, 21 August 1874.   [4] *Ibid.*

bothered to visit their factory even once during the whole year.[1] There were other cases as well but the scope of our work does not allow us to go into the subject in more detail.

The tendency towards reforms had in fact started as early as 1872–3. We have many examples of contracts in which the method of remuneration, the tenure of office and the administrative powers of the managing agents were considerably varied.[2] The effort to devise a satisfactory method of remuneration led to many complicated formulas.[3] The introduction of the final mode of reform was left to the genius of an Englishman, James Greaves, the pioneer of the cotton ginning and pressing industry in the Bombay Presidency. Born in Lancashire in 1820, Greaves came out to India in 1866 after experience of factory life in his own native place, and began business in Broach in partnership with George Cotton in 1868.[4] In 1877 the firm of Greaves, Cotton & Company were appointed managing agents of the Empress Mill on a commission of 10% on net profits for a term of ten years.[5] Nearly eighty years afterwards the Government of India followed suit and provided in the *Companies Act of 1956* that a managing agent could not be appointed for a greater period than ten years or be paid more than 10% of the net profits of a company in remuneration. The newspapers in Bombay welcomed the agreement made by Greaves,

[1] Report of the shareholders' meetings in T.O.I., 22 May 1875.

[2] (*a*) Merwanji & Company were appointed managing agents of a cotton mill in place of Forbes & Company resigning, for a period of only ten years. T.O.I., 27 October 1873.

(*b*) The firm seeking the agency of the Great Eastern Spinning & Weaving Company had, despite their holding 600 shares out of the total issue of 695 shares, offered to work under the control and supervision of the Board with the power to hire and fire officers of the Company. What is more, the aspirants also stated that they did not want any tenure of office to be fixed but if they were removed for any cause other than gross misfeasance or misconduct, they should be paid five years' remuneration in compensation. *Ibid.*, 28 November 1873.

(*c*) The remuneration in the case of Khatau Muccunji & Company who replaced Mangaldas Nathubhoy was fixed at 1 pie per pound weight of production or a third of the standard rate, so long as the company paid less than 4% in dividends, but, over that rate of dividend payment, they were to receive the standard rate. *Ibid.*, 10 September 1874.

(*d*) The Bhownugger Mills and Press Company paid its managing agents—Forbes & Company—5% on the procurement of machinery, 1% on the net profits of the Company and Rs.450 per month as office allowance. *Ibid.*

[3] *Ibid.*, 25 September 1874—see an article on Mandvie Spg. & Wvg. Co.

[4] Rutnagur, p. 708.

[5] See article on Empress Cotton Mills in T.O.I., 20 March 1887.

Cotton & Company and hoped that the agreement would become a model for future managing agency appointments.

But such hopes remained unrealised and it became increasingly clear that nothing short of legislation would stop the agents in Bombay from 'sucking the lifeblood out of the concerns they were supposed to manage'.[1] This does not, however, mean that the new system was not followed at all. J. N. Tata, who arrived on the scene soon afterwards, was not only a staunch supporter of the new system, but he revolutionised the whole concept of management. He showed a steady will for a new industrial order rather than mild yearnings to come to somewhat more palatable terms with the existing one, and that is what marks the dividing line between his spirit of adventure and his avaricious contemporaries.[2] The words 'Tata' and 'good management' became synonymous. Apart from Greaves, Cotton & Company and Tata & Sons there were only a few others who took up the new system.[3] Yet, save for such persons as M. Petit, Morarji Gockuldas, and Mangaldas Nathubhoy who managed their mills very well indeed,[4] the mounting criticism from all sides made it very difficult for others to work on the old system.

Editorial attacks such as 'no class of capitalists in the world ever invented such an extravagant system as the present [old] plan of agency'[5] or 'the absurd, hated and pernicious principle . . .'[6] of managing agency were bound to produce some benefits, however small. For a time all efforts to promote mills on the basis of a commission of $\frac{1}{4}$ anna per pound of yarn and/or cloth produced,

---

[1] It was reported that forty-five cotton mills in Bombay were working on the old system of remuneration. T.O.I., 20 March, 1887.

[2] In a letter to the T.O.I., J. N. Tata solicited public support to start a cotton mill to spin higher counts than 20 and offered to undertake the management of the mill at a remuneration of 10% on net profits which were to be calculated after deductions of 10% on the assets for depreciation. *Ibid.*, 17 August 1886. Moreover, it was then generally said that only Tata could have resurrected the dead Dhurrumsey Mill and turned it into one of the most prosperous mills in the Presidency.

[3] One Scott was appointed to the agency of the People of India Cotton Mill, Ltd., on a 10% on net profits basis. The contract was said to have been free from any fettering clauses. T.O.I., 11 May 1883.

[4] *Ibid.*, Mr Mangaldas Nathubhoy, who was not particularly mentioned, was the agent of the Bombay United Spg. & Wvg. Co. Ltd., since its foundation in 1860 until 1874 when he resigned. During this time the Mill had paid a sum in dividends which was equivalent to the paid-up capital of the company, Rs.900,000 and then had assets worth Rs.1,200,000. *Ibid.*, 26 August 1874.

[5] T.O.I., 27 March 1885.   [6] *Ibid.*, 7 January 1887.

ended in failure[1] and such mills as were floated on that basis were all private concerns.[2] During 1887 promoters were wandering 'from door to door with copies of deeds in their arms, like the Brahmins with *tipnas* . . .'[3] spreading false hopes of a 'large Chinese market'[4] for Indian cloth and yarn, and 'begging'[5] people to subscribe for shares. By and large, however, the old system of agency continued during the later eighties and nineties, although with mitigated evils and with changes here and there, in the ranks of the managing agents. More and more experienced and otherwise competent mill managers and engineers were appointed managing agents and mill agencies were also taken up by European firms but to chronicle all the developments would fill many more pages. It is sufficient to note here that the struggle for reforms continued and was particularly strong during the trade depression of 1898–1900. At least twenty-three firms gave up their managing agencies, it is said 'voluntarily and in the interest of the share-holders'[6] in the decade following 1895.

Before, however, we leave the subject of managing agency in Bombay, it would be useful to look at the following figures:

Table 19

Number of Managing Agents and Companies Controlled by them in Bombay in 1871[a]

M/Agency Firms Type	No.	Cotton Mills	Cotton Presses	Insurance	Others	Total
European	16	2	15	11	6	34
Indian	9	10	4	—	—	14

[a] Compiled from the *Times of India Directory*, 1872.

The table does not claim to be exhaustive, for the analysis of the companies included in it are only those which were given in the

---

[1] T.O.I., 7 January 1887.

[2] It was reported in the T.O.I. that the Bhatias, who started a mill and became its managing agents on a remuneration which was related to the profits on a sliding scale, could promote the mill by subscribing only privately because the public did not like the idea of a remuneration based on the sliding scale of profits. *Ibid.*, 4 January 1889. It is interesting to note that the National Council of Applied Economic Research recommended a sliding scale of remuneration for managing agents. See *The Managing Agency System, op. cit.*

[3] T.O.I., 6 September 1887.   [4] *Ibid.*   [5] *Ibid.*

[6] Rutnagur, p. 53.

Times of India Directory for 1872. Apart from the firms included in the table, there were eight individuals who were described as 'secretary'. Only one of them was a European who was in charge of an insurance company. The remaining seven were Indians—two in cotton mills, two in cotton presses, and three in other fields. Some of these may have held managing agencies in their individual capacities, as Cowasjee did. The main fact revealed by the table is that the number of European firms holding managing agencies was larger than the number of Indian firms, and that the former controlled more companies and had more diversified interests than the latter.

Table 20

Frequency Distribution of Companies Controlled by Managing Agents[a]

Managing Agents	Number of Companies							Total Companies
	1	2	3	4	5	6	7	
Europeans	9	4	–	1	–	1	1	34
Indians	6	2	–	1	–	–	–	14

[a] Compiled from the *Times of India Directory*, 1872.

The frequency analysis shows that the Europeans managed more companies from the same establishment than the Indians, and so reinforces the conclusion drawn from the earlier table.

The only Indian firm which controlled as many as four companies was that of Kessowjee Naik & Company, two of them cotton mills and the other two cotton presses, with an aggregate paid-up capital of Rs.2,733,000. The three European firms controlling seven, six and four companies respectively were Forbes & Company, Ewart, Latham & Company, and Remington & Company. Half or more companies held in each case were insurance companies originating in Bombay or elsewhere. Apart from the insurance companies included in this analysis, there were at least fifty-two marine, seventeen fire, and twelve life insurance companies which originated outside but operated in India through agencies mainly held by Europeans.[1] Of all the companies

[1] Byramjie Jeejibhoy, the promoter of the Bombay Fire Insurance Company in 1870 estimated that as far back as 1830 something like a sum of Rs.5 crores or £5 million was carried away from India by different European fire insurance offices that had agencies in India. See his obituary in T.O.I., 19 September 1890.

included in the *Times of India Directory*, 1872, there were only three companies excluding banks,[1] which functioned without a managing agent. These were the Bombay Gas Company (a sterling company), the Bombay Mechanics Building Company (a building society), and Treacher & Company (a trading concern) which had a capital of Rs.1,000,000. Another interesting fact that may be noted here is that not all the managing agencies were partnership concerns. One of them was a limited company, the London, Asiatic and American Company, Limited, incorporated in London with a paid-up capital of £1,000,000 which managed the Colaba Press Company, Limited, of Bombay which, in 1871, had a capital of Rs.940,000.[2] The cotton textile industry in Bombay could be said to have assumed a national importance from the year 1871, and the industrial eminence of Indians is primarily connected with the growth of this industry, but our analysis so far does not fully reflect their part. Their contribution is clearly shown by the following figures:[3]

Table 21

The Number of Managing Agencies and the Managed Mills in Bombay, 1895

Communities	Agencies	Mills
Hindus	27	30
Parsees	15	22
Mohammedans	4	4
Jews	1	8
Europeans	3	6
All	50	70

In interpreting the relative influence of the various Indian communities it should be remembered that the Parsees were well in the lead during the first two to three decades of the founding of the cotton mill industry in India. As the years advanced, the Hindus outstripped the Parsees. The table also shows that the influence of the European community in this field remained rather limited.

Forty-five companies were also analysed to find out the com-

---

[1] The banks did not have managing agents but see pp. 421–2.
[2] The *Times of India Directory*, 1872.   [3] Rutnagur, p. 54.

position of their boards of directors. One hundred and thirty-one persons held a total of 223 directorships available on the boards of these companies in 1871. The following results were obtained:[1]

Average number of directorships on a board	5
Average number of directorships held by one person	1·7
Total number of European directors	39
Total number of Indian directors	92
Number of directorships held by Europeans	50
Number of directorships held by Indians	173
Ratio of Europeans to Indian directors	1:2·36
Ratio of European to Indian-held directorships	1:3·46

More interesting results were obtained by analysing the frequency distribution of the directorships held by the two communities: Indians and Europeans. Whereas no European was a director of more than three companies at the same time, in the case of Indians as many as twelve held between four and eleven directorships. This is shown by the following table:

Table 22

Frequency Distribution of Directorships held in Bombay in 1871[a]

Directors	Number of Directorships held											Total
	1	2	3	4	5	6	7	8	9	10	11	
Europeans	29	9	1	–	–	–	–	–	–	–	–	39
Indians	67	9	4	4	2	–	3	1	–	1	1	92
All	96	18	5	4	2	–	3	1	–	1	1	131

[a] Compiled from the *Times of India Directory*, 1872.

Of those analysed, only twenty companies had European directors. The boards of three companies—Treacher & Company, Bombay Mechanics Building Society, and the Landing, Shipping Company of Kurranchi—were made up entirely of Europeans. Similarly, twenty-five companies had only Indians on their boards. The rest were mixed. Finally, a surprising finding was that though the boards of two companies were purely Indian, their managing agency was held by A. C. Brice & Company, probably a European firm.[2]

Lack of sufficient material makes it difficult to draw any detailed picture of the managing agency system in Calcutta. A search through the journals and newspapers of the day has produced very little which would give a vivid account of the system there. In

[1] Compiled from the *Times of India Directory*, 1872.   [2] *Ibid.*

contrast to the verbatim reports of the meetings of shareholders in Bombay newspapers, such a leading newspaper as the *Friend of India* in Calcutta completely ignored these occasions. The *Pioneer* published from Allahabad, although containing intelligent comments on financial matters, also failed to report on these meetings. The *Englishman* of Calcutta did report on almost every general meeting of the shareholders held in the City but these reports contained only such matters as the names of the shareholders present at the meeting and the resolutions proposing the adoption of the final accounts, the election of directors and the appointment of auditors. This may be because these meetings were unruffled and quiet. A more probable reason may be that the composition of the shareholders of companies in Calcutta was different. One would suspect that the independent shareholders in Calcutta companies were largely Europeans who were more interested in dividends than capital gains. Also that they were either in occupations not connected with trade, or were absentees in Britain. This would account for the non-turbulent meetings even in decidedly bad times. We know enough, however, from the occasional 'letter to the editor' and the comments of financial reporters that the management of companies in Calcutta was no better than in Bombay.

Commenting on the heavy fall in the price of jute shares, which, in some cases, amounted to up to 50% of their value, in 1874, the correspondent of the *Times of India* for the 'Commercial Affairs in Bengal' wrote:[1]

But, taking into account the necessary economies which can be readily effected on extravagant managements, in reduced commissions, highly paid managers, steam yachts, and many other matters which passed unquestioned when the Directors met their shareholders annually with over a 30% dividend in many instances; then also the stoppage of further competition [i.e. erecting new mills]. . . .

the situation can be much improved. The foregoing remarks of the Correspondent became more illuminating when seen in the light of the following letter by a shareholder of a tea company to the editor of the *Friend of India*:[2]

[1] T.O.I., 22 March 1875.
[2] F.O.I., 12 June 1887. The reporter further observed that the jute companies pay a commission of $2\frac{1}{4}$% on outturn to their agents which would, on a mill of 300 looms, amount to Rs.40,000.

... managing agents charge 5% commission on the gross proceeds of the outturn which may amount to Rs.40,000 to Rs.60,000 while the unhappy shareholders will not receive a pie. They go on producing whatever the state of the market. ...

Similar charges were made by an 'Unfortunate Scripholder' against the managing agents of tea companies. According to him many agents charged office allowance, commission on stores and coolies, etc. and there were others 'who could not account for funds'[1]. In appraising the Directors' Report of the Budge Budge Jute Mills, the *Friend of India* commented that the management was infested with such abuses as dealing in its own shares and influencing their price; a disease which the shareholders ought to cure by proper provisions in the Articles of the Company.[2] In a further series of articles on the jute and cotton mills in Calcutta, the newspaper unearthed many other undesirable practices carried on by the management of these mills. Amongst the more serious allegations were the declaring of dividends without making any provision for depreciation, as if, as the paper wrote, 'a jute mill, like port wine, improves in value';[3] 'forward sale' of the products of a mill which it believed were not made genuinely;[4] and window-dressing of balance sheets by constant over-valuation of stock.[5] These articles suggested further that money was being siphoned away by the managing agents in the shape of remuneration and allied matters.[6] The continuing attacks by the newspaper produced a climate for the reforms in accounting methods which

---

[1] F.O.I., 24 March 1880.   [2] *Ibid.*, 28 November 1881.

[3] See an article on the Fort Gloster Mill, F.O.I., 9 November 1877.

[4] See two articles—Our Jute Mills—F.O.I., 28 September and 5 October 1877.

[5] See an article on the Howrah Jute Mills, F.O.I., 6 August 1881.

[6] According to a shareholder, Schoene, Kilburn & Company, the managing agent of the Dunbar Cotton Mill, had drawn away half the profits amounting to Rs.115,643 in commission and Rs.23,100 in office allowance earned during a period of 5½ years since the founding of the Mill in 1874. Of the total profits of Rs.281,172 earned during this period, the shareholders received only 21% in dividends part of which must have been a return of capital, as sufficient depreciation was not provided. F.O.I., 6 August 1881.

In the case of the Baranggore Jute Mills which was a sterling company, the managing agents' commission amounted to £10,696 7s. 0d. and the six London directors together drew in fees a sum of £1,500 in the course of one year. Together this amounted to 40% more than what the shareholders had received and was considerably more than the remuneration drawn by other agencies in Calcutta. F.O.I., 9 November 1877. See also the issue of 9 May 1882, for comments on Bowreah Cotton Mill.

followed, but the attitude of the management changed only slowly. The boards of these companies were show pieces, much as in Bombay. Complaining, a shareholder wrote that they were 'self-perpetuating, irresponsible and provided no information'.[1] The safeguard of qualification shares suggested in the articles, with the intention of making the directors exert themselves in the interests of the company, resulted only in the election of wealthy persons, and in the opinion of this shareholder, of 'fools who let themselves in the hands of one or two clever directors'.[2] Moreover, these directors, as another shareholder wrote, were 'frequently under pecuniary obligations to their agents, or members of, or assistant to, the agent's firm.'[3] No wonder the paper advocated the abolition of these boards altogether as superfluous.[4] But the suggestion to abolish the boards must be regarded as retrogressive for it is in the development of a genuine board of directors that the much needed control can be exercised on the activities of the managing agents.

A tendency to employ highly paid European staff in preference to Indians was another serious criticism levelled against the European management,[5] a tendency which had been consistently followed throughout British Rule and only gave way after Independence under pressure from the Government of India.[6]

[1] F.O.I., 28 November 1881. [2] *Ibid.* [3] *Ibid.*, 24 March 1880.
[4] See the Commercial Report on jute companies, T.O.I., 29 March 1875.
[5] The T.O.I. reporter on the Commercial Affairs in Bengal wrote: 'Indo-European youths can replace European staff for 10% of their salary, i.e. Rs.25 or Rs.30 p.m. after three months training.' T.O.I., 29 March 1875.
[6] The figures for the employment of Indians in foreign firms in India during 1954–6 were as follows:

Salary Group (in Rupees)	Indians as % of the total Employees		
	1954	*1955*	*1956*
1000–1500	54·0	61·5	66·7
1501–3000	23·0	27·4	33·3
Highest	6·5	7·9	10·0

(Information was not collected with regard to salaries below Rs. 1000 per month.)
Categories of firms employing more than 79% non-Indians which showed no change between 1955 and 1956 were as follows: Plantation companies (86·1%); jute companies (84·8%): and banking companies (75·6%). The managing agencies employed 64·0% non-Indians in 1955 and 59·3% in 1956. There were in all 6,566 foreigners employed by the foreign companies in India on salaries of Rs.1,000 or more. 86·7% of these were British, 3·9% American (their number had increased from 227 in 1954 to 259 in 1956), 108 Swiss (as compared to 121 in 1955). In 1956 the total number of foreigners employed had declined by 244 as compared to 1955 but this was primarily due to a decrease of 216 in the managerial posts. (Source: confidential.)

Calcutta also nourished an element of professional promotors in the ranks of its industrialists. This is what the Registrar of the Joint Stock Companies in Calcutta had to say about them:[1]

Not infrequently, a joint stock company is started as speculation; a few speculators club together and seek to raise the wind; they fix upon a stock and block, set a nominal value upon them, fill their pockets by sending forth glowing prospectus of the projected company. Thus for instance, they start a mill, appoint a trustee for its sale to a company, set their own valuation upon it, and stipulate with the trustees an upset price; then they join with a few persons to get up a memorandum of association; they thus form a company with a certain capital; the bulk of the capital is absorbed by the purchase of the mill, the sale proceeds go to the original founders of the mill. These persons take over such a large number of shares, representing their respective value of the mill, in addition to what they may receive in cash; they speculate with the shares, and, after the market is excited, they take advantage of it and sell their shares at high rates; then some of them become directors, one of them or his firm becomes managing agents, or agent, and one of the members of the firm is appointed a managing director; the same firm does business with the company by supplying goods or lending money, they secure public credit by voting substantial dividends, though little business may have been done; the credit once established brings in more credit; they then reduce the dividend and put the company in liquidation; they become the liquidator themselves; they next get up another company, and make the new company purchase the old; they pay the value of the business or property of the company in liquidation with the shares of the purchasing company, and then go on building one house of cards on another. When the smash comes the innocent and the credulous public, represented in the shareholders and the creditors, suffer.

But competence for the jobs was not the only consideration. Here is what the Viceroy, Sir John Lawrence wrote to the Secretary of State in a letter (17 August 1867) on the question of changing the manner of recruitment to the Indian Civil Service:

'The chief objection to a change is that of policy. We have conquered India mainly by force of arms, though policy and good management have largely aided us. In like manner we must hold it. The Englishman must always be in the front rank, holding the post of honour and of power as the condition of our retaining our rule.'

Quoted in B. B. Misra, *The Indian Middle Classes*, 1961, p. 372.

[1] See memorandum by P. C. Ghosha, Registrar, Joint Stock Companies, Calcutta to Government of Bengal, No. 66, 14 November 1881. J.P., 1882, Departmental No. 446.

This explicit account of outright swindling from such an authoritative source contained in a report to the Government of India, can lead to only one conclusion: the promotion and management of companies in Calcutta was badly infected. It must not, however, be inferred that every managing agent in Calcutta was a swindler. It is more likely, in the days when joint stock companies were still few, that a few cases had an exaggerated effect on the minds of the people. But, taking the criticisms as a whole, it cannot be denied that '. . . the interests of the shareholders and consequently of the people who seek to invest their capital in joint stock enterprises, [were] not sufficiently protected . . .'.[1]

Finally, a statistical investigation was carried out to determine the extent of the managing agencies, the number and categories of companies controlled by them, and to find out about the composition and character of the boards of directors of companies in Calcutta to put the matter in proper perspective. An analysis of the share market report showed that there were at least thirty-one managing agents in Calcutta during 1875 who were responsible for the management of ninety companies out of a total of 128 listed.[2] The rest of the companies, which included all the twelve banks and four railway companies listed in the report, were under the managership or secretaryship of individuals. These individuals, excluding those connected with the banks and the railways, may well, in fact, have been managing agents like Davar.[3] Some of them certainly were, as is evident from the fact that no less than three tea companies—Dehradoon, Tukvar, and Hoolungoorie—were under the management of the same person, R. S. Staunton.[4]

Table 23 is an industrial breakdown of the companies included in the list.[5] Nineteen out of the thirty-one managing agencies were managing either only one company or companies only in one field of enterprise. Of these, twelve were exclusively in tea, two had a jute mill each, another three had one jute press each; one was running a printing press and the last one was a distiller. Schoene, Kilburn & Company were the most important managing agents both from the viewpoint of the number of companies managed and the

---

[1] See memorandum by P. C. Ghosha, Registrar, Joint Stock Companies, Calcutta to Government of Bengal, No. 66, 14 November 1881, J.P., 1882, Departmental No. 446.

[2] Compiled from the Share Market Report in F.O.I., 5 November 1875.

[3] See pp. 228-9.   [4] F.O.I., 5 November 1875.   [5] *Ibid.*

Table 23

Calcutta Managing Agencies in 1875

Number of Companies	Industry	Number of Companies Controlled by Individuals	by Firms
12	Banks	12	—
5	Coal Mines	1	4
4	Cotton Mills	1	3
10	Jute Mills	—	10
9	Jute Presses	1	8
4	Railways	4	—
66	Tea	10	56
18	Miscellaneous	9	9
128	All	38	90

diversification of interest. Besides controlling four tea companies, they had such other enterprises under their wing as the Ranigunj Coal Association, the Bengal Jute Company, the Dunbar Cotton Mills, the Bengal Jute Pressing Company, the Merchant Steam Tug Company, and lastly, but perhaps the most important of them all, the India General Steam Navigation Company. The firm of Williamson, Magor & Company, which only controlled eight tea companies, was undoubtedly the leader of the tea industry and has remained prominent in this field down to this day. A comparison of the 'Share and Stock Market' list in 1875 with that of 1879 showed negligible changes in the composition, control or rank of managing agents, except in the tea industry where, at least, seventeen companies had changed hands.[1] The causes of the change of managing agencies are not explicitly stated, but selling out, insolvency, and death were generally the most important factors.

An analysis of the boards of directors of seventy-seven companies showed that 148 people held the 241 directorships available on these boards, or, roughly, there were three directors on the board of a company. The frequency distribution was as follows:[2]

---

[1] F.O.I., 5 November 1875.
[2] Compiled from *Thacker's Bengal Directory*, 1875.

Number of Directorships Held by a Person	Number of Persons Holding
7	1
5	3
4	6
3	18
2	21
1	99
Average 1·6	Total 148

The largest number of directorships was held by J. H. Williamson, the senior partner of the firm of Williamson, Magor & Company. The other partner of this firm, R. B. Magor, was the director of three companies which were different from those on which Williamson sat. Thus, between them they were directors of ten different companies. The three persons occupying five seats each were Leo Zender who was the partner in India of the firm of Robert & Charriol; R. S. Staunton, partner in Staunton & Company; and C. N. Kernot, a medical doctor. Assistants in the managing agency firms also acted as directors in some cases. There were only six Indian directors, namely, Peary Charan Mitra who was a director in the Great Eastern Hotel, the Bengal Tea Company, and the Durrung Tea Company; Manockjee Rustomjee, the promoter of the ill-fated Rustomjee Twine & Canvas Company, who was a director in the Howrah Docking Company, and the Triton Marine Insurance Company which was the only insurance company promoted by Indians in Calcutta, as can be gathered from the same source;[1] and the remaining three, Baiconthonath Sein, G. C. Paul and H. Seal, held only one directorship each.

There were some directors in India who held seats on the London board of some companies[2] and similarly, there were people in London who were directors of one or two companies in India.[3] But any relationship between the directorship of a company and its managing agency, and the nature of such a relationship, can only be established if individual cases are studied. Such

---

[1] Compiled from *Thacker's Bengal Directory*, 1875.

[2] For instance, Seth A. Apcar of Calcutta was on the London Board of the National Bank of India, Limited. *Ibid.*

[3] An example is David Wilson on the Board of the Great Eastern Hotel Company, Limited. *Ibid.*, p. 380.

studies generally fall outside the scope of this work, but the firm of Williamson, Magor & Company was studied to see what these relationships may have been. All the companies in which the two partners of this firm were directors were analysed, and it was found that the managing agency of all the companies except the Soom Tea Company was held by firms other than Williamson, Magor & Company. Similarly, the boards of all the companies of which this firm was a managing agent, were analysed. In 1879 the firm had the agencies of eleven tea companies, five of which were sterling companies. Information regarding the directors of two of the sterling companies was not available, but George Williamson, probably a partner in the London branch of the firm, was a director in two of the remaining three companies' boards. No information was available about the boards of two Indian companies. The directors of other companies, except the Soom Tea Company, were not partners in the firm of Williamson, Magor & Company. Some of the directors on the boards of some of these companies were common also to the boards of some of the companies of which one of the two partners was a director, but for which the firm of Williamson, Magor & Company did not hold the managing agency.[1] The conclusion, therefore, if any, would be that the link between the directorship and the managing agency of a company was rather weak. But the surprising fact from the standpoint of business secrecy was that the partners of the managing agency firm of one tea company should have been allowed to act as directors in another tea company of which they were not managing agents.

The response of the Indian community in Calcutta to the promotion and financing of industrial enterprises was decidedly poor. Without a share in the risks, they were naturally without any share in the control of these concerns. But any inference about their inability to manage industrial concerns economically and efficiently would be far from the truth. This is well illustrated by the history of the Empress Cotton Mill Company Limited, which was founded in Calcutta in 1877, a solitary instance but a bright one nonetheless. The great bulk of the shareholders as well as all the directors of this company were Indians and so were its managing agents, D. B. Mehta & Company. The Company's share capital of Rs.625,000 was divided into 1,250 shares of Rs.500 each and was

[1] Namely Dr. Kernet, S. N. Smellie, and R. S. Staunton. *Ibid.*

fully paid-up. In the words of the Financial reporter of the *Friend of India*, the mill was 'the latest and also the cheapest cotton mill erected on the Hooghly'.[1] Its gross profit, which included all manufacturing expenses, amounted in a year to 30% of its equity and loan capital combined. This was the highest profit earned by any mill in that part of the country. The mill pursued a policy of steady expansion by ploughing back from its profits. In 1882 it capitalised Rs.250,000 of its reserves by issuing bonus shares which formed an addition of 40% to its existing capital. The mill was constantly referred to in the newspaper as the 'best of all'. The financial help given by its managing agents may also be noted here. In 1882 the balance sheet of the Company showed a loan from them to the extent of Rs.105,642-6-0.[2]

The management of business corporations in other parts of India seems also to have suffered from the same sort of malaise as was present in Bombay and Calcutta. This is what the Secretary of the Chief Commissioner of Coorg had to say about the practice in Mysore:[3]

Composed of unlettered and helpless *raiyats* [subjects] as shareholders, and managed by astute and unscrupulous men, they [companies] have too often been worked solely for the benefit of the directors and their friends and entirely at the cost of the shareholders' interests, and it has been found that even where the provisions of the Act [*Companies Act, 1866*] are sufficient for men of education and ordinary intelligence to protect themselves, the shareholders have been powerless to look after their own interests, and the interference of the Government Officer, the Registrar, on their behalf has, one way or another, frequently been defeated.

As a matter of fact, the people of this part of India seem to have had a very peculiar notion about joint stock institutions. A most ingenious device which struck at the very basis of the joint stock principle was observed in, of all places, the articles of companies formed in Mysore. This was a clause whereby the shareholders could claim back the amount of their paid-up shares from the company and thus withdraw from it.[4] Not only had this amazing provision been incorporated in the articles but as the Registrar of

---

[1] F.O.I., 11 June 1881.   [2] *Ibid.*
[3] J.P., Departmental No. 332. The *Companies Act, 1866* was never applied to Coorg. *Ibid.*
[4] *Ibid.*

Companies for that area wrote: 'it was worked by the few who were behind the scenes, in favour of a few chosen shareholders, and at the expense and to the detriment of the honest and general body of shareholders.[1] It is difficult to conceive a more novel method of cheating and one wonders if it had any parallel elsewhere in the world. The tragedy of it all was that the courts in Mysore, rightly or wrongly, upheld these articles of association[2] which were so manifestly dishonest, against public policy and the interests of the companies.

In the North-West Province, the only other province relatively important from the point of view of company formation, the situation does not seem to have been any better. The case of the Punjab Bank Limited, illustrates the practices in this part of the country. In 1877, when the Bank went into liquidation after fourteen years of service, on account of gross mismanagement, it had a paid-up capital of Rs.2,000,000 and a reserve fund amounting to Rs.150,000. At this time its bad debts amounted to Rs.1,127,713 or more than half of the paid-up capital and the reserve fund combined. The result was that during the three years preceding its liquidation, the Bank had spent Rs.300,000 in buying its own shares 'to conciliate shareholders who had been clamorous because of the depreciated state of their shares'.[3]

To conclude, the management of corporate enterprises in India was seriously diseased. Its harmful effects were felt by many and this must have deterred the potential investors to some significant extent. It would be wrong, however, to tar all the managing agents with the same brush. There were certainly some who were very jealous of their reputation and who always strove to achieve something more than the mere pursuit of private gains at all costs. Yet, when all is said, one is still left wondering whether the mismanagement was not the rule rather than the exception. There is certainly nothing which is inherently wrong in the institution. It arose out of necessity. It is a unique system inasmuch as it makes it possible to appoint management experts to run the affairs of a single company or group of companies without the necessity

---

[1] J. P., Department No. 332. The *Companies Act, 1866* was never applied to Coorg. *Ibid.*

[2] *Ibid.* The quotations relate mostly to *nidhis*. At a later date the High Court ruled that the shareholders who had thus withdrawn their capital remained liable for the debts of the company. See p. 188.

[3] *Beacon*, 5 July as reported in the T.O.I., 13 July 1877.

for the managing agent to invest, and, although its fate in India now seems to be sealed,[1] it is playing a useful part in other developing countries.[2] Whether the big managing agency firms, in the words of the Industrial Commission, 'were unduly conservative in their method of business'[3] so that they preferred 'commerce rather than industries'[4] is difficult to say, but there is no doubt that during the nineteenth century the bait of potential profits from a managing agency impelled many merchants to start cotton, tea and jute companies.

Obviously unaware that the ground has already been broken, B. B. Kling has written an article on 'The Origin of the Managing Agency System in India'.[5] The scope of his article is limited to the story of six joint stock companies promoted and/or acquired by the firm of Carr, Tagore & Company between 1836 and 1846. His researches, however, confirm the findings reported in this chapter though there is a great difference in what he emphasises.

Kling dates the beginning of the system as 1836, when Carr, Tagore & Company were appointed the managing agents of the Steam Tug Association and dismisses the earlier developments in the following words:[6]

The agency houses also conducted the handful of joint stock associations founded before 1834. Though the joint stock form was limited to

---

[1] The Lok Sabha (Lower House of Indian Parliament) adopted by 58 votes to 19 a motion sponsored by 72 members seeking to abolish managing agencies in cement, sugar, jute, cotton textiles and paper industries in three years from 2 April 1967. *The Overseas Hindustan Times*, 1 December 1966. See also Michael Kidron, *Foreign Investments in India*, 1965, pp. 52–3.

[2] In Nigeria many industries are being developed under the managing agencies of foreign firms. For instance, the managing agency of the Nigerian Cement Company Limited, at Nkalagu in the Eastern Region, is held by Tunnel Portland Cement Company. Tunnel Portland and its subsidiary, F. L. Smith & Company, hold between them only 10·8% of the equity which now amounts to over £4 million. The company was incorporated on 13 November 1954.

Similarly, the Indian Head Inc. of America have started the Aba Textiles, Limited, at Aba, Eastern Nigeria, under a managing agency contract. Arrangements made by companies manufacturing products under licence from foreign firms and many agreements on technical collaboration between foreign firms partake of the managing agency system.

[3] Report of the Industrial Commission, 1916–18, p. 9.   [4] Ibid.

[5] 'The managing agency has been a dominant form . . . yet no one has described the circumstances surrounding its first emergence.' Kling, JAS, Vol. XXVI. No. 1. November 1966, pp. 37–47. The quotation is on p. 37. See my Ph.D. Thesis, London, 1965, Chapter 14, pp. 415–81. The chapter was, in fact, written during the 1960–1 academic session.   [6] Kling, p. 38.

insurance and laudable societies, the employment of agency houses as managers provided the organisational model for the later managing agency system.

In his zeal to prove that the managing agency system was entirely an Indian contribution, Kling has, to my mind, completely misplaced the emphasis. As mentioned earlier in this chapter, the system had already been developed in its essential features at least twenty years before the Steam Tug Association was formed.[1] The terms of appointment of Carr, Tagore & Company were similar to those on which earlier European houses conducted the insurance business, and the former, thus, do not provide a point of departure.[2] Even if we were to assume that Kling's concern was with the application of this system to only such joint stock businesses as steam tugs and coal mines, we cannot be at all certain, without further research, whether the system had not already been applied for the management of other such companies existing between 1818 and 1836.[3] His lamentation: 'it is ironical that a system whose invention is always attributed to British mercantile houses and associated with colonialism, should have begun with an Indian owned firm'[4] rings, therefore, a bit hollow even if we were to imagine Carr, Tagore & Company as an *Indian owned* firm in which Tagore was only an equal partner with a European.[5] But apart from a minor imaginative stretch[6]

[1] See pp. 223–6.

[2] The Steam Tug Association was formed for a term of five years and its affairs were conducted by a committee of five elected directors under whose control Carr, Tagore & Company were appointed as Secretaries to manage the details of the business at a remuneration of 5% on the net earnings of the steamers. These terms of what Kling calls the first 'managing agency contract' were provided in the deed of association (equivalent to the Regulations of the insurance societies or the present memorandum of association of companies). Kling, p. 40.

[3] See list of companies in Appendix 4. Particularly list of references under 'Y' on Bowreah Cotton Mills. See also Chapter 1, Appendix 3, and Bishnupodo Guha, 'The Coal Mining Industry' in V.B. Singh (Ed.), *The Economic History of India*, 1965, pp. 304–11.

[4] Kling, p. 47.

[5] Kling, pp. 38–59.

[6] Kling asks 'Why did Tagore form a joint stock association instead of operating the Forbes [steamer] as an adjunct of his agency house?' Apart from the need for capital he says, 'The very title of the new company—Steam Tug Association—provides another clue. Associations were promoted in Calcutta for civic and economic improvements and people invested in them to support "good causes" as well as to earn a return. To promote his plan Tagore took

and a serious error of fact,[1] his article makes some useful additions to our knowledge of Carr, Tagore & Company.

---

advantage of this connection in the public mind between civic improvement and the joint stock form of organisation' (p. 39).

Kling has read a little too much into the choice of the word 'association'. Whereas there were some joint stock undertakings called associations, there were many more named companies. There is no suggestion that the Bengal Tea Association, also a Carr, Tagore & Company's enterprise, had this in mind or for that matter the Ranigunj Coal Association, Ltd. formed much later. Companies certainly did not find it more difficult to raise capital than associations, by reason of this difference alone. Very likely, whether an undertaking was called an association or a company only reflected personal taste rather than shrewd judgement about the motivation of investors. The words agent, manager, secretary, or secretaries and treasurers, mostly the latter, were also used in the same sense of a managing agent, and it is interesting to note that the office of Secretaries and Treasurers had been codified in the Companies Act, 1956.

[1] The first limited liability Act in India was not passed in 1866 as mentioned by Kling in footnote eighteen of his article. The first Act to accord limited liability to joint stock companies, excepting banking and insurance undertakings was passed in 1857. In 1860 it was extended to banking and in 1866 to insurance companies. See pp. 65–8 70 and 212.

S

CHAPTER 13

CONCLUDING OBSERVATIONS

By the end of March 1901 the paid-up capital of the 1,364 companies registered in India still in operation amounted to no more than 370 million rupees—hardly an impressive growth record over a period of fifty years for a country of the size and resources of India.[1] This chapter summarises the main features which characterise the growth of the Indian corporate sector in the nineteenth century, and examines why this growth remained so poor.

Corporate institutions had been known in ancient India and corporations of the guild type survived throughout the Hindu period, lingering on into the Moghul era. No direct link, however, can be traced between these institutions and the modern joint stock company. Development of the latter in India was conditioned by the examples of European chartered companies operating in the country. Joint stock companies engaged in trading were first formed in the 1660's. After flourishing for some sixty years, these companies gradually dwindled away during the eighteenth century. Not until the end of the first quarter of the nineteenth century did the growth of modern companies get under way, and though the managing agency system had come into existence earlier, its development was as yet in its infancy.

The first spurt in Indian company formation followed in the wake of the break-up of the European agency houses, itself arising from the commercial crisis of the 1820's. Progress was assisted by the application of steam power to manufacture and the coming of the steamships.[2] In the main, the banking, manufacturing, mining and navigation companies owed their creation to European initiative but the Indian element was nevertheless quite significant. Alongside the agency houses, the military and the civil servants of the East India Company played a very important role in promoting and financing banking and certain industrial companies. The success of the few manufacturing companies promoted during this

---

[1] See Appendix 20.   [2] See Chapter 1.

period was limited for a number of reasons, not least that of poor management. Scarcity of capital as such did not make itself felt in this period since enterprises were few; nevertheless, it does not appear to have been easy to raise venture capital, very likely due to the poor performance of industrial companies already in operation. The lack of an organised capital market at that time forced company promoters to rely on newspaper advertisements and personal contacts for raising funds.[1] The treatment of companies as large partnerships made going more difficult still, particularly for the banks, since to recover debts, every shareholder had to be joined as a plaintiff in law suits. Conditions changed radically after 1850.[2]

The Companies Act of 1850 made it easier to raise finance and the beginning of the railroads in the early fifties opened up further possibilities for industrialisation. A few cotton and jute mills were started soon afterwards.[3] In 1859, pressure was brought on the Government to relax the Assam clearance rule of 1845. As a result, 'the practice of requiring applicants to show that they had means to cultivate the land was forbidden'.[4] A rush of applications followed this decision, culminating in 1863–4 in a virtually reckless promotion of tea companies. The boom ended in 1866 and the industry remained in a depressed state until 1870.[5]

In the meantime, by an Act of 1860, limited liability had been extended to the banking companies. Soon afterwards, the American Civil War cut off cotton supplies to Britain and made her dependent on India. As a result cotton prices soared in Bombay. The four years 1862 to 1865 saw a four-fold increase in the value of cotton exports from Bombay; the total amounting to £82·5 million. An orgy of speculation ensued. The paid-up capital of companies registered from 1863 to 1865 amounted to 206 million rupees. Of this large sum, 94·4% belonged to the banks, financial and land reclamation companies. Almost all companies floated during this period had to be wound-up after the crash in 1865.[6] One important result of the episodes in Bombay and Calcutta was to bring the share markets in these cities into the limelight, and expose their organisational weaknesses.

The Bombay share market was formally organised in 1875. In

---

[1] See Chapter 2.   [2] See Chapter 3.   [3] See Chapter 4.
[4] See Edgar's 'Note on the Tea Industry in Bengal', *Papers Regarding the Tea Industry in Bengal*, 1873, p. 11.
[5] See Chapter 6.   [6] See Chapter 5.

Calcutta attempts to organise a stock exchange seem to have been made as early as 1858 but not until the first decade of the present century did these attempts succeed. In Bombay, the business of stock brokering was almost exclusively in the hands of Indians. In Calcutta, on the other hand, the Bengalis worked alongside the Europeans, particularly in the earlier years, but during the last two decades of the nineteenth century, the Marwaris came to dominate the scene. Indians were quite at home in the art of stock market operations and their love of *satta* (time bargains in which difference in price alone is passed) was a common feature of both the Bombay and Calcutta stock markets.[1]

By the beginning of the 1870's the aftermath of the boom was over and the three major industries of the country were able to resume the path of prosperity.[2] The share markets embraced a much wider public than ever before within their folds. Transfer of savings through the share markets to entrepreneurs by those not interested in undertaking investment themselves helped the corporate sector to grow. At the same time the experience industrialists had gained in the working of companies prior to 1870 brought home to them the need for alterations in the capital structure of companies if they were to reap the full benefits of the share market facilities. They realised, for instance, that the face value of shares needed to be drastically reduced to attract small investors. They also found that the practice of private borrowing had to be discarded in favour of issuing debentures and preference shares.[3] Without the aid of the Bombay share market it is highly doubtful whether the cotton industry in particular could have expanded at the rate it did.

Among the factors which improved the climate for investment on a larger scale and hence the growth of the corporate sector, one can list the substantial railroad development which unified the country, the 'Rule of Law' established under the Crown Government, advances in liberal education, depreciation of the rupee which favoured exports, and the enterprise of a body of British and Indian managing agents.[4]

The idea of the managing agency system was born at the turn of the eighteenth century. During its first seventy years it served the cause of industrial development very well indeed, though the

---

[1] See Chapter 11. [2] See Chapters 7 and 9.
[3] See Chapter 11. [4] See Chapter 9.

managing agency contract had become impregnated with seeds of possible abuse. The system came under considerable strain during the last quarter of the nineteenth century. In the seventies and eighties many unscrupulous people had joined the ranks of managing agents and severely abused their powers under the managing agency contract. Public demand for voluntary reforms failed to produce significant results and it was realised that the abuses could be stopped only by legislative measures. The Government, however, was in no mood to listen to public out-cries. Influenced by a *laissez-faire* philosophy, the Government considered it more important to keep Indian law in line with British law so that British investors would know where they stood; however, greater emphasis was placed on the publication of accounts in Indian law.[1]

Many other factors make the last three decades of the nineteenth century important from the viewpoint of corporate history. These include the gold mining speculation in South India,[2] the growth of a host of small savings and loan societies, the episode of the assessment insurance companies and the Bengal gold craze. The Bengal gold craze showed, incidentally, the fallacy of regarding the European houses as irreproachable in business morality. Not only did they originate the idea of 'catch-penny' gold mining com-panies, they promoted every single one of these companies and kept the ball rolling for as long as they could.[3]

In the nineties, the demand from railways gave the coal mining industry its first big impetus to create new capacity. The counter-vailing duty on imports of Continental beet sugar led to increased investment in the sugar industry.[4]

Modern methods of factory production were meanwhile spreading through the urban society. Urbanisation and a very limited relaxation of the rules governing the purchase of Govern-ment stores encouraged investment in flour, rice, oil, paper and other miscellaneous trading and manufacturing enterprises. This overall development further necessitated and brought about a gradual but noteworthy increase in the banking capital of the country.[5] The share of the various industries in the total paid-up capital of companies at the end of the nineteenth century is shown in the table on p. 260.

[1] See Chapter 12.   [2] See Chapter 8.   [3] See Chapter 10.
[4] See Chapter 9.   [5] *Ibid.*

Cotton mills, Jute mills, Tea companies,	
Cotton and Jute Screws and Presses	56·0%
Banking Companies	12·4%
Railways and Tramways	8·6%
Coal mining Companies	3·5%
Miscellaneous	19·5%
	100·0%

The amount of total paid-up capital invested was, however, only Rs.370 million or £25 million (converted at the then rate of 1s. 4d.). The question arises, why was the amount of investment so small?

Certain other students of Indian economic history have asked much the same question and the debate continues. Anstey wrote of 'arrested development',[1] Rosen of 'aborted growth',[2] Morris[3] and Dhairyabala Pandit of a 'century of gestation',[4] Bhatt of 'stagnation',[5] and Thorner of a 'possibility of decline'.[6] One can possibly divide these studies into two broad categories: some sketch a general trend of development over the past century or a longer period; others see in India between 1860 and 1900 'some visible signs' such as a large amount of foreign investment or the growth of a host of cotton or jute mills as indicative of further sizeable growth which, however, failed to occur. The explanations given for this failure vary from largely economic[7] to largely non-

[1] Anstey, pp. 5, 8, 154, 399, 471, 472.

[2] George Rosen, 'A Case of Aborted Growth: India, 1860–1900, Some Suggestions for Research', EW, 11 August 1962, pp. 1299–1302. It should, however, be noted that India as a case of aborted growth was discussed a good deal by Mathur and others at the International Economic Association's conference at Konstanz in September 1960. The 'leading sectors' such as the railways and the cotton mills and their 'linkage effects' were particularly examined in some detail. The proceedings of this conference was later edited by Rostow and published in 1963 under the title of *The Economics of Take-Off into Sustained Growth.*

[3] M. D. Morris, 'Towards a Reinterpretation of the Nineteenth Century Indian Economic History', JEH,Vol. XXIII, No. 4, December 1963.

[4] Dhairyabala Pandit, 'India: A Century of Gestation, Relevance of Non-Economic Facts in Development Studies', EW, 22 September 1962, pp. 1503–8.

[5] V. V. Bhatt, 'A Century and a Half of Economic Stagnation in India', EW, Vol. XV, combined numbers 28 and 29, (30 July 1963), pp. 1229–36.

[6] Daniel Thorner, 'Long-term Trends in Output in India', in Kuznets *et al*, (Eds.) pp. 103–28.

[7] See, for instance, Rosen, EW, 11 August 1962, pp. 1299–302.

economic reasons.[1] As very little reliable information is available for the economy of that period, and as the relationship between social conditions and economic development has hardly yet gone beyond the speculative stage, endless controversy and confusion has been the inevitable result of these attempts.

Two studies, one by Morris which deals with the trend of development from 1800 to 1947[2] and another by Rosen which examines economic development during 1860–1900[3] will serve to illustrate the nature of this problem. Morris sees the nineteenth

[1] See, for instance, W. C. Neale, 'A Case of Aborted Growth, India: 1860–1900, A Comment', EW, 1 December 1962, and Dhairyabala Pandit, EW, 22 September 1962.
In addition to the studies referred to above, see the following:
A. K. Sen, 'Sociological and Economic Explanations: An Illustration from the Indian Iron and Steel Industry', EW, Annual Number, February 1963, pp. 183–6 is particularly important for distinguishing and showing the relevance of two types of explanations. See also 'Comments' on his article in the same journal by N. Sen, 18 May, 1963, pp. 812–14; S. Dasgupta, 7 August 1963, pp. 1411–15; and A. K. Sen's reply, 17 August 1963, pp. 1416–18.
Lamb in Kuznets *et al.* (Eds.).
N. V. Sovani, 'British Impact on India', *Cahiers d'Historie Mondiale*, No. 4, (April 1954), pp. 857–82 and No. 1, (July 1954), pp. 77–105.
V. N. Murti, 'Indian Economy During the British Rule', IEJ, April 1961.
S. Bhattacharya, '*Laissez-faire* in India', IESHR, January 1965.
D. H. Buchanan, *Op. cit.*
D. R. Gadgil, *The Industrial Evolution of India in Recent Times*, 4th Edn., 1942.
A. L. Basham, *The Indian Sub-Continent in Historical Perspective*, 1958.
K. Davis, *The Population of India and Pakistan*, 1951.
George Blyn, *Op. cit.*
Dharma Kumar, *Land and Caste in South India*, 1965.
Parimal Ray, *India's Foreign Trade Since 1870*, 1934.
M. D. Morris and B. Stein, 'The Economic History of India: A Bibliographic Essay', JEH, Vol. XXI, No. 2, June 1961, pp. 179–207.
S. J. Patel, 'Long-term Changes in Output and Income in India; 1896–1960'. IEJ, January 1958, pp. 233–46.
Alice Thorner, 'Secular Trends of the Indian Economy, 1881–1951', EW, July 1962, Special Number.
M. Mukherjee, 'A Preliminary Study of the Growth of National Income in India, 1857–1957', *Asian Studies in Income and Wealth*, 1965, a version of which was presented first to the Asian Conference of the International Association for Research in Income and Wealth at Hongkong in 1960. For a theoretical background on the various aspects of economic growth and a critical evaluation of the 'Rostow Doctrine' see Gerald M. Meier, *Leading Issues in Development Economics*, 1964.
B. R. Mitchell with the Collaboration of Phyllis Deane, *Abstract of British Historical Statistics*, 1962, and Phyllis Deane and W. A. Coles, *British Economic Growth, 1688–1959*, published in 1962, are useful for comparing the British with the Indian economic growth.
[2] Morris, JEH, December 1963, Vol. XXIII, No. 4.
[3] Rosen, EW, 11 August 1962, pp. 1299–1302.

century 'as a period too brief to achieve all the structural changes needed to provide the pre-conditions for an industrial revolution'.[1] His explanation starts with the observation that India lacked political unity and stability, not only immediately prior to British rule, but almost all through her history. To substantiate his statement he says, 'Despite of Hindu tradition of imperial expansion, at no time in Indian history over any large region did a stable political unit survive for more than a century or a century and a half. There was nothing that compares with the imperial chronologies of Rome, Egypt or China. A crucial consequence is that no tradition of continuous administrative institutions and no persistent bureaucracy ever developed . . . the political instability had obvious effects through the eighteenth century. Commerce and capital accumulation certainly were kept to low levels.'[2]

If a period or periods of a century or a century and a half are not big enough for developing administrative institutions, how long must the period be? And what if India cannot compare with the imperial chronologies of Rome, Egypt or China? Many countries are far more advanced than any of these mentioned, which never had any imperial chronologies of that kind. We must also ask whether Egypt or China were more advanced than India at the end of the eighteenth century for that particular reason or for any other. India certainly experienced periods of political instability due to internal conflicts and external aggressions which inevitably affected commerce and capital accumulation adversely, but she is by no means unique in that. Actually political stability over large regions during periods as long as 150 years has been the exception rather than the rule of history.

Other notions put forward by Morris such as 'Indian society has been based historically on a non-animal-powered agriculture'[3] and the conclusions he bases on them are equally questionable. His statement, 'once having established a settled irrigation agriculture (*c.* 1000 B.C.?) the population apparently quickly expanded to limits of vegetal production'[4] seems inconsistent with his statement only a little later that 'much of the Indian sub-continent seems to have been a virgin land as late as 1800';[5] nor does he explain how 'extensive tracts' remained virgin partly as a result of pre-1800 technology'.[6] What are the limitations of this tech-

---

[1] Morris, JEH, December 1963, Vol. XXIII, No. 4.
[2] *Ibid.*   [3] *Ibid.*   [4] *Ibid.*   [5] *Ibid.*   [6] *Ibid.*

nology ? And if 'technology' here means 'non-animal-power' he is surely wrong on points of fact.

Elsewhere Morris says, 'while British cloth was competitive with Indian handloom production, machine-made yarn seems to have strengthened the competitive position of the indigenous handloom sector despite the fall in cloth prices'.[1] In the paragraph which follows Morris states that 'there is evidence of a rising demand for cotton cloth during the nineteenth century. My tentative conclusion is that, at worst, the vast expansion of British cloth exports to India skimmed off the expanding demand. The handloom weavers were at least no fewer in number and no worse off economically at the end of the period than at the beginning. The net effect for the economy was a positive one in terms of per capita real income.'[2]

The trouble is that nowhere does Morris mention any figures. In saying that the 'machine-made yarn seems to have strengthened the competitive position of the indigenous handloom sector' he at least implies that the spinning industry was seriously affected although he does not say so in so many words. He talks of 'rising demand'. Did the demand expand at such a rate that it not only compensated for the lost exports from India, but also made up for the large imports of cloth into the country without affecting the handloom sector ? There can be little doubt that the hand spinning and weaving of cotton textiles was seriously disrupted during the 1820's.[3] A major factor for the survival of the handloom industry as a whole was probably the Indian preference for the products of this sector such as *sarees*, *gamachhas* (towels), and silk cloth. And

[1] Morris, JEH, December 1963, Vol. XXIII, No. 4.   [2] *Ibid.*

[3] In 1813–14 cotton goods imported into Bengal Presidency from Britain amounted to 91,000 *sicca* rupees and by 1822–3 its value went up to *sicca* Rs.6,777,279. During the same period exports of piece goods to Britain from Bengal fell from *sicca* Rs.4·6 million to only *sicca* Rs.300,000. H. R. Ghosal, 'Changes in the Organisation of Industrial Production in the Bengal Presidency in the Early Nineteenth Century', in Ganguli (Ed.), p. 128.
Like the weavers, a 'vast body of spinners' was also seriously affected, particularly after 1825. 'Nearly half a million women, engaged in spinning, were seriously affected, a great many of them being completely deprived of their means of livelihood. Women, consequently, became virtually an unnecessary factor in industrial organisation.' *Ibid.*, p. 129. In 1832, the Governor-General wrote: 'cotton piece goods for so many ages the staple manufacture of India, seems . . . for ever lost. . . . The sympathy of the Court is deeply excited by the Report of the Board of Trade exhibiting the gloomy picture of the effects of a commercial revolution, productive of so much present suffering to numerous classes in India, and hardly to be paralleled in the history of commerce.' Quoted, *Ibid.*, pp. 129–30.

even if we were to ignore the production of the Indian mills (numbering around 190 by the end of the nineteenth century), and accept for the sake of argument Morris's thesis that the 'vast expansion of British cloth exports' only 'skimmed off the expanding demand' and his further assertion that 'the handloom weavers were at least no fewer in number and no worse off economically at the end of the period [1900?] than at the beginning [1800?] it does not warrant the conclusion that the 'net effect for the economy was a *positive* one *in terms of per capita real income*'.[1] At best one could conclude that the economy stagnated.

In his study of the nineteenth century Morris arrives at two main conclusions. One is that India started from such a low level of economic and social development that one century was 'too brief a period to provide pre-conditions for an industrial revolution'. We have indicated above the inadequacy (and sometimes inaccuracy) of the arguments which he has produced in support of this conclusion. His arguments for the other main conclusion that the per capita national income of India grew during this period, also falls to the ground for the same reasons. Although Morris's explanations of why the national per capita income must have grown do not stand critical analysis, there is, however, a more direct and convincing evidence, not considered by him, to show that the national per capita income did in fact grow. M. Mukherjee after considering the nine point estimates of national income made up to 1903, and on the basis of some direct estimates, constructed a series of per capita national income from 1857 onwards and concluded that 'we may safely think in terms of a very slowly growing per capita income during the second half of the nineteenth century'.[2] At the sectoral level Blyn has shown that the agricultural output and the yield per acre increased, at least in the last

[1] Italics supplied.
[2] AVERAGE PER CAPITA NATIONAL INCOME OF INDIA AT 1948–9 PRICE FOR OVERLAPPING 9–YEAR PERIODS.

Period	Centring	Per Capita Income
1857–1863	1860 (7 year)	169
1861–1869	1865	172
1871–1879	1875	177
1876–1884	1880	197
1881–1889	1885	216
1886–1894	1890	204
1891–1899	1895	201
1896–1904	1900	199

Source: Table IV.I, p. 103, Mukherjee, For quotation see p. 79.

decade of the nineteenth century.[1] It was stated in Chapter 9 that the paid-up capital invested in the corporate sector as a whole went up by 4.5% annually during 1882–83 to 1900–01.[2]

The main burden of Rosen's thesis is that the absence of a significant rate of growth can be explained by economic factors alone. Among the economic factors, he considers the lack of effective demand as the most significant. He argues that demand was low because per capita income was low. However, before we examine his argument it is appropriate to consider briefly his method of analysis.

The enigma Rosen set out to explain is that there was little change in annual per capita income during 1860–1900 despite a 'major inflow of foreign investment', 'much domestic investment', and 'an infra-structure of railroads and irrigation works'.[3]

The foreign investment was comprised of about £300 million from British sources.[4] Much of this sum was invested in the railways and a substantial amount was put into Government securities.[5] The aggregate sterling capital employed (ordinary shares, preference shares and debentures) in the tea, jute and coal industries at the end of 1900 did not exceed £15 million.[6] The cotton textile mills, another large and by all accounts a paying industry, was very largely financed by indigenous capital. It is noteworthy that foreigners almost completely ignored this industry.[7]

Rosen analyses the impact of foreign investment in terms of 'leading sectors' and 'linkage effects' and concludes that, unlike Britain and the U.S.A., the 'backward linkage' did not occur in India except in the case of the coal industry. According to him the

[1] Blyn, Appendix 4C, p. 316, and Appendix Table 5a, pp. 327–30.
[2] See p. 150. [3] Rosen, EW, 11 August 1962, pp. 1299–1302.
[4] From A. K. Cairncross, *Home and Foreign Investment, 1870–1913*, 1953, p. 185 and Jenks, pp. 213 and 219. Rosen derived a figure of £351 million as an approximate figure for 1900. EW, 11 August 1962.
[5] Rosen, EW, 11 August 1962. [6] See pp. 170, 168, and 174.
[7] For figures of mills managed by various communities see table on p. 241. See also Dhairyabala Pandit who posed the question why was the cotton textile industry of the modern type developed by Indians; and why for a long time only one industry and no other and why in more or less the same region of Guzerat.
It is suggested that an answer to why certain industries were developed first, and why certain communities invested in some and not other industries, can in general be obtained if the relevant factors for the flow of capital such as comparative cost advantage, government policy, expected yield, location of industries, location of business communities, potential demand, familiarity with the market, etc., were assigned weights, say, between one and ten and the industries were ordered along a preference scale according to the aggregate weights.

coal industry grew under the stimulus of the leading sectors because 'it is a bulk product whose transport cost is extremely high relative to its total price if it must be shipped from Europe to India. It would be far cheaper to mine it in India and use it nearer to the point of origin, and India had the coal which could be mined and used.'[1]

But this is precisely what did not happen. Freight rates were such that it was cheaper to import coal into India than to buy the Ranigunj coal, except in the Calcutta region. The fortunes of the coal industry changed only in the 1890's when the price of British coal rose very sharply.[2]

Apart from this industrial growth, Rosen mentions that 'there was a major investment in irrigation works and the area under irrigation rose from 29 million acres in 1880 to 44 million in 1903'.[3] Government investment in irrigation did pay off, in higher yields and in protecting agriculture against the vagaries of nature to some extent, but the acreage increased at the same time and there was not much change in the proportion of irrigated area to total cultivated area which remained, between 20 to 23% of the total.[4] The effect of the increase in irrigation was thus limited, because Government investment in infra-structure for economic purposes was restricted by its concern for a balanced budget, as well as its policy that such investments must pay their way quickly at the ruling interest rate.[5]

Although Rosen does not analyse backward linkages in detail and does not even consider possible forward linkages,[6] his conclusion

---

[1] *Op. cit.*

[2] COAL IMPORTS INTO INDIA AND ITS PRICE

Year	Value (Rs.)/Quantity (tons)	Average Price (Rs. per ton)
1880–1	6,884,030/648,201	10·6
1885–6	11,429,600/805,700	14·1
1890–1	14,198,030/817,004	17·3
1895–6	16,275,401/848,637	19·1
1899–1900	14,944,395/481,190	31·0

For figures of output of Indian mines see p. 173. The value and output figures can be found in S.T.B.I. The Calcutta price of Indian coal worked out at round Rs.3·3 per ton throughout the nineties. It was about the same in the eighties.　　　　　　　　　　　　　　　　[3] Rosen, EW, 11 August 1962.

[4] Blyn, Appendix Table 8A, pp. 340–1 and pp. 184–8.

[5] Morris, JEH, December 1962, on railway finance see Macpherson, EHR, December 1955.

[6] For instance the rise of the textile industry led to the development of the 'Dressmaking' industry in the U.S.A. But in India there is relatively little demand for tailored clothing so the scope for a forward link was severely limited.

that the leading sectors did not generate backward linkage in India is not disputed. With regard to the coal industry, the linkage possibility no doubt existed, as in fact it did in the case of other leading sectors, but this possibility was not realised for the reason mentioned above until almost the end of the nineteenth century. Nor is it disputed that the real wages were low or that the per capita income was low, but his thesis that there was no effective demand because per capita income was low cannot be sustained.

Per capita income is relevant in studying the pattern of demand. For the *level* of demand it is the total income which matters more. In fact, much more *direct* evidence of the *existence* of effective demand, despite the low per capita income, can be given. India imported over Rs.700 million worth of goods annually during the last decade of the nineteenth century and a study of the items shows that much of what was imported could have been produced in India.[1] Assuming that only two-thirds of these imports could have been manufactured locally, this alone would have absorbed capital to the extent of Rs.1,400 million, given the usual capital-output ratio of 3 to 1 and ignoring the multiplier and acceleration effects.[2] Against this the capital employed in the industrial sector of India at the end of last century amounted to only about Rs.400 million.[3] The possibility of further capital investment thus represented a three-to-four-fold industrial growth, which makes Rosen's argument that lack of effective demand was the main hindrance to growth completely unacceptable. This, nevertheless, leaves us with the question of why industrialisation did not proceed further in the second half of the nineteenth century.

In Chapter 9 it has been shown that the domestic private investment in the modern sector was small, not because capital was not

[1] See the part on Foreign Trade in the *Financial and Commercial Statistics for British India, 1901*. Cotton goods alone amounted to over Rs.327 million in 1894–5.

[2] My guess is though the capital-output ratio was much smaller in those days which would, of course, reduce the quantum of potential investment, on the other hand, the labour-output ratio was likely to be higher. With only about 0·4% annual rate of population growth, this would mean that a much higher proportion of industrially trained labour force would have been available in later periods.

[3] At the end of 1900–1 the paid-up capital of all companies classified as 'Mills and Presses' amounted to Rs.183,965,073. A further Rs.30 million was invested in mining, quarrying, breweries, ice and sugar factories. Considering the debenture and private loans and reserves of these companies, about Rs.400 million would seem to be the total capital employed. See Appendix 17.

forthcoming, as the growth of cotton, jute and tea industries out-paced the demand for their products. Neither was it a fact that entrepreneurs were not alive to seize opportunities. Morarji's memorandum,[1] Tata's efforts[2] and the existence of nearly two hundred cotton mills in 1900 clearly demonstrate their zeal. Moreover, the impelling force of the managing agency profits was always there to beckon them.[3] One can therefore say with con-fidence that by and large potential opportunities were realised to the extent possible without government support.

Britain had an early start in industrialisation so that other countries trading with her needed to make up a degree of economic backwardness. Other nations were able to develop their industries under the umbrella of protective tariffs,[4] but the Government of India (or rather the Secretary of State for India) stubbornly main-tained a policy of *laissez-faire*, prepared neither to impose protec-tive tariffs nor actively to encourage domestic industries in other ways. The Government was not even willing to assure local indus-trialists that it would buy their products at the same price as the landed cost of imported goods, which deprived the indigenous entrepreneurs of opportunities to develop local sources of supply as an alternative to the large-scale overseas purchases made by the Government and its units.[5]

---

[1] See pp. 129–30.

[2] On Tata's efforts to establish an iron and steel factory see Harris, *op. cit.*, Fraser, *op. cit.*, Elvin, *op. cit.* Also A. K. Sen, EW, Annual number, February 1963. On his efforts to beat the monopoly of British shipping to the Far East, see S. D. Mehta, *op. cit.*

[3] See pp. 159–60, 214–16, and 228–39.

[4] In the case of Japan which could not impose tariffs, it was done through subsidising industries.

[5] See Chapter 7. The value of Government stores manufactured in India was only Rs.3,942,421 in 1882–3. After the rules were relaxed in 1883, the value of stores obtained in India gradually rose and fluctuated between Rs.9–13 million during the last decade of 1900. See S. K. Sen, *Economic Policy*, p. 23 for annual figures.

But the restriction on buying locally manufactured 'iron, steel, tools, and plant, and especially . . . machinery' was not lifted on the instruction of the Secretary of State. See *Financial Despatch from the Secretary of State*, No. 192, 28 July 1888, quoted in S. K. Sen, p. 19. The annual value of 'Stores for India' on an average amounted to £1,270,433 from 1877–8 to 1899–1900 (*ibid.*, p. 25).

On the question of iron and steel works, the Stores Committee in its report published in 1906, took the view that the Government purchase was inadequate and irregular, though the railways could assure 'continuity of orders' and it concluded 'it seems improbable that any such industry can be profitable if largely dependent on private demands, especially in view of the very considerable

Concluding Observations

Thus the period, 1870–1900 represents an era of frustrated ambition for Indian entrepreneurs. The question of State aid or the lack of it looms so large that in the present state of our knowledge, it is difficult to single out any other major explanation.

---

imports from the United Kingdom and the Continent', p. 15 quoted in *ibid.*, p. 44. Kidron, p. 12, quotes the following passage from Lord Hardinge's *My Indian Years: 1910–1916*, 1948, pp. 3–4, 'Lord Morley came up to us, and taking me aside asked if I would like to succeed Lord Minto as Viceroy of India. . . . What struck me as curious at the time was that the only question he put to me was whether I was a free-trader, and I was honestly able to say that I was and always had been a free-trader. He told me that I might regard the matter as settled. . . .' In November 1915 the same Lord Hardinge wrote in a despatch to the Secretary of State for India:

'It is becoming increasingly clear that a definite and self-conscious policy of improving the industrial capabilities of India will have to be pursued after the war, unless she is to become the dumping ground for the manufacture of foreign nations who will be competing the more keenly for markets, the more it becomes apparent that the political future of the large nations depends on their economic position. . . . After the war India will consider herself entitled to demand the utmost help which her government can afford, to enable her to take her place, so far as circumstances permit, as a manufacturing country.' (Quoted in A. R. Desai, *Social Background of Indian Nationalism*, 1959, p. 98. See also Lamb in Kuznets *et al.* (Eds.).)

Early European Chartered Companies in India

The Portuguese, who were the first Europeans to visit India by way of the Cape of Good Hope, doubled by da Gama, 22 November 1497, never put their Eastern trade into the hands of an incorporated company, except in the year 1731, when the King gave permission to one ship to make one voyage to Surat and the Coromandel Coast to the exclusion of other ships. Except in this instance, the monopoly of the Portuguese East India trade was always vested immediately in the Crown, until it was abolished in 1752. Even then, various important articles still continued subject to royal privileges.

The 'Dutch East India Company' was formally instituted in 1602 by the union of the funds of various rival companies which had sprung up in Holland in consequence of the success of Houtman's voyage in 1596–7.

The first English East India Company was incorporated by Queen Elizabeth on 31 December 1600, under the title of 'The Governor and Company of Merchants of London trading to the East Indies'. Courten's Association, the Assada Merchants, established in 1635 united with the 'London Company' in 1650. The 'Merchant Adventurers', chartered in 1654–5, united with the 'London Company' in 1655–7. The 'English Company (or the "General Society") trading to the East Indies' was incorporated in 1698. This company of Merchants of London and the English Company were finally incorporated under the name of 'The United Company of Merchants of England trading to the East Indies' in 1702–8–9'.

The first French East India Company was formed in 1604. The second in 1611. The third in 1615. The fourth (Richelieu's) in 1642–3. The fifth (Colbert's) in 1644. The sixth was formed by the French East and West India, Senegal and China Companies, united under the name of 'The Company of the Indies, 1719'. The exclusive privileges of the Company were, by the King's decree, suspended in 1769, and it was finally abolished by the National Assembly in 1790.

The first Danish East India Company was formed in 1612 and the second in 1670.

'The Ostend Company' was incorporated by the Emperor of Austria in 1723, its factors chiefly being people who had served the Dutch and English East India Companies; but the opposition of the maritime powers forced the Court of Vienna in 1727 to suspend the Company's charter for seven years. The company, after passing through a most trying existence, prolonged by the Austrian Government's desire to participate in the growing East India trade, became bankrupt in 1784 and was finally extinguished.

When the Ostend Company was suspended (1727) and a number of its servants thrown out of employment, Henry Koning of Stockholm took advantage of their special knowledge of the East and obtained a charter for the Swedish Company, dated 13 June 1731. The Swedes were thus the last of the European nations to engage in the ocean trade with India.

Excerpt from *Report on the Miscellaneous Old Records of the India Office, 1 November, 1878,* London, 1879, p. 77 (footnote).

APPENDIX 2

Institution of Guilds in Ancient India

The origin of the institutions of guilds, 'Nigam' or 'Sreni' as they were called in Sanskrit, is traced as far back as 800 B.C., but they became firmly established only towards the third century B.C. Many facts are known about these guilds (for example, that they owned property in their corporate capacity, employed a variety of staff, undertook diplomatic, legislative, administrative and other functions at times, enjoyed immunity under charters and were generally a most important 'pressure group' in the community), but the legal basis of the institution has never been established nor, which concerns us more closely, the exact procedure by which the component or constituent members for the time being invested their capital, the conditions under which managers were appointed and profits realised, those under which members might withdraw their investments or influence the manner in which enterprises were begun or stopped. The bare features of these 'guilds' that may be gathered from copies of deeds and other documents which have survived in the form of inscriptions have been described in the following books and articles:

R. C. Majumdar, *Corporate Life in Ancient India* (Calcutta, 1922, 2nd Edn.). (This is the most complete and original work. The others, though important, contain little that is new so far as we are concerned.)

Pran Nath, *A study of Economic Conditions in Ancient India*, Royal Asiatic Society, 1929.

A. Bose, *Social and Rural Economy of Northern India, 1942–1945*, 2 vols., 1949–52.

A. Appadorai, *Economic Conditions in Southern India (1000–1500 A.D.)*,1936.

S. K. Maity, *Economic Life in Northern India in the Gupta Age*, 1957.

A. S. Altekar, *Rastrakutas and their Times*, 1934.

T. Mahalingham, *South India Polity*, 1955.

P. V. Kane, *History of Dharmasastra*, Vol. II and III, 1930.

Journal of Indian History, 1947, Vol. XXV, pp. 269–80.

Quarterly Journal of Mythic Society, New Series, 1948–9, Vol. XXXIX, pp. 158–71.

Half-yearly Journal of the Mysore University, 1928, Vol. II, 2, pp. 196–233.

(The above account is taken from a letter to the author from Professor J. D. M. Derrett. The comment on Majumdar's book is my own.)

APPENDIX 3

List of Indian and Foreign Banks to 1850

Joint Stock Banks established between 1829 and 1850			
In India	Name	Hd. Office	Remarks
1829	Union Bank	Calcutta	Failed 1848
1833	Agra & United Services Bank Limited	Agra (N.W.P.)	
1840	Bank of Bombay	Bombay	
1840	N.W. Bank of India	Meerut	
1842	Agra Savings Fund	Agra (N.W.P.)	
1842	Oriental Bank Corp.	Bombay	
1843	Bank of Madras	Madras	
1844	Delhi Bank Corp.	Delhi	
1844	Simla Bank	Simla (N.W.P.)	
1844/5	Benares Bank	Benares (N.W.P.)	Failed 1848/9
1845	Cawnpore Bank	Cawnpore (N.W.P.)	
1845	Commercial Bank of India	Bombay	
1845	Uncovenanted Service Bank	Agra (N.W.P.)	
1846	Dacca Bank	Dacca (Bengal)	
Abroad	*Name*	*Hd. Office*	*Remarks*
1841	Bank of Asia	London	Wound-up 1842
1841	Bank of Ceylon	Ceylon	Taken over by Oriental Bank 1849
1842	East India Bank	London	Did not commence business
1848	Comptoir d'Escompte	Paris	Still operating

(*India and Bengal despatches, Finance, Bengal Letters and enclosures, letters received, 1848*) India Office Library.

List of Industrial Companies in India, 1817–50

Name	Year Founded (F) or Existed (E)	Source
Companies connected with sea, river trade or transport (11 companies)		
Bengal Bonded Warehouse Assoc.	Calcutta 1838	C.D. 1838
Calcutta Docking Company	Calcutta E. 1830	E; D.
Steam Tug Association	Calcutta F. 1837	E; D; L, p. 9
Union Steam Tug Association	Calcutta E. 1850	D.
Eastern Steam Navigation Co.	Calcutta E. 1848	D.
Benares & Mirzapore Steam Co.	Calcutta E. 1847	A, p. 266
Ganges Steam Navigation Co.	Benares F. 1845	A, p. 273 D; L, p. 20
Calcutta Steam Ferry Bridge Co.	Calcutta F. 1839	X, p. 46
P. & O. Steam Nav. Co. (Reg. U.K.)	— F. 1840	D.
India Gen. Steam Nav. Co.	Calcutta F. 1844	D.
Bombay Steam Navigation Co.	Bombay —	E.
Coal (3 companies)		
Bengal Coal Company	Calcutta F. 1820[a]	E.
Sylhet Coal Company	Sylhet E. 1847	A, p. 274
Mirzapore Coal Company	Mirzapore F. 1830	A, p. 266
Iron & Steel (1 company)		
Porto Novo Steel & Iron Co.	Porto-Novo F. 1825–30	B, p. 65
Indigo (1 company)		
Bengal Indigo Company	Calcutta, E. 1848	E.
Sugar (1 company)		
Nischindpore Sugar Co.	Nisch're E. 1847	A, p. 261
Plantations (2 companies)		
Assam Company (U.K.) (Tea)	Calcutta F. 1839[a]	G.
Pew Estate (Coffee)	Malabar Coast E. 1847	A, p. 273
Cotton Mills (5 companies)		
Bowreah Cotton Mills	Calcutta F. 1817–18	Y, p. 22; Z, N.
New Fortgloster Mills Co.	Calcutta F. 1830 E. 1848	H; E; I.
Broach Cotton Mills Co.	Broach F. 1845 E. 1850	J.

Name Unknown	Travancore F. 1830	
Blin & Delbuck	Pondichery	F; N, pp. 6–7
	F. 1829	

Cotton Bale Screwing &
Pressing (2 companies)

Apollo Company	Bombay E. 1850	M; N, p. 4
Colaba Company	Bombay E. 1850	N, p. 4
Bengal Salt Company	Calcutta F. 1838	X, p. 45

A. Cooke, *op. cit.*
B. Brown, *op. cit.*
C. Theobald, *op. cit.*
D. *The Bengal and Agra Directory and Annual Register*, 1850.
E. J. C. Stewart, *Facts and Documents relating to the Affairs of the Union Bank of Calcutta*, Calcutta, 1848, Appendix E.
F. S.T.B.I., 1893.
G. Antrobus, *A History of the Assam Company.*
H. P.P. 1831–2, Pt. 2. *Digest of Evidence* p. 154.
I. N. Das, *Industrial Enterprise in India* 1938.
J. *Indian Economist*, 10 December 1869.
K. F.O.I., 30 January 1850, leading article.
L. Brame, *op. cit.*
M. L.P., 28 December 1850. Letter from the Secretary to the Government of Bombay to the Secretary of India, dated 24 October 1850.
N. S. D. Mehta, *op. cit.*
X. B. Kling, *op. cit.*
Y. M. D. Morris, *Emergence of an Industrial Labour Force in India.* It was part of a complex which included a distillery, a foundry, an oil pressing and oil mill. The total cost seems to have been about £200,0000. The entire complex went bankrupt, not because the cotton mill was unprofitable but apparently because the original managing agency house, Messrs. Fergusson & Company, failed during the Calcutta crisis of the early 1830's. 'When purchased from the bankrupts, the cotton mill and other enterprises were restarted and functioned at least until 1840'. *Ibid.* In 1830 it was probably re-named New Fortgloster Mill Company.
Z. S. K. Sen, *Economic Policy.*
Note: Altogether about 70 banking, insurance and other companies seem to have been formed by 1850.
The names of the following firms were also found in Source D (Trade List). All of them are still in existence as joint stock companies:

F. & C. Osler	Chandeliers and Glass Dealers. (Now makers of Electric Lamps.)
Bathgate & Co.	Chemists and Druggists. (Chemical manufacturing)
Smith & Stainstreet & Co.	(Pharmaceuticals)
Burn & Company	Builders (multifarious business)
Hamilton & Co.	Jewellers (same)
Manton & Co.	Gunmakers (same)
Jessop & Co.	Millwrights & Founders (Wagon manufacturers)
Thacker & Co.	(Thacker, Spink & Co) publishers (same)
Rankin & Co.	Tailors and Outfitters (same)

[a] These companies are still in existence.

Brief History of the Iron and Steel Industry in India

The date of the discovery of iron in India, or its first manufacture in the country, is not known but the Indian iron ore deposits have certainly been worked for thousands of years. The indigenous Indian iron industry, 'until it almost succumbed in comparatively recent times under the competition of imported metal, was both widespread and prosperous, capable of meeting all the internal demands of the country.'[1] All early attempts ('largely on account of the lack of official support and encouragement at critical times'[2]) to introduce European methods and to manufacture iron on a large scale failed. About 1825 Josiah Marshall Heath, of the Madras Civil Service, obtained from the directors of the East India Company an exclusive right to manufacture iron on a large scale in the Madras Presidency. In 1830 works were established at Porto Novo in the South Arcot district, with the aid of advances received from the Government, and in 1833 the business was taken over by a company, the Porto Novo Steel & Iron Company. The works were enlarged, and a new plant was erected at Beypore on the Malabar Coast. The product was of good quality and some of it was exported to England for use in the construction of the Menai and Britannia bridges. But his venture proved to be a failure. Among the reasons were poor management, inadequacy of capital, technical inexperience and the use of charcoal as fuel. In 1853 the Porto Novo Steel & Iron Company was taken over by a new company—the East India Iron Company—formed primarily by merchants, and the efforts continued until they were finally given up in 1874, when the company went into liquidation. Before Heath started on his venture, he was advised by a European merchant in Calcutta to consider whether the works would not be more suitably erected in the district of Burdwan in Bengal, which abounded in the supply of coal, but Heath rejected this idea. One wonders whether the fate of the iron and steel industry in India might not have been different if he had taken this advice; however, the consequences might have been similarly unfortunate. The experiment by Jessop & Company of Calcutta in 1839 had ended in failure. The history of the attempts made to manufacture iron on a large scale in Bengal, in fact, is a

---

[1] J. Coggin-Brown, *The Iron and Steel Industry of India*, p. 2. Reprinted from the *Mining Magazine* for June and July 1921. (India House Library).
[2] Verrier Elvin, *The Story of Tata Steel*, 1958, p. 10.

long one, and dates back to the year 1774, when Motte and Farquhar started their concern. The hook-iron produced by them sold in the market at less than half the price of the imported product. Disputes, however, with the local *Zamindar* soon led to the abandonment of the project and it was not until 1855 that efforts were renewed in that area. In that year Mackay & Company opened the Birbhum Iron Works. Attempts were also made in other places to manufacture iron on a large scale, notably in Kumaon, Indore and Chanda, but they all failed more or less for the same reasons as had led to the abandoning of efforts at Porto Novo, leaving nothing but the 'ruins of furnaces and workshops to stand as silent witnesses to misguided effort'. The Barakar Iron Works Company formed in 1874 with works at Kulti emerged as the lone survivor in this long struggle. This company also came to an end in 1879 after producing some 13,000 tons of pig iron. A letter published in the *Friend of India* by its European managing agents suggests that the chief reason why they had to close down the works was the uncertain purchasing policy of the Government of India.[1] In 1882 the concern was taken over by the Government and was resold in 1889 to the U.K. registered Bengal Iron and Steel Company which completely remodelled the works and gradually developed them.

In the 1890's Belgium had started to compete seriously with Britain in exporting iron and steel to India as the following figures show:

Imports of Iron and Steel into India (£1,000)

From	Steel		Iron	
	1885–6	*1895–6*	*1885–6*	*1895–6*
U.K.	98	274	1,120	1,076
Belgium	8	280	43	418

Source: S. B. Saul, *Studies in British Overseas Trade, 1870–1914*, 1960, p. 199 quoted by A. K. Sen, EW, Annual, No. February, 1963.

This, Sen thinks, caused a shift in the Government policy.[2] In 1896 the Government of India did agree with the Bengal Iron and Steel Company to purchase annually 10,000 tons of pig iron and castings for ten years but only at '5% below English rates'.[3] Even this proved a great help to the Company. In 1901 it was producing 25,000 tons of pig iron

[1] F.O.I., 18 April 1881. By the Managing Agents, Marillier and Edwards.

[2] A. K. Sen, EW, February 1963, see also comments on his article by N. Sen, EW, 18 May 1963.

[3] Government of India, Commerce Department, Iron and Steel, January 1897 (National Archives, New Delhi) quoted in S. K. Sen, p. 43.

of which the railways bought 10,000 tons. At least seventeen attempts were made to manufacture iron and steel in India.[1]

[1] M. G. Ranade, *Essays in Indian Economics*, 1906, Chapter VI, pp. 170–92.
See also:
Hilton Brown, *op. cit.*
P.P., *Minutes of Evidence Before Select Committee on the Affairs of East India Company*, Pt. II., Finance, 24 March 1832, Evidence of Thomas Bracken, p. 150.
Report of the Famine Commission, 1880.
Report of the Stores Committee, 1906.
For a detailed account of the works at Porto Novo, R. H. Mahon, *Report Upon the Manufacture of Iron and Steel in India*, Commerce Department, Coal and Iron, October 1899, National Archives, New Delhi.
G. L. Molesworth, *Notes on Iron Manufacture*, Commerce Department, Coal and Iron, September, 1882, National Archives of India.
Lovat Fraser, *Iron and Steel in India*, 1919, pp. 3–9.
F. R. Harris, *Jamshetji Nusserwanji Tata*, 1958.
D. H. Buchanan, pp. 278–82.
William A. Johnson, *The Steel Industry of India*, 1966, pp. 8–10.
S. G. T. Heatly, 'Contributions towards a history of the Development of the Mineral Resources of India: No. 2, Memoranda relative to the working of Iron in Bengal', *Journal of the Asiatic Society of Bengal*, Vol. XII, 1843.
W. Jackson, 'Memorandum on the Iron Works of Birbhum', *Journal of the Asiatic Society of Bengal*, Vol. XIV, Part III, 1845.

APPENDIX 6

Tea Companies of Northern India Incorporated in U.K.

Serial No. in P.P.	Name	Date of Incorpn.	Nominal Capital £	Face Value of Shares £	Capital Subscribed £	Paid-up Capital £	No. of Share-holders	Date Wound-up & Amount of Liability
(1) —	Assam Co.	1845	5,000,000	150	500,000	200,000	—	
(2) 988	Jorehaut Tea Co. Ltd.	29.6.59	80,000	20	80,000	66,000	23	
(3) 1056	Darjeeling Tea Co. Ltd.	3.10.59	80,000	10	50,000	50,000	21	
(4) 1816	Lower Assam Co. Ltd.	8.10.61	120,000	10	86,000	21,325	112	9.3.64 £1,365
(5) 1832	Northern Bengal Tea Co. Ltd.	17.10.61	60,000	5	19,495	10,626	54	21.12.66
(6) 2093	Eastern Bengal Tea Co. Ltd.	16.6.62	100,000	5	50,000	16,425	168	£5,886
(7) 2220	Upper Assam Tea Co. Ltd.	9.10.62	250,000	10	250,000	13,185	111	
(8) 2285	Debroogurh Tea Co. Ltd.	25.11.62	20,000	20	20,000	11,500	35	Not known
(9) 2302	Lebong Tea Co. Ltd.	5.12.62	100,000	10	80,000	28,000	80	
(10) 2326	Himalayan Tea Co. Ltd.	18.12.62	100,000	25	50,000	16,000	32	

APPENDIX 6 (Cont'd)

Tea Companies of Northern India Incorporated in U.K.

Serial No. in P.P.	Name	Date of Incorpn.	Nominal Capital £	Face Value of Shares £	Capital Subscribed £	Paid-up Capital £	No. of Share-holders	Date Wound-up & Amount of Liability
(11) 2410	Anglo Indian Tea Co. Ltd.	29.1.63	10,000	100	6,100	—	7	
(12)a 2540	Oriental Tea Co. Ltd.	24.4.63	250,000	20	8,000	—	8	
(13) 2562	Indian Tea Co. (Cachar)	5.5.63	100,000	10	350	—	7	
(14) 2842	Land Mortg. Bank	5.10.63	2,000,000	20	74,000	—	8	
(15) 2857	British India Tea Co. Ltd.	10.10.63	250,000	20	6,020	—	7	
(16) 2927	Indian Tea Co. of Darjeeling	11.11.63	60,000	10	70	—	7	
(17) 2992	Brahmapootra Tea Co. Ltd.	10.12.63	120,000	25	7,250	—	7	
(18) 2994	Central Darj. Tea Co. Ltd.	11.12.63	50,000	10	7,020	—	7	19.1.64 £7,885
(19) 3038	Kumaon & Oudh Plantation	31.12.63	100,000	10	350	—	7	2.7.66 £2,067
(20) 3530	Borokai Tea Co. Ltd.	24.6.64	10,000	10	38,150	25,372	68	
(21)a 3614	Rinchington Tea Co. Ltd.	23.7.64	60,000	10	4,000	—	7	

(22) 3717	Aumchong Tea Co. Ltd.	1.9.64	25,000	10	800	—	8		
(23) 3785	Eastern Assam Co. Ltd.	11.10.64	250,000	10	180,000	59,785	158	12.1.67	£120,000
(24) 3855	Banghorah Tea Estates Co. of Assam Ltd.	22.11.64	200,000	10	74,810	14,777	103		
(25) 3934	Darjeeling Co. Ltd.	31.12.64	250,000	20	112,740	43,776	94		
(26) 3941	Nowgong Tea Co. Assam Ltd.	2.1.65	250,000	10	250,000	72,630	280	15.12.66	£115,306
(27) 4196	Luckimpore Tea Co. Assam Ltd.	18.4.65	150,000	10	100,000	33,496	94		
(28) 4354	Gawhatty Tea Co. Ltd.	15.6.65	100,000	10	70	—	7		
(29) 4363	Chubwa Tea Co.	19.6.65	300,000	10	140,670	26,615	130	1.7.67	£15,915
(30) 4564	Cachar Co. Ltd.	11.9.65	500,000	10	9,150	—	7		
(31) 4922	Koomtage Tea Co. of Assam	1.2.66	150,000	15	105	—	7		

Sources:

Antrobus, *Assam* (for Assam Co. only).

P.P., LVIII, 1864, pp. 513–52 (for rest of the list).

P.P., LXVI, 1866, pp. 551–660.

P.P., LVI, 1868–9, (104–1) pp. 1–60.

London Stock Exchange Official Year Book (or Burdette's Intelligence) 1882.

[a] These two companies, found listed in the P.P., *Op. cit.*, have been taken as working in India, although the place of business was not clear from their 'listed' objects. They were not quoted on the London Stock Exchange.

Companies included in this appendix are only those which were formed for the purpose of working in Northern India. Such as were incorporated to work in Southern or Western India, have been excluded.

The figures given in this table relate to dates (i) for companies formed up to May 1864—returns filed with the Registrar by that date (ii) for companies formed after May 1864—returns received by the Registrar up to May 1866.

The figures for paid-up capital are rather incomplete as they were taken from returns filed soon after the companies had been formed. This would be evident if one compared the figures of paid-up capital given in P.P. up to 1866 (*op. cit.*) and those given in P.P. 1868–9 (*op. cit.*) relating to companies would up in the above list:

Company Number	Paid up Capital (£)	Company Number	Paid up Capital (£)
5	15,866	23	85,275
6	50,000	26	87,085
7	164,636	30	45,209
18	4,654		
19	33,182	Total	485,907

A note is also needed to clarify the somewhat odd appearance of the Land Mortgage Bank of India (company No. 14), as a tea company. Details of this Bank's activity are not available but it is sufficiently known that it had large proprietory interest in the tea industry. (Sources —*Commission on Tea Cultivation in Assam* (*1868-9*) and Gow, Wilson and Stanton, *Tea Producing Companies of India and Ceylon.*)

It would not be out of place to make a few observations here. First thing to notice is the pace of development of tea companies in Britain. Summarised annually, it is as follows:

	Number of Companies			
Up to	1861	5	1864	6
	1862	5	1865	5
	1863	9		

Thus the period of greatest activity was between 1862 and 1865 with 1863–4 as the peak years.

Secondly, it will be noticed that, although the paid-up capital of companies, where given, was quite reasonable, and in some cases, very high, the percentage of nominal capital paid-up, generally speaking, was very low. Similarly, the number of shareholders in thirteen out of thirty-one companies was near the very minimum required by law for a company to be incorporated. The later companies were formed during the years 1863–4, i.e. at the height of the boom, but some of them, like the Brahmapootra, the British Indian and the Land Mortgage Bank, were really sound companies and the low number of shareholders may be because these figures probably relate to the time of incorporation of these companies.

Number and Paid-up Capital of Companies Registered in India From January 1866 to March 1882

Year	Number of Companies Registered	Aggregate Capital in Rs.(000's)	Number of Companies for which figures of Paid-up Capital are available
1866	41	8,538	23
67	27	24,552	17
68	15	3,826	12
69	23	16,181	15
70	22	3,561	15
71	24	5,994	20
72	44	10,762	39
73	71	26,484	66
74	96	57,042	89
75	60	8,135	58
76	57	10,721	51
77	41	6,460	36
78	55	8,388	48
79	43	4,922	41
80	55	8,871	42
81	77	4,367	42
82[a]	25	283	7
Total	776	209,087	621
1851–65	373	130,070	214
Grand Total	1149	339,157	835 (80% of 1,149)

[a] 3 months

APPENDIX 8[a]

*Industrial Breakdown of the Number of Companies Registered,
Wound-up and Working between 1851 and 1865, 1866 and 1882, and
1851 and 1882*

Industry	Registered 1851–65	Registered 1866–82	1851–82	Wound-up 1851–82	Working 1882
Banking	77	246	323	182	141
Tea	62	106	168	55	113
Cotton Mills	13	52	65	34	31
Multiple Textile Mills[b]	1	41	42	11	31
Jute Mills	2	14	16	8	8
Screws & Presses	35	53	88	58	30
Coal	5	5	10	3	7
Navigation	30	14	44	36	8
Railways	—	9	9	5	4
Ship/Agents	5	2	7	5	2
Co-operatives	—	21	21	10	11
Sugar Mills	1	5	6	3	3
Breweries	3	3	6	3	3
Insurance	14	25	39	34	5
Miscellaneous	125	180	305	199	106
Details Misc.					
Gold	—	11	11	3	8
Coffee	12	5	17	15	2
Printing	12	10	22	17	5
Sundry Manfg.	37	56	93	55	38
Sundry Trading	49	72	121	81	40
Paper Mills	—	2	2	1	1
Land Reclamation etc.	10	14	24	21	3
Formation of Bazaar	2	9	11	2	9
Indigo	3	1	4	4	—
Total	373	776	1149	646	503

[a] The period 1882 runs from 1 January to 31 March only.
[b] Multiple textile mills are those which were classified in the official records as 'Mills for Cotton, Wool, Jute, Silk, Hemp, etc.' If the 'Object Clause' in the memorandum of association specified the manufacture of more than one variety

of textiles, the company was classified in this category. On scrutinising the list of companies formed up to the end of March 1882, these companies, except for those mentioned below, appeared to be manufacturing only cotton textiles.

Name	Region	Paid-up Capital Rupees	Year Regd.	Year Wound-up	Capital of those working
George III. Jute & Wool	Bombay	453,150	1865	1867	
Bombay Hemp & Jute	Bombay	599,200	1874	1879	
Sassoon Silk	Bombay	350,000	1875		350,000
Rustomjee Twine & Canvas	Bengal	777,200	1875	1879	
Bengal Silk	Bengal	Not specified	1881	1881	
Egerton Woollen	Punjab	192,000	1880		192,000
		2,371,550			542,000

Double Frequency Table showing the Number of Companies formed during 1863–5 and wound-up by 31 March 1882, by the size of Capital and Age

Life Span	Paid-up Capital Groups in Rs.(000's)										
Years	6–10	11–25	26–50	51–100	101–500	501–1,000	1,001–2,500	2,501–5,000	5,001–10,000	None[a]	Total
0				1		1				16	18
1		1			4		1			6	12
2			1	1	10	1	1	2		13	29
3	1	1	1		10		1			5	19
4				1	2		1	1		14	19
5				1	8	4				10	23
6			1	3	5	1			1	16	27
7										11	11
8–10				2	3	2				18	25
11–15			2	1	13	4				10	30
16–over			3	3	5	2				2	15
Not known[b]	1	2	2	1	2		3			10	18
Total	2	4	7	13	63	15	7	3	1	131	246

[a] Paid-up capital not specified for these companies.
[b] The dates of winding-up for these companies were not available

Double Frequency Table showing the Number of Companies formed in India between 1851 and 1882[a] by Capital and Age

Life Span Year	Paid-up Capital Groups in Rs. (000's)												Total
	None[b]	1–5	6–10	11–25	26–50	51–100	101–500	501–1,000	1,001–2,500	2,501–5,000	5,001–10,000	Over	
0[c]	54	7	—	—	1	1	2	1	—	—	—	—	66
1	48	12	8	12	4	5	15	1	2	—	—	—	107
2	37	6	6	10	5	10	34	4	2	3	—	—	117
3	18	10	4	6	11	11	24	3	3	—	—	—	90
4	23	8	5	16	6	8	17	4	3	2	—	—	92
5	17	5	4	5	3	7	30	9	1	—	—	—	81
6–10	63	22	23	35	27	34	97	30	22	4	4	1	362
11–15	17	1	1	3	9	13	32	12	5	—	—	2	95
16–20	2	—	—	1	2	4	24	14	11	—	—	—	58
21–25	—	—	—	—	1	1	7	5	3	1	—	—	18
Not known[d]	35	1	5	5	5	2	8	1	—	—	—	—	63
Total	314	72	56	93	74	96	290	84	52	10	5	3	1,149

[a] The period 1882 runs from 1 January to 31 March 1882.
[b] Figures of paid-up capital were not found for these companies.
[c] These are companies which were wound-up or otherwise defunct in the same year in which they were registered.
[d] The date of winding-up is not known for these companies.

APPENDIX 11[a]

Double Frequency Table showing the Life Span of Companies by Capital Groups between 1851 and 1882

Life Span (Year)	Paid-up Capital Groups in Rs. (000's)												Total
	None	1–5	6–10	11–25	26–50	51–100	101–500	501–1,000	1,001–2,500	2,501–5,000	5,001–10,000	Over	
0	36	2	—	—	—	1	1	1	—	—	—	—	41
1	14	1	1	5	2	—	7	1	1	—	—	—	32
2	29	3	3	2	4	1	20	3	1	2	—	—	68
3	18	3	2	3	3	6	15	2	—	2	—	—	54
4	23	6	3	5	3	2	9	2	2	—	—	—	55
5	17	3	3	3	3	—	18	6	1	—	—	—	54
6–10	60	18	15	16	9	15	37	12	17	2	2	1	204
11–15	17	1	—	1	4	8	16	8	1	—	—	1	57
16–20	2	—	—	—	1	6	6	1	—	—	—	—	16
21–25	—	—	—	—	—	1	1	—	—	—	—	—	2
Not known	35	1	3	5	2	5	8	2	1	—	1	—	63
Total	251	38	30	40	31	45	138	38	24	6	3	2	646

[a] This table should be read subject to the same qualifications as in Appendix 10.

APPENDIX 12

Paid-up Capital of Companies registered in India between 1851 and 1882, by Industries
(Capital in Rs.000's)

Industry	1851–1865 Capital	No. of Co.	1866–1882[a] Capital	No. of Co.	1851–1882[a] Capital	No. of Co.
Banking	44,895	30	31,639	277	76,534	257
Tea	21,725	53	17,692	91	39,417	144
Cotton Mills	7,276	8	35,767	42	43,043	50
Jute Mills	1,800	2	11,933	13	12,833	15
Multiple Textile Mills[c]	453	1	31,257	30	31,710	31
Screws & Pressing	5,514	17	12,681	39	18,195	56
Coal	4,495	4	1,695	3	6,190	7
Navigation	9,115	14	3,465	8	12,580	22
Railways	—	—	2,416	4	2,416	4
Ship/Agents	1,071	4	122	1	1,193	5
Co-operatives	—	—	288	17	288	17
Sugar Mills	253	1	716	3	969	4
Breweries	600	1	384	2	984	3
Insurance	1,472	5	2,569	19	4,041	24
Miscellaneous	31,401	74	57,363	122	88,764	196
All	130,070	214[b]	209,087	621[b]	339,157	835[b]

[a] The period 1882 ends on 31 March 1882.
[b] The total number of companies formed in each of the three periods were 373; 776; and 1,149 respectively. The companies included here are only those for which figures of both nominal and paid-up capital were available, hence the difference.
[c] See Appendix 8.

APPENDIX 13

Number of Companies registered annually 1851 to 31 March 1901 in Select Industries

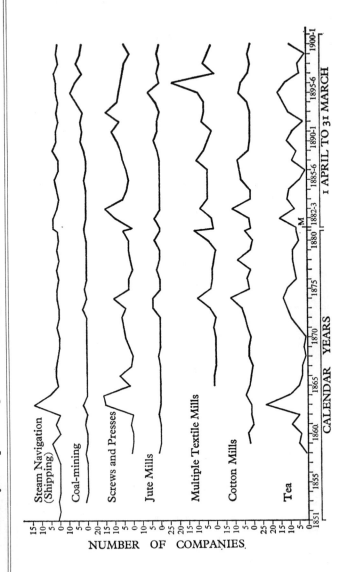

ources and Uses of Funds in the Cotton Mills of Bombay, 1893–4

The figures mentioned below give a synopsis of the published accounts of the principal cotton spinning and weaving mills whose shareholders were in Bombay, though some of the mills were in the *Mofussil*. Some of the accounts are for the whole year 1893, while others are for the year ending with the first half of 1894.

The mills are divided into three groups, the first comprising mills whose market value on 1 November 1894 showed a premium over the par value of their capital; the second those whose capital was between par and 50% discount, and the third whose capital showed a depreciation of more than 50%.

	Group I (15 Mills)	Group II (15 Mills)	Group III (9 Mills)	Total (39 Mills)
Paid-up Capital Rs.	18,426,400	14,108,550	8,916,500	41,451,450
Reserves etc.	11,093,300	3,941,200	1,583,200	16,617,700
Outlay on Block, value of goods in hand and other assets	16,282,300	8,069,400	3,746,200	28,097,900
Loan Capital	15,502,000	10,506,200	7,550,600	33,558,800
Paid in Interest	994,700	632,500	536,000	2,163,200
Paid in Commission to Managing Agents	558,850	510,900	173,950	1,243,700
Paid in Dividends	1,681,100	386,000	26,000	2,093,100
Carried to Reserve	1,009,700	439,500	98,000	1,547,200
Value of Capital on 1 November 1894	30,543,000	9,940,100	2,931,500	43,414,600

Compiled from an article in the T.O.I., 10 November, 1894.

The sources and uses of funds show the difference in the working of mills and the high ratio of loan to equity capital. The market value of share capital reveals a lack of relationship with the yield in the three groups of mills. These figures show why shareholders of the mills in the second and third groups would look with envy at the earnings of their managing agent.

APPENDIX 15

History of the Shipping Industry in India

Until the end of the eighteenth century, India was a maritime nation, making her own ships, manned by Indian crews, carrying the trade of Indian merchants.[1] During the early nineteenth century, however, the shipping industry declined rapidly. The trade with the West was the monopoly of the East India Company. Ships trading with England were liable to forfeiture under an Act of 1814, unless their captain and 75% of the crew were British, with the result that Indian crews could not acquire experience in Western waters, and it would have been very difficult, if not impossible, for Indian shippers to recruit a crew which was 75% British. The reason for this Act, as stated in the supplement of the *Fourth Report of the East India Company*, App. 47, pp. 23–4, was that 'The native sailors of India are to the disgrace of our national morals, on their arrival here led into scenes which soon divest them of the respect and awe they had entertained in India for the European character. The contemptuous reports which they disseminate on their return cannot fail to have a very unfavourable influence upon the minds of our Asiatic subjects, whose reverence for our character, which has hitherto contributed to maintain our supremacy in the east will be gradually changed for most degrading conceptions . . . and if an indignant apprehension having hitherto rated us too highly or respected us too much should once possess them, the effects of it may prove extremely detrimental. . . . Considered, therefore, in a physical, moral, commercial and political view, the apparent consequences of admitting these Indian sailors largely into our navigation form a strong additional objection to the concession to the proposed privilege manned by them'.[2] (Despatch dated 27 January 1801).

The Government tariff policy deliberately discouraged Indian shipping since, from 1812, the general import duty on goods brought into the country in Indian ships was raised to 15% as against 7½% in the case of British ships.[3]

Since the Indian shipping industry was in such a poor condition it is

---

[1] The Sanskrit work of great antiquity, *Yuktikalpatru*, describes in detail the several classifications, sizes, proportions, materials of construction, etc., of sea and river craft in the ancient India. See Central Water and Power Commission, *Water Transport in India*, Bulletin of Public Education No. 1., Government of India, n.d., see also Radha Kumud Mookerjee, *Indian Shipping*, Bombay, 1912.

[2] Quoted in Sarda Raju, p. 223.   [3] *Ibid.*

largely an academic question whether shipbuilding could have been adapted to meet the additional demand imposed by the advent of steel steamships. The general absence of an iron and steel industry would have been a grave impediment although it is impossible to say to what extent the Porto Novo Steel & Iron Company could have supplemented this want, or to what extent the needs of the shipping industry could have encouraged the growth of an iron and steel industry. But the possibility has led to the expression of bitter sentiments by Indians. For instance, the Reconstruction Policy Sub-Committee on Shipping observed, 'It was not the advent of the steamship that led to the decline of Indian shipbuilding industry. It was the acts of hostility of the British Government such as the banning of Indian ships from British waters and the imposition of discriminating and crushing import duties by the Government of India on goods imported in Indian bottoms that led to the decline of the shipbuilding industry in India and its ultimate ruin. Indian shipbuilding industry had thus to perish so that British shipbuilding industry could flourish'.[1]

From the 1830's onwards, attempts were made by Indians to compete in shipping in coastal waters, but they were largely unsuccessful as they did not, like some of the European-owned companies, possess Government contracts to carry mails, a source of steady income. Since their history is obscure, the precise reasons for failure of companies on the western coast cannot be stated, but probably there is some truth in the view that it was due to inexperienced management and lack of capital, etc. In the East, a number of companies were started in Calcutta by Indians and Europeans working together but these gradually passed almost completely into the hands of the Europeans and in the violent competition described in Chapter 7 all, except one or two, were eliminated. As regards the Far East, the mill owners in Bombay showed some interest in trade there from the 1880's but by that time the large number of international lines working on these routes and the vested interest of European lines made success by Indians almost impossible.

It was for these reasons that the Indian National Steamship Owners' Association observed:[2]

By their powerful financial resources and the ruthless trade wars, British shipping interests wiped out one Indian shipping company after another

[1] Quoted in the *Silver Jubilee Issue* of the Indian National Steamship Owners' Association, Bombay, 1958, p. 3.

[2] *Ibid.*

See also:

Walchand Hirachand, 'Why Indian Shipping Does Not Grow', *Bombay Investors' Year Book*, 1940.

Indian Ship. Why Shipowners Oppose Indo-Foreign Combine for Shipping, Bombay, (1958 ?), published by Navin Khandwallah.

from the coastal waters of India. As observed by the Committee [Reconstruction Policy Sub-Committee on Shipping], instead of giving protection to any of the several Indian enterprises that started operations in the field of shipping during the preceding sixty or seventy years against this unfair and anti-national rate wars, the Government of India missed not a single opportunity to extend its patronage during the last century to the British interests and thus encouraged them in every way to act against the national economic interests of the country.

Dividend paid by Gold Mining Companies operating in Mysore
(As a percentage of paid-up capital)

Year	Mysore	Nundydoorg	Champion	Ooregum
1886	20			
87	10			
88	20			
89	75			
90	75	$19\frac{1}{8}$	—	20
91	65	25	—	45
92	50	$28\frac{3}{4}$	—	85
93	50	$12\frac{1}{2}$	—	115
94	25	15	35	85
95	$47\frac{1}{2}$	25	65	85
96	100	$32\frac{1}{2}$	$67\frac{1}{2}$	$72\frac{1}{2}$
97	110	$42\frac{1}{2}$	100	35
98	150	$27\frac{1}{2}$	100	40
99	140	30	125	50
1900	135	$33\frac{3}{4}$	130	90

Balaghat declared its first dividend of 10% in 1900.

Source: Ahmed, p. 346.

APPENDIX 17

Number and Paid-up Capital (in rupees) of Each Class of Company in Existence at the end of Each Year since 1881-2 (ending 31 March)

| | Banking, Loan, and Insurance | | | | | | | | Trading | | | | | | | |
| | Banking and Loan | | Insurance | | Navigation | | Railways and Tramways | | Co-operative Associations | | Shipping, Landing, and Warehousing | | Printing, Publishing, and Stationery | | Other Trading | |
	No.	Capital	No.	Capital	No.	Capital	No.	Capital	No.	Capital	No.	Capital	No.	Capital	No.	Capital
1881-2	139	2,09,30,080	5	9,15,640	7	39,87,500	5	37,88,510	11	1,36,890	2	3,42,400	6	2,11,250	55	1,11,13,510
1882-3	135	2,13,20,600	5	27,00,750	9	40,31,920	3	38,09,340	13	1,79,690	2	4,20,000	6	5,33,150	69	1,10,78,050
1883-4	175	2,67,31,790	9	27,00,750	10	58,56,640	6	41,88,610	14	1,96,560	4	4,24,000	5	4,35,400	71	1,59,42,330
1884-5	198	2,80,16,880	11	11,69,990	8	87,16,130	6	20,32,990	14	1,98,250	4	5,06,600	8	5,78,100	82	1,75,22,090
1885-6	287	2,99,97,900	14	14,48,270	7	73,03,950	8	67,02,760	13	1,75,670	8	5,17,150	10	6,34,320	83	1,26,49,910
1886-7	355	3,05,31,340	15	18,62,980	9	73,60,070	10	68,54,600	15	1,97,460	6	6,24,200	11	6,23,120	88	1,61,00,500
1887-8	362	3,24,63,370	17	16,99,230	7	89,45,720	11	68,89,720	18	3,09,180	6	6,48,950	11	6,16,090	96	1,68,37,4900
1888-9	314	3,27,37,870	17	21,90,840	7	92,60,930	12	69,58,450	20	3,77,140	5	6,29,100	16	6,34,810	101	1,76,72,18
1889-90	291	3,22,73,370	16	20,79,130	9	90,71,910	12	78,56,730	18	3,09,880	5	6,29,100	17	7,35,210	104	1,75,21,570
1890-1	275	3,09,58,930	13	20,06,640	7	91,96,620	11	87,46,410	18	3,63,150	6	6,29,100	13	3,53,560	104	1,82,53,970
1891-2	259	3,73,32,930	14	20,58,730	8	89,11,650	11	95,89,580	24	3,85,490	6	6,39,100	15	3,89,310	115	1,82,44,320
1892-3	256	3,74,98,620	8	7,93,070	7	87,39,400	10	97,95,820	24	5,13,960	5	5,68,890	16	3,87,640	112	1,84,73,920
1893-4	271	3,74,39,820	75	8,35,650	8	87,39,400	12	99,08,000	25	3,80,550	7	5,90,890	17	4,60,710	121	1,88,35,840
1894-5	295	4,01,21,960	156	6,05,940	8	87,45,460	10	82,06,750	24	5,96,260	5	6,00,100	19	4,27,240	124	1,88,31,930
1895-6	299	4,04,66,720	183	8,99,010	9	87,45,460	14	89,71,100	27	5,94,410	5	4,77,600	23	5,93,620	142	2,15,98,770
1896-7	353	4,15,65,670	373	11,41,920	8	1,05,16,850	20	1,04,82,710	29	6,42,600	5	5,51,100	22	5,67,120	146	2,26,33,680
1897-8	389	4,31,75,420	285	9,21,250	9	1,06,16,660	20	1,42,49,860	28	4,39,900	5	13,46,100	27	4,38,840	169	2,49,80,750
1898-9	405	4,41,13,580	105	14,60,620	9	1,23,73,000	19	1,97,01,200	32	4,39,820	5	14,31,600	29	4,10,220	186	2,86,27,210
1899-1900	407	4,57,41,459	43	16,86,533	9	26,24,904	18	2,28,45,826	29	6,41,826	6	15,04,420	32	7,99,682	185	3,00,67,169
1900-1	430	4,51,57,522	33	16,86,025	9	26,26,102	18	3,16,69,541	28	6,32,938	5	15,04,100	30	5,15,372	190	3,27,11,225

APPENDIX 17 (*contd.*)

| | Tea and Other Planting Companies | | | | | | Mining and Quarrying | | | | | |
| | Tea | | Coffee and Chinchona | | Other Plantation | | Coal | | Gold | | Other Mining and Quarrying | |
	No.	Capital	No.	Capital	No.	Capital	No.	Capital	No.	Capital	No.	Capital
1881–2	113	2,75,89,930	5	1,97,500	4	1,81,360	6	38,95,000	8	20,52,800	6	14,44,000
1882–3	121	2,92,22,180	2	1,28,240	7	5,02,580	8	48,20,180	9	25,08,650	3	4,34,000
1883–4	121	3,05,91,970	7	3,81,720	5	4,61,870	6	50,45,000	11	27,05,840	8	9,03,000
1884–5	127	3,30,56,050	8	4,13,110	3	4,52,270	6	51,77,870	10	25,10,270	9	29,39,250
1885–6	130	3,27,73,950	7	4,42,030	5	4,57,190	7	52,00,000	9	19,75,730	10	31,37,080
1886–7	131	3,52,48,430	7	4,67,430	5	4,84,180	7	51,95,000	9	19,15,830	9	27,36,480
1887–8	127	3,54,36,070	7	4,81,810	7	5,60,480	7	51,95,000	8	19,33,970	8	29,66,540
1888–9	129	3,52,91,400	7	5,14,290	9	5,41,830	7	51,95,000	6	18,79,030	7	8,60,830
1889–90	133	3,55,17,340	7	5,26,710	4	4,58,280	8	52,05,000	6	15,63,730	7	8,76,130
1890–1	140	3,54,62,510	6	4,61,890	8	4,62,420	10	52,29,000	27	29,75,250	26	9,52,810
1891–2	144	3,64,88,340	5	3,83,290	9	6,31,000	11	61,66,800	19	77,11,230	27	22,80,920
1892–3	142	3,63,68,980	5	3,83,390	10	9,56,280	14	64,78,700	17	72,21,190	23	29,11,710
1893–4	148	3,71,30,890	5	3,89,990	12	9,56,280	16	79,46,710	15	71,84,330	22	28,59,140
1894–5	154	3,67,23,550	5	3,91,990	13	10,07,250	20	79,77,550	16	71,84,330	22	28,49,750
1895–6	156	3,52,20,590	3	2,76,800	13	12,47,250	28	96,68,880	14	71,84,330	21	23,84,770
1896–7	156	3,60,04,640	2	1,61,500	13	12,42,250	34	1,02,79,350	13	57,83,550	17	25,08,720
1897–8	137	3,21,85,020	1	39,000	14	12,31,660	34	1,14,83,230	13	58,09,900	16	24,82,780
1898–9	135	3,21,23,100	2	39,000	13	10,92,860	34	1,27,48,620	12	59,08,420	17	24,82,780
1899–1900	129	3,25,38,118	4	1,96,800	15	18,39,660	34	1,32,95,435	7	17,27,694	13	15,62,389
1900–1	135	3,32,13,192	4	1,57,570	12	12,12,472	34	1,40,01,120	9	21,27,699	15	16,16,682

APPENDIX 17 (contd.)
Mills and Presses

	Cotton Mills		Jute Mills		Mills for Cotton, Jute, Wool, Silk, Hemp, etc.		Cotton and Jute Screws and Presses		Paper Mills		Rice Mills		Flour Mills		Saw and Timber Mills		Other Mills and Presses	
	No.	Capital	No.	Capital	No.	Capital	No.	Capital	No.	Capital	No.	Capital	No.	Capital	No.	Capital	No.	Capital
1881-2	28	1,92,60,640	8	74,64,900	31	2,33,78,270	30	82,56,000	1	5,28,730	..	..	1	..	2	6,40,000	3	79,10,450
1882-3	31	2,67,22,750	12	87,17,400	33	2,81,46,870	38	88,59,250	2	5,63,670	..	..	1	..	2	6,40,000	1	31,07,300
1883-4	42	2,70,11,350	12	1,00,17,820	38	2,71,40,540	52	1,07,66,830	2	10,42,640	1	4,01,900	3	6,85,000	2	6,40,000	..	..
1884-5	44	3,40,85,030	11	1,03,62,970	42	3,20,96,260	55	1,12,77,010	3	11,71,740	1	4,10,000	3	4,00,000	2	6,40,000	..	..
1885-6	40	3,35,02,110	10	1,03,32,040	45	3,42,49,120	61	1,21,77,600	4	13,83,490	1	4,10,000	6	6,00,980	2	6,40,000	3	..
1886-7	46	3,43,10,980	10	1,03,56,230	47	3,03,88,370	60	1,26,58,810	4	16,69,030	..	..	9	9,31,830	1	6,00,000	4	17,780
1887-8	51	3,60,76,440	10	1,04,43,800	50	3,29,61,050	60	1,21,50,510	4	18,66,050	..	..	9	15,48,530	1	6,00,000	4	1,999,450
1888-9	58	3,97,61,660	10	1,07,11,200	58	3,53,85,650	63	1,26,41,120	4	18,71,120	..	..	9	15,96,070	1	..	4	2,334,010
1889-90	56	4,38,73,720	10	1,02,11,200	61	3,84,58,030	68	1,27,79,940	5	20,92,950	..	..	7	9,97,550	2	40,700	4	2,61,880
1890-1	56	4,68,66,920	11	1,10,86,200	63	4,93,29,600	76	1,32,02,580	5	27,67,660	..	..	8	11,22,550	2	40,700	2	1,07,960
1891-2	57	4,85,48,440	11	1,17,85,250	63	4,24,81,760	83	1,33,46,970	6	27,79,250	..	..	8	11,22,220	3	2,40,700	3	39,530
1892-3	59	4,96,50,260	12	1,20,94,850	68	4,18,89,520	87	1,37,40,810	6	34,48,380	2	..	11	14,91,220	3	2,40,700	4	69,250
1893-4	57	4,84,19,970	12	1,48,58,130	71	4,40,30,770	101	1,41,68,030	6	41,50,630	4	1,15,000	11	15,07,740	3	2,40,700	7	99,000
1894-5	57	4,85,72,340	13	1,46,34,760	75	4,42,04,840	105	1,42,43,150	6	44,66,370	4	1,29,840	15	17,20,370	3	2,40,700	12	2,13,180
1895-6	62	4,91,70,420	19	1,72,21,960	84	4,72,74,580	111	1,51,92,580	6	46,68,590	5	1,87,340	17	26,86,740	2	2,40,700	16	2,35,070
1896-7	67	5,10,04,620	19	2,12,76,430	104	5,27,50,280	112	1,55,37,040	7	47,15,910	5	1,86,760	18	28,38,200	4	2,40,700	16	2,46,990
1897-8	68	5,38,24,470	21	2,31,97,040	111	6,11,67,590	115	1,59,93,630	7	47,23,000	4	1,73,730	17	29,21,980	3	2,00,000	18	5,94,590
1898-9	66	5,52,69,340	20	2,57,10,630	113	6,92,78,030	116	1,60,72,810	7	47,34,850	4	1,18,520	17	29,64,250	4	3,88,400	19	8,52,070
1899-1900	67	5,65,40,106	21	2,87,94,525	110	6,77,40,454	113	1,63,97,165	7	52,47,375	3	1,18,525	18	27,99,870	3	4,03,400	22	12,20,045
1900-1	66	5,86,95,452	21	3,03,27,800	113	6,90,49,306	116	1,64,85,374	7	52,49,620	3	1,23,766	20	30,49,738	3	4,05,000	19	5,79,017

APPENDIX 17 (concluded)

	Land and Building		Breweries		Ice		Sugar		Others		Total of All Companies	
	No.	Capital	No.	Capital	No.	Capital	No.	Capital	No.	Capital	No.	Capital
1881–2	3	62,82,090	3	9,84,000	5	10,85,970	4	19,97,820	14	22,42,320	505	15,68,17,560
1882–3	3	62,82,300	4	10,48,050	10	12,17,450	3	21,99,300	15	17,65,370	547	17,09,59,040
1883–4	4	62,82,300	5	12,50,000	11	15,75,340	2	18,50,680	23	22,76,230	649	18,75,06,110
1884–5	4	63,42,580	3	11,00,000	14	18,03,360	4	18,51,830	14	15,27,810	694	20,63,58,440
1885–6	4	63,52,230	3	12,00,000	12	19,85,180	4	18,51,830	13	19,25,190	806	21,00,25,680
1886–7	3	62,08,830	3	12,00,000	12	20,96,310	2	16,09,430	8	15,55,200	886	21,38,04,420
1887–8	3	62,08,830	3	12,00,000	12	18,71,020	1	16,00,000	10	15,52,620	910	22,32,61,920
1888–9	3	63,46,130	3	12,00,000	13	19,59,930	1	16,00,000	11	19,24,490	895	22,99,75,080
1889–90	4	63,46,130	3	16,95,400	13	19,76,040	1	16,00,000	15	18,84,390	886	23,68,42,020
1890–1	5	65,99,330	3	16,95,400	12	18,97,520	2	16,06,360	19	12,09,410	928	24,45,84,450
1891–2	5	66,73,917	3	16,95,400	12	19,71,820	2	16,06,360	27	23,50,503	950	26,58,54,810
1892–3	4	65,58,005	3	16,95,400	12	18,63,870	3	16,22,040	33	24,75,985	956	26,79,31,860
1893–4	4	65,59,100	3	16,95,400	10	17,17,170	3	16,32,190	19	22,48,560	1,065	27,51,00,590
1894–5	4	65,59,100	3	16,95,400	11	17,28,040	5	16,37,250	20	23,72,330	1,204	27,66,87,730
1895–6	4	65,59,100	3	17,00,000	11	17,28,270	6	22,32,990	26	64,45,140	1,309	29,38,72,790
1896–7	4	65,59,100	3	17,00,000	10	16,22,240	8	23,02,360	28	65,03,350	1,596	31,15,65,590
1897–8	4	65,59,100	3	17,00,000	11	16,42,060	10	25,35,990	33	65,99,670	1,572	33,12,33,220
1898–9	4	65,59,100	3	17,00,000	11	16,46,820	10	31,97,970	20	45,44,670	1,417	35,59,89,490
1899–1900	4	65,59,100	3	17,00,000	10	15,97,537	11	36,98,849	17	44,98,883	1,340	35,43,87,749
1900–01	5	65,59,100	4	17,00,000	10	15,97,537	10	36,66,651	17	43,09,965	1,366	37,06,29,886

Source: *Financial and Commercial Statistics For British India*, (Calcutta, 1902), pp. 371–2.

APPENDIX 18

Number of Companies at Work in India, and their Nominal and Paid-up Capital (*in rupees*), at the end of each year since 1884-5

	Companies at work	Nominal capital	Paid-up capital	Increase or decrease in paid-up capital	per cent
1884-5	694	27,88,76,910	20,63,58,440	+ 1,88,52,330 =	10
1885-6	806	28,54,34,370	21,00,25,680	+ 36,67,240 =	2
1886-7	886	29,13,61,650	21,38,04,420	+ 37,78,740 =	2
1887-8	910	30,25,42,840	22,32,61,920	+ 94,57,500 =	4
1888-9	895	31,33,98,450	22,99,75,080	+ 67,13,160 =	3
1889-90	886	32,32,17,310	23,68,42,020	+ 68,66,940 =	3
1890-1	928	35,05,87,760	24,45,84,450	+ 77,42,430 =	3
1891-2	950	36,02,32,380	26,58,54,810	+ 2,12,70,360 =	9
1892-3	956	35,37,28,420	26,79,31,860	+ 20,77,060 =	0·8
1893-4	1,065	36,25,11,880	27,51,00,590	+ 71,68,730 =	2·7
1894-5	1,204	38,15,85,180	27,66,87,730	+ 15,87,140 =	0·6
1895-6	1,309	41,89,14,470	29,38,72,790	+ 1,71,85,060 =	6
1896-7	1,596	49,56,22,860	31,15,65,590	+ 1,76,92,800 =	6
1897-8	1,572	50,13,96,370	33,12,33,220	+ 1,96,67,630 =	6·3
1898-9	1,417	51,30,97,190	35,59,89,490	+ 2,47,56,270 =	7·5
1899-1900	1,340	50,16,59,366	35,43,87,749	− 16,01,741 =	0·4
1900-01	1,366	51,74,18,551	37,06,29,886	+ 1,62,42,137 =	4·6

Source: *Financial and Commercial Statistics for British India*, Calcutta, 1902.

APPENDIX 19

Number of Companies and their Paid-up Capital in each Province, at the end of each year since 1891-2

Number of Companies

Province	1891-2	1892-3	1893-4	1894-5	1895-6	1896-7	1897-8	1898-9	1899-1900	1900-1
Burma	17	17	16	16	17	17	17	18	18	22
Assam	1	2	2	2	2	2	2	3	4	6
Bengal	322	325	402	508	560	761	666	487	402	398
North-West Provinces and Oudh	55	55	55	61	64	65	68	67	71	75
Ajmer-Merwara	6	7	7	7	8	8	10	9	9	9
Punjab	20	21	21	20	26	31	39	50	52	50
Bombay	229	233	249	264	295	331	349	350	344	342
Central Provinces	9	10	12	12	12	10	10	11	11	12
Berar	3	4	3	3	3	3	4	4	4	3
Madras	203	188	195	206	217	257	307	321	335	361
Mysore	85	94	103	105	105	111	100	97	90	88
TOTAL	950	956	1,065	1,204	1,309	1,596	1,572	1,417	1,340	1,366

Paid-up Capital (in Rupees)

Province	1891-2	1892-3	1893-4	1894-5	1895-6	1896-7	1897-8	1898-9	1899-1900	1900-1
Burma	15,51,620	16,12,070	14,94,050	17,19,740	18,29,670	19,56,670	17,71,050	18,62,830	20,16,880	38,57,100
Assam	a	5,000	7,820	11,160	11,420	21,590	21,850	1,30,290	1,45,726	1,90,433
Bengal	11,72,97,610	11,91,06,510	12,52,06,630	12,53,71,480	13,14,36,320	13,92,97,600	14,11,20,250	14,98,43,510	15,03,32,742	15,47,11,734
North-Western Provinces and Oudh	97,62,880	1,00,05,340	91,69,230	93,18,020	1,12,26,390	1,19,80,200	1,27,76,800	1,41,74,920	1,51,66,108	1,71,97,630
Ajmer-Merwara	6,70,570	6,73,370	7,58,690	7,55,060	7,56,480	7,57,200	8,18,910	8,34,770	9,97,975	9,98,275
Punjab	42,55,770	44,33,380	46,26,850	47,81,000	53,27,610	54,98,240	58,87,270	65,07,390	74,11,504	72,55,752
Bombay	10,78,87,710	10,67,40,730	10,79,02,650	10,91,38,570	11,66,74,260	12,53,53,070	13,82,43,610	14,82,20,210	14,69,00,094	15,60,33,551
Central Provinces	20,50,030	24,37,210	26,12,220	26,46,070	26,63,650	25,50,130	26,20,840	26,49,800	27,52,770	30,59,058
Berar	25,720	36,060	29,910	29,910	29,910	29,910	1,43,660	1,54,910	1,54,910	1,45,000
Madras	1,90,73,870	1,94,58,270	1,94,60,820	1,92,26,160	2,04,11,620	2,04,93,220	2,43,91,320	2,82,91,320	2,53,04,921	2,43,56,104
Mysore	32,79,030	34,23,920	38,31,720	36,90,560	36,05,160	36,27,760	34,37,660	33,19,240	32,04,119	28,25,249
TOTAL	26,58,54,810	26,79,31,860	27,51,00,590	27,66,87,730	29,38,72,790	31,15,65,590	33,12,33,220	35,59,89,490	35,43,87,749	37,06,29,886

Source: *Financial and Commercial Statistics for British India*, 1902.
a Not reported.

Number of Companies registered, ceased, and working, with Capital, at the end of March, from 1882–3 to 1900–1

Number of Companies			Year	Capital of companies working In Rs. (000's)[b]		Number of Companies
Regd.	Ceased	Workg.		Nominal	Paid-up	
1149	646	503[a]	Up to March 1882			
74	30	547	1882–83	206,936	160,224	449
147	45	649	–84	239,420	187,028	550
82	35	696	–85	258,002	206,211	618
155	46	805	–86	266,526	209,606	714
133	52	886	–87	265,360	213,608	780
116	92	910	–88	283,843	231,297	829
94	109	895	–89	295,736	229,745	789
83	92	886	–90	304,225	236,609	791
134	92	928	–91	319,969	244,318	796
106	84	950	–92	335,732	265,526	810
72	66	956	–93	330,556	267,896	850
163	54	1,065	–94	343,943	275,066	893
194	55	1,204	–95	354,176	275,999	963
167	62	1,309	–96	373,969	293,775	1,049
388	101	1,596	–97	495,622	311,565	1,045
179	203	1,572	–98	501,396	331,233	1,019
116	271	1,417	–99	513,097	355,989	([c])
91	170	1,338	–1900	501,659	354,387	([c])
89	63	1,364	1900–01	517,418	370,629	([c])
3,732	2,368	1,364	Total (50 years)			

[a] The figures in the first three columns: 'Number of companies registered, ceased and working' are derived from the summaries of company data in S.T.B.I. and *Moral and Material Progress of India*. It is therefore not possible to account for the slight difference in the number of companies styled 'working' in this table and the tables in Appendices 17, 18, and 19.

[b] The figures are slightly different from those shown in Appendix 17. The figures in Appendix 17 are given for *all* companies, whereas the figures shown here are for only those companies for which both figures of nominal and paid-up capital were available. Hence the difference. (Since information was not available separately for the companies formed in any particular year, more interesting figures such as the total amount of capital lost by companies which ceased to exist etc. could be extracted only if enormous manual labour was employed).

[c] It was not possible to extract the required information from the data available in these years.

Sources: Various issues of S.T.B.I. and *Statement Exhibiting Moral and Material Progress of India*.

Company Registrations and dissolutions, 1851 to 1900[1]

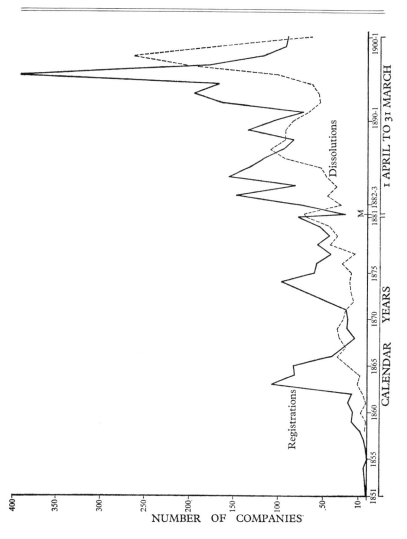

[1] Excluding thirty-seven 'defunct' companies up to March 1822.
M = January–March 1882.

Paid-up capital of jute, cotton, tea and all companies in operation,
1866–81.   In millions of rupees

Number of Companies in 1881		
Type	Total	Included here
All	586	505
Cotton[a]	59	48
Tea	114	105
Jute	8	8

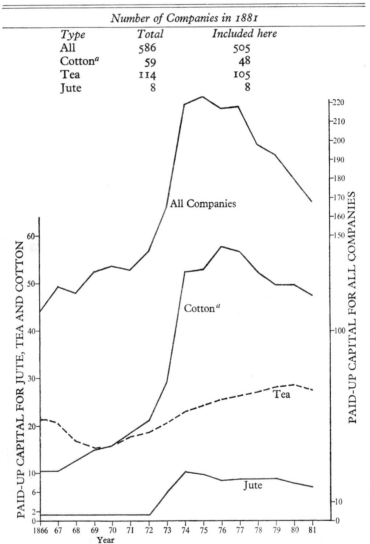

[a] Includes those classified as Multiple Textile Mills (See Appendix 8).

Paid-up capital of companies, 1 January 1851 to 31 March 1882. In millions of rupees

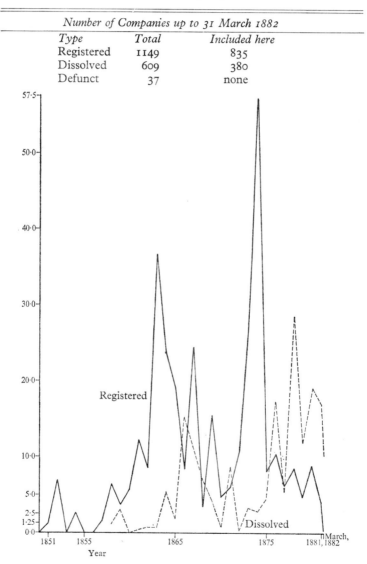

Number of Companies up to 31 March 1882		
Type	Total	Included here
Registered	1149	835
Dissolved	609	380
Defunct	37	none

SELECT BIBLIOGRAPHY

ARRANGEMENT

PRIMARY SOURCES
1. Archive Records
   1.1 India Office Library, London
   1.2 National Archives, Delhi
   1.3 Others
2. Official Publications
3. Statutes
   3.1 Indian
   3.2 British
4. Law Cases
   4.1 Indian
   4.2 British
5. Indian Law Reports and Digests
6. Directories, Almanacs, Stock Exchange Year Books, Trade Association Reports

SECONDARY SOURCES
Books, Theses, Monographs and Articles

PRIMARY SOURCES

1. ARCHIVE RECORDS

1.1 India Office Library, London.
India and Bengal Despatches, 1851.
Finance. Bengal Letters and Enclosures Received, 1848.
Judicial and Public Department Register, 1881 and 1882.
Legislative Proceedings of India, 27 December 1850.
List of Factory Records, Original Correspondence, Vol. 50.
Madras Public Proceedings, 1720.
Princep, H. T., *Four Generations in India*, MS. Eur.C.97.
Proceedings of the Council of the Governor General of India, assembled for the purpose of making laws and regulations, from 1862.
Proceedings of the Governor General-in-Council in the Financial Department, 27 May 1848. (No. 29 of 1848.)
Report on the Miscellaneous Old Records of the India Office, 1 November 1878, London, 1879.
1.2 National Archives, Delhi.
Commerce Department: *Coal and Iron*, from 1832.

Commerce and Industry Department: *Companies* (1912–14).

Commerce Department: *Stores*, from 1887.

Finance Department: *Despatches from the Secretary of State*, from 1858.

1.3 Algemeen Rijksarchief, The Hague.

Memoir of Governor Laurence Pit to his successor Cornelis Speelman, Koloniaal Archief, Overgekomen Brieven 1664, inv. nr. 1132 fo. 791–811, 25 June, 1663.

2. OFFICIAL PUBLICATIONS

Banking Enquiry Committee. The Indian Central, Report, 1931–32.

Bengal. Report on the Industries of, (J. G. Cummings), 1908.

Coal Mining Committee. Report of the Indian, 2 Vols., 1936–1937.

Coal Resources and Production of India. Report by T. Oldham, 1867.

Company Law Committee, Report, 1952.

Companies Act Amendment Committee, Report, 1957.

Cotton Mill Industry. Report of the Statutory Enquiry into the Indian, 1927.

Cotton. Statistical Tables Relating to Indian, 1889.

Currency. Report of the Fowler Committee on Indian, 1898.

Currency. Report of the Herschell Committee on Indian, 1893.

Factories in the Bombay Presidency. Report and Proceedings of the Commission Appointed to consider the Working of, 1885.

Factory Act. Report of the Commission Appointed by the Governor of Bombay in Council to Enquire into the Condition of the Operatives in the Bombay Factories, and the necessity or otherwise for the passing of a, 1875.

Famine Commission Report, 1880.

Financial and Commercial Statistics for British India.

Fiscal Commission, (1921–2), *Report of the Indian,* Simla, 1922.

Hazari, R. K., *The Structure of the Corporate Private Sector,* Report to the Government of India Research Programme Committee, Bombay, 1963.

Howard, Sir Albert, and Voelcker, J. A., *Report on the Improvement of Indian Agriculture,* London, 1893.

Imperial Legislative Proceedings.

Index Number of Indian Prices, 1861–1918, 1919.

Index Number of Prices, 1861–1931, 1953.

Indian Railways—One Hundred Years: 1853–1953, Indian Railway Board, New Delhi, 1953.

Industrial Commission. Report of the Indian, 1916–18.

Kaldor, N., *Indian Tax Reform,* New Delhi, 1956.

Labour Commission. Report of the Indian Factory, 1908, Vol. 1.

Labour in India. Report of the Royal Commission on, 1931.

Legislative Council. Abstract of the Proceedings of,

Madras Provincial Banking Enquiry Committee. Report of the, Vol. 1, 1930.

Mahon, R. H., *Report upon the Manufacture of Iron and Steel in India*, 1899.
Mineral Resources of India, Report by T. H. Holland, 1908.
Molesworth, G. L., *Notes on Iron Manufacture*, September 1882.
Moral and Material Progress of India. Statement Exhibiting the,
Nicholson, F., *Report on the Possibility of Introducing Land Banks into India*, 1895–8.
Nigam, Raj K. and Chaudhuri, N. C., *Corporate Sector in India*, New Delhi, 1960.
P.P., 1831–32, *X*, Pt. I & II; P.P., 1840, H. C., *VIII*; P.P., 1854 (299), LXV; P.P., 1864, LVIII; P.P. 1866, LXVI; P.P., 1868–69, XV; P.P., 1868–69 (104–1), LVI; P.P. 1893–94, LXV.
Prices in India. Report on the Enquiry into the Rise of, 5 vols., Calcutta, 1914 (K. L. Datta Report).
Railway Report, 1921. Cmd. 1512.
Railways. Report on the Working of the Indian, 1875.
Railways. Wedgewood Committee Report, 1937.
Statistical Tables for British India. From 1877.
Stock Exchange Enquiry Committee. Report of the, Bombay, 1924.
Stores Committee. Report of, 1906.
Tea Cultivation in Assam, Cachar and Sylhet. Report of the Commissioners Appointed to Enquire into the State and Prospects of, Calcutta, 1868.
Tea in India. Report on the Production of, Statistical Department, India, (Published in Calcutta, 1903 ?).
Tea Industry in Bengal. Papers regarding, Calcutta, 1873.

3.   STATUTES

3.1   *Indian.*

Theobald, G. W., *Legislative Acts of the Governor General of India-in-Council, 1834–71.*
Act V of 1838.
Act IX of 1843.
Act XIX of 1845.
Act XXIII of 1845.
Companies Act (LXIII of 1850).
Companies Act (XIX of 1857).
Companies Act (VII of 1860).
Act XXVIII of 1865.
Companies Act (X of 1866).
Companies Act (VI of 1882).
Companies Act (VI of 1887).
Companies Act (XII of 1891).
Companies Act (XII of 1895).
Companies Act (IV of 1900).
Companies Act 1913.
Companies Act 1936.
Companies Act 1956.

Select Bibliography

3.2 *British.*
    6 Geo. I, c. 18.
    47 Geo. III, c. 68.
    3 and 4 Wm. IV, c. 85.
    19 and 20 Vic. c. 47.

4. LAW CASES

4.1 *Indian.*
    Pillay Appavu vs.Kamakshi, I, Madras High Court Reports, **448**.

4.2 *British.*
    Andrews vs. Gas Meter Co. (1897) 1 Ch. 361 C. A.
    Ashbury Carriage Co. vs. Riche (1875) L.R. 7 H.L. 653.
    Erlanger vs. New Sombrero Phosphate Co. (1878) 3 App. Cas. **1218**, H.L.
    Gluckestein vs. Barnes (1900) A.C. 240, H.L.
    Hutton vs. Scarborough Cliff Hotel Co. (1865) 2 Dr. and sm. **521**.
    Ooregum Gold Mining Co. vs. Roper (1892) A.C. 125, H.L.
    Solomon vs. Solomon (1897) A.C. 22, H.L.
    Trevor vs. Whitworth (1887) 12 App. Cas. 409, H.L.

5. INDIAN LAW REPORTS AND DIGESTS
    A Digest of Indian Law Cases (1836–1909) 16 Pt. Calcutta, 1912–20 (compiled by B. D. Bose).
    Bengal Law Reports—Digest of Cases Reported. Vol. I to XV. Calcutta, 1878 (by J. V. Woodman).
    Indian Law Reports: Bombay, Allahabad, Calcutta and Madras. From 1876.
    Reports of Cases decided in the High Court of Bombay, Bombay, 1875. (by C. W. L. Jackson).
    Reports of Cases decided in the High Court of Madras, 1862 to 1874 (by W. Stokes).

6. DIRECTORIES, ALMANACS, STOCK EXCHANGE YEAR BOOKS, TRADE ASSOCIATION REPORTS, ETC.
    The Bengal Almanac and Directory for 1815, Calcutta.
    The Bengal and Agra Directory and Annual Register, 1850.
    Bengal Chamber of Commerce—Half-Yearly Reports, 1854 to 1869.
    Bengal Directory, Thacker's, Various issues.
    Bengal National Chamber of Commerce. Report, 1887.
    Bombay Chamber of Commerce, Reports.
    Bombay Mill Owners Association, Annual Reports.
    The Bombay Times Calendar of 1855.
    Calcutta Exchange Price Current, 1820–4.
    Calcutta Stock Exchange Official Year Book, 2 Vols., 1940–2.
    Calcutta Trade Association, Report of Proceedings, 1830–50.
    Calcutta Weekly Price Current, 1828.
    Indian Insurance Manual, Thacker, Spink & Co., 1907.

Business Corporations in India, 1851–1900

Dictionary of National Biography, London, 1885 and 1932.
Investors' India Year Book, Place, Siddons & Gough, first published in 1912.
London Stock Exchange Year Books (from Burdett's Intelligence of 1882).
Times of India Calendar and Directory, 1864–1929.
Madras Stock Exchange Official Year Book.

SECONDARY SOURCES

A Manchester Man, *A Guide to Indian Investments*, London, 1861.

Acharya, Hemlata (Mrs), 'Creative Response in Indian Economy— A Comment'. *Economic Weekly*, 27 April 1957.

Adarkar, B. N., *The Indian Tariff Problem*, Bombay, 1936.

Adarkar, B. P., *The Indian Monetary Policy*, Kitabistan, 1939.

Ahmed, N. Z., *Some Aspects of the History of British Investment in the Private Sector of the Indian Economy, 1874–1914*. (Unpublished Thesis, M.Sc.Econ.) London, 1955.

Altekar, A. S., *Rastrakutas and their Times*, Oriental Book Agency, Poona, 1934.

Ambedkar, B. R., *The Problem of the Rupee*, London, 1923.

Andrew Yule & Company, 1863–1963 (Managing Agents of the Bengal Coal Company), Calcutta, 1963.

Anstey, V., *The Economic Development of India*, 4th Edn., London, 1952

Antia, F. P., *Inland Transport Costs*, Bombay, 1932.

Antrobus, H. A., *A History of the Assam Company, 1839–1953*, Edinburgh, 1957.

A History of the Jorehaut Tea Co. Ltd., 1859–1946, London, 1948.

Appadorai, A., *Economic Conditions in Southern India (A.D. 1000–1500)* Madras, 1936.

Arasaratnam, S., 'Indian Merchants and Their Trading Methods (*circa* 1700)', *Indian Economic and Social History Review*, March 1966.

Ashley, P., *Modern Tariff History*, 2nd Edn., London, 1910.

Badshah, B. R., *The Life of Rao Bahadur Ranchodlal Chotalal, C.I.E.*, Bombay, 1899.

Bagchi, R., *Banks and Industrial Finance in India*, Ph.D. Thesis, London, 1957.

Bagchi, S. C., *Principles of the Law of Corporations with Special Reference to British India*, Calcutta, 1914 ?

Ballhatchet, Kenneth, *Social Policy and Social Change in Western India, 1817–30*, London, 1957.

Banerjee, H., *The House of the Tagores*, Calcutta, 1965.

Basham, A. L., *The Indian Sub-Continent in Historical Perspective*, London, 1958.

Basu, S. K., *Industrial Finance in India*, Calcutta, 1939.

The Managing Agency System—In Prospect and Retrospect, Calcutta, 1958.

Beauchamp, J., *British Imperialism in India*, London, 1934.

Bell, H., *Railway Policy in India*, London, 1894.

Select Bibliography

Berg, N. P. V. D., *The Money Market and Paper Currency of India*, Batavia, 1884.

Berle, A. A. and Means, G. C., *The Modern Corporations and Private Property*, New York, 1933.

Berle, A. A., *The Twentieth Century Capitalist Revolution*, New York, 1954.

Berrill, Kenneth, 'Foreign Capital and Take-Off' in Berrill, K. (Ed.) *Economic Development with Special Reference to East Asia*, London, 1964.

Bhardwaj, Khrishna R., 'Linkages', *Economic Weekly*, 18 August 1962.

Bhatia, B. M., *Famines in India*, Bombay, 1962.

Bhatnagar, B. G., *Currency and Exchange in India*, Allahabad, 1924.

Bhatt, V. V., 'A Century and a Half of Economic Stagnation in India', *Economic Weekly*, July 1963.

Bhattacharya, S., 'Laissez-faire in India', *Indian Economic and Social History Review*, January 1965.

Blake, G., *B. I. Centenary (1856–1956)*, London, 1956.

Blyn, George, *Agricultural Trends in India, 1891–1947: Output, Availability and Productivity*, Philadelphia, 1966.

Bose, A., *Social and Rural Economy of Northern India, 1942–1945*, 2 Vols. University of Calcutta, 1949–52.

Boserup, Mogens, 'Agrarian Structure and Take-Off' in Berrill, K. (Ed.) *Economic Development with special reference to East Asia*, London, 1964.

Brame, Alfred, *The India General Steam Navigation Company*, London, 1900.

Brimmer, A., 'The Setting of Entrepreneurship in India', *Quarterly Journal of Economics*, Vol. LXIX, November 1954.

Brown, Hilton, *Parry's of Madras*, Madras, 1954.

Buchanan, D. H., *The Development of Capitalist Enterprise in India*, New York, 1934.

Buchanan, N. S., *The Economics of Corporate Enterprise*, New York, 1940.

Bulsara, Navaroji Jamshedji, *Guide to Indian Securities, Stocks and Currency Notes*, Bombay, 1897.

Bye, Maurice, 'Le Rôle du Capital dans le développement économique', *Economie Appliquée*, 1958, No. 3.

Cairncross, A. K., *Home and Foreign Investment, 1870–1913*, Cambridge, 1953.

'Capital Formation in the Take-Off' in Berrill, K. (Ed.) *Economic Development with special reference to East Asia*, London, 1964.

Cambridge History of India, Vol. VI. London, 1932.

Cawston, G., and Keane, A. H., *The Early Chartered Companies, 1296–1858*, London, 1896.

Chablani, H. L., *Indian Currency and Exchange*, London (Madras printed), 1925.

Chandra, Bipan, *The Rise and Growth of Nationalism in India*, New Delhi, 1966.

Chaudhuri, Nirad C., *The Continent of Circe*, London, 1965.

Chatterson, A., *Agricultural and Industrial Problems in India*, Madras, 1903.

Choksey, R. D., *Economic Life in the Bombay Deccan, 1818–1839*, Bombay, 1955, also *Economic Life in the Bombay Konkan, 1818–1839* Bombay, 1960.

Cirvante, V. R., *The Indian Capital Market*, Bombay, 1956.

Clarke, H., *Gold in India*, London, 1881.

Coggin-Brown, J., *Iron and Steel Industry of India*, Reprint of articles from *Mining Magazine*, 1921.

Cola, P. R., *How to Develope (sic) Productive Industry in India and the East*, London, 1867.

Colar Gold Field in the State of Mysore. (Reprinted from the *Madras Mail*, Madras, 1885).

Condon, J. K., *The Bombay Plague*, Bombay, 1900.

Cooke, C. N., *The Rise, Progress and Present Conditions of Banking in India*, Calcutta, 1863.

Copper, John, *The Three Presidencies of India*, London, 1853.

Das, N., *Industrial Enterprise in India*, London, 1938.

Dasgupta, Samir, 'Sociological and Economic Explanations—A Comment', *Economic Weekly*, 7 August 1963.

Davis, K., *The Population of India and Pakistan*, Princeton, 1951.
  'Social and Demographic Aspects of Economic Development in India' in Kuznets, Moore and Spengler (Eds.) *Economic Growth: Brazil, India and Japan*, Duke University Press, Durham, N.C., 1955.

Deane, P., and Cole, W. A., *British Economic Growth, 1688–1959, Trends and Structure*, Cambridge, 1962.

Deb, Raja Binaya Krishna, *The Early History and Growth of Calcutta*, Calcutta, 1905.

Delden, Wilhelm van, *Studien uber die indische Jute Industrie* (Dresden, Technische Hochschule, Volkswirtschaftliches Seminar, Abhandlungen 9 Heft), Munich, 1915.

Dhume, S. M., *The Evolution of Banking in India from Earliest Times to Present Day*, D.Sc.Econ. Thesis, London, 1948.

Dobb, M., *Studies in the Development of Capitalism*, Cambridge, 1951.

Du Bois, A. B., *The English Business Company after the Bubble Act, 1720–1800*, New York, 1938.

Dutt, R. C., *The Economic History of India in the Victorian Age*, 2nd Edn., London, 1906.

Edwardes, S. M., *K. R. Cama (1831–1909): A Memoir*, Oxford University Press, London, 1923.
  Memoir of Rao Bahadur Ranchhodlal Chhotalal, Exeter, 1920;
  The Gazetteer of Bombay City and Island etc. (compiled by S. M. Edwardes), 3 Vols., Bombay, 1909–10.
  The Rise of Bombay: A Retrospect, Bombay, 1902.

Ellison, Thomas, *The Cotton Trade of Great Britain*, London, 1866.

Elvin, Verrier, *The Story of Tata Steel*, Bombay, 1958.

Employers Association, *Achievements of Managing Agency System*, Calcutta, 1954.

Select Bibliography

Enthoven, R. E., *The Cotton Fabrics of the Bombay Presidency*, Bombay, 1897.

Evans, G. H., *British Corporation Finance, 1775–1850*, Baltimore, 1936.

Financial Institutions in India, International Monetary Fund (Research Dept.), [Typescript], 1950.

Florence, P. Sargant, *Ownership, Control and Success of Large Companies*, London, 1961

Foster, W., *The English Factories in India, 1618–1621*, Oxford, 1906.

Fraser, Lovat, *Iron and Steel in India*, Bombay, 1919.

Fraser, W. M., *Recollections of a Tea Planter*. Tea and Rubber Mail, 1935.

Gadgil, D. R., *Origin of the Indian Business Class*, Mimeographed, Gokhle Institute, Poona, [1951 ?].

The Industrial Evolution of India in Recent Times, Calcutta, 1942.

Ganguli, B. N., *Dadabhai Naoriji and the Drain Theory*, Bombay, 1965.

Ganguli, B. N. (Ed.), *Readings in Indian Economic History*, Bombay, 1964.

Garg, K. L., *Stock Exchanges in India*, 2nd Edn., Calcutta, 1950.

Ghosal, H. R., *Economic Transition in the Bengal Presidency, 1793–1833*, Calcutta, 1966.

'Changes in the Organisation of Industrial Production in the Bengal Presidency in the Early Nineteenth Century' in Ganguli, B. N. (Ed.), *Readings in Indian Economic History*, Bombay, 1964.

Ghosh, K. M., *The Indian Company Law*, 2 Vols., 11th Edn., Calcutta, 1963.

Ghurye, G. C., *Caste and Class in India*, 2nd Edn., London, 1957.

Gopal, S., *The Viceroyalty of Lord Ripon*, Oxford, 1953.

Gopalkrishnan, P. K., *Development of Economic Ideas in India, 1880–1950*, New Delhi, 1959.

Gow, Wilson and Stanton, *Tea Producing Companies of India and Ceylon*, London, 1897.

Gower, L. C. B., *The Principles of Modern Company Law*, London, 1957.

Grant, C. W., *Bombay Cotton and Indian Railways*, London, 1850.

Griffiths, P., *The British Impact on India*, London, 1952.

Habakkuk, H. J., 'Free Trade and Commercial Expansion, 1853–1870' in *Cambridge History of the British Empire*, II, Cambridge, 1940.

Habib, Irfan, *The Agrarian System of Mughal India*, London, 1963.

Haji, S. N., *Economics of Shipbuilding*, Bombay, 1924.

Hardinge, Charles, *My Indian Years: 1910–1916. The Reminiscences of Lord Hardinge of Penhurst*, London, 1948.

Harnetty, Peter, 'The Imperialism of Free Trade: Lancashire and Indian Cotton Duties, 1859–1862,' *Economic History Review*, 1965.

Harris, F. R., *Jamshetji Nusserwanji Tata*, Bombay, 1958.

Harrison and Crosfield Ltd., *100 Years as East India Merchants*, 1943.

Heatly, S. G. T., 'Contributions towards a history of the Development of the Mineral Resources of India: No. 2, Memoranda relative to the working of Iron in Bengal,' *Journal of the Asiatic Society of Bengal*, Vol. XII, 1843.

Heaton, H., *Economic History of Europe*, Revised Edn., New York, 1948.

Hirachand Walchand, 'Why Indian Shipping does not Grow', *Bombay Investors' Year Book*, 1940.

Hobson, C. K., *The Export of Capital*, London, 1914.

Howard, H. F., *India and the Gold Standard, 1911*, London, 1911.

Howard, Louise, E., *Sir Albert Howard in India*, London, 1953.

Hubbard, G. E., *Eastern Industrialisation and its Effects on the West*, London, 1938.

Hunt, B. C., *The Development of the Business Corporation in England, 1800–1867*, Cambridge, Mass., 1936.

Hunter, W. W., *The Annals of Rural Bengal*, 7th Edn., London, 1897.

Indian National Steamship Owners' Association: Silver Jubilee Issue, Bombay, 1958.

Indian Ship. Why Shipowners Oppose Indo-Foreign Combine for Shipping. Published by Navin Khandwallah, Bombay, 1958?

Islam, Nurul, *Foreign Capital and Economic Development: Japan, India and Canada*, Tokyo, 1960.

Iyer, G. S., *Some Economic Aspects of British Rule in India*, Madras, 1903.

Jackson, W., 'Memorandum on the Iron Works of Birbhum' *Journal of the Asiatic Society of Bengal*, Vol. XIV, Part III, 1845.

Jain, L. C., *Indigenous Banking in India*, London, 1929.

Monetary Problems of India, London, 1933.

Jain, P. C., *Industrial Finance in India*, New Delhi, 1961 ?

James Finlay and Company Limited, 1750–1950, Glasgow, 1951.

Jather, G. B. and Beri, S. G., *Indian Economics*, 9th Edn., 1952, 2 Vols.

Jeffreys, J. B., *Trends in Business Organisation in Great Britain since 1856*, Ph.D. Thesis, London, 1938.

Jenks, L. H., *The Migration of British Capital to 1875*, New York, 1927, and London, 1963.

Jennings, S., *My Visit to the Goldfields in the S.E. Wynaand*, London, 1881.

Jevons, H. S., *Money, Banking and Exchange in India*, Simla, 1922.

Johnson, William A., *The Steel Industry of India*, Harvard, 1966.

Joshi, M. D., 'Currency' in Singh, V. B. (Ed.) *The Economic History of India 1857–1956*, Bombay, 1965.

Jute Mills of Bengal described by the Special Correspondent of the Dundee Advertiser in Calcutta, 1880.

Kane, P. V., *History of Dharmasastra*, Vol. II and III, Poona, 1930.

Keynes, J. M., *Indian Currency and Finance*, London, 1913.

Khala, K. P., *Industrial Protection in India*, Bombay, 1939.

Kidron, Michael, *Foreign Investments in India*, London, 1965.

Kling, Blair, B., 'The Origin of the Managing Agency in India', *Journal of Asian Studies*, Vol. XXVI, No. 1, November 1966.

Knowles, L. C. A., *Economic Development in the 19th Century*, London, 1948.

Economic Development of the British Overseas Empire, London, 1924.

Industrial and Commercial Revolutions in Great Britain during the Nineteenth Century, London, 1937.

Kodanda, Rama Aiyer, *Law of Corporate Bodies and Registration*, Madras, 1903.

Krishnaswami, A., *Capital Development of India, 1860–1913 [Typescript]*, 1941. (London School of Economics Library).

Kumar, Dharma, *Land and Caste in South India*, Cambridge, 1965.

Lamb, Helen B., 'The Development of Modern Business Communities in India', *Proceedings of the Conference on Human Resources and Labour Relations in Under Developed Countries*, Ithaca, 1954 [Mimeograph].

'The "State" and Economic Development in India' in Kuznets, Moore and Spengler (Eds.) *Economic Growth: Brazil, India and Japan*, Durham, N.C., 1955.

Lees-Smith, H. B., *India and the Tariff Problem*, London, 1909.

Leighton, D. E. W., *The Indian Gold Mining Industry*, Madras, 1883.

Levy, A. B., *Private Corporations and Their Control*, Vols. I and II, London, 1950.

Lindsay, H. R. S., *The Role of Foreign Enterprise in a Developing Economy*, The Metal Box Co. of India Ltd., Calcutta, 1965 ?

Lokanathan, P. S., *Industrial Organisation in India*, London, 1935.

'Entrepreneurship: Supply of Entrepreneurs and Technologists with Special Reference to India' in Berrill, K. (Ed.) *Economic Development with special reference to East Asia*, London, 1964.

Macaulay, The Works of Lord, Vol. II. *Historical Essays*, The Universal Library, London, n.d.

Mackenzie, C., *Realms of Silver, 100 Years of Banking in the East*, London, 1954.

Maclean, J. M., *A Guide to Bombay*, 3rd Edn., Bombay, 1877.

Macpherson, W. J., 'Investment in Indian Railways, 1845–1875', *Economic History Review*, December 1955.

Madon, B. F., *India's Exchange Problem*, Parts I & II, Bombay, 1925.

Mahalingham, T., *South India Polity*, University of Madras, 1955.

Maity, S. K., *Economic Life in Northern India in the Gupta Period A.D. 300–550*, Calcutta, 1957.

Majumdar, R. C., *Corporate Life in Ancient India*, Calcutta, 1922.

Malhtora, D. K., *History and Problems of Indian Currency, 1835–1943*, Lahore, 1944.

Marx, Karl, *Das Kapital*, Vol. I, London, 1938.

Mathur, J. S., *Indian Working Class Movement*, Allahabad, 1964.

Mazumdar, Harendra Kumar, *Business Savings in India*, Bombay, 1959.

Mehta, M. M., *Structure of Indian Industries*, Bombay, 1955.

Mehta, N. B., *Indian Railways*, London, 1927.

Mehta, R. C., *Capital Market in India for Planned Growth*, Gwalior, 1965.

Mehta, S. D., *The Cotton Mills of India, 1854–1954*, Bombay, 1954.

Meier, Gerald M., *Leading Issues in Development Economics*, New York, 1964.

Milburn, W., *Oriental Commerce*, London, 1813 and 1825.

Mishra, Vikas, *Hinduism and Economic Growth*, Oxford University Press, India, 1962.

Misra, B. B., *The Indian Middle Classes: Their Growth in Modern Times*, London, 1961.

Mitchell, B. R., with collaboration of Deane, Phyllis, *Abstract of British Historical Statistics*, Cambridge, 1962.

Mittra, Kissory Chand, *Memoir of Dwarkanath Tagore*, Calcutta, 1870.

Mookerjee, Radha Kumud, *Indian Shipping*, Bombay, 1912.

Moore, R. J., 'Imperialism and Free Trade Policy in India, 1853–54,' *Economic History Review*, 1964.

Moreland, W. H. and Chatterjee, A. C., *A Short History of India*, London, 1957.

Morison, Sir T., *The Economic Transition in India*, London, 1911.

Morris, M. D., *The Emergence of an Industrial Labour Force in India: A Study of the Bombay Cotton Mills, 1854–1947*, Berkeley and Los Angeles, 1965.

'Some Comments on the Supply of Labour to the Bombay Cotton Textile Industry', *Indian Economic Journal*, I, No. 2, October 1953.

'Towards a Reinterpretation of Nineteenth Century Indian Economic History', *Journal of Economic History*, December, 1963.

Morris, M. D. and Stein, B., 'The Economic History of India: A Bibliographic Essay', *Journal of Economic History*, Vol. XXI, No. 2, June 1961.

Mukherjee, M., 'A Preliminary Study of the Growth of National Income in India, 1857–1957', in *Asian Studies in Income and Wealth*, Bombay, 1965.

Mulky, M. A., *New Capital Issues Market in India*, Bombay, 1947.

Mulky, M. A. and Samant, D. R., *Organisation and Finance of Industries in India*, London, 1937.

Mullick, K. M., *A Brief History of Bengal Commerce, 1814–1870*, Calcutta, 1871–2.

Muranjan, S. K., *Modern Banking in India*, Bombay, 1940.

Murti, V. N., 'Indian Economy during the British Rule', *Indian Journal of Economics*, April, 1961.

Myint, H., 'An Interpretation of Economic Backwardness' in Agrawal, A. N. and Singh, S. P., (Eds.), *The Economics of Underdevelopment*, New York, 1963.

Myres, Charles A., *Industrial Relations in India*, Bombay, 1958.

Labour Problems in the Industrialisation of India, Harvard, 1958.

'Recent Development in Management Training', *Indian Journal of Public Administration*, April–June 1958.

Namjoshi, M. V., *The Development of the Large-Scale Private Sector in India*, Thesis, Gokhle Institute of Politics and Economics, Poona, 1956.

Naoroji, Dadabhai, *Poverty and UnBritish Rule in India*, London, 1901.

Nath, Pran, *A Study of Economic Conditions in Ancient India*, London, 1929.

National Council of Applied Economic Research, *The Managing Agency System*, Delhi, 1959.

Capital Market in a Planned Economy, Delhi, 1966.

Nazir, Cooverjee Sorabjee, *The First Parsee Baronet*, Bombay, 1866.

Neale, W. C., 'A Case of Aborted Growth, India: 1860–1900, A Comment', *Economic Weekly*, 1 December 1962.

Nef, J. V., 'What is Economic History?', *Journal of Economic History* (Supplement), December 1944.

Nehru, Jawaharlal, *A Bunch of Old Letters*, Bombay, 1958.

Nigam, Raj K., *Managing Agencies in India*, New Delhi, 1957.

Paish, F. W., *Business Finance*, London, 1957.

Pandit, D. P. (Mrs), 'Creative Response in Indian Economy—A Regional Analysis', *Economic Weekly*, 23 February and 2 March 1957.

Pandit, Dhairyabala, 'India: A Century of Gestation, Relevance of Non-Economic Facts in Development Studies', *Economic Weekly*, 22 September 1962.

Patel, S. J., 'Long Term Changes in Output and Income in India: 1896–1960', *Indian Economic Journal*, January 1958.

'Main Features of Economic Growth Over the Century', *Indian Economic Journal*, Vol. XI, No. 3, 1964.

Philips, C. H., *The East India Co., 1784–1834*. Manchester, 1940.

Pillai, P. P., *Economic Conditions in India*, London, 1925.

Playne, Somerset, (comp.), *The Bombay Presidency, The United Provinces, The Punjab, etc.*, London, 1917–20.

Prakash, Om, 'The European Trading Companies and the Merchants of Bengal, 1650–1725', *Indian Economic and Social History Review*, Vol. I, No. 3.

Prasad, Amba, *Indian Railways*, Asia Publishing, Bombay, 1960.

Prasad, B., *The Effects of Improved Transport upon the distribution of Industry in India*, M.Sc. Thesis, London, 1954.

Premchund Raychund and Sons, 1856–1956, Bombay, 1957?

Ranade, M. G., *Essays on Indian Economics*, Bombay, 1899 and 1906.

Rangnekar, D. K., *Poverty and Capital Development in India*, London, 1947.

Ray, Parimal, *India's Foreign Trade Since 1870*, London, 1934.

Ray, R. M., *Life Insurance in India*, Bombay, 1941.

Raychaudhuri, Tapan, 'European Commercial Activity and the Organisation of India's Commerce and Industrial Production, 1500–1750' in Ganguli, B. N. (Ed.) *Readings in Indian Economic History*, Asia Publishing House, 1964.

Jan Company in Coromandel, 1605–1960 The Hague, 1962.

Raynes, Harold E., *A History of British Insurance*, London, 1948.

Robertson, Ross M., *History of the American Economy*, New York, 1955.

Rosen, George, *Some Aspects of Industrial Finance in India*, New York, 1962.

'A Case of Aborted Growth: India, 1860–1900, Some Suggestions for Research', *Economic Weekly*, 11 August 1962.

Rostow, W. W., *The Stages of Economic Growth*, London, 1960 (Paperback).

Process of Economic Growth, Oxford, 1960.

(Ed.) *The Economics of Take-off into Sustained Growth*, London, 1963.

Rungta, R. S., *The Rise of Business Corporations in India and their Development during 1851–1900*, Ph.D. Thesis, London, 1965.

'Indian Company Law Problems in 1850', *American Journal of Legal History*, Vol. 6, No. 3, July 1962.

'Promotion of Indian Companies before 1850', *Indian Journal of Economics*, Vol. XLVI, Part IV, No. 183, April 1966.

'The Bengal Gold Craze', *Indian Economic and Social History Review*, Vol. III, No. 1, March 1966.

Russell, L. P., *The Indian Companies Acts, 1882–1887*, Bombay, 1888.

Rutnagur, S. M., *Bombay Industries: The Cotton Mills*, Bombay, 1927.

Sanyal, N., *Development of Indian Railways*, Calcutta, 1930.

Sarda Raju, A., *Economic Conditions in the Madras Presidency, 1800–1850*, Madras, 1941.

Saul, S. B., *Studies in British Overseas Trade, 1870–1914*, Liverpool, 1960.

Savkar, D. S., *Joint Stock Banking in India*, Bombay, 1938.

Seminar on Current Problems in Corporate Law, Management and Practice, Proceedings, Delhi, 1964

Sen, A. K., 'Sociological and Economic Explanations: An Illustration from the Indian Iron and Steel Industry', *Economic Weekly*, Annual Number, February 1963.

'Reply', *Economic Weekly*, 17 August 1963.

Sen, Nabendu, 'Sociological and Economic Explanations—A Comment', *Economic Weekly*, 18 May 1963.

Sen, S. K., *Studies in Industrial Policy and Development of India, 1858–1914*, Calcutta, 1964.

Studies in Economic Policy and Development of India, 1848–1926, Calcutta, 1966.

Shah, K. T., *Sixty Years of Indian Finance*, Bombay, 1921.

Shelvankar, K. S., *The Problem of India*, Harmondsworth, 1940.

Shirras, G. Findlay, *Indian Finance and Banking*, London, 1919.

'Gold and British Capital in India', *Economic Journal*, December, 1929.

Simha, S. L. N., *The Capital Market of India*, Bombay, 1960.

Singh, S. B., *European Agency Houses in Bengal, 1783–1833*, Calcutta, 1966.

Sinha, H., *Early European Banking in India*, London, 1927.

Sinha, J. C., *Economic Annals of Bengal*, London, Calcutta printed, 1927.

Sinha, N. C., *Studies in Indo-British Economy*, Calcutta, 1946.

Sinha, N. K., *Economic History of Bengal*, Vol. I, Calcutta, 1956.

Slater, D. M., *Rise and Progress of Native Life Assurance in India*, Bombay, 1897.

Smallwood, R. P. F., 'Transacting Fire Business in India and Pakistan', *Journal of the Chartered Insurance Institute*, Vol. 46, 1957–8.

'The Nature and Structure of Insurance Markets in the Far East', *Journal of the Chartered Insurance Institute*, Vol. 59.

Smetham, E. R., *Indian Companies Act, 1882*, Bombay, 1902.

Sovani, N. V., 'British Impact on India', *Cahiers d'Histoire Mondiale*, April 1954.

Select Bibliography

Srinivas, M. N. (Ed.), *India's Villages*, Asia Publishing House, 2nd Edn., 1960.

Srinivas, M. N. and Shah, A. M., 'The Myth of Self-Sufficiency in the Indian Village', *Economic Weekly*, 10 September 1960.

Srinivasachari, Rao Sahib C. S., *History of the City of Madras*, Madras Tercentenary Celebration Committee, Madras, 1939.

Stewart, J. C., *Facts and Documents relating to the Affairs of the Union Bank of Calcutta*, Calcutta, 1848.

Stokes, Eric, *The English Utilitarians and India*, Oxford, 1959.

Stokes, Whitley, *Indian Companies Act, 1866*, Calcutta, 1866.

Strachey, John, *The End of Empire*, London, 1959.

Strachey, Sir John and Lt. Gen. Richard, *The Finances and Public Works of India from 1869 to 1881*, London, 1882.

Sullivan, R. J. F., *One Hundred Years of Bombay—History of the Bombay Chamber of Commerce, 1836–1936*, Bombay, 1937.

Sur, A. K., *The New Issue Market and the Stock Exchange*, Calcutta, 1961.
(Ed.), *The Stock Exchange—A Symposium*, Calcutta, 1958.

Thadani, J. N., 'Transport and Location of Industries in India', *Indian Economic Review*, August 1952.

Thorner, Alice, 'Secular Trends of the Indian Economy, 1881–1951', *Economic Weekly*, Special Number, July 1962.

Thorner, Daniel, 'Emergence of an Indian Economy, 1760–1960', in *The Encyclopedia Americana*, Vol. 15, reprinted in *Land and Labour in India*, See Thorner, Daniel and Alice.
'Long-Term Trends in Output in India', in Kuznets, Moore and Spengler (Eds.), *Economic Growth: Brazil, India and Japan*, Durham, N.C., 1955.
Investment in Empire, British Railway and Steamshipping Enterprise in India, 1825–1849, Philadelphia, 1950.

Thorner, Daniel and Alice, *Land and Labour in India*, Bombay, 1962 (Paperback).

Tiwari, R. D., *Railways in Modern India*, Bombay, 1941.

Toussaint, A., *History of the Indian Ocean*, London, 1966.

Trevor, H. E., *Railways in British India*, London, 1891.

Tripathi, A., *Trade and Finance in Bengal Presidency, 1793–1833*, Calcutta, 1956.

Turle, H. B., *An Outline of Indian Currency*, Calcutta, 1927.

Tyson, Geoffrey, *Managing Agency—A System of Business Organisation*, Calcutta, 1961.
The Bengal Chamber of Commerce and Industry, 1853–1953, A Centenary Survey, Calcutta, 1952.

Vakil, C. N., *Financial Development in Modern India, 1860–1924*, Bombay, 1924.

Vakil, C. N. and Muranjan, S. K., *Currency and Prices in India*, Bombay, 1927.

Wacha, D. E., *A Financial Chapter in the History of Bombay City*, Bombay, 1900.
The Rise and Growth of Bombay Municipal Government, Madras, 1913.

Shells from the Sands of Bombay—Being my recollections and reminiscences: 1860–1875, Bombay, 1920.

Premchund Raychund—his early life and career, Bombay, 1913.

Wadia, R. A., *The Bombay Dockyard and the Wadia Master Builders*, Bombay, 1955.

Wadia, P. A. and Joshi, G. N., *Money and the Money Markets in India*, London, 1926.

Wallace, D. R., *The Romance of Jute: A Short History of Calcutta Jute Mill Industry from 1855 to 1909*, Calcutta, 1909.

Wanliss, W., *A Three Months Prospecting Trip to the Indian Gold Fields*, London, 1881.

Watt, Sir George, *The Commercial Products of India*, London, 1908.

West, Edward, *On Emigration to British India. Profitable Investments for Joint Stock Companies and for emigrants who possess capital, etc.*, London, 1857.

Young, H. A., *The East India Company's Arsenals and Manufactories*, Oxford, 1937.

INDEX

accountants, firms of, 214
accounts of companies, 39, 65, 213–14,
230, 259; in Companies Acts,
(1850) 42, (1857) 69, 70; of cotton
mills in Bombay, 291
agency houses, 5–6, 18, 21, 221; break
up of, in Calcutta (1829), 9, 13,
27, 256; in development of companies, 12, 13, 22, 26–7, 59, 61;
see also managing agency system
Agra, cotton mills in, 153
Agra Savings Fund, 19 n, 273
Agra and United Services Bank, 30 n,
65 n, 67, 221, 273
agriculture, development of commercial, 55–6; and industrialisation,
124–7, 135; productivity of, 6 n–
7 n, 127, 264
Ahmedabad, assessment insurance
companies in, 194; cotton mills
in, 49, 60, 153
Ajmer-Merwar, companies in, 150,
301; cotton mills in, 153
Ajodhia Bank, 176
Albert Life Assurance Co., 13 n,
64
Alexander and Co., agency house,
Calcutta, 6 n, 22 n, 224–5
Allahabad Bank, 176
Alliance Bank of India, 75, 176
Alliance Financial, 75, 84
Amarapolliem Raj Estates and Mines
Co., 140
American Civil War, and banking in-
flation in Bombay, 72–3, 87, 208
Amritsar, cotton mills in, 153
Apcar and Co., agency house, Cal-
cutta, 225 n
Apollo Press Co., 46 n, 275
Arbuthnot and Co., agency house,
Madras, 140
artisans, English ban on emigration
of, 15
Asiatic Bank, 75, 77–8
Asiatic Financial, 76
Assam, companies in, 150, 301; tea
plantations in, 95, 171; transport
in, 49

Assam Clearance Rule, for tea companies, 257
Assam [Tea] Co., 20, 25, 96, 274;
capital of, 30; dividends of, 34 n,
103; incorporation of, 37 n;
labour for, 53; prices of shares of,
102
assessment insurance companies, 149,
181, 186, 190–4
Auckland and Sen, Calcutta, jute mill
of, 48, 59, 61
auditors, 119, 159–60, 213–14; Companies Acts and, 42, 65, 69
Australia, gold in, 139; trade with, 63

Back Bay Co., see Bombay Reclama-
tion Co.
Balaghat Gold Mining Co., 140, 148
Bangalore, cotton mills in, 153
Bangalore Bank, 176
banias, 165 n
Bank of Asia, 28 n, 31 n, 36, 273
Bank of Bengal, 11, 19 n, 27, 155, 200;
notes of, 26; price of shares of, 32
Bank of Bombay, 37, 92, 273; capital
of, 29 n; in cotton boom, 78–9,
82, 90; notes of, 26; price of
shares of, 32–3; shareholders in,
23–4
Bank of Calcutta, 11, 37
Bank of Ceylon, 37 n, 273
Bank of India, Australia, and China,
36, 63 n
Bank of Madras, 37, 273; notes of, 26,
32; shareholders in, 23, 24
Bank of Upper India, 176
bank rate, rises to 15% in Calcutta
(1866), 101
banking companies, 113–15, 176–81,
273; borrowing from, by companies, 33, 204; capital of, 106,
152, 289, 296; cash balances of,
180; establishment of, 9, 10–11,
13, 107; foreign, operating in
India, 63; Government and, 11,
23, 37; Indian promoters and
directors of, 19, 23, 24; limited
liability provisions and, 47, 64,

321

banking companies, (*cont.*) 68, 70, 255 n, 257; managing agencies and, 5–6, 221; numbers of, (registered) 46, 73, 284, (wound up) 47, 111, 284; percentage of total capital in, 260; percentage of total increase of capital in, 152; *see also* exchange, joint stock, *mofussil, and* Presidency banks

Barakar Iron Works Co., 277

Baranggore Jute Mills, 244 n

bazaars, companies to form, 284

Belgium, imports of iron and steel from, 134, 277

Benares Bank, 13, 19 n, 30–1, 221, 273; dividends of, 34 n; failure of, 40, 66

Benares and Mirzapore Steam Co., 274

Bengal, assessment insurance companies in, 193; companies in, 46, 62, 106, 112–13, 149–50, 301; companies wound up in, 106; cotton mills in, 153; gold mania in (1890), 149, 151, 166, 194–202; growth of industries in, 163–7; savings and loan companies in, 114, 188; tea plantations in, 171

Bengal Bonded Warehouse Association, 37 n, 274; shareholders of, 25–6

Bengal Chamber of Commerce, 207, 216

Bengal Coal Co., 46 n, 58, 225 n, 274

Bengal Gold Syndicate, 196, 197

Bengal Indigo Co., 274

Bengal Iron and Steel Co., 277

Bengal Jute Co., 248

Bengal Jute Pressing Co., 248

Bengal Rivers Steamship Co., 123

Bengal Salt Co., 275

Bengal Tea Association, 19–20, 25, 58, 96, 255 n

Bengal Tea Co., 249

Bengal Trust and Loan Co., 66 n, 200

Bengali, Sorabji, Sapruji, on managing agency system, 117

Bengali merchants in Calcutta, 25, 26, 28, 57, 163

Berar, companies in, 150, 301; cotton mills in, 153

Bethune, J. E. D., and company law, 41, 68n

Bishwanath [Tea] Co., prices of shares of, 102

Bohras, trading community, 164

Bombay (City), 91–3; banking inflation in (1861–5), 71–91, 257; cotton mills in, 15, 50, 153; railways from, 17, 92, 120; riots in, 161; share market in, 158–9, 211, 257; Stock Exchange in, 208–10

Bombay (Province), companies in, 112–13, 149–50, 301; cotton mills in, 153; promotion of companies in, 46, 60, 62; savings and loan companies in, 188

Bombay Chamber of Commerce, 40, 92

Bombay Fire Insurance Co., 240 n

Bombay Gas Co., operated without managing agents, 241

Bombay Mechanics Building Co., 242; operated without managing agents, 241

Bombay Reclamation Co. (Back Bay Co.), 74, 75, 78, 87, 88, 90

Bombay Steam Navigation Co., 43 n, 92, 274

Bombay Telephone Co., 157 n

bonus shares, 158, 251; bonuses on shares, 34

Borneo Jute Co., 61

Bowreah Cotton Mills, 27 n, 274

brewery companies, 183, 284; capital in, 289, 299

Brice, A. C., and Co., agency house, Bombay, 242

British India Steam Navigation Co., 123

Broach Cotton Mills Co., 60, 274

Brokers' Exchange, Calcutta, 206, 208

Bruce brothers, tea planters, 95

Bubble Act, 38

Budge Budge Jute Mills, 244

bullion, flow of, into Bombay (1865), 79

Burdwan coal district, 17

Burkinyoung, Henry, tea company promoter, 61

Burma, companies in, 150, 301

Index

Cachar, tea plantations in, 96, 98

Calcutta, break-up of agency houses in (1829), 9, 13, 27, 256; promotion of companies in, 60–1; railways from, 17, 120, 160–2; share market in, 166, 206–7, 211, 257–8; speculative manias in, (gold) 149, 151, 166, 194–202, (tea) 95–107, 230, 257

Calcutta and Burma Steam Navigation Co., 48, 61

Calcutta Docking Co., 225 n, 274

Calcutta Laudable [Life Insurance] Company, 12; Third, 223–4; Fourth, 32 n

Calcutta Steam Ferry Bridge Co., 274

Calcutta Steam Tug Association, 20, 58, 225 n

Cama, B. H., cotton shipper, 85, 87, 90

Cama, Khurshedjee Rustomjee, merchant, 57

Campbell, Mitchell and Co., Bombay, 78 n

Canning, Lord, Viceroy, 97

capital, British, 16–17, 59, 184–5, 265; of companies, see under companies and individual industries; dividends paid from, 34, 100, 145, 213; divorced from technology, 9; rate of formation of, 150–2, 265; supply of, for industry, 27–9, 53–4, 127–8

Carr, Tagore, and Co., agency house, Calcutta, 20, 28 n, 58, 59, 225 n, 226, 253–5

case law, and companies, 216–18

castes, and employment in factories, 53; size of trading community limited by, 8; trading, 3, 163

Cawnpore, cotton mills in, 153

Cawnpore Bank, 273

Central Bank, 76,

Central Cachar [Tea] Co., prices of shares of, 102

Central Provinces, companies in, 150, 301; cotton mills in, 153

Chambers of Commerce, and company law, 40

Champion Reef Gold Mining Co., 148; dividends paid by, 295

chartered companies in India, 1–5, 256, 270; see also East India Co., Dutch East India Co., etc.

Chartered Mercantile Bank of India, London, and China, 20 n, 64 n

Chettis, in banking, 24, 28, 165 n

Chhotanagpur Gold Mining Co., 196, 197

Chotanagpur, Gold mining in, 195

China, export of cotton yarn and textiles to, 155–6, 161–2; tea from, 95; trade with, 57, 63

chinchona plantation companies, 183, 297

Chitfunds, 188–9, 190

City Bank, 76

City of Glasgow Bank, failur of, 138, 139, 143, 234

civil services, Bengalis in, 163

Clive, Lord, and Exclusive Society of Trade, 10 n

coal, exports of, 175; imports of, 121, 174–5, 185, 266 n; for iron and steel industry, 131; output of, 173

coal mining companies, 21, 119, 172–5; capital in, 106, 173, 289, 297; managing agencies and, 22, 248; numbers of, (registered) 46, 284, (wound up) 47, 284, 290; percentage of total capital in, 260; percentage of total increase of capital in, 152; railways and steamships and, 14, 172, 259

coffee plantation companies, 14, 183, 284, 297

Colaba Co., 46 n

Colaba Land Co., 76

Colaba Press Co., 241, 275

Colaba Spinning and Weaving Co., 204; New, 236

Colvin and Co., agency house, Calcutta, 6 n

Commercial Bank of India, 19 n, 32 n, 38 n, 273

Commercial Finance and Stock Exchange Co., prosecution of directors of, 89

Commercial and Land Mortgage Bank, 176

Commercial Steamship Co., 123

commission to managing agents, from assessment insurance companies, 192; from Bombay cotton mills, 291; on output, 117, 118, 159, 162, 214, 225, 228, 230; on profits, 160, 162, 237

323

communications, difficulties of, 14, 31, 171; improvements in, 120, 156–7
companies (in India), foreign, operating in India, 63; growth of, (to 1850) 18–35, (1851–60) 46–70, (1861–5) 71–108, (1866–82) 109–48, 283, (1882–1901) 149–86, 300, 302; law relating to, (to 1850) 36–45, (later) 312–18; life span of, 286, 287, 288; liquidation of, *see* liquidation of companies; managing agencies and, *see* managing agency system; numbers of, (by industries) 46, 47, 115, (by provinces) 112; numbers and capital of, 109, (by industries), 152, 284, 289, 290 296–9, 304, (by provinces) 62, 113, 150, 301, (by years) 116–17, 150–1, 300; origins of, 1–17, 256; *see also individual industries*
Companies Acts, (1850), 17, 35, 41–5, 212, 214, 257; (1857), 46–7, 48, 64–71, 212, 214, 255 n; (1860), 70, 255 n; (1866), 212, 213, 255 n; (1882, 1887, 1891, 1895, 1900), 212–13; (1914), 215, 216; (1936), 219; (1956), 219, 220, 237, 255 n
Comptoir National d'Escompte de Paris, 64, 273
conspicuous consumption, 55, 125
Cooperative Associations, 183 n, 284; capital in, 289, 296
Coromandel, joint-stock companies in (17th century), 2
cotton, acreage under, 73 n; dependence of Britain on U.S.A. for, 16, 17; exports of, 72 n; long-staple, 154, 162; price of, 72, 85–6; speculation in, 78, 234; trade with China in, 57
cotton mill companies, 152–62; accounts of, 291; boom in shares of, 71–93, 181, 208, 257; capital of, 113, 116, 117, 153, 157–8, 265, 289, 298, 304; establishment of, 14, 22 n, 48, 49, 60, 71, 107; Europeans employed in, 50; losses of (1893), 156; managing agencies and, 159–60, 227–41 *passim*, 248; numbers of, (registered), 46, 115, 284, 290, (wound up), 47, 284; as percentage of all

cotton mill companies, (*cont.*)
companies, 152; percentage of total capital in jute companies and, 260; percentage of total increase of capital, in, 152
cotton textiles, Chinese and Japanese, 156; excise duties on, 160; exports of, 1, 8 n, 156, 161–2, 263 n; handloom production of, 14 n–15 n, 263–4
cotton yarn, exports of, 155
credit, in Bombay (1861–5), 76, 77, 79; ingredients of, 58
Credit Mobilier of Calcutta, 75, 104
crises, commercial, (mid 1820s) 221, 256, (mid 1840s) 6 n, 24, 47, 59; financial, 11, 87–90
cultivation, area under, 126–7
currencies, multiplicity of, 27
Curzon, Lord, Viceroy, 134

Dacca Bank, 19 n, 273
Danish East India Co., 270
Davar, Cowasjee Nanabhoy, cotton-mill promoter, 228–9
debentures, 33, 158, 170, 205, 258
Delhi, cotton mills in, 153; railway to, 120
Delhi Bank Corporation, 19 n, 273
depreciation of assets, 159, 160, 170, 205, 213
Dhadka Gold Co., 200–1, 202
Dibrugarh, steamship to, 49; tea plantation at, 96
directors, in English and Indian Law, 217; of gold mining companies, 145–6; and limited liability, 67, 213; loans to, 43; local boards of, for branches of banks, 221; in London and India, 227; managing agencies and, 232, 236, 242, 249; misdeeds of, 40, 66, 88–9
Diver, Dr, company promoter, 84, 85
dividends, bearer warrants for, 205–6; in Companies Act (1857), 69; of cotton mills, 159, 291; fluctuation in, 34, 205; of gold mining companies, 295; managing agencies and, 231; paid from capital, 34, 100, 145, 213; stabilization of, 160; of tea companies, 102–3, 171

Index

Dunbar Cotton Mill, 244 n, 248
Durrung Tea Co., 249
Dutch East India Co., 2, 4 n–5 n, 270

East India Bank, 273
East India Co. (English), 2, 4–6, 18, 119, 270; end of trade monopoly of, 14, 95; and Indian shipping, 292; and incorporation of companies, 36–7; ordnance factory of, 92; Salt and Opium Department of, 58; servants of, in promotion of companies, 20–1, 25, 29, 32, 56, 66, 221, 256
East India Iron Co., 62, 276
East India Railway Co., 17 n, 58, 172
Eastern Financial Co., 83
Eastern Steam Navigation Co., 274
Edgar, J. W., Secretary, Department of Agriculture, 98
electricity, in textile mills, 158, 168
Elphinston Land Reclamation Co., 85
Empress Cotton Mill Co., 250–1
Enthoven, R. E., Secretary, Department of Commerce and Industry, 215
European Life Assurance Co., 13 n, 64
Europeans, in banking, 23; in cotton mills, 50; in foreign firms in India, 245; in insurance companies, 19; in managing agencies, 241, 242
Ewart, Latham, and Co., agency house, 240
exchange banks, 64, 86, 114, 177, 178; and Bombay Stock Exchange, 210; cash balances of, 180
Exclusive Society of Trade, 10 n
exports from India, coal, 175; cotton, 72n, 73 n; cotton textiles and yarn, 1, 8 n, 155–6, 161–2, 263 n; iron and steel, 276

factory system, 9, 259
family businesses, 4, 165
famine, 117, 121 n, 156, 161, 171–2
Fergusson and Co., agency house, Calcutta, 275
Financial Association of India and China ("Old Financial"), 73, 75, 78, 104
financial companies, 73, 75, 76
financial institutitons, needed for establishment of industry, 49, 53

Finlay, Clark, and Co., Bombay, 78 n
fire insurance companies, 182; managing agencies and, 240
Fleming, John, merchant, 84–5
flour mill companies, 183, 259, 298
food grains, acreage under, 126; prices of, 155
Forbes and Co., agency house, Bombay, 78 n, 140–1, 237 n. 240
foreign exchange, 154–6; banks responsible for, 114; earned by agriculture, 125; fluctuations in rate of, 155, 179; manipulation of rate of, by East India Co., 37
foremen jobbers, in cotton mills, 51, 52
founders' shares in companies, 195
"free merchants", licensed by East India Co., 5, 18, 20; form agency houses, 21
free trade, policy of, and industrialisation, 128–9, 269
French East India Cos., 270
Frere, Sir Bartle, Governor of Bombay, 81
Frere Land Co., 76, 85
friendly societies, 194; no separate statute for, 115
"futures" in share market, 76, 77, 86, 158, 166, 210, 211, 258

Ganges Steam Navigation Co., 123, 225 n, 226, 274
General Bank of India, 10–11, 21, 34, 65 n, 221
Gisborne and Co., agency house, Calcutta, 225 n
glass manufacturing company, 164
Gockuldas, Morarji, cotton mill manager, 129–30, 133, 238, 268
gold, hoarding of, 55
gold mining companies, in Bengal, 149, 151, 166, 194–202; dividends paid by, 295; in Madras and Mysore, 119, 136–48, 259; numbers and capital of, 144, 183, 284, 297
gold standard, 143
Gorakhpore Bank, 176
Government of India, and banking, 11, 23, 37; borrowing by, 32, 127, 156, 158–9, 185–6, 265; import of supplies by, 129–30, 134, 185, 259, 268; and iron and steel

Index

Government of India, (cont.)
industry, 130–4, 277; and land reclamation companies, 104; and limited liability, 68; and managing agency system, 135, 214–15, 237, 259; and public works, 128; and railways, 54 n, 63, 120, 121, 127 n, 129, 175–6; and tea cultivation, 96; see also Companies Acts

Grant, Andrew, promoter of financial companies, 78 n

Great Eastern Hotel Co., Calcutta, 249

Great Eastern Spinning and Weaving Co., face value of shares of, 203–4

Great Indian Peninsular Railway Co., 17 n

Great Southern Mysore Gold Mining Co., 148

Greaves, Cotton, and Co., agency house, Bombay, 160, 204 n, 237–8

Greaves, James, 237

guilds, in ancient India, 1, 256, 272

Guezrat, assessment insurance companies in, 194; cotton mills in, 265

Hannay, Col., tea planter, 96

Hardinge, Lord, Viceroy, 269 n

Hastings, Warren, and banking, 10 n

Heath, J. M. founder of iron works, 21, 276

Heilgers and Co., agency house, Calcutta, 196, 199, 200

Henderson, George, jute-company promoter, 61

Hindus, in banking, 23; in managing agencies, 241

Hongkong and Shanghai Banking Corporation, 114, 151, 176, 177

Hope Town Association, tea company, 96–7

Howrah Docking Co., 249

Howrah Jute Mills, 244 n

Hyderabad, cotton mills in, 153

ice manufacturing companies, 183, 299

Imperial Bank of India, 11

Imperial Silver Lead Mining Co., 141

imports into India, 267; coal, 121, 174–5, 185, 266 n; iron and steel, 131, 134, 277; metals, 8 n; supplies for Government, 129–30, 134, 185, 259, 268

income, annual per head, 6 n, 54, 263, 264, 267

income-tax, paid by bankers and moneylenders, 181

incorporation of companies, 36–7

India General Steam Navigation Co., 46 n, 49, 123, 204, 274; Carr, Tagore, and Co. as managing agents for, 20, 58, 226, 248; transferred to British register, 151

Indian and Colonial Goldfields Co., 148

Indian Consolidated Mines, 148 n

Indian Glenrock Co., 144

Indian Gold Mining Co., 138, 139, 147

Indian Guarantee Suretyship Association, 182

Indian Life Association Co., 182

Indian National Steamship Owners' Association, 293

indigo factories, 14, 22, 284

Indore, cotton mills in, 153

industrialisation, agriculture and, 124–7; reasons for slowness of, 260–9

inflation, 155; in banking in Bombay (1861–5), 71–93

inheritance, laws of, and agricultural development, 126

insolvency, Companies Acts on, 44, 65; see also liquidation

insurance companies, 181–2; capital in, 289, 296; establishment of, 9, 11–13, 92; Europeans in, 19; limited liability provisions and, 47, 64, 68, 70, 212, 255 n; managing agencies and, 22, 239 240; numbers of, (registered) 46, 284, (wound up) 111, 284; see also assessment insurance, fire insurance, life insurance, and marine insurance companies

interest, rate of, 28 n, 156, 178

iron and steel industry, 118 n, 130–4, 185, 276–8

irrigation, 127 n, 265, 266

Jamnadass and Devidass, brokers, 84

Japan, 16, 156, 161

Jeejibhoy, Byramjie, fire insurance promoter, 240 n

Jeejibhoy, Sir Jamshedji, merchant, 57

Jehangir, Sir Cowasji, company director, 77 n, 78 n, 84
Jews, in agency houses, 241
Jharia coalfields, 50, 175, 185
joint stock banks, 177, 178, 220–1
joint stock companies, concept of, 9; in industry, 119; in South India (17th century), 1–4
Jorehaut Tea Co., 61, 102–3
Jut Put Gold Co., 200
jute mill companies, 167–70; capital in, 106, 116, 166, 167, 289, 298, 304, (British) 54, 61, 168, 185, 265; establishment of, 48, 59, 70, 107, 257; incorporated in Britain, 63; managing agents and, 248; markets for products of, 168, 169; numbers of, (registered) 46, 115 284, 290, (registered in Britain) 63, (wound up) 284; percentage of total capital in cotton mills and, 260; percentage of total increase in capital in, 152; stimulus to shipping from, 123; transfer of capital for, from Britain to India, 16 n

Kaiser-i-Hind Gold Mining Co., 141, 148
Karo Gold Mining Co., 196
Kessowji, Naik, and Co., agency house, Bombay, 160, 234, 236, 240
Kenrick, G. H. B., Advocate General of Bengal, 215
khados, 75; *see also* land reclamation companies
Kharswan gold syndicate, 195
Kilburn and Co., *see* Schoene, Kilburn, and Co.
Kolar Gold Mining Co., 148
Kotagiri District Estates, 140

labour, industrial force of, 49, 51, 119; shortage of skilled, 50; for tea plantations, 53, 100, 101; turnover of, 51–2
Lahiri, Ramtanu, promoter of insurance companies, 13
Lahore, cotton mills in, 153
laissez-faire, doctrine of, 36, 42, 128, 162, 259, 268

land, alteration in law relating to, 18, 55, 97; investment in, 18–19, 56, 163; revenue from, 125; tenure of, and agricultural development, 126; vendors of, to gold mining companies, 145, 146
land and building companies, 183, 299
Land Mortgage Bank of India, 282
land reclamation companies, 74, 75, 76, 104–5, 284
Landing, Shipping Co. of Kurranchi, 242
Landon, James, cotton mill promoter, 60
law, British "rule of", in India, 6, 107, 258; company, (to 1850) 36–45, (later) 212–18; *see also* Companies Acts
lawyers, in company promotion, 81–2; in financial crisis of 1865, 87
life insurance companies, 12–13; foreign, operating in India, 63; managing agencies and, 223, 240
life span of companies, 286, 287, 288
limited liability, 10, 33, 37, 45; case law and, 217; Companies Acts and, 46–7, 48, 64–71, 212, 255 n, 257
liquidation of companies, (1851–82) 47, 109–11, 284, 286, 305, (1851–1901) 303, (1882–1901) 149, 302; in Bengal (1861–9), 106–7; in Bombay (1865), 88–90; in Companies Acts, (1850) 44, (1857) 69, (1865) 88; of tea companies, 103; time lag in, 117 n
London, demand for gold mining shares in, 139, 140–1, 143–6; railways controlled from, 227
London, Asiatic, and American Co., agency house, 241
London and Eastern Banking Corporation, 222

machinery, difficulties of importing, 15, 49; for gold mining, 146; improved, for cotton mills, 157–8
Mackenzie, Capt. A. G., and India General Steam Navigation Co., 226
Mackinnon, William, 61
Mackinnon, Mackenzie, and Co., merchants, Calcutta, 61, 172 n

Index

Mackintosh, Fulton, and McClintock, agency house, Calcutta, 225

Madhevji, Atmaram, Bombay broker, 84

Madras (City), cotton mills in, 153; free merchants in, 5; railways from, 120; telephones in, 157 n

Madras (Province), companies in, 46, 62, 112–13, 149–50, 301; cotton mills in, 153; gold mining in, 136–9; savings and loan companies in, 109, 113, 114–15, 149, 177, 188

Madras Gold Mining Co., 140, 147, 148

Madras Spinning and Weaving Co., 225 n, 236

Magor, R. B., managing agent, 249

Mail Coach Carrying Co., 62

mails, contracts for carriage of, 61, 293

managers, during banking inflation, 80; of tea plantations, 99

managing agency system, 22, 59, 219–55, 258, 268; in assessment insurance, 192; in cotton industry, 117–18, 159–60, 227–9, 237–9, 241; and gold mining companies, 142, 146, 194–202 passim, 259; government and, 135, 214–16, 237, 259; in jute industry, 169–70; see also agency houses

Manbhoom Gold Co., 196, 197

Marco Polo, 136

marine insurance companies, 11–12, 73, 182; managing agencies and, 223, 240

Marwaris, as stockbrokers, 166, 207, 211, 258; as trading community, 164, 165–7, 197, 199

Mazagon Reclamation Co., 75, 84, 85, 88

Mehta, D. B. and Co., agency house, Calcutta, 250

Mehta, Sir Pheroz Shah, lawyer, 159

Memons, trading community, 164

Merchant Steam Tug Co., 248

merchants, investment in industry by, 55–6, 107

metallurgy, Indian, 8 n

middlemen, Indian merchants as, for European companies (18th century), 18, 58

mining companies, 183, 184; see also coal and gold mining companies

mining and quarrying companies, 297

mints for free coinage of rupees, closed, 155, 156

Mirzapore, coal district, 17

Mirzapore Coal Co., 274

mofussil banks, 27, 66, 113

Mohammedans, in managing agencies, 241; as shareholders in Bank of Bengal, 23; and trade and industry, 164

moneylenders, interest rates charged by, 28 n; land reform and, 55–6

Motilal, Choonilal, Bombay broker, 84

multiple textile mills, 284, 285, 290; capital in, 289, 298

Mysore, companies in, 149–50, 301; gold mining in, 139, 147; management of companies in, 251–2; savings and loan companies in, 109, 114, 177, 188; war in, 11

Mysore Gold Mining Co., 147, 148; dividends paid by, 295

Nagpur, cotton belt near, 17

Nathubhoy, Mangaldas, cotton mill manager, 238

National Bank of India, 249 n

Native Share and Stock Brokers' Association, Bombay, 209, 210

navigation companies, see steam navigation companies

New Fortgloster Mills Co., 274, 275 n

Nicol and Co., Bombay merchants, 138, 139

Nicol and Sons, 84–5

nidhis, 187–8, 190; see also savings and loan companies

Nigeria, managing agents in, 253 n

Nilgiri Hills, gold workings in, 136

Nine Reefs Gold Mining Co., 148

Nischindpore Sugar Co., 225 n, 274

North-West Provinces, companies in Oudh and, 46, 150, 301; management of companies in, 252; mofussil banks in, 113; savings and loan companies in, 188

North Western Bank of India, 30 n, 273

notes, of Presidency banks, 26

Nundydoorg Gold Mining Co., 148; dividends paid by, 295

oilseeds, 259
Ooregum Gold Mining Co., 139, 148;
  dividends paid by, 295
opium trade, 22, 57, 234
ordnance factory of East India Co.,
  at Bombay, 92
Oriental Bank, 19 n
Oriental Bank of Bombay, 38 n, 43 n
Oriental Bank Corporation, 34 n, 37,
  64 n, 222, 226, 273
Oriental Gold Mining Co., 148
Oriental Government Security Life
  Association, 182
Oriental Life Insurance Co., 12–13;
  New, 46
Oriental Loan Association, 114
Oriental Steamship Co., 123
Ostend Company, 270–1
Oudh Commercial Bank, 176

Palmer and Co., agency house, Calcutta, 6 n
paper mill companies, 183, 259, 284,
  298
Parry and Co., agency house, Madras,
  142
Parsees, in banking, 19 n, 23, 26, 28;
  as company promoters, 57, 61,
  107; in managing agencies, 57,
  241
partnerships, between family businesses, 4; joint stock companies
  as, 37–9, 68, 257; law of, and company law, 216, 217, 218
Pat Pat Gold Co., 197, 199
Peninsular and Oriental Steamship
  Co., 17 n, 63n, 124, 274
Petit, M., cotton-mill promoter, 209,
  238
Pew Estate (coffee), 274
Pilgrimage Provident Fund, 193
Pioneer Glass Manufacturing Co.,
  164 n
Pit, Laurens, Dutch Governor of
  Coromandel, 1 n
plague, epidemics of, 51 n, 161, 166,
  169
plantation companies, 183, 297; *see
  also* chinchona, coffee, *and* tea
  plantation companies
Pondicherry, cotton mills in, 153
population, of Bombay, 93; rate of
  increase of, 126 n

Port Canning Land Investment Co.,
  75, 104, 143
Porto Novo Steel and Iron Co., 21,
  27 n, 33, 62, 274, 276
Portuguese in India, 270
Posner and Co., agency house, Calcutta, 200
postal services, 92, 156–7; contracts
  for, 61, 293
preference shares, 33, 170, 205, 258;
  case law on, 217
Presidency banks, 37 n, 177, 178
press, the, and assessment insurance,
  192; and Calcutta gold mania,
  198; and Companies Act (1850),
  44–5; and company financing,
  170, 205, 214, 243–4; and stock
  exchanges, 209, 210
pressing and screwing (baling) companies (cotton and jute), capital
  in, 106, 183, 289, 290, 298; establishment of, 92; managing agents
  and, 239, 240, 248; Marwaris in,
  166; numbers of, (registered) 46,
  47, 73, 284, 290, (wound up) 111,
  284
price level, general (1886–97), 155;
  of Indian manufactures, 180
printing, publishing and stationery
  companies, 183, 284, 296
productivity, agricultural, 6 n–7 n,
  27, 264; industrial, 8 n
profits, bank managers' commission
  on, 221, 222; managing agencies'
  commission on, 160, 162, 237;
  ploughing back of, 34, 125, 251
public works, Government policy on,
  128
Punjab, companies in, 150, 301; cotton
  mills in, 153; *mofussil* banks in,
  113; savings and loan companies
  in, 188
Punjab Bank, liquidation of, 252
Punjab Banking Co., 176
Punjab National Bank, 176–7

railways, 120–2, 175–6; capital in, 289,
  296, (British) 17, 54 n, 63, 265;
  in China, 157; controlled from
  London, 227; establishment of,
  10, 17, 48, 70, 92, 107, 257;
  freight charges of, 121 n–122 n;
  Government and, 54 n, 63, 120,

Index

railways, (cont.)
121, 127 n, 129, 175–6; iron and steel for, 278; managing agents and, 248; percentage of total capital in, 260; percentage of total increase of capital in, 152; rate of increase of mileage of, 156; number of companies registered and wound up (1851–82), 284

Ranchhodlal, cotton mill promoter, 49, 60

Ranigunj Coal Association, 248, 255 n

Ranigunj coalfieds, 14, 49; railway to, 59, 172, 173

Ratnagiri Provident Association,191–2

registration of companies, case law and, 218; in Companies Acts, (1850), 44, 45, 62, (1857) 68

Remington and Co., agency house, 240

reserve funds of companies, 34, 160, 170, 205

revenue of Government, 185–6; from agriculture, 125; from borrowing, 127 n

rice mill companies, 183, 259, 298

Richmond and Co., agency house, Bombay, 225 n, 226

Ripon, Lord, Viceroy, 131, 134

Ritchie, Stuart, and Co., Bombay merchants, 77 n, 84, 126 n

Rivers Steamship Co., 123

roads, building of, 14, 120

Robert and Charriol, agency house, 249

Roberts, William, tea company promoter, 61

Royal Cotton Mills, Bombay, face value of shares of, 203

Roychand, Premchand, director of Bank of Bombay, 77, 78, 81–3, 84, 85, 90, 104, 208

Roychund, Deepchund, 81

rupee, value of, 127 n–128 n, 154–6, 175–6, 184–5, 258

Rustomjee, Manockjee, managing agent, 249

Rustomjee Twine and Canvas Co., 249

Rustomji, Cowasji, agency house, Calcutta, 13, 225 n

Salt Water Lakes Reclamation Co., 105

Sassoon, E. D., and Co., Bombay, 78 n

sattas, 76, 88, 258; see also time bargains

savings and loan companies, 114–15, 187–90; capital of, 109, 113, 149, 177; included in banking statistics, 176; liquidations of, 110, 188

saw and timber mill companies, 183, 298

Schoene, Kilburn, and Co., agency house, Calcutta, 197, 199, 202, 244 n, 247–8

Scott, Michael, of Ritchie, Stuart, and Co., 77 n, 84

Seal, Motilal, promoter of insurance company, 13

Sepoy Rebellion (1857), 48, 122; life insurance payments after, 64

shareholders in companies, in Britain, 24, 64, 114, 226–7; case law and protection of, 217, 218; classification of, 23, 24; in Companies Act (1857), 69, 70; in companies as partnerships, 39–41; and managing agents, 118, 220, 233–4

shares, companies dealing in own, 43, 244, 252; face value of, 31, 59–60, 203–4, 258; in tea companies, prices of (1863–7), 102

shipping, Indian, 292–4; see also steam navigation companies, steamships

shipping agencies, 73, 284; capital in, 106, 289

shipping, landing, and warehousing companies, 183, 296

short-time working, in cotton mills, 162; in jute mills, 168

shroff, Prestonji Cursetji, 83–4

shroffs (moneylenders and bankers), 204

silver, fall in price of, 127; hoarding of, 55

silver standard, 156

Simla Bank, 221, 222, 273

Singbhoom Gold Co., 196

Smyth, R. Borough, mining engineer, 138

social overheads, 6, 125, 128, 185, 186

Sonapet Gold Syndicate, 196, 197, 199

Index

Soom tea Co., 250

South Cachar [Tea] Co., 101

South India, gold rush in, 136–48, 259; joint stock companies in (17th century), 1–4

Southern India Alpha Gold Mining Co., 136, 137

speculation, in Bombay (1861–5), 75–93, 107; in Calcutta, (1861–5) 95–107, 230, 257, (1890–1) 149, 151, 166, 194–202

Staunton, R. S., managing agent, 247, 249

steam navigation companies, 122–4; capital in, 106, 183, 289, 296; establishment of, 22, 107; foreign, operating in India, 63; numbers of, (registered) 46, 47, 73, 284, 290, (wound up) 111, 284

Steam Tug Association, Calcutta, 225 n, 226, 253, 254, 274

steamships, 10, 13, 256; losses of, 123

Stephenson, Macdonald, railway promoter, 17 n

Stephenson, R. M., railway engineer, 63

stock exchanges, 119, 206–11, 258

stockbrokers, 31, 119; in Bombay, 29, 108, 158, 208–9; in Calcutta, 29, 206; Marwaris as, 166, 207, 211, 258

stone quarrying companies, 184

Suez Canal, opening of, 118, 120

sugar, duties on imports of, 184, 259; West Indian interest and, 15

sugar mill companies, 183, 184, 284; agency houses and, 15, 22; capital in, 289, 299

Sunderbund [Land Reclamation] Co., 48, 105

Surat, joint stock companies in (17th century), 2

Swedish East India Co., 271

Sylhet, coal district, 14; tea in, 96

Sylhet Coal Co., 274

Tagore, Dwarka Nath, founder of Carr, Tagore, and Co., 13, 58

tariff policy, and development of industry, 70, 132 n, 268

Tata, J. N., cotton mill of, 162, 238, 268; P. and O. and, 124

Tata, Nusserwanji and Jamshedji, merchants, 57

taxes, 186; on agriculture, 125

Taylor, George, lawyer, 84

tea, market for, 118, 171

tea plantation companies, 170–2, 279–82; capital in, 103, 106, 113, 116, 152, 170, 289, 297, 304, (British) 54, 170, 185, 265; establishment of, 14, 71; incorporated in Britain, 63; labour for, 53, 100, 101; managing agents and, 248; numbers of, (registered) 46, 95, 115, 284, 290, (registered in Britain) 63, 95, 116, (wound up) 47, 103, 284; speculation in shares of, 95–107, 230, 257; stimulus to shipping from, 123

technicians, European, 49, 50, 154

technology, Indian, 7–9; in establishment of industries, 49, 165 n

telegraph lines, opening of, 92, 120, 156–7

telephones, 157

Temple Block Wynaad Gold Mining Co., 141, 142

time bargains ("futures") in share markets, 76, 77, 86, 158, 166, 210, 211, 258

time deposits at banks, 178

trade, end of East India Co.'s monopoly of, 14, 95; external, in European hands, 179; internal, 18; railways and, 10, 16–17; steamships and, 10, 13–16; terms of, between Britain and India, 155; through Bombay, 91

trading companies, 113, 183, 184; in Calcutta, 94–5; capital in, 106, 152, 296

transport, agricultural development hampered by lack of, 125–6; difficulties of, 14, 16, 17, 49, 185; improvements in, 120, 156–7; and value of land, 56

Travancore, cotton mills in, 153

Treacher and Co., trading company, 242; operated without managing agents, 240

Tremayne and Co., fraudulent company promoters, 66 n, 141–2

331

Index

Trevelyan, Sir Charles, Finance Minister, 86

Triton [Marine] Insurance Co., 182

Uncovenanted Service Bank, Agra, 273

Union Bank of Calcutta, 19 n, 27, 58, 273; capital of, 29 n, 33; dividends of, 34–5; failure of, 13, 40, 65

Union [Life Insurance] Society of Calcutta, 224–5

Union Steam Tug Association, 225 n, 274

United Services Bank, 65 n

United States of America, assessment insurance in, 191; Sherman Act in, and value of rupee, 155

universities, 119

urbanisation, agriculture and, 124; rate of, 7–8

Vansittart, C. G., in gold mania, 200–1

Viger, George, gold miner, 136, 137

Wadia, N. N., engineer, 120 n

wages, in cotton mills, 51, 52; general level of, 155, 267; in tea plantations, 171

Wallace and Co., Bombay, 78 n

wars, frontier, 127, 156, 186; internal, 6, 262

Western Ghats, stimulation of trade by road through, 14 n, 91

Whithers, George, gold miner, 136, 137

Williamson, Magor, and Co., agency house, Calcutta, 248, 249, 250

women, employed in hand-spinning, 263 n

woollen mill companies, 119

Wynaad Consols, 140

Wynaad district, gold mining in, 136

Wynaad Gold Mining Co., 141

Wynaad Prospecting Co., 137

Zender, Leo, managing agent, 249

zilla bankers, 28